THOMAS SANKARA SPEAKS

THOMAS SANKARA SPEAKS

SPEAKS

The Burkina Faso Revolution
1983–1987

Pathfinder

New York ~ London ~ Montreal ~ Sydney

Edited by Michel Prairie

ISBN 978-0-87348-986-7
Library of Congress Catalog Card Number 2007932253
Manufactured in Canada

First edition, 1988
Second edition, 2007
Twelfth printing, 2023

COVER DESIGN: Eva Braiman

FRONT COVER PHOTO: J. Langevin/Sygma-Corbis

BACK COVER PHOTOS: *Top*: Burkinabè children in Young Pioneers welcome delegates to international conference against South Africa's racist apartheid regime, Ouagadougou, Burkina Faso, October 8, 1987 (Margaret Manwaring/*Militant*). *Middle*: Women march at celebration of second anniversary of Burkina revolution, Ouagadougou, August 4, 1985 (Marla Puziss/*Militant*). *Bottom*: Thomas Sankara planting tree during mobilization to halt the spread of the desert, August 1985 (Marla Puziss/*Militant*).

FACING TITLE PAGE: Portrait of Thomas Sankara, painted by Lyne Pelletier and Luis Perrero, from Pathfinder Mural in New York City, which existed from 1989 to 1996 on the wall of the Pathfinder Building in New York City and included portraits of revolutionary leaders published by Pathfinder Press.

The interview with Jean-Philippe Rapp is published by permission of Editions Favre of Lausanne, Switzerland. The interview with Mongo Beti is published by permission of Odile Biyidi Awala, cofounder of *Peuples noirs Peuples africains*. The interview with Elisabeth Nicolini is published by permission of *Jeune Afrique*.

PATHFINDER PRESS
www.pathfinderpress.com
Email: pathfinder@pathfinderpress.com

Contents

Preface

This preface is taken from remarks by Mary-Alice Waters, president of Pathfinder Press, to a February 10, 2005, presentation in Havana, Cuba, of the Spanish-language edition of *We Are Heirs of the World's Revolutions* by Thomas Sankara, a booklet published in French in 2001 and in English the following year containing five of the thirty speeches and interviews that are in this new edition of *Thomas Sankara Speaks*. The event was organized as part of the annual Havana International Book Fair.

Also speaking on the panel were Manuel Agramonte, Cuba's ambassador to Burkina Faso during the four years of the revolutionary government led by Thomas Sankara; Armando Hart, one of the historic leaders of the Cuban Revolution and long-time minister of culture; and Ulises Estrada, director of *Tricontinental* magazine and himself an internationalist combatant with a long record of missions in Africa and Latin America.

This booklet by Thomas Sankara, the leader of Burkina Faso's popular revolutionary government from 1983 to 1987, was published by Pathfinder Press in French and then English some three years ago. The publication of *Somos herederos de las revoluciones del mundo* means that now, for the first time ever, a few of Sankara's most important speeches are also available in Spanish. It is a powerful new weapon in the hands of those fighting to advance along the road first charted in the Communist Manifesto more than 150 years ago by Karl Marx and Frederick Engels and their comrades.

In October 1984, adopting a practice employed so effectively by Fidel [Castro] and Che [Guevara] before him, Thomas Sankara used the platform of the United Nations

General Assembly to speak for and on behalf of the oppressed and exploited of the world. "I come here to bring you fraternal greetings from a country . . . whose seven million children, women, and men refuse to die from ignorance, hunger, and thirst any longer," Sankara told the assembled delegates of 159 nations.

"I make no claim to lay out any doctrines here. I am neither a messiah nor a prophet. I possess no truths. My only aspiration is . . . to speak on behalf of my people . . . to speak on behalf of the 'great disinherited people of the world,' those who belong to the world so ironically christened the Third World. And to state, though I may not succeed in making them understood, the reasons for our revolt."

Sankara voiced the determination and dignity of the people of one of the poorest countries of imperialist-ravaged Africa—one that then had the highest infant mortality rate in the world, a rural illiteracy rate approaching 98 percent, and an average life expectancy of some forty years. He reached out to, and spoke on behalf of, all those the world over who refuse to accept the economic bondage of class society and its consequences, including ecological devastation, social disintegration, racism, and the wars of conquest and plunder inevitably wrought by the workings of capitalism itself. Sankara knew such conditions are not "natural" phenomena, but the products of today's imperialist world order.

That world order, Sankara explained, can be fought, and must be destroyed. What marked him above all was his confidence in the revolutionary capacities of ordinary human beings to accomplish this. Like Fidel and Che, Sankara *believed* in the men and women so arrogantly dismissed by the rulers of the imperialist world. Sankara, as Fidel so memorably said of Che, did not think that man is "an incorrigible little animal, capable of advancing only if you feed him grass or tempt him with a carrot or whip him with a stick." Sankara, like Che, knew that anyone who thinks like that "will never be a revolutionary, . . . never be a socialist, . . . never be a communist."[1]

Sankara believed that a world built on different economic and social foundations can be created not by "technocrats," "financial wizards," or "politicians," but by the masses of workers and peasants whose labor, joined with the riches of nature, is the source of all wealth. By ordinary human beings who transform themselves as they become an active, conscious force, transforming their conditions of life. And the revolutionary government he headed set out along this course, mobilizing peasants, workers, craftsmen, women, youth, the elderly, to carry out a literacy campaign, an immunization drive, to sink wells, plant trees, build housing, and begin to eliminate the oppressive class relations on the land.

❖

Sankara stood out among the leaders of the struggles for national liberation in Africa in the last half of the twentieth century because he was a communist. Unlike so many others, he did not reject Marxism as a set of "European ideas," alien to the class struggle in Africa. He understood that Marxism is precisely *not* "a set of ideas," but the generalization of the lessons of the struggles of the working class on the road to its emancipation the world over, enriched by every battle. And he drew from those lessons to the best of his abilities.

Speaking before the United Nations in 1984, he linked the freedom struggle of the people of Burkina Faso to the

---

1. Fidel Castro, October 8, 1987. Published as "Che's Ideas Are Absolutely Relevant Today," in Ernesto Che Guevara and Fidel Castro, *Socialism and Man in Cuba* (New York: Pathfinder, 1989).

centuries of revolutionary struggle from the birth of capitalism to today—from the American and French revolutions at the end of the eighteenth century to the great October Revolution of 1917 that "transformed the world, brought victory to the proletariat, shook the foundations of capitalism, and made possible the Paris Commune's dreams of justice." We are the heirs of those revolutions, he said—hence the title of this small book.

We are "open to all the winds of the will of the peoples of the world and their revolutions, having also learned from some of the terrible failures that led to tragic violations of human rights," he noted. "We wish to retain only the core of purity from each revolution. This prevents us from becoming subservient to the realities of others."

And along that line of march, Sankara looked to Cuba as the preeminent example of revolutionary struggle in our times.

❖

Sankara was not only a leader of the people of Africa. He was not only a spokesman for the oppressed and exploited of the semicolonial countries. He gave leadership to working people in the imperialist world as well. In the last decades of the twentieth century, proletarian leaders with the world stature of Thomas Sankara, Maurice Bishop of Grenada, and in a similar way Malcolm X in the United States, have emerged from the ranks of the oppressed peoples of all lands—even the most economically undeveloped—to give leadership to the international struggle for national liberation and socialism. And thus to take their rightful place in history.

That fact is a measure of the vast changes that have marked the past century—the strengthening of revolutionary forces worldwide foreseen by [V.I.] Lenin and the leaders of the Communist International in the first years after the victory of the October Revolution.

This is the tradition in which we can today place the example given us by our five Cuban brothers who continue to fight not as victims, but as combatants of the Cuban Revolution placed by circumstances beyond their will on the front lines of the class struggle in the United States.[2] Within the federal prisons, where they are serving the draconian sentences the U.S. rulers imposed on them, they are carrying out their political work among some two million others who are the recipients of what Washington calls justice. That is where we see the original of the face that the whole world has witnessed so clearly at Guantánamo Bay Naval Base and in Iraq.[3]

❖

The books produced by Pathfinder are not sold only in bookstores or through the worldwide web. Most are

---

2. The Cuban Five—Fernando González, René González, Antonio Guerrero, Gerardo Hernández, and Ramón Labañino—were convicted in 2001 of charges including conspiracy "to act as an unregistered foreign agent," "to commit espionage," and "to commit murder." Sentences were handed down ranging from fifteen years, to terms of double life plus fifteen years. The five—each of whom has been named "Hero of the Republic of Cuba"—had accepted assignments to infiltrate counterrevolutionary groups in the United States and keep the Cuban government informed about terrorist attacks being planned against the Cuban people. Millions worldwide have mobilized to condemn the convictions, sentences, and harsh conditions of detainment and to demand their release.

3. Since early 2002, the U.S. government has used its Guantánamo naval base in eastern Cuba—a piece of Cuba's territory held by Washington against the will of the Cuban people—for a prison housing hundreds seized primarily in Afghanistan as part of imperialism's "war on terror." Deemed "enemy combatants," these prisoners have not been charged with any crimes and have been subjected to brutality and torture, denied contact with their families, and prevented from challenging their detention in any court of law.

sold on the streets—from sidewalk tables in working-class districts of the cities and towns of the United States and Europe, at mine portals and factory gates, on university campuses and at high school doors, at demonstrations or meetings where those who are fighting and seeking a way forward for working people are likely to gather.

At those tables, the face of Thomas Sankara has a powerful, indeed unique impact. Many passing by are literally stopped in their tracks when their eye falls on the book *Thomas Sankara Speaks*—a substantial selection of his speeches that Pathfinder published in English very soon after he was assassinated in 1987. Some do not know who Sankara is. But they are attracted to the confidence, character, and integrity they see in his face, and want to know more about him.

It is among the growing tens of thousands of immigrant workers from West and Central Africa who today are swelling the ranks of the working class in the imperialist centers, driven there by the whiplash of capital, that Sankara is best known and respected. Many are astonished to see the face of Sankara on a street table in the neighborhood where they live or work, on the cover of a book of his speeches, edited, printed, and distributed in the United States by working people there who look to Sankara as a revolutionary leader. That fact alone leads a good number to begin to think about the working class in the United States in a different way, and to be open to seeing the importance of the traditions of struggle they bring into what is the growing resistance by working people in North America to the bosses' assaults on our wages, job conditions, hours of work, and basic social and political rights.

And it is important to add that the converse is equally true. Reading Sankara is for us an important part of broadening the historical and cultural horizons of those who have been born or lived for years in the imperialist centers.

❖

Since it first appeared in 1988, close to 7,000 copies of *Thomas Sankara Speaks* have been sold in English alone, and many thousands more of the first French edition, *Oser inventer l'avenir*—Dare to invent the future.

From the very beginning, one of the hallmarks of the revolutionary course Sankara fought for was the mobilization of women to fight for their emancipation. As he says in one of the speeches published here, an October 1983 talk that presents the program of the government he headed, "The revolution and women's liberation go together. We do not talk of women's emancipation as an act of charity or out of a surge of human compassion. It is a basic necessity for the revolution to triumph. Women hold up the other half of the sky."

Sankara's powerful speech to a gathering of several thousand women on International Women's Day, March 8, 1987—also contained in *Thomas Sankara Speaks*—has been published by Pathfinder as a pamphlet, *Women's Liberation and the African Freedom Struggle* that is available in four languages—French, English, Spanish, and Farsi. Some 12,000 copies of that title have been sold since it first appeared in English translation almost fifteen years ago—more than 1,500 in Farsi in Iran alone.

We are proud that with the publication of this selection of some of the most representative of Sankara's other speeches, his voice will now be heard more broadly in Spanish. *Somos herederos de las revoluciones del mundo* includes, for example, his powerful speech on imperialism's destruction of the trees and forests of Africa, given to an international conference in Paris in 1986.

Before top dignitaries of the French imperialist government, Sankara affirmed:

> The battle against the encroachment of the desert is a battle to establish a balance between man, nature, and society. As such, it is a political battle above all, and not an act of fate. . . .
>
> As Karl Marx said, those who live in a palace do not think about the same things, nor in the same way, as those who live in a hut. This struggle to defend the trees and forests is above all a struggle against imperialism. Imperialism is the arsonist setting fire to our forests and our savannas.

That speech by Sankara is cited extensively in the recently produced issue number 13 of *New International* magazine, which is also being presented here today. From its lead article, entitled "Our Politics Start with the World," by Jack Barnes, to the photo of Earth at Night on its back cover—a photo that captures the economic and cultural inequalities, the veritable abyss, that exists between the imperialist and semicolonial countries, and among classes within almost every country—this issue of the magazine of Marxist politics and theory distributed by Pathfinder deals in depth with many of the same political issues and the course of action Sankara fought to advance.

❖

To end, I want to point to the depth of Sankara's internationalism so evident in these pages. For him, the popular, democratic, revolutionary struggle of the people of Burkina Faso was one with the struggles to bring down the apartheid regime of South Africa; it was one with the anti-imperialist struggles of the people of Angola, Namibia, Palestine, Western Sahara, and Nicaragua; it was one with the people of Harlem who so warmly welcomed him there in 1984; it was one with the working people of France, the United States, and across the imperialist world.

It was in Managua in 1986 that I had the pleasure of meeting and coming to know Sankara as a leader. We were both delegates to an international conference marking the twenty-fifth anniversary of the founding of the Sandinista National Liberation Front (FSLN) and the tenth anniversary of the fall in combat of founding FSLN leader Carlos Fonseca. Sankara was chosen to speak at the rally on behalf of the 180 international delegations present there.

When he learned that a delegation from the Socialist Workers Party in the United States was present, he made a point of heading straight to our table to greet us. It was not just as an act of diplomacy; he came to talk politics with fellow revolutionists. He knew that the *Militant* newsweekly was one of the few papers outside Africa that regularly wrote about the revolutionary course unfolding in Burkina Faso, carrying interviews and speeches by Sankara whenever we could get them.

❖

The presentation of *Somos herederos de las revoluciones del mundo* here in Cuba is especially appropriate because of the final selection it contains, Sankara's tribute to Che on October 8, 1987. That twentieth anniversary of Che's fall in combat was barely a week before the counterrevolutionary coup d'état that ended Sankara's own life.

It is only because of a fortunate combination of circumstances that Sankara's words at that memorable event are available to us today. The exhibition focusing on Che's revolutionary course and example, inaugurated that day by

Sankara, coincided with the opening of an international antiapartheid conference in Ouagadougou attended by delegations from some twenty-nine countries. Among them were compañeros from the United States and Canada, supporters of the *Militant* newspaper, and of Pathfinder Press. They were looking at the displays when Sankara arrived together with Che's son Camilo and a number of other Cuban compañeros. When Sankara began his impromptu remarks, one of the Canadian compañeras pulled out a tape recorder she had in her backpack and recorded them. The *Militant* transcribed and published them shortly afterward, and they are included here in their totality.

Che taught us "we could dare to have confidence in ourselves and our abilities," Sankara pointed out on that occasion. Che instilled in us the conviction that "struggle is our only recourse."

Che, Sankara insisted, was "a citizen of the free world— the free world that we're building together. That's why we say that Che Guevara is also African and Burkinabè."

What more appropriate place to end?

Mary-Alice Waters

Introduction

On August 4, 1983, a popular uprising in the West African nation then known as Upper Volta initiated one of the most profound revolutions in Africa's history. A former colony of France, Upper Volta, with more than seven million inhabitants, was among the world's poorest countries. The central leader of the revolution was Thomas Sankara, who became president of the new government at the age of thirty-three. A year later the people of Upper Volta adopted the name Burkina Faso—the Land of Upright Men.

Thomas Sankara was born in December 1949 in Yako in the center of the country. His father was an assistant policeman, at that time one of the country's few inhabitants to work for the colonial administration. His family moved to Gaoua near the border with Côte d'Ivoire (Ivory Coast) in the country's southwest, where Sankara attended elementary school and was among the tiny handful of African youth fortunate enough to gain a high school education in Bobo-Dioulasso. He then entered the Kadiogo military school in Kamboinsé—one of the few avenues for young people of his generation in sub-Saharan Africa to receive a higher education.

While Sankara was continuing his training in Madagascar, tens of thousands of workers and students organized mass demonstrations and strikes in 1972 that toppled the government. The scope and character of the popular mobilization had a deep impact on him. It was also in Madagascar that Sankara first became acquainted with Marxism, through study groups and discussions with students from France who had been part of the May 1968 prerevolutionary upsurge there. During a subsequent stay in France in the late 1970s, taking training as a paratrooper, Sankara scoured bookstores for revolutionary literature, studying, among other things, works by communist leaders Karl Marx and V.I. Lenin.

A lieutenant in Upper Volta's army, Sankara came to prominence as a military leader during a border conflict with Mali in December 1974 and January 1975, a war he later denounced as "useless and unjust." Over the next several years, he linked up with other junior officers and soldiers dissatisfied with the oppressive conditions in Upper Volta perpetuated by the imperialist rulers in Paris and elsewhere, with the support of landlords, businessmen, tribal chieftains, and politicians at home.

Jailed briefly in 1982 after resigning a government post to protest the regime's repressive policies, Sankara was appointed prime minister in January 1983 in the wake of a coup that made Jean-Baptiste Ouédraogo the president of the country. Sankara used that platform to urge the people of Upper Volta and elsewhere in Africa to advance their interests against the propertied exploiters at home and abroad. This uncompromising course led to growing conflict with proimperialist forces in the government. In May Ouédraogo had Sankara and some of his supporters arrested. But, in face of street protests by thousands, Ouédraogo transferred Sankara from prison to house arrest. In the following months, social tensions deepened across the country, heading toward a political showdown.

On August 4, 1983, some 250 soldiers led by Captain Blaise Compaoré marched from an insurgent military base in Pô to the capital of Ouagadougou. The regime of Jean-Baptiste Ouédraogo was overthrown in a popular uprising. Sankara became president of the new National Council of the Revolution. Over the next four years the popular

revolutionary government under Sankara's leadership organized the peasants, workers, and young people to carry out
deep-going economic and social measures that curtailed
the rights and prerogatives of the region's landed aristoc-
racy and wealthy merchants. They joined with working
people the world over to oppose imperialist domination.
Mass organizations of peasants, craftsmen, workers, youth,
women, and elders were initiated.

With broad popular support, the government abolished
tribute payments and compulsory labor services to village
chiefs. It nationalized the land to guarantee rural toilers—
some 90 percent of the population—access to the fruits
of their labors as productive farmers. The prices peasants
received from the government for basic food crops were
increased. The government launched tree-planting and
irrigation projects to increase productivity and stop the
advance of the desert in the Sahel region in the north of
the country. It organized massive immunization campaigns, and made basic health care services available to
millions. By 1985 infant mortality had fallen from 208 for
every 1,000 live births at the beginning of the decade to
145, and the accelerated spread of parasite-induced river
blindness had been curbed. In a country where illiteracy
was 92 percent—and even higher in the countryside—literacy campaigns in its indigenous languages were initiated. Steps were taken to combat the age-old subjugation
of women, who were encouraged to organize to fight for
their emancipation. The government funded public works
to build roads, schools, and housing. Trusting in the justice of the working class and peasantry, it set up popular
revolutionary courts to try former leaders and high officials accused of corruption.

Led by Sankara, the Burkinabè Revolution charted a
course of internationalist solidarity with those fighting

oppression and exploitation in Africa and worldwide. Sankara championed the fight of the people of Western Sahara against the occupation of their country by Morocco and helped lead a successful fight to admit the Saharawi representatives to the Organization of African Unity. He actively organized support, in Africa and beyond, for the struggle against the apartheid regime in South Africa and for the Palestinians' fight to reestablish their homeland. Sankara campaigned for cancellation of the onerous debt imposed on semicolonial countries by imperialist governments and banks. He spoke in New York City's Harlem to demonstrate support for African-Americans' fight against racist oppression and for other struggles by working people in the United States. He extended Burkina's hand to rising revolutionary struggles in Central America and the Caribbean, visiting Cuba in 1984 and 1986, and Nicaragua in 1986, where he spoke on behalf of all the international guests at a 200,000-strong rally marking the twenty-fifth anniversary of the Sandinista National Liberation Front.

In August 1987, speaking in Burkina Faso on the anniversary of the revolutionary uprising four years earlier, Sankara emphasized that, "The democratic and popular revolution needs a convinced people, not a conquered people—a convinced people, not a submissive people passively enduring their fate." Growing numbers of workers, peasants, and youth issuing from the ranks of such a people were becoming involved in social and political life in Burkina Faso, setting an example that was already reverberating throughout Central West Africa—far beyond the borders of that landlocked country. On October 15, 1987, Capt. Blaise Compaoré led a military coup serving the interests of those—at home and abroad—whose property and class domination were threatened by this deep-going revolutionary mobilization. Sankara and twelve of his aides and bodyguards were assassinated and the revolutionary government destroyed.

A week before his death, at a special commemoration in the capital of Ouagadougou, Sankara had spoken about Ernesto Che Guevara, the Argentine-born leader of the Cuban Revolution who died in combat twenty years earlier during an internationalist mission in Bolivia. In a speech reproduced in this book, Sankara, speaking of Che's legacy, noted that revolutionaries as individuals can be killed but "you cannot kill ideas." Thomas Sankara has himself become a symbol for millions of workers, peasants, and youth throughout Africa especially, who recognize in the Burkinabè Revolution—and in its continuing political heritage—a source of political ideas and inspiration for the battles for genuine liberation on the continent.

❖

The present collection of speeches and interviews is a new edition, entirely revised and expanded, of two earlier books. The first, *Thomas Sankara Speaks*, was rapidly published in English by Pathfinder in the months following the assassination of Sankara. The second, *Oser inventer l'avenir* [Dare to invent the future], was copublished in French in 1991 with l'Harmattan in Paris. This new edition, published in French and English with identical title and contents, appears on the twentieth anniversary of the coup in which Sankara was murdered. Its presentation will coincide with events in several countries celebrating the political accomplishments and living legacy of the revolutionary government he led.

Particular attention has been paid to placing the Burkinabè Revolution in its historical and international context. A new preface—along with a new introduction, maps, photo pages, explanatory notes, and index—will help readers unfamiliar with events, places, and people mentioned in the book to find their way. The chronology and glossary have been updated and expanded in the same spirit.

This edition includes five new documents:

- Substantial extracts of a previously unpublished interview conducted by writer Mongo Beti from Cameroon.
- The message sent by Sankara to the First Francophone Summit in Paris, February 1986.
- The remarks Sankara made at an official reception in Ouagadougou for French president François Mitterrand, November 17, 1986.
- A speech on the foreign debt given during a conference of the Organization of African Unity in Addis Ababa, Ethiopia, in July 1987.
- And the last major speech given by Sankara, October 2, 1987, on the fourth anniversary of the Political Orientation Speech, the programmatic document of the Burkinabè Revolution.

The French version of these documents has been revised to eliminate errors and misprints in the first edition. The translation to English has been carefully checked to ensure accuracy. Both have been reset in larger, easier-to-read type.

❖

This new edition of *Thomas Sankara Speaks* could not have seen the light of day without the help and encouragement of numerous people.

First and foremost, our thanks go to Mariam Sankara, wife of Thomas Sankara, and to Paul Sankara, his brother. Both of them were generous in helping to clarify a number of questions about Thomas Sankara's words as well as various events of the revolution.

Our thanks also go to Germaine Pitroïpa, high commissioner of Kouritenga province during the revolution. In addition to lending us a number of her personal photos, she patiently answered numerous questions directed her way as we prepared footnotes, revised the English translation of the text, and prepared the maps.

Jean-Louis Salfati in Paris devoted many hours to finding photographs and researching the glossary, chronology, and footnotes.

A number of people around the world gave generous assistance in assembling the photos and maps illustrating this new edition. Special mention goes to Augusta Conchiglia of the magazine *Afrique Asie*, Thuy Tien Ho of the agency Orchidées, and Didier Yara in Paris; to photographer Dany Be of Madagascar; to Balozi R. Harvey in New Jersey; and to Elombe Brath, Kwame Brathwaite, and Rosemari Mealy in New York.

Production of this book in two languages was made possible by the work of more than 200 volunteers in the Pathfinder Print Project who offered their time and skills to review the documents and their translation, set and proofread the type, prepare the many digital files for printing, and, finally, to help get out the finished product, making possible its distribution in bookstores, on street corners, at factory gates—wherever the workers, farmers, and youth to whom these books are dedicated can be found. It is they who will respond to Thomas Sankara's call, "dare to invent the future."

Michel Prairie
JULY 2007

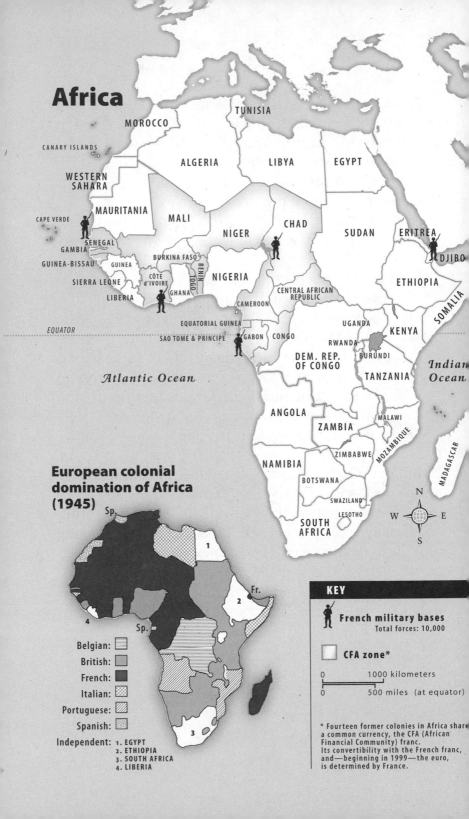

Africa

TUNISIA
MOROCCO
CANARY ISLANDS
WESTERN SAHARA
ALGERIA
LIBYA
EGYPT
CAPE VERDE
MAURITANIA
MALI
NIGER
CHAD
SUDAN
ERITREA
SENEGAL
GAMBIA
GUINEA-BISSAU
GUINEA
BURKINA FASO
DJIBO
SIERRA LEONE
CÔTE d'IVOIRE
BENIN
TOGO
NIGERIA
ETHIOPIA
LIBERIA
GHANA
CENTRAL AFRICAN REPUBLIC
SOMALIA
CAMEROON
EQUATORIAL GUINEA
UGANDA
KENYA
EQUATOR
SAO TOME & PRINCIPE
GABON
CONGO
RWANDA
BURUNDI
DEM. REP. OF CONGO
TANZANIA
Indian Ocean
Atlantic Ocean
ANGOLA
MALAWI
ZAMBIA
MOZAMBIQUE
ZIMBABWE
MADAGASCAR
NAMIBIA
BOTSWANA
SWAZILAND
N
LESOTHO
W   E
SOUTH AFRICA
S

European colonial domination of Africa (1945)

Sp.
1
Fr.
2
Sp.
4
3

Belgian:
British:
French:
Italian:
Portuguese:
Spanish:
Independent: 1. EGYPT
              2. ETHIOPIA
              3. SOUTH AFRICA
              4. LIBERIA

KEY

French military bases
Total forces: 10,000

CFA zone*

0   1000 kilometers
0   500 miles (at equator)

* Fourteen former colonies in Africa share a common currency, the CFA (African Financial Community) franc. Its convertibility with the French franc, and—beginning in 1999—the euro, is determined by France.

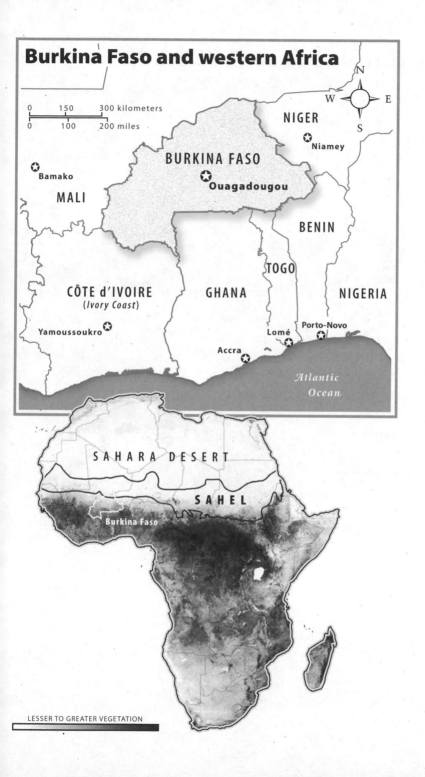

Burkina Faso and western Africa

0   150   300 kilometers
0   100   200 miles

N
W   E
S

NIGER

Niamey

BURKINA FASO

Bamako

Ouagadougou

MALI

BENIN

TOGO

CÔTE d'IVOIRE
(Ivory Coast)

GHANA

NIGERIA

Yamoussoukro

Porto-Novo

Lomé

Accra

Atlantic
Ocean

SAHARA DESERT

SAHEL

Burkina Faso

LESSER TO GREATER VEGETATION

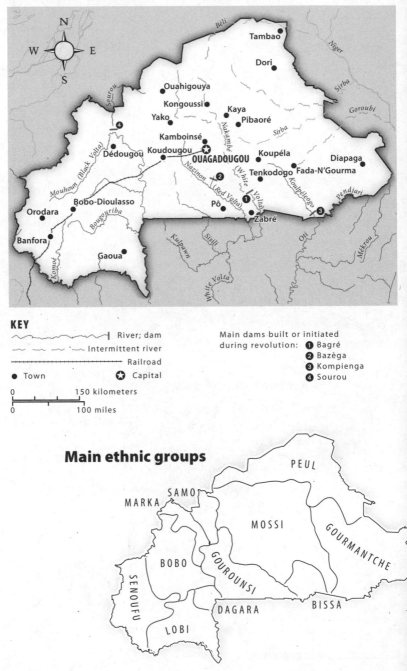

Burkina Faso (1983-87)

N
W   E
S

Tambao
Dori

Ouahigouya
Kongoussi
Kaya
Yako   Pibaoré
Kamboinsé
Dédougou   Koudougou
★ OUAGADOUGOU
Koupéla
Diapaga
Tenkodogo   Fada-N'Gourma
②
①
Orodara
Bobo-Dioulasso
Pô
③
Banfora
Zabré
Gaoua

Béli
Niger
Sirba
Gorouби
Sourou
Nakambé
Sirba
Mouhoun (Black Volta)
White Volta
Koulpéléogo
Pendjari
Nazinon (Red Volta)
Bougouriba
Komoé
Kulpawn
Sisili
Oti
Mékrou
White Volta

KEY

River; dam
Intermittent river
Railroad
● Town   ★ Capital

Main dams built or initiated
during revolution:
① Bagré
② Bazèga
③ Kompienga
④ Sourou

0   150 kilometers
0   100 miles

Main ethnic groups

PEUL
SAMO
MARKA
MOSSI
GOURMANTCHE
BOBO
GOUROUNSI
SENOUFU
DAGARA
BISSA
LOBI

Burkina Faso at the time of the revolution

POPULATION	7,964,705 (1985) (90% in rural areas)
NONAGRICULTURAL WORKERS	40,000 government 20,000 industrial (handicrafts & manufacturing) 10,000 construction
SURFACE AREA	105,869 sq. mi. / 274,200 sq. km
CAPITAL	Ouagadougou
AVERAGE YEARLY INCOME	US$150 (1981)
CURRENCY	CFA franc During 1983–87, this fluctuated between 300 and 500 to the US dollar
NATIONAL BUDGET	58 billion CFA francs (1985)
MAIN PRODUCTION & EXPORT GOODS	cotton, hides and skins, livestock, shea nut products, gold
ETHNIC GROUPS	Over 60, among them: 　Mossi　　　　　53.0% 　Peul　　　　　　7.8% 　Gourmantche　7.0% 　Gurunsi　　　　6.0% 　Bissa　　　　　3.0% 　Samo　　　　　2.0% 　Lobi　　　　　　2.5% 　Senufo　　　　2.2% 　Marka　　　　　1.7% 　Bobo　　　　　1.6%
LANGUAGES SPOKEN	Official language: French. Over 60 spoken, among them: 　Mooré　　　　53.0% 　Diula　　　　　8.8% 　Fulfulde　　　6.6%
ILLITERACY	92% (98% in rural areas)

HEALTH	Life expectancy	43.8 years (1980)
	Infant mortality rate	208 per 1,000 live births (1981)
	Maternal mortality rate	610 per 100,000 live births (1985)
	Doctors Nurses Midwives Assistant midwives	1 for every 37,494 (1988) 1 for every 12,366 (1988) 1 for every 28,397 (1988) 1 for every 31,267 (1988)

List of initials and acronyms

ANC	African National Congress
CDR	Comités de défense de la révolution / Committees for the Defense of the Revolution
CEAO	Communauté économique de l'Afrique de l'Ouest / West African Economic Community
CMRPN	Comité militaire de redressement pour le progrès national / Military Committee for Redressment and National Progress
CNR	Conseil national de la révolution / National Council of the Revolution
CSP	Conseil du salut du peuple / Council of Popular Salvation
CSR	Caisse de solidarité révolutionnaire / Revolutionary Solidarity Fund
DOP	Discours d'orientation politique / Political Orientation Speech
EPI	Effort populaire d'investissement / Popular Investment Effort
FPV	Front progressiste voltaïque / Voltaic Progressive Front
FRELIMO	Frente de Libertação de Moçambique / Mozambique Liberation Front
FSLN	Frente Sandinista de Liberación Nacional / Sandinista National Liberation Front
IMF	International Monetary Fund
MNP	Mouvement national des pionniers / National Movement of Pioneers
NGO	Non-Governmental Organizations
OAU	Organization of African Unity

OPEC	Organization of Petroleum Exporting Countries
PAI/LIPAD	Parti africain de l'indépendance–Ligue patriotique pour le développement / African Independence Party–Patriotic Development League
PLO	Palestine Liberation Organization
POLISARIO FRONT	Popular Front for the Liberation of Saguía el-Hamra and Río de Oro
PPD	Programme populaire de développement / Popular Development Program
RENAMO	Resistência Nacional Moçambicana / Mozambican National Resistance
SADR	Saharawi Arab Democratic Republic
SNEAHV	Syndicat national des enseignants africains de Haute-Volta / National Union of African Teachers of Upper Volta
SWAPO	South West Africa People's Organisation
TPC	Tribunaux populaires de conciliation / Popular Courts of Conciliation
TPR	Tribunaux populaires de la révolution / People's Revolutionary Courts
UFB	Union des femmes du Burkina / Women's Union of Burkina
UN	United Nations
UNAB	Union nationale des anciens du Burkina / National Union of Elders of Burkina
UNESCO	United Nations Educational, Scientific and Cultural Organization
UNITA	União Nacional para a Independência Total de Angola / National Union for the Total Independence of Angola
UNPB	Union nationale des paysans du Burkina / National Peasants Union of Burkina

Chronology

1945

August 15 – End of World War II.

At the time, European powers are colonial masters over all of Africa, with the exception of four independent states (Egypt, Ethiopia, Liberia, South Africa). Over the next two decades, struggles against colonial domination sweep Africa, Asia, and the Caribbean.

After initially attempting to drown these struggles in blood, the regimes of France, the United Kingdom, and other colonial powers are eventually forced to cede direct rule to independent governments across most of Africa and elsewhere in their former overseas empires.

1949

December 21 – Thomas Sankara born in Yako, Upper Volta, a French colony at the time.

1953

July 26 – Attempting to spark popular insurrection against Batista dictatorship, some 160 revolutionaries attack Moncada garrison in Santiago de Cuba and garrison in nearby Bayamo. Attacks fail but mark beginning of Cuban revolutionary struggle against Batista tyranny.

July 27 – End of Korean War. Workers and peasants of Korea and People's Liberation Army of China inflict first military defeat on U.S. imperialism in its attempt to destroy north Korean workers state and roll back Chinese Revolution, which had triumphed in 1949. Under United Nations banner, Washington maintains military occupation of south Korea to preserve the forcible partition of the country it had imposed in 1945.

1954

May 7 – In historic defeat for French colonialism, French forces surrender to combatants of Vietnam's national liberation movement at Dien Bien Phu.

November 1 – Start of Algeria's war of independence from French colonial rule.

1955

April 18–24 – Under impact of colonial revolution, representatives from 29 countries of Africa and Asia hold conference in Bandung, Indonesia. Six years later, in 1961, many of these governments and others will form the Movement of Nonaligned Countries.

December 5 – Boycott of racially segregated buses begins in Montgomery, Alabama. Marks beginning of mass civil rights movement to overturn racist "Jim Crow" system in southern United States.

1956

July 26 – Egyptian government headed by Gamal Abdel Nasser nationalizes Suez Canal, largely owned by British and French capital.

1958

December 11 – Upper Volta is declared to be self-governing. It becomes a member of the "French Community," a Paris-dominated organization whose members include France and its colonial territories and protectorates. Maurice Yaméogo is elected Upper Volta's president in December 1959.

1959

January 1 – Revolutionary war triumphs in Cuba, opening door to first socialist revolution in the Americas.

1960

March 21 – Sharpeville massacre in South Africa. Apartheid police fire on peaceful demonstration, killing 69 and wounding 180.

June 30 – Congo wins independence from Belgium. Patrice Lumumba becomes prime minister.

July – USSR withdraws advisers from People's Republic of China, registering deepening of Sino-Soviet conflict.

August 5 – Upper Volta becomes independent.

September 14 – With collaboration of UN troops, Colonel Joseph Mobutu (later Mobutu Sese Seko) overthrows Congo prime minister Patrice Lumumba. Lumumba is murdered January 17 with the direct participation of Belgian imperialism and the support of Washington.

1961

September 1–6 – Nonaligned Movement founded in Belgrade, Yugoslavia.

1962

July 5 – After an eight-year war of liberation and bloody attempts by Paris to crush it, Algeria wins independence from France. A workers and peasants government, led by Ahmed Ben Bella, soon comes to power.

1963

April–May – "Battle of Birmingham." In face of police billy clubs, dogs, fire hoses, and tear gas, Black-rights fighters conduct mass marches and sit-ins to desegregate public facilities in Birmingham, Alabama.

1964

June 12 – Nelson Mandela, arrested in 1962, is sentenced to life in prison in South Africa.

August 7 – U.S. government begins bombing of North Vietnam. Rapid U.S. escalation of war against Vietnamese liberation forces soon starts. By 1969 some 540,000 U.S. troops are in Vietnam.

1965

April – After resigning all leadership responsibilities in Cuba, Ernesto Che Guevara goes to Congo, where he heads more than 100 Cuban volunteers assisting popular forces fighting proimperialist regime.

April 17 – First national demonstration in Washington against war in Vietnam. In the following years, the opposition to this imperialist war will lead to mass mobilizations of millions of youth and working people throughout the world.

June 19 – Workers and peasants government in Algeria overthrown in military coup.

1966

January 3 – Mass demonstrations in Ouagadougou, capital of Upper Volta, against government austerity policies. President Maurice Yaméogo is overthrown and replaced by military regime led by Aboubakar Sangoulé Lamizana.

October – Thomas Sankara begins military school in Kamboinsé; graduates in 1969.

1967

June 5–10 – Six-Day War between Israel and Egypt, Jordan, and Syria. Tel Aviv wins rapid military victory and occupies West Bank, Gaza Strip, Golan Heights, and Sinai Peninsula.

October 8 – While leading revolutionary front in Southern Cone of Latin America, Ernesto Che Guevara is wounded and captured by Bolivian army. Assassinated next day with Washington's approval.

1968

May–June – Student revolt sparks general strike and factory occupations by workers, leading to prerevolutionary situation in France. Regime of President Charles de Gaulle is saved as Communist and Socialist parties demobilize movement.

1969

October 1 – Sankara enters Antsirabé military academy in Madagascar.

1972

May – While Sankara is in Madagascar, workers and students organize wave of strikes and demonstrations and overthrow regime of President Tsiranana.

June – Sankara finishes training at Antsirabé. In fall, begins additional year of "civic service" in Madagascar.

1973

October – Sankara returns to Upper Volta. Assigned to Bobo-Dioulasso to train new recruits.

1974

April 25 – Beginning of "Revolution of the Carnations" in Portugal. Dictatorship collapses, in large part under impact of advancing national liberation struggles in its African colonies of Angola, Guinea-Bissau/Cape Verde, and Mozambique.

December–January – Border conflict between Mali and Upper Volta, in which Sankara becomes widely known in Upper Volta for his military conduct.

1975

April 30 – Troops from Democratic Republic of Vietnam and National Liberation Front take Saigon, ending three decades of imperialist-imposed division of the country. Victory of national liberation movement and Washington's defeat in Vietnam War deal historic setback to U.S. imperialism.

June 25 – Independence of Portuguese colony of Mozambique.

November 11 – Independence of Angola. Prior to this date, South African and Zairean troops invade country to install proimperialist regime. By early 1976 they are stopped by arrival of thousands of Cuban volunteers who respond to Angolan government's call for help.

December 17–18 – General strike in Upper Volta. Government employees obtain wage increases and tax reductions.

1976

Middle of year – Sankara takes command of new national commando training center in Pô.

June 16 – Beginning of Soweto revolt in South Africa. Encouraged by defeat of South African army in Angola, thousands of young people confront apartheid regime's cops and armed forces.

1978

January–May – Sankara and Blaise Compaoré train at paratrooper school in Rabat, Morocco. Sankara then pursues his training in Pau, France.

1979

February 11 – Popular insurrection in Iran. Workers and peasants overthrow brutal U.S.-backed monarchy and prevent installation of Washington's designated replacement regime.

March 13 – Armed popular uprising overthrows Eric Gairy dictatorship on Caribbean island of Grenada. A workers and farmers government is established led by Maurice Bishop, who becomes prime minister.

May 24–31 – Four union federations strike in Upper Volta. They win liberation of imprisoned unionists.

July 19 – Under leadership of Sandinista National Liberation Front, workers and peasants overthrow Anastasio Somoza dictatorship in Nicaragua.

December 25 – Invasion of Afghanistan by Soviet troops.

1980

September 22 – With complicity of Washington and Paris, Iraqi army invades Iran to seize oilfields and strike at Iranian Revolution. Opens war in which hundreds of thousands of Iranian and Iraqi soldiers and civilians will be killed over next eight years.

October 1–November 22 – Teachers strike against drop in buying power in Upper Volta. Actions twice become general strikes, October 4–5 and November 4–5.

November 25 – Coup overthrows Lamizana government. Colonel Saye Zerbo heads Military Committee for Redressment and National Progress (CMRPN).

1981

February – Thomas Sankara is promoted to captain.

May 10 – François Mitterrand, Socialist Party candidate, elected president of France.

Middle of year – Beginning of contra war initiated by Washington against workers and peasants government in Nicaragua.

September 9 – Asked by Saye Zerbo to become state secretary for information, Sankara first refuses, later accepts.

December 31 – Jerry Rawlings carries out coup in Ghana and becomes president of National Provisional Defense Council of Ghana, set up by junior officers and civilians.

1982

April – Voltaic Union Federation organizes three-day strike against ban on strikes decreed by Saye Zerbo government.

April 12 – Protesting government attacks on democratic rights, Sankara resigns as state secretary for information. In following days he is arrested, demoted, and sent to Dédougou. In protest, Henri Zongo and Blaise Compaoré resign from government. They are sent to remote garrisons of Fada and Ouahigouya.

November 1 – CMRPN government confirms ban on strikes.

November 7 – Coup led by Colonel Somé Yoryan overthrows CMRPN. Junior officers do not participate. New Provisional Council of Popular Salvation (later Council of Popular Salvation) appoints Commander Jean-Baptiste Ouédraogo president.

1983

January 10 – Council of Popular Salvation appoints Sankara prime minister.

February 28 – Attempted coup against Council of Popular Salvation.

March 7–12 – At Nonaligned summit in New Delhi, India, Sankara meets Cuban president Fidel Castro, Mozambican president Samora Machel, prime minister of Grenada Maurice Bishop.

March 26 – Sankara addresses mass meeting in Ouagadougou.

April 30 – Libyan head of state Muammar al-Qaddafi visits Ouagadougou.

May 15 – Sankara gives speech in Bobo-Dioulasso, where he criticizes France's actions in Africa.

May 16 – Guy Penne, African affairs adviser to French president François Mitterrand, arrives in Ouagadougou.

May 17 – Colonel Somé Yoryan leads coup. Sankara, Jean-Baptiste Lingani, Henri Zongo arrested. Blaise Compaoré escapes and functions as government opponent from Pô military base he commands.

May 20–22 – Huge street demonstrations in Ouagadougou demand release of Sankara.

May 27 – Sankara placed under house arrest.

June 9–16 – Sankara, Lingani, and Zongo are jailed again. Upon their release they're again put under house arrest. But in fact they actively work to organize the forces opposing the regime issuing from the coup.

June–August – Sankara supporters flock to Pô, where Compaoré remains entrenched, to receive accelerated military training.

August 4 – Compaoré and 250 men march on Ouagadougou and overthrow government of Jean-Baptiste Ouédraogo. National Council of the Revolution takes power, names Sankara president. His first speech, broadcast countrywide by radio, calls for immediate formation of Committees for the Defense of the Revolution.

August 5–7 – Mass demonstrations in support of new regime sweep Ouagadougou.

August 24 – First government of National Council of the Revolution (CNR) formed and includes five leaders of the African Party for Independence/Patriotic League for Development (PAI/Lipad).

September 30 – Sankara meets Jerry Rawlings, head of state in Ghana, in Pô.

October 2 – In name of CNR, Sankara gives Political Orientation Speech, broadcast on radio, television.

October 13 – Coup in Grenada overthrows workers and farmers government led by Maurice Bishop. Six days later, as thousands of workers and farmers attempt to reinstall former government, Bishop and other revolutionary leaders are executed. Taking advantage of counterrevolution, U.S. government invades the island six days later.

October 31 – Upper Volta elected non-permanent member of UN Security Council for two-year term.

November 4–8 – Ghana and Upper Volta hold joint military exercises.

December – Agreement on scientific, economic, technical cooperation signed with Cuba.

December 21 – Angolan president Eduardo dos Santos visits Ouagadougou.

1984

January 3 – First session of People's Revolutionary Courts. Sessions are broadcast by radio.

February – CNR abolishes all compulsory payments and unpaid labor to traditional chiefs.

February 10–12 – Jerry Rawlings makes official visit to Ouagadougou.

February–March – Angola, Mozambique sign nonaggression pacts with South Africa, aimed at stopping attacks by apartheid regime.

March 20–21 – Strikes organized by National Union of African Teachers of Upper Volta, whose leadership is linked to the National Liberation Movement/Progressive Front of Joseph Ki-Zerbo.

March 22 – CNR fires 1,500 striking teachers.

March 31 – Sankara begins official visits to Algeria, Mauritania, Saharawi Arab Democratic Republic.

April 8 – Plots of land distributed in Ouagadougou to alleviate housing crisis.

April 26 – Sourou valley project launched with goal of irrigating 39,500 acres (16,000 hectares).

May 20–21 – Committees for the Defense of the Revolution's General National Secretariat and PAI/Lipad organize competing demonstrations to mark first anniversary of May 1983 mass demonstrations protesting coup against Sankara.

May 26–27 – Discovery of plot linked to exiled Joseph Ki-Zerbo. Seven in plot are executed June 11.

May 27 – Official visit to Côte d'Ivoire (Ivory Coast) canceled when President Houphouët-Boigny says Sankara can't meet with Voltaic students and workers living in Abidjan.

June 23 – Sankara begins official trip in Africa, visiting Ethiopia, Angola, Congo, Mozambique, Gabon, Madagascar.

July 12 – Compulsory military service introduced.

August 4 – First anniversary of revolution marked with parade of people's militias in Ouagadougou. Upper Volta is renamed Burkina Faso, or Land of Upright Men, words taken from Mooré and Diula, the two languages most used in the country. Land, mineral resources are nationalized.

August 19 – First CNR government is dissolved, which becomes annual practice. New government formed August 31, without any member from PAI/Lipad.

September 22 – Day of solidarity with housewives in Ouagadougou. Men encouraged to shop, prepare meals so as to see women's living conditions.

September 25–30 – Sankara's first visit to Cuba. Receives Order of José Martí.

October – Sankara becomes president of West African Economic Community.

October 1 – CNR abolishes poll tax, launches Popular Development Program, which lasts until December 1985.

October 4 – Sankara addresses 39th Session of United Nations General Assembly in New York.

November 5–9 – Sankara visits China.

November 12–15 – Sankara attends OAU summit, Addis Ababa, Ethiopia. Supports OAU recognition of Saharawi Arab Democratic Republic against opposition by Moroccan government, which withdraws from OAU when SADR is admitted.

November 25 – Two-week campaign begins to vaccinate all Burkinabè under 15 against meningitis, yellow fever, German measles. Cuban volunteers participate. 2.5 million children vaccinated, including some from neighboring countries.

December 3 – At national budget conference in Ouagadougou, 3,000 delegates decide to fund development projects by payroll deductions—one month's pay from upper-level government employees, two-weeks' pay from others.

December 31 – Sankara announces abolition of housing rents for 1985, launches housing construction program.

1985

1985 – Reforestation campaign launched: ten million trees to be planted during the year to stop "creeping desert" in the Sahel region.

January 12 – In New Caledonia, French occupation forces assassinate Eloi Machoro, central Kanak leader of independence movement in South Pacific colony.

February 1 – "Battle for the Railroad" begins. Goal is to build new rail line from Ouagadougou to Tambao in north.

February 12 – Sankara attends Entente Council meeting in Yamassoukro, Côte d'Ivoire. Population greets him with enthusiasm.

March 1–8 – 3,000 delegates attend national conference on women's emancipation.

March 17–23 – Joint military exercises with Ghana.

May 8 – Leader of Burkinabè Trade Union Federation and of African Party of Independence, Soumane Touré, is arrested after charging CNR with embezzlement. Remains in prison 21 months.

August 4 – Second anniversary of revolution. In Ouagadougou, parade composed entirely of women illustrates progress toward women's equality.

September 10 – Special meeting of Entente Council in Yamoussoukro, Côte d'Ivoire, which displays the hostility of governments beholden to imperialism in region to Burkina.

December 25 – "Christmas War" begins. Troops and planes from Mali attack and bomb Burkina Faso. Close to 100 deaths and more than 300 wounded overall on both sides. Ceasefire signed December 29.

1986

January 3 – Sankara frees all Mali prisoners of war.

February – Sankara visits France, where he attends First Silva Conference on Trees and Forests and sends message to First Francophone Summit.

February–April – Literacy campaign in national languages involves 35,000 people in rural areas.

March 31–April 4 – First National Conference of CDRs.

April 15 – U.S. Air Force bombs city of Tripoli and Benghazi region in Libya. Kills over 100, among them the daughter of Libyan leader Muammar al-Qaddafi.

May 19 – South African warplanes, helicopters, and commandos carry out raids in Gamborone, Botswana; Harare,

Zimbabwe; and Lusaka, Zambia, allegedly to destroy bases used by African National Congress (ANC).

August 4 – Third anniversary of revolution. CNR announces launch of five-year development plan.

August 27 – Nicaraguan president Daniel Ortega arrives on official visit to Ouagadougou.

September 3 – Sankara participates in Eighth Summit Conference of Movement of Nonaligned Countries, Harare, Zimbabwe.

October 6–12 – Sankara visits Soviet Union.

October 19 – Mozambican president Samora Machel dies in plane crash in South Africa. Many African and anti-apartheid leaders believe this was planned assassination carried out by the apartheid government.

November 8 – Sankara stops in Cuba, meets with Fidel Castro, on way to Nicaragua. Later the same day, Sankara, on behalf of 180 foreign delegations, addresses rally of 200,000 in Managua on 25th anniversary of founding of Sandinista National Liberation Front.

November 9 – Sankara receives Order of Carlos Fonseca. On return trip, spends two days in Cuba during which he meets with Raúl Castro, vice president of Council of State and Council of Ministers.

November 17 – French president François Mitterrand stops in Ouagadougou during tour of Africa. At official reception for him, Sankara criticizes French policy in Africa.

1987

Early 1987 – At beginning of year, program organized with UN help eliminates onchocerciasis (river blindness), for a long time one of Burkina's worst medical problems.

March 8 – On International Women's Day, Sankara gives speech to meeting of several thousand women.

March 30–April 3 – Second National Conference of CDRs.

April 11 – Sankara announces creation of National Union of Peasants of Burkina.

April 28–May 2 – National Peasant Symposium in Ouagadougou.

May – Scurrilous anonymous leaflets attacking several CNR leaders circulate widely.

May 30 – Arrests begin of union leaders associated with PAI/ Lipad and Voltaic Revolutionary Communist Party, eventually reaching 200. The arrests are initiated by forces in CNR and CDRs that will subsequently support coup.

August 4 – Fourth anniversary of revolution celebrated in Bobo-Dioulasso. In speech, Sankara launches political counteroffensive against measures by currents in CNR that increasingly undermine revolution and functioning of mass organizations.

August 7 – Esquipulas Accords signed in Central America, marking strategic defeat of U.S.-backed contras in Nicaragua.

August 21 – Letter by Sankara asks government ministers to rehire teachers and government employees fired for opposing revolution. Initiative meets strong opposition in CNR and from political organizations in it.

August 22 – Sankara creates special six-member cabinet to advise and aid in organizing his work.

October 2 – Fourth anniversary of revolution celebrated in Tenkodogo, addressed by Sankara. Before Sankara's talk, a student leader associated with Blaise Compaoré gives speech publicly attacking central aspects of course Sankara is fighting for.

October 8 – Opening in Ouagadougou of exhibition on Che Guevara's life, marking 20th anniversary of his death in combat in Bolivia.

October 8–10 – Bambata conference against apartheid held in Ouagadougou, with 40 organizations from 29 countries represented. Closing address by Sankara.

October 15 – Around 4:30 p.m., Thomas Sankara and 12 others are assassinated by military detachment from

Pô commando base led by an aide of Blaise Compaoré.

Among dead are five of Sankara's six special cabinet members: Paulin Bamouni, Bonaventure Compaoré, Frédéric Kiemdé, Christophe Saba, Patrice Zagré. Not killed was Alouna Traoré. Seven soldiers also killed (four presidential guards, two drivers, and one police officer), making 13 victims in all. Blaise Compaoré takes power, dissolves CNR, replacing it with Popular Front of October 15. Coup is supported by Jean-Baptiste Lingani, Henri Zongo (both of whom are executed by Compaoré without trial in 1989), many organizations that had been in CNR, and organizations that had opposed revolution.

Over following days, targeted killings, arrests, and torture hit Sankara's supporters across the country. Thousands go to his grave, condemning crime and coup.

1988

March – Internationalist Cuban combatants, together with troops from Angola and the South West Africa People's Organisation (SWAPO), inflict decisive defeat on South African forces in southern Angolan town of Cuito Cuanavale. In response to the changed relationship of forces this defeat registers, the white supremacist government of South Africa is forced to withdraw its troops from Angola and grant Namibia its independence. The defeat sets in motion a chain of events within South Africa itself that leads to the downfall of the apartheid system in the first years of the 1990s.

Speeches & interviews

Who are the enemies of the people?

At mass rally in Ouagadougou
March 26, 1983

Speaking as prime minister of the Council of Popular Salvation (CSP), Sankara delivered this speech to a rally of several thousand in the country's capital city. The text appeared in the April 1, 1983, issue of the weekly *Carrefour africain*, published in Ouagadougou.

Thank you for having gathered here at January 3 Square. I salute you for answering the call of the Council of Popular Salvation. By doing so you are showing that the people of Upper Volta are coming of age.[1]

When the people stand up, imperialism trembles. As it watches us, imperialism is worried. It is trembling. Imperialism is wondering how to break the bond that exists between the CSP and the people. Imperialism trembles. It is trembling because it is afraid. It is trembling because right here in Ouagadougou we are going to bury it.

---

1. Sixteen months later Upper Volta was renamed Burkina Faso.

I also salute you for coming to show that all our de-
tractors, who are both inside and outside the country, are
wrong. They have misjudged us. They thought they could
stop the CSP's march toward the people with their maneuvers of propaganda and intimidation. By coming here,
you have shown that the opposite is true. Imperialism is
trembling and will keep trembling.

People of Upper Volta, represented here by the inhabitants of the city of Ouagadougou, thank you. Thank you
for giving us the opportunity to provide you with truthful
information, information that comes up from the ranks.

What is our purpose here? Our purpose is to tell you
exactly what our enemies want, what the CSP wants, and
what the people have a right to. The people love liberty
and they love democracy. Consequently, the people will
take on all enemies of liberty and democracy.

But who are the enemies of the people?

The enemies of the people are both inside and outside
the country. Right now they are trembling, but you must
expose them. You must combat them even holed up in
their burrows. The enemies of the people inside the country are all those who have taken advantage of their social
position, of their bureaucratic position, to enrich themselves illicitly. In this way, through maneuvers, through
graft, and through forged documents, they find themselves
corporate shareholders, they find themselves financing
some company, they find themselves seeking approval for
this or that company. They claim they are serving Upper
Volta. These are enemies of the people. They must be exposed. They must be combated. We will combat them together with you.

Who are the enemies of the people? The enemies of the
people are also that section of the bourgeoisie that enriches
itself dishonestly through fraud and bribery, through the

corruption of state officials, so they can bring into Upper Volta all kinds of products, whose prices have been multiplied tenfold. These are the enemies of the people. This section of the bourgeoisie must be combated, and we will combat it.

Who are the enemies of the people? The enemies of the people are also the politicians who travel throughout the countryside only at election time. The politicians who are convinced that only they can make Upper Volta work. However, we, the CSP, are convinced that Upper Volta's seven million people represent seven million politicians capable of running this country. Those are the enemies of the people, who we must expose and combat. And we will combat them together with you.

The enemies of the people are also the forces of obscurantism who, under spiritual cover, under cover of tradition, are exploiting the people instead of genuinely serving their moral interests, instead of genuinely serving their social interests. They must be combated, and we will combat them.

Let me ask you a question: Do you like these enemies of the people, yes or no?

[*Shouts of "No!"*]

Do you like them?

[*Shouts of "No!"*]

So we must combat them.

Will you combat them inside the country?

[*Shouts of "Yes!"*]

On with the fight!

The enemies of the people are also outside our borders. They base themselves on unpatriotic people here in our midst at every level of society—civilians as well as in the army; men as well as women; young as well as old; in the town as well as the country. The enemies of the people are there. The enemies outside the country are there: these enemies are neocolonialism; they are imperialism.

So, basing itself on these unpatriotic people, on those who have rejected their homeland, those who have rejected Upper Volta—who have, in fact, rejected the people of Upper Volta—the enemy outside the country is organizing a series of attacks. Attacks in two phases: the nonviolent phase and the violent phase.

Currently we are in the nonviolent phase. The enemy outside the country—that is, imperialism; that is, neocolonialism—is attempting to sow confusion among the Voltaic people. Thus, through their newspapers, their radios, and their television they would make us believe that Upper Volta is being laid waste by armed conflict. But you are here, people of Upper Volta, and your presence proves that imperialism is wrong, and that its lies won't stick. You are present, you are standing up, and it is imperialism that is trembling today.

A foreign journalist in a faraway country, sitting in his swivel chair, in his air-conditioned office, dared to report that the CSP's informational tours are a failure. Are they failures? You are here, answer me.

[*Shouts of "No!"*]

Are they failures?

[*Shouts of "No!"*]

I would like imperialism to be here, so it can hear you say no. Repeat: are they failures?

[*Shouts of "No!"*]

You see, imperialism is wrong. But imperialism is a bad student. When it's been defeated, when it's been sent out of the classroom, it goes back in again. It's a bad student. It never learns the lessons of its failures, it never draws the lessons from its failures. It's over there in South Africa cutting African throats, just because those Africans are thinking about freedom, as you are today. Imperialism is over there in the Middle East crushing the Arab peoples. That's Zionism.

Imperialism is everywhere. Through the culture that it spreads, through its misinformation, it gets us to think like it does, it gets us to submit to it, and to go along with all its maneuvers. For goodness' sake, we must stand in imperialism's way.

As I've already told you, it will move on to a violent phase. It is imperialism that has organized troop landings in certain countries that we know. It is imperialism that has armed those who are killing our brothers in South Africa. It is imperialism that assassinated the Lumumbas, the Cabrals, and the Kwame Nkrumahs.

But I'm telling you and I'm promising you—because I have confidence in you and you have confidence in the CSP, because we are part of the people—when imperialism comes here, we will bury it. We will bury imperialism here. Ouagadougou will be the *bolibana* of imperialism, that is, the end of its road. Through very sophisticated methods, imperialism has tried to sow division within the CSP itself. It has created anxiety and hysteria among the Voltaic people themselves. But we are not afraid.

For the first time, something fundamental is happening in Upper Volta, something completely new. The people have never had the power to establish a political democracy here. The army has always had the possibility of taking power, but it never wanted democracy. For the first time, we see an army that wants power, that wants democracy, and that genuinely wants to link up with the people. For the first time, too, we see the people coming forward in massive numbers to stretch out their hands to the army. That's why we believe that this army, which is taking control of the destiny of Upper Volta, is the people's army. That is why I also salute those placards that speak of the people's army.

In order to do us harm, our enemies within as well as without rely on a certain number of factors. I'll mention some and will let you complete the list. They are trying to make us believe that the CSP is going to halt the normal functioning of the state apparatus as a result of taking decisions against high-level government employees.[2] We have taken these decisions simply because we feel that there are those who, at this stage of our struggle, cannot keep pace. There are civil servants who don't come to the office until 9:00 a.m. and who leave again at 10:30 a.m. to go to their orchards and watch over their houses. Is that normal? When we want to get rid of this kind of civil servant, our enemies say the CSP wants to bring the state apparatus to a standstill. But who is afraid of whom?

We are with the people. They are against the people. So we will take decisions that will be against the enemies of the people, because these decisions will be in favor of the people—the militant people of Upper Volta. Are you in favor of us keeping corrupt civil servants in our administration?

[*Shouts of "No!"*]

So we must get rid of them. We will get rid of them.

Are you in favor of us keeping corrupt soldiers in our army?

[*Shouts of "No!"*]

So we must get rid of them. We will get rid of them. Perhaps this will cost us our life, but we are here to take

------

2. The Council of Popular Salvation had decided to punish civil servants who spent time in bars during their workday—the first time by naming them on the radio; the second time by giving them an official reprimand; the third time by dismissing them.

risks. We are here to dare. And you are here to continue the struggle at all costs.

Our enemies say that the CSP is preparing to nationalize, that the CSP is preparing to confiscate their property. Who is afraid of whom?

When you go around Ouagadougou and you make a list of all the houses there are, you'll see that these houses belong to only a minority. How many of you, consigned to Ouagadougou from the farthest corners of the country, have had to move every night because of being thrown out of the house you had rented? Every day the owner raised the price a little more. For those who acquired their houses normally, there's no problem, there's no need to worry. However, for those who acquired their land and their houses through corruption, we say to them: start trembling. If you have stolen, tremble! Because we are going to come after you. Not only is the CSP going to come after you, but the people will take care of you. Yes or no?

[*Shouts of "Yes!"*]

Honest citizens, even if you own 1,000 houses, have no fear! Dishonest citizens, however, even if you own only a half square, an *entrée-coucher*[3] without sanitation, start trembling, the CSP is coming! We did not come this far only to stop after such a promising start. We are not here to sell out, we are not here to betray the people.

They say we want to nationalize. The CSP does not understand and will never understand—just as you too will never understand—how someone can come and get set up in Upper Volta, start a company in Upper Volta, succeed in obtaining favors—all kinds of tax exemptions—on the

---

3. A half square is the equivalent of approximately 12.5 square meters, or 15 square yards. An *entrée-coucher* is a small house with only one entrance and one bedroom.

pretext of wanting to create jobs, of wanting to contribute to economic development, and then, after a certain number of years of brazen exploitation, announce cuts in personnel.

On what condition were you granted these favors? On the condition that you create jobs for Voltaics. Today, when you've squeezed the lemon dry, you want to throw the lemon out. No! That is what we say no to!

Our enemies say that the CSP proclaimed freedom of expression and of the press, but that the CSP is beginning to restrict this freedom. Comrade Jean-Baptiste Lingani said earlier, and later Comrade Jean-Baptiste Ouédraogo will say it better than I can: we do not want to put an end to freedom. We say only that the freedom to criticize also brings with it the freedom to protest. And freedom for sincere men should not mean freedom for dishonest men.

We will take away the freedom of those who use the freedom created by the CSP to attack the CSP, in fact, to attack the Voltaic people. We are taking away their freedom to do harm, and we are giving them the freedom to serve the people. We cannot grant the freedom to lie, to brainwash the collective Voltaic consciousness. That would be to work against the popular masses of Upper Volta.

It is also said that some of the CSP's members, such as Captain Thomas Sankara, have been to Libya and north Korea, and that this is dangerous for Upper Volta. People of Upper Volta, one question: Libya has never done anything to us. Korea has never exploited Upper Volta. Libya has never attacked Upper Volta. Yet we know countries that *have* attacked Upper Volta, that put our parents in prison. Our grandparents died on the battlefield for these countries. When we cooperate with them, no one complains.

Sangoulé [Lamizana] went to Libya. Saye Zerbo has

been to Libya and Korea. Why didn't anyone complain? There's something crooked here. Yesterday, preparations were made for an official visit by Saye Zerbo to [Libyan head of state Muammar al-] Qaddafi in Qaddafi's plane, and this was publicized. Today when we go to Libya, there are complaints.

But we went to Libya in a responsible and an intelligent manner! We went to Libya after Colonel Qaddafi had sent us emissaries three times. We told the Libyan leaders that we had nothing against Libya, but that we have positions of our own. When it comes to ideology, we're not virgins. We are ready to collaborate with Libya, but we are also ready to tell them, in a responsible manner, whatever we might criticize. It was after being approached three times that we decided to go, and we laid down concrete conditions, in accordance with the interests of the Voltaic people.

When the cement starts to arrive from Tripoli and we sell it at a cheap price, will the people be pleased, yes or no?

[*Shouts of "Yes!"*]

Why is Qaddafi's cement desirable while negotiating with Qaddafi is undesirable? When we negotiate deals with certain countries worth 2 million, 3 million CFA francs,[4] it's talked about on the radio. With Qaddafi, we negotiated a deal worth 3.5 billion. And so, are the people pleased, yes or no?

[*Shouts of "Yes!"*]

The people like cooperation between states that respect their peoples. The people of Upper Volta don't want to be

---

4. Many of the former French colonies in Africa share a common currency, the CFA (African Financial Community) franc, whose convertibility with the French franc (and now the euro) is determined by Paris. At the time of the revolution, 1 French franc equalled 50 CFA francs. Based on the French franc's exchange rate, during 1983–87 the CFA franc fluctuated between 300 and 500 to the U.S. dollar.

told what road to take. We say no to housebroken Voltaic diplomacy! We say no to bossed-around Voltaic diplomacy! We are free to go wherever we wish. And I'll tell you something, a secret. Don't tell this to the imperialists. Those who criticize us for having been to Libya took Qaddafi's dollars to develop their countries. Do they think they're smarter than we are? They go deal with Qaddafi. Why? Who is smarter than whom?

We will go wherever the interests of the Voltaic masses are to be found. We saw social achievements in Libya—hospitals, schools, houses, and all of it available for free. How has Libya managed to carry out these social investments? Thanks to oil. This oil existed under the former regime of King Idriss. But this oil was exploited by the imperialists and for the benefit of the king. The people drew absolutely no benefit from it. Today, Libyans have free houses and paved roads. If we could transform Upper Volta tomorrow the way Qaddafi has transformed Libya, would you be pleased, yes or no?

[*Shouts of "Yes!"*]

So in our relations with other states, when we take their good aspects, we're simply carrying out a policy of diplomatic independence and applying one of the CSP's rules: to work for the people. There is no shame in getting on one's knees when it is in the interests of the people.

As we speak to you, we know that in this crowd are people who would very much like to shoot us right now. Those are the risks we take, convinced that it is in the interests of the people. We say to them: "Shoot!" When you shoot, your bullets will turn around and hit you. That is what is called the victory of the people over the enemies of the people. Today we speak with the strength of the people, and not our own.

The enemies of the CSP say that certain factions of the CSP look favorably on this or that country, this or that camp, or the pro-Western camp, and so on. We say that we are not against any camp. We are for all the camps. We repeated this in New Delhi at the summit of the Movement of Nonaligned Countries:[5] we are for all the camps. We say too that he who loves his own people loves the other peoples. We love the Voltaic people, and we love the peoples of Nicaragua, Algeria, Libya, Ghana, Mali, and all the other peoples.

Those who do not love their own people do not love the Voltaic people. Those who are worried today by the transformations occurring in Upper Volta do not love their own peoples. They impose their will through dictatorship and through police operations against their peoples. We are not of that type.

We are told that the CSP has a certain admiration for Flight Lieutenant Jerry Rawlings. Rawlings is a man. Every man must have friends and enemies. If Rawlings has admirers in Upper Volta, whose fault is that? It's imperialism's fault. It's because a situation was created in Ghana in which the new authorities were compelled to fight for the interests of the Ghanaian people. When Ghana was prosperous, we Voltaics took full advantage of it! Today, when Ghana is experiencing difficulties, why should we forget Ghana?

No, we are sincere. The people keep their attachments. Men perhaps may betray, but peoples do not betray each other. The Ghanaian people need the Voltaic people, just as the Voltaic people need the Ghanaian people.

When Flight Lieutenant Rawlings closed his borders, there were protests.[6] You don't like Rawlings. Yet when

---

5. The Seventh Summit of the Movement of Nonaligned Countries was held March 7–12, 1983.

6. Ghana closed its borders following an attempted coup on November 23, 1982.

he closes his borders in order to stay at home, you protest!

Ghana cannot impose anything on us. Nor can we impose anything on Ghana. Rawlings can't give us lessons. But neither can we give lessons to Rawlings. However, when Rawlings says, "No way for *kalabule*!"—that is, stop the corruption—he says this in the interests of the Ghanaian people. But in fact it is in the interest of all peoples, because the Voltaic people too are against corruption.

The enemies of the CSP also say that we are "reds," communists. That pleases us! Because it proves that our enemies are in disarray. They are lost. They no longer know what has to be done, what has to be said. We have done nothing communist here, we have simply talked about improving living conditions, about social justice, liberty, and democracy.

When we took the decision to revoke the decree issued by the Military Committee for Redressment and National Progress prohibiting the opening of bars at certain hours, we heard people say: These folks in the CSP, whether they're red or green, communists or not—we have our interests and we prefer them. That's what's called being close to the popular masses. It's not the labels that count.

They call us communists in order to frighten the people. They accuse us of being communists, and they tell the people that communism is bad. We have no intention of telling you that communism is good, nor of telling you the opposite. We intend only to tell you that we will take actions with you and for you. The label that will be pinned on these actions matters little.

The enemies of the people also say that we are going after foreigners. No. We love all foreigners—those who are here today and those who will come. We love them because we assume they love the Voltaic people. We don't believe they are foreigners who want to exploit us.

The CSP intends to create, together with you, the conditions for mobilization and work. We want the people to get organized for work, for the battle we are going to wage. For example, we know that certain regions of Upper Volta, such as Orodara, have been very successful in growing fruits and vegetables. But we know too that in these regions the fruits and vegetables rot for lack of means to get them out of the area. We say that the people should be mobilized in Orodara to build landing strips so planes will land there. The mangoes will come to Ouagadougou, will go to Dori, and that will be good for the people of Upper Volta.

This is the kind of work we're talking about. Every day now—because we are going to begin big construction projects—we want you to come out in massive numbers to build. We are going to build a monument and a people's theater in Ouagadougou. We'll build the same things in all the administrative regions, and it will be done with the youth. You are going to build in order to prove that you're capable of transforming your existence and transforming the concrete conditions in which you live. You don't need us to go looking for foreign financial backers, you only need us to give the people their freedom and their rights. That will be done.

The CSP also intends to put a stop to certain practices. When you go to a hospital with a hemorrhage or a fracture, even if you're about to pass out, they'd rather ignore you and take care of the cold of some president, prime minister, or minister, simply because you're a common man, a worker. We should denounce that every day. We will put a stop to it. Have confidence. We are going to put a stop to speculation, to the misappropriation of funds, and to illicit enrichment. That is why we are locking up—and we will continue to lock up—all those who steal the people's money.

We tell the people to be ready to fight, to be ready to take up arms, to resist whenever it's necessary. Have no fear, nothing will happen. The enemy knows that the Voltaic people are now mature.

That's why, when we're told that two years is too short a time for returning to normal constitutional life, we say it's quite sufficient. Because when you let the people speak in complete freedom and complete democracy, the people will tell you in thirty minutes what they want. We don't need two years.

The CSP thanks you because you are mobilized. We were right to have confidence in you, and we were right to side with you in the fight against the enemies of the people—imperialism. That's why we should shout together:

Down with imperialism, down with imperialism, down with imperialism!

Down with the enemies of the people!

Down with the embezzlers of public funds!

Down with the fakers in Upper Volta!

Fakery is over!

Down with the owls with the shady look in their eyes!

Down with the fence-sitting chameleons!

Down with the hungry jackals!

Down with the cornered foxes!

Down with the lepers who know only how to knock things over!

Down with those who hide behind the diplomas paid for by the people's sweat, and who, because of their diplomas, think they have the right to speak in the name of the people, but are incapable of serving in the name of the people!

Down with those who are against the bonds between the army and the people!

Down with those who are against the bonds between the people and the army!

Down with those who hide in various clothes—white or black—against the people!

Imperialism will be buried in Upper Volta! Its lackeys will be buried in Upper Volta!

Long live Upper Volta!

Long live democracy!

Long live liberty!

Thank you, and see you very soon!

A radiant future for our country

Proclamation of August 4
August 4, 1983

On May 17, 1983, Thomas Sankara, Jean-Baptiste Lingani, and other supporters of the political course defended by Sankara within the Council of Popular Salvation (CSP) were arrested in a coup organized by President Jean-Baptiste Ouédraogo and senior officers belonging to the CSP. The coup took place the day after the arrival in Ouagadougou of Guy Penne, special adviser on Africa to French president François Mitterrand.

Thousands took to the streets of Ouagadougou to demand Sankara be freed. On May 30 Sankara and Lingani were placed under house arrest. The officers and personnel of the armed forces and the political parties supporting Sankara's political course launched a sustained effort to prepare for an inevitable confrontation with the proimperialist forces who had carried out the May 17 coup.

On August 4, 1983, Captain Blaise Compaoré and 250 men marched on Ouagadougou and overthrew the Ouédraogo regime. At 10:00 p.m. that evening, Sankara, now president of the National Council of the Revolution (CNR) and head of state, addressed the country in this radio broadcast.

People of Upper Volta:

Today, once again, soldiers, noncommissioned officers, and officers of the national army and the paramilitary forces found themselves compelled to intervene in the running of state affairs in order to restore independence and liberty to our country and dignity to our people.

The patriotic and progressive objectives that justified the formation of the Council of Popular Salvation on November 7, 1982, were betrayed on May 17, 1983—that is, only six months later—by individuals vehemently opposed to the Voltaic people's interests and their aspirations for democracy and liberty.

You know these individuals, because they fraudulently wormed their way into the history of our people. They became notorious, first through their two-faced policies, and later through their open alliance with all the conservative and reactionary forces who are capable only of serving the interests of the enemies of the people, the interests of foreign domination and neocolonialism.

Today, August 4, 1983, soldiers, noncommissioned officers, and officers from all military services and all units, in a surge of patriotism, have decided to sweep away this unpopular regime—the submissive and groveling regime established on May 17, 1983, by doctor and commander Jean-Baptiste Ouédraogo, under the tutelage of Colonel Gabriel Somé Yoryan and his henchmen.

Today, August 4, 1983, the patriotic and progressive soldiers, noncommissioned officers, and officers have thus restored the honor of our people and their army and have given them back their dignity, enabling them to enjoy once again the esteem and respect that everyone, both in

Upper Volta and abroad, accorded them from November 7, 1982, to May 17, 1983.

In order to achieve these goals of honor, dignity, genuine independence, and progress for Upper Volta and its people, the current movement of the Voltaic armed forces, having drawn the lessons of the bitter experiences of the CSP, has on this day, August 4, 1983, formed the National Council of the Revolution. This body now assumes state power, putting an end to the bogus regime of the CSP of Commander Jean-Baptiste Ouédraogo, who moreover had arbitrarily dissolved it.

People of Upper Volta, the National Council of the Revolution calls on all Voltaics—men and women, young and old—to mobilize and remain vigilant, in order to give the CNR their active support. The National Council of the Revolution invites the Voltaic people to form Committees for the Defense of the Revolution everywhere, in order to participate in the CNR's great patriotic struggle and to prevent our enemies here and abroad from doing our people harm. It goes without saying that the political parties are dissolved.[1]

On the international level, the National Council of the Revolution pledges to respect the agreements between our country and other states. Likewise, it maintains our country's membership in regional, continental, and international organizations.

The National Council of the Revolution is not directed against any country, state, or people. It proclaims its solidarity with all peoples and its intention to live in peace and friendship with all countries, in particular with all

---

1. Only parties associated with the former neocolonial regime were dissolved. A number of groups and organizations that supported the revolution were able to function openly.

of Upper Volta's neighboring countries.

The basic purpose and objective of the National Council of the Revolution is to defend the interests of the Voltaic people and to achieve their deep aspirations for liberty, for genuine independence, and for economic and social progress.

People of Upper Volta:

Let us all move forward with the National Council of the Revolution in this great patriotic battle for the radiant future of our country!

Homeland or death, we will win!

Long live the Voltaic people!

Long live the National Council of the Revolution!

Power must be the business
of a conscious people

Press conference
August 21, 1983

On August 21, 1983, Sankara gave his first news conference as president of Upper Volta to the international press. It was broadcast live over national radio. Below are major excerpts.

QUESTION: Mr. President, August 4 is seen by some as an act of revenge against those who held power after May 17. How would you portray this action?

THOMAS SANKARA: I too have heard such analyses. But after all, you have to understand that for some people the Voltaic people's problem is just a matter of cliques. You have to understand, too, that it is completely normal for some people to view every action as an act of revenge, as taking back and going back, and so on.

We believe that August 4 was simply the logical outcome—the concretization—of the popular will that you have been able to witness here in Upper Volta. Moreover, we say that all the Voltaics who mobilized in Ouagadougou and elsewhere, after the famous coup of May 17, did not

71

mobilize just because of Captain Sankara and his comrades, but because of a process to which they were very committed—the process of freeing the Voltaic people. They mobilized so that the people might take charge of their destiny and their development. They fought because they did not accept how the Voltaic people were being pushed around. They fought because the Voltaic people's interests had been betrayed—a betrayal they could not accept.

If there was revenge, it was the revenge of the people against the forces of reaction, which had taken form around a few men, a few individuals. There was no revenge of one group against another.

QUESTION: Mr. President, is the National Council of the Revolution [CNR] a continuation of the pre–May 17 Council of Popular Salvation [CSP]?

SANKARA: Yes. We affirm that the CNR both continues the pre–May 17 CSP and goes beyond it. It was the pre–May 17 CSP that enabled us to link up with the Voltaic people, to get them to express themselves and tell us what their deepest and most sincere aspirations were, to get to know them. This then made it possible to define a policy—that of the CSP at the time—which was to get the Voltaic people to increasingly take power and run it genuinely in their own interests.

As you know, the pre–May 17 CSP ended precisely on May 17—that is, someone, somewhere, betrayed the people. That betrayal took place on May 17.

QUESTION: Mr. President, in an interview you had with reporters from *Carrefour africain* when you were prime minister, you said that the CSP was looking for a strategy that would put an end to military coups in Upper Volta. Now that you preside over the destinies of the Voltaic people, do you think the CNR might be the army's last intervention in the political affairs of the Voltaic state?

SANKARA: We hope so at any rate. We are convinced that the best way to limit the usurpation of power by a group of individuals, military or otherwise, is to place responsibility in the hands of the people from the outset. Plots and coups can be perpetrated between factions and between cliques. No lasting coup can be perpetrated against the people. Consequently, the best way to avoid the army usurping power by and for itself is to already have the Voltaic people sharing this power. That is our goal.

QUESTION: Mr. President, many political observers said you were behind the CSP's coming to power on November 7, 1982. If this was true, why did you not assume the political leadership of the CSP? Could the May 17 events also have been avoided that way?

SANKARA: It is really a shame that there are observers who look at political problems as if they were comic strips. There must be a Zorro, there must be a star. No, the problem in Upper Volta is more serious than that. It was a serious error to have looked for one man, a star, whatever the cost, even going so far as to create one—that is, going so far as to say that the person behind the scenes was Captain Sankara, who was supposed to be the mastermind, and so on.

Let me tell you that November 7 has a complex history. There are plenty of episodes to tell about. November 7 gave birth to a government that was quite heterogeneous, with many components and inevitable contradictions. On November 7 all the efforts of my comrades and myself were aimed at preventing the coup from going ahead. Curiously, we were in Ouagadougou only by coincidence. And curiously, we had done everything possible to convince those who had an interest in making November 7 happen to abandon their project. But you understand that not everyone has the same political views. For some, it's enough to have arms and to have a few army units with you in order to take power. Others believe differently. Above all, power must be the business of a conscious people. Arms therefore constituted only a limited, occasional, and complementary solution.

You should know that on November 7 some well-hidden players were trying to win support for their project, or in any case to achieve their ambitions, by using and exploiting others. These were the people who wanted to put a particular man in office. I'm alluding to Colonel Somé Yoryan, who they sought to put in as president of the Republic of Upper Volta. These were also the men who wanted to free certain figures of the Third Republic held at the time by the Military Committee for Redressment and National Progress.[1]

To succeed in this project, to attain that goal, they needed military backing. And the best way for them to get military backing—since they found themselves isolated within the army—was to float the idea in some army units that all those should participate, they said, who wanted to free the arrested officers—Captain Blaise Compaoré, Captain Henri Zongo, Captain Sankara, and others, such as Commander Lingani, who were in danger.[2]

This approach was successful, since many military men felt a moral obligation to back these officers. They agreed to fight, unaware that all the officers I named were themselves against this coup. They had said so to officers such as Captain Kamboulé, such as doctor and commander Jean-Baptiste Ouédraogo, just to name a few. They had

1. Sankara is referring here to members of the government of President Sangoulé Lamizana imprisoned during a 1980 coup.

2. See chronology, April 12, 1982.

explained to them, they had impressed upon them all the risks and all the dangers involved in such a coup.

But there were different political views. We spent hours, entire nights discussing, trying to convince those officers. Nevertheless, they went into action and November 7 happened. Of course, faced with the contradictions that arose among them, they were unable to put Colonel Somé Yoryan in as head of state. Many were pleased to have been able to free some Third Republic figures, but at the same time were disappointed that other figures from that same Third Republic had also been set free. These are contradictions that must be appreciated.

They did not hesitate to say that Captain Sankara was the strongman and to blame Captain Sankara for the coup, saying to themselves that in any case, once the first step was taken, he would not be able to turn back.

I know the press repeated this information, thus forcing us to accept political responsibilities we had previously refused because of our political convictions. There again, we were beginning to be forced to take on responsibilities for strictly political reasons. As you can understand, a regime born in this way could not last very long.

You should also know that despite all the contradictions, differences, and opposing views existing among us, and although the military and political forces were ours, we had always attempted through democratic debate to argue against the putschist clique—perhaps out of sentimentality, perhaps too from being naive, or perhaps out of honesty— to bring the putschists around to a better understanding of things. We also attempted to avoid any violent clashes, from which we, naturally, would have emerged victorious.

You know that Commander Jean-Baptiste Ouédraogo was protected and guarded by commandos we had trained. They retain all the loyalty and faithfulness to us that elite troops are capable of forging between men and their leaders. So at any time we could have carried out a coup against him had we wanted to. We even took risks to avoid coups being carried out against him.

It must be said that November 7 was a very hard blow to us—very, very hard. At a certain point we had even submitted our resignation to President Jean-Baptiste Ouédraogo. He never made it public, but he remembers it. We had given him our resignation because we disagreed with his policies. We knew he was still receiving orders from somewhere. We also knew we could not win him to our positions. But neither did we want to carry out a coup. We preferred, purely and simply, to submit our resignation, to be honest. He never accepted it.

So that reveals the hidden side of November 7. There are mysteries that remain under wraps. Perhaps history will be able to speak on this at greater length and assign responsibility more clearly.

QUESTION: To go back to one of your earlier answers, can you already envision a date for the army to return to the barracks? On another point, what kind of relations do you wish to establish with the civilian political forces that existed in the country and, more generally, how do you plan to preserve freedom of speech to which, I believe, you have declared yourself personally very much attached in the past?

SANKARA: First question, the army returning to the barracks. You would like that, that's your right. But you should understand that for us, it's not that there are revolutionaries in the barracks and others outside the barracks. The revolutionaries are everywhere. The army is a component of the Voltaic people, a component subject to the same contradictions as the other layers of the Voltaic people. We have taken the power out of the barracks.

You will have noticed that we are the first military regime not to have established our headquarters in a military camp. That is highly significant. Better yet, we set it up at the Entente Council.[3] You know what this means.

It is not a question of the military taking power one day and giving it up the next. It is about the military living with the Voltaic people, suffering with them, and fighting by their side at all times.

So there is no deadline that will work. Of course, I am sure you are referring to those who stated that the military should no longer be involved in politics. These people had delighted certain Voltaic milieus, who thought that certain officers should no longer be involved in politics. This is all that was meant. The proof is that there were officers in power who stated this in order to keep other officers under house arrest.

As for our relations with the political class: What kind of relations would you have liked us to forge? We had it out directly, face to face, with the leaders, the former leaders of the former political parties. As far as we're concerned, these parties no longer exist, they have been dissolved.

That is quite clear. The relations we have with them are simply the same relations we have with Voltaic citizens or, if they want, relations among revolutionaries, if they want to become revolutionaries. Outside of that, there remain only relations between revolutionaries and counterrevolutionaries.

You spoke of freedom of speech, to which I was "very

---

3. A reference to a group of buildings erected in the 1960s to welcome the heads of state and distinguished guests of the Entente Council, a regional economic body dominated by Paris. It included a tunnel connecting these buildings to the French Embassy across the street. The revolutionary government later blocked off this tunnel.

attached." I would say that I am very consistent, even if I sometimes change hats. I am very consistent and am still attached to freedom of speech. I'm simply saying that every Voltaic will always be able to defend freedom, to defend justice, and to defend democracy. That is all we will allow.

All those who wish to commit themselves to this fight will find space in our press, in the columns of our newspapers, within our media, and even in the streets as long as they want to defend freedom of speech, democracy, and justice.

Outside of that fight, there is only the fight between revolutionaries and counterrevolutionaries. That means we will do battle.

Building a new society, rid of social injustice and imperialist domination

Political Orientation Speech
October 2, 1983

In the name of the National Council of the Revolution (CNR), Sankara presented this speech over radio and television. The speech became the Burkinabè Revolution's fundamental programmatic document, known as the Political Orientation Speech. It was published in pamphlet form in October 1983 by the Upper Volta Ministry of Information. The subtitles are from that pamphlet.

People of Upper Volta;
Comrade militants of the revolution:

In the course of this year, 1983, our country has gone through some particularly intense moments, whose impact still remains indelibly stamped on the minds of many of our fellow citizens. During this period, the struggle of the Voltaic people has experienced ebbs and flows.

Our people went through the test of heroic struggles and finally triumphed on the now historic night of August 4, 1983. The revolution has been irreversibly marching forward in our country now for almost two months. Two months during which the fighting people of Upper Volta have mobilized as one behind the National Council of the Revolution in order to build a new, free, independent, and prosperous Voltaic society; a new society rid of social injustice and of the age-old domination and exploitation by international imperialism.

At the end of the short road traveled thus far, I invite you to take a look back with me, to draw the lessons necessary for accurately assessing the revolutionary tasks that are posed presently and for the near future. By equipping ourselves with a clear view of unfolding events, we strengthen ourselves all the more in our struggle against imperialism and reactionary social forces.

To sum up: Where have we come from? And where are we going? Those are the questions of the moment that demand a clear, resolute, and unequivocal answer from us, if we wish to march boldly forward to greater and more resounding victories.

The August revolution is the successful result of the Voltaic people's struggle

The triumph of the August revolution is due not only to the revolutionary takeover against the sacrosanct reactionary alliance of May 17, 1983. It is the result of the Voltaic people's struggle against their long-standing enemies. It is a victory over international imperialism and its national allies. A victory over backward, obscurantist, and sinister forces. A victory over all the enemies of the people who have plotted and schemed behind their backs.

The August revolution is the culmination of the popular insurrection launched following the imperialist plot of May 17, 1983, which aimed to stem the rising tide of this country's democratic and revolutionary forces.

This insurrection was symbolized not only by the courageous and heroic stance of the commandos of the city of Pô, who were able to put up fierce resistance to the proimperialist and antipopular regime of Commander Jean-Baptiste Ouédraogo and Colonel Somé Yoryan, but also by the courage of the popular, democratic, and revolutionary forces, who were able to put up exemplary resistance in alliance with the patriotic soldiers and officers.

The insurrection of August 4, 1983, the victory of the revolution, and the rise of the National Council of the Revolution thus unquestionably represent the culmination and logical outcome of the Voltaic people's struggles against neocolonial domination and exploitation, against the subjugation of our country, and for the independence, freedom, dignity, and progress of our people. On this point, simplistic and superficial analyses, limited to reproducing predetermined patterns, cannot change the facts of reality in any way.

The August revolution thus triumphed by presenting itself both as heir to and as a deepening of the popular uprising of January 3, 1966. It is both the continuation, and the development at a qualitatively higher level, of all the great popular struggles, whose number has increased in recent years. They have all shown the systematic refusal of the Voltaic people—in particular the working class and toilers—to let themselves be governed as before. The most notable and significant milestones of these great popular struggles are December 1975, May 1979, October and November 1980, April 1982, and May 1983.[1]

It is a well-established fact that the great movement of popular resistance immediately following the reactionary and proimperialist provocation of May 17, 1983, created

---

1. See chronology.

favorable conditions for the events of August 4, 1983. Indeed, the imperialist plot of May 17 precipitated a large-scale regroupment of the democratic and revolutionary forces and organizations, which mobilized during this period, taking initiatives and carrying out unprecedented and audacious actions. During this time, the sacrosanct alliance of reactionary forces around the moribund regime labored under its inability to block the breakthrough of the revolutionary forces, which were mounting an increasingly open attack on the antipopular and antidemocratic forces in power.

The popular demonstrations of May 20, 21, and 22 met with a broad national response essentially due to their great political significance. They provided concrete proof that an entire people, especially the youth, subscribed openly to the revolutionary ideals defended by the men who the forces of reaction had treacherously moved against. These demonstrations were of great practical significance, since they expressed the determination of an entire people and all its youth, who stood up to confront concretely the forces of imperialist domination and exploitation. This was the most obvious illustration of the truth that when the people stand up, imperialism and the social forces allied with it tremble.

History and the process by which the popular masses develop political consciousness follow a dialectical progression that defies reactionary logic. That is why the May 1983 events greatly contributed to accelerating the process of political clarification in our country, reaching a level whereby the popular masses as a whole made an important, qualitative leap in their understanding of the situation. The May 17 events greatly contributed to opening the eyes of the Voltaic people. In a cruel and brutal flash, imperialism was revealed to them as a system of oppression and exploitation.

There are days that hold lessons incomparably richer than those of an entire decade. During such days, the people learn with such incredible speed and so profoundly that a thousand days of study are nothing in comparison.

The events of May 1983 allowed the Voltaic people to get to know its enemies better. Henceforth in Upper Volta, everyone knows who's who; who is with whom and against whom; who does what and why.

This kind of situation, which constituted a prelude to great upheavals, helped lay bare the sharpening class contradictions of Voltaic society. The August revolution thus came as the solution to social contradictions that could no longer be suppressed by compromise solutions.

The enthusiastic adherence of the broad popular masses to the August revolution is the concrete expression of the immense hopes that the Voltaic people place in the rise of the CNR. They hope that their deep-going aspirations might finally be achieved—aspirations for democracy, liberty, independence, genuine progress, and the restoration of the dignity and grandeur of our homeland, which twenty-three years of neocolonial rule have treated with singular contempt.

The legacy of twenty-three years of neocolonialism

The formation of the CNR on August 4, 1983, and the subsequent establishment of a revolutionary government in Upper Volta opened a glorious page in the annals of the history of our people and our country. However, the legacy bequeathed to us by twenty-three years of imperialist exploitation and domination is weighty and burdensome. Our task of building a new society cleansed of all the ills keeping our country in a state of poverty and economic and cultural backwardness will be hard and arduous.

In 1960 French colonialism—hounded on all sides, defeated at Dien Bien Phu, and grappling with tremendous difficulties in Algeria[2]—drew the lessons of those defeats and was compelled to grant our country its national sovereignty and territorial integrity. This was greeted positively by our people, who had not remained impassive, but rather had been developing appropriate struggles of resistance. This move by French colonial imperialism constituted a victory for the people over the forces of foreign oppression and exploitation. From the popular masses' point of view, it was a democratic reform, whereas from imperialism's point of view, it was merely a transformation of the forms of its domination and exploitation of our people.

This transformation nevertheless resulted in a realignment of classes and social layers and the formation of new classes. In alliance with the backward forces of traditional society, the petty-bourgeois intelligentsia of the time—with total contempt for the great masses, who they had used as a springboard to power—set about laying the political and economic foundations for the new forms of imperialist domination and exploitation. Fear that the struggle of the popular masses might radicalize and lead to a genuinely revolutionary solution had been the basis for the choice made by imperialism: From that point on, it would maintain its stranglehold over our country and perpetuate the exploitation of our people through the use of Voltaic intermediaries. Voltaic nationals were to take over as agents of

---

2. Dien Bien Phu was the decisive final battle in Vietnam's war of national liberation against French colonialism. The surrender of the French forces there in May 1954 led to the end of French colonial presence in Indochina.

In November 1954 the National Liberation Front (FLN) of Algeria began a revolutionary war against French colonial occupation that led to the country's independence in 1962.

foreign domination and exploitation. The entire organization of neocolonial society would be nothing more than
a simple operation of substituting one form for another.

In essence, neocolonial society and colonial society do
not differ in the least. Thus, we saw the colonial administration replaced by a neocolonial administration identical to it in every respect. The colonial army was replaced
by a neocolonial army with the same characteristics, the
same functions, and the same role of safeguarding the
interests of imperialism and its national allies. The colonial schools were replaced by neocolonial schools, which
pursued the same goals of alienating the children of our
country and reproducing a society fundamentally serving imperialist interests, and secondarily serving imperialism's local lackeys and allies.

With the support and blessing of imperialism, Voltaic
nationals set about organizing the systematic plunder of
our country. With the crumbs of this plunder that fell to
them, they were transformed, little by little, into a genuinely parasitic bourgeoisie that no longer knew how to
control its voracious appetite. Driven only by their own
selfish interests, they no longer hesitated at employing
the most dishonest means, engaging in massive corruption, embezzlement of public funds and properties,
influence-peddling and real estate speculation, and practicing favoritism and nepotism.

This is what accounts for all the material and financial
wealth they've been able to accumulate on the backs of
working people. Not satisfied with living off the fabulous
incomes they derive from shamelessly employing their ill-
gotten wealth, they fight tooth and nail to monopolize
political positions that will allow them to use the state
apparatus for their own exploitative and wasteful ends.

Never do they let a year go by without treating themselves

to extravagant vacations abroad. Their children desert the country's schools for prestigious educations in other countries. At the slightest illness, all the resources of the state are mobilized to provide them with expensive care at luxurious hospitals in foreign countries.

All this unfolds in full view of the honest, courageous, and hard-working Voltaic people, mired nonetheless in the most squalid misery. While Upper Volta is a paradise for the wealthy minority, for the majority—the people— it is a barely tolerable hell.

As part of this great majority, the wage earners, despite the fact that they are assured a regular income, suffer the constraints and pitfalls of capitalist consumer society. Their entire wage is spent before it has even been received. And this vicious cycle goes on and on with no perspective of being broken.

Within their respective trade unions, workers join in struggles around demands to improve their living conditions. The breadth of those struggles sometimes compels the neocolonial authorities to grant concessions. But they simply take back with one hand what they give with the other.

Thus a 10 percent wage increase is announced with great fanfare, only to be immediately taxed, wiping out the expected benefits. After five, six, or seven months, the workers always end up seeing through the swindle, and mobilize for new struggles. Seven months is more than enough for the reactionaries in power to catch their breath and devise new schemes. In this never-ending fight, the worker is always the loser.

Among this great majority are the peasants, the "wretched of the earth," who are expropriated, robbed, mistreated, imprisoned, scoffed at, and humiliated every day, and yet are among those whose labor creates wealth. Thanks to their productive labor, the country's economy stays afloat despite its frailty. It is from their labor that all those Voltaics for whom Upper Volta is an El Dorado line their pockets.

And yet, it is the peasants who suffer most from the lack of buildings, of road infrastructure, and from the lack of health care facilities and personnel. It is the peasants, creators of the nation's wealth, who suffer most from the lack of schools and school supplies for their children. It is their children who will swell the ranks of the unemployed after a brief stint on benches in schools that are poorly adapted to the realities of this country. It is among the peasants that the illiteracy rate is the highest—98 percent. Those who most need to learn, in order to improve the output of their productive labor, are again the ones who benefit the least from investments in health care, education, and technology.

The peasant youth—who have the same attitudes as all young people, that is, greater sensitivity to social injustice and a desire for progress—end up rebelling and they desert the countryside, thus depriving it of its most dynamic elements.

These youths' initial impulse drives them to the large urban centers, Ouagadougou and Bobo-Dioulasso. There they hope to find better-paying jobs and enjoy, too, the advantages of progress. The lack of jobs drives them to idleness, with all its characteristic vices. Finally, so as not to end up in prison, they seek salvation by going abroad, where the most shameless humiliation and exploitation await them. But does Voltaic society leave them any other choice?

Stated as succinctly as possible, such is the situation of our country after twenty-three years of neocolonialism— a paradise for some and hell for the rest.

After twenty-three years of imperialist domination and exploitation, our country remains a backward agricultural country, where the rural sector—employing 90 percent of the workforce—accounts for only 45 percent of the gross domestic product (GDP) and supplies 95 percent of the country's total exports.

More simply, it should be noted that in other countries, farmers constituting less than 5 percent of the population manage not only to feed themselves adequately and satisfy the basic needs of the entire nation, but also to export enormous quantities of their agricultural produce. Here, however, more than 90 percent of the population, despite strenuous exertions, experiences famine and deprivation and, along with the rest of the population, is compelled to fall back on imported agricultural products, if not on international aid.

The imbalance between exports and imports thus created accentuates the country's dependence on foreign countries. The resulting trade deficit has grown considerably over the years, and the value of our exports covers only around 25 percent of imports. To state it more clearly, we buy more from abroad than we sell abroad. And an economy that functions on such a basis increasingly goes bankrupt and is headed for catastrophe.

Private investments from abroad are not only insufficient, but also constitute a huge drain on the country's economy and thus do not help strengthen its ability to accumulate wealth. An important portion of the wealth created with the help of foreign investments is siphoned off abroad, instead of being reinvested to increase the country's productive capacity. In the 1973–79 period, it's estimated that 1.7 billion CFA francs left the country each year as income from direct foreign investments, while new investments came to only an average of 1.3

billion CFA francs a year.[3]

The insufficient level of productive investments has led the Voltaic state to play a fundamental role in the nation's economy through its efforts to compensate for the lack of private investment. This is a difficult situation, considering that the state's budgeted income basically consists of tax revenues, which represent 85 percent of total revenues and largely come from import duties and taxes.

In addition to making national investments, this income finances government spending, 70 percent of which goes to pay the salaries of civil servants and to ensure the functioning of administrative services. What, then, can possibly be left over for social and cultural investments?

In the field of education, our country is among the most backward, with 16.4 percent of children attending school and an illiteracy rate that reaches 92 percent on average. This means that of every 100 Voltaics, barely 8 know how to read and write in any language.

On the level of health, the rate of illness and mortality is among the highest in the subregion due to the proliferation of communicable diseases and nutritional deficiencies. How can such a catastrophic situation be avoided when we know that our country has only one hospital bed per 1,200 inhabitants and one doctor per 48,000 inhabitants?

These few elements alone suffice to illustrate the legacy left to us by twenty-three years of neocolonialism, twenty-three years of a policy of total national neglect. No Voltaic who loves and honors his country can remain indifferent to this most desperate situation.

Indeed our people, a courageous, hardworking people,

---

3. At 1983 exchange rates, these figures equaled approximately US$6.8 million leaving the country, compared with new investments of US$5.2 million.

have never been able to tolerate such a situation. Because they have understood that this was not an inevitable situation, but a question of society being organized on an unjust basis for the sole benefit of a minority. They have therefore waged different types of struggles, searching for the ways and means to put an end to the old order of things.

That is why they enthusiastically greeted the National Council of the Revolution and the August revolution. These constitute the crowning achievement of the efforts they expended and the sacrifices they accepted so as to overthrow the old order, establish a new order capable of rehabilitating Voltaic man, and give our country a leading place within the community of free, prosperous, and respected nations.

The parasitic classes that had always profited from colonial and neocolonial Upper Volta are, and will continue to be, hostile to the transformations undertaken by the revolutionary process begun on August 4, 1983. The reason for this is that they are and remain attached to international imperialism by an umbilical cord. They are and remain fervent defenders of the privileges acquired through their allegiance to imperialism.

Regardless of what is done, regardless of what is said, they will remain true to themselves and will continue to plot and scheme in order to reconquer their "lost kingdom." Do not expect these nostalgic people to change their mentality and attitude. The only language they respond to and understand is the language of struggle, the revolutionary class struggle against the exploiters and oppressors of the people. For them, our revolution will be the most authoritarian thing that exists. It will be an act by which the people impose their will on them by all the means at their disposal, including arms, if necessary.

Who are these enemies of the people?

They revealed themselves in the eyes of the people during the May 17 events by their viciousness against the revolutionary forces. The people identified these enemies of the people in the heat of revolutionary action. They are:

1. The Voltaic bourgeoisie, which can be broken down, by the functions of its various layers, into the state bourgeoisie, the comprador bourgeoisie, and the middle bourgeoisie.

The state bourgeoisie. This is the layer known by the label political-bureaucratic bourgeoisie. This is a bourgeoisie that has enriched itself in an illicit and criminal manner through its political monopoly. It has used the state apparatus just as an industrial capitalist uses his means of production to accumulate surplus value drawn from the exploitation of workers' labor power. This layer of the bourgeoisie will never willingly renounce its former privileges and sit by passively observing the revolutionary transformations under way.

The commercial bourgeoisie. This layer, by virtue of its business activity, is tied to imperialism through numerous bonds. For this layer, elimination of imperialist domination means the death of "the goose that lays the golden egg." That is why it will oppose the present revolution with all its might. Coming from this category, for example, are the corrupt merchants who seek to starve the people by taking food supplies off the market for purposes of speculation and economic sabotage.

The middle bourgeoisie. Although this layer of the Voltaic bourgeoisie has ties to imperialism, it competes with the latter for control of the market. But since it is economically weaker, imperialism supplants it. So it has grievances against imperialism. But it also fears the people, and this fear can lead it to make a bloc with imperialism. Nevertheless, since imperialist domination of our country prevents this layer from playing its real role as a national bourgeoisie, some of its members could, under certain circumstances, be favorable to the revolution, which would objectively place them in the people's camp. However, we must cultivate revolutionary mistrust between the people and individuals like these who come over to the revolution. Because all kinds of opportunists will rally to the revolution under this guise.

2. The reactionary forces that base their power on the traditional, feudal-type structures of our society. In their majority, these forces were able to put up staunch resistance to French colonial imperialism. But ever since our country attained its national sovereignty, they have joined with the reactionary bourgeoisie in oppressing the Voltaic people. These forces have put the peasant masses in the position of being a reservoir of votes to be delivered to the highest bidder.

In order to safeguard their interests, which they share with imperialism in opposition to those of the people, these reactionary forces most frequently rely on the decaying and declining values of our traditional culture that still endure in rural areas. To the extent that our revolution aims to democratize social relations in the countryside, giving more responsibilities to the peasants, and making more education and knowledge available to them for their own economic and cultural emancipation, these backward forces will oppose it.

These are the enemies of the people in the present revolution, enemies that the people themselves identified during the May events. These are the individuals who made up the bulk of the isolated marchers who, protected by a cordon of soldiers, demonstrated their class support for the already moribund regime that had emerged from the reactionary and proimperialist coup.

The rest of the population, aside from the reactionary

and antirevolutionary classes and social layers enumerated above, is what comprises the Voltaic people. A people who consider imperialist domination and exploitation to be an abomination and who have continually demonstrated this by concrete, daily struggle against the various neocolonial regimes. In the present revolution the people consist of:

1. The Voltaic working class, young and few in number, but which, through unremitting struggle against the bosses, has been able to prove that it is a genuinely revolutionary class. In the present revolution, it is a class that has everything to gain and nothing to lose. It has no means of production to lose, it has no piece of property to defend within the framework of the old neocolonial society. It is convinced, however, that the revolution is its business, because it will emerge from it in a stronger position.

2. The petty bourgeoisie, which constitutes a vast, very unstable social layer, that quite often vacillates between the cause of the popular masses and that of imperialism. In its large majority, it always ends up by taking the side of the popular masses. It includes the most diverse components, including small shopkeepers, petty-bourgeois intellectuals (civil servants, college and high school students, private sector employees, etc.), and artisans.

3. The Voltaic peasantry, which in its big majority consists of small peasants, who are tied to small plots of land because of the gradual disintegration of collective property forms since the introduction of the capitalist mode of production in our country. Market relations have increasingly dissolved communal bonds and replaced them with private property over the means of production. In the new situation thus created by the penetration of capitalism into our countryside, the Voltaic peasant, tied to small-scale production, embodies bourgeois productive relations. Given all these considerations, the Voltaic peasantry is

an integral part of the category of the petty bourgeoisie.

Because of the past and its present situation, the peasantry is the social layer that has paid the highest toll for imperialist domination and exploitation. The economic and cultural backwardness that characterizes our countryside has long kept the peasantry isolated from the great currents of progress and modernization, relegating it to the role of reservoir for reactionary political parties. Nevertheless, the peasantry has a stake in the revolution and, in terms of numbers, is its principal force.

4. The lumpenproletariat. This is the category of declassed individuals who, since they are without jobs, are prone to hire themselves out to reactionary and counterrevolutionary forces to carry out the latter's dirty work. To the extent that the revolution can provide them something useful to do, they can become its fervent defenders.

The character and scope of the August revolution

The revolutions that occur around the world are not at all alike. Each revolution presents original features that distinguish it from the others. Our revolution, the August revolution, is no exception. It takes into account the special features of our country, its level of development, and its subjugation by the world imperialist capitalist system.

Our revolution is a revolution that is unfolding in a backward, agricultural country, where the weight of tradition and ideology emanating from a feudal-type social organization weighs very heavily on the popular masses. It is a revolution in a country that, because of imperialism's domination and exploitation of our people, has evolved from a colony into a neocolony.

It is a revolution occurring in a country still characterized by the lack of an organized working class conscious of its historic mission, and which therefore possesses no tradition of revolutionary struggle. It is a revolution occurring in a small country on the continent, at a time when, on the international level, the revolutionary movement is coming apart day by day, without any visible hope of seeing a homogenous bloc arise capable of giving a stimulus and practical support to nascent revolutionary movements. This set of historical, geographic, and sociological circumstances gives a certain, specific stamp to our revolution.

The August revolution exhibits a dual character: It is a democratic and a popular revolution.

Its primary tasks are to eliminate imperialist domination and exploitation; and to purge the countryside of all the social, economic, and cultural obstacles that keep it in a backward state. Its democratic character flows from this.

It draws its popular character from the full participation of the Voltaic masses in the revolution, and their consistent mobilization around democratic and revolutionary slogans that concretely express their own interests in opposition to those of the reactionary classes allied with imperialism. The popular character of the August revolution also lies in the fact that, in place of the old state machinery, new machinery is being built, capable of guaranteeing the democratic exercise of power by the people and for the people.

Our present revolution as characterized above, while being an anti-imperialist revolution, is still unfolding within the framework of the limits of the bourgeois economic and social order. By analyzing the social classes of Voltaic society, we have put forward the idea that the Voltaic bourgeoisie does not constitute a single, homogenous, reactionary, and antirevolutionary mass. Indeed, what characterizes the bourgeoisie in underdeveloped countries under capitalist relations is its congenital inability to revolutionize society as the bourgeoisie of the

European countries did in the 1780s, that is, at the time when it still constituted a rising class.

Such are the characteristics and limitations of the present revolution launched in Upper Volta on August 4, 1983. Having a clear view and precise definition of its content guards us against the dangers of deviation and excesses that could be detrimental to the victorious march of the revolution. All those who have taken up the cause of the August revolution should fix firmly in their minds the guiding principles laid out here. By doing so they can assume their role as conscious revolutionaries. And, as genuine, bold, and tireless propagandists, they can disseminate these principles among the masses.

It is no longer enough to call oneself a revolutionary. We also need to be absolutely clear on the profound meaning of the revolution we fervently defend. This is the best way to defend it from the attacks and distortions that the counterrevolutionaries will not fail to use against it. Knowing how to link revolutionary theory to revolutionary practice will be the decisive criterion from now on in distinguishing consistent revolutionaries from all those who flock to the revolution under motives that are alien to the revolutionary cause.

On popular sovereignty in the exercise of revolutionary power

As we have said, one of the distinctive traits of the August revolution and which endows it with its popular character, is that it is a movement of the vast majority for the benefit of the vast majority.

It is a revolution made by the Voltaic popular masses themselves, with their own slogans and aspirations. The goal of this revolution consists in having the people assume power. That is the reason why the first act of the revolution, following the August 4 proclamation, was the appeal addressed to the people to create Committees for the Defense of the Revolution [CDRs]. The National Council of the Revolution is convinced that for this revolution to be a genuinely popular revolution, it must proceed to destroy the neocolonial state machinery and organize new machinery capable of guaranteeing popular sovereignty. The question of knowing how this popular power will be exercised, how this power should be organized, is an essential question for the future of our revolution.

Until today, the history of our country has essentially been dominated by the exploiting and conservative classes, which have exercised their antidemocratic and antipopular dictatorship through their stranglehold on politics, the economy, ideology, culture, the administration, and the judicial system.

The primary goal of the revolution is to transfer power from the hands of the Voltaic bourgeoisie allied with imperialism to the hands of the alliance of popular classes that constitute the people. This means that from now on the people, who hold power, will have to counterpose their democratic and popular power to the antidemocratic, antipopular dictatorship of the reactionary alliance of social classes that favor imperialism.

This democratic and popular power will be the foundation, the solid basis, of revolutionary power in Upper Volta. Its chief task will be the total conversion of the entire state machinery with its laws, administration, courts, police, and army, which have been fashioned to serve and defend the selfish interests of the reactionary social classes and layers. Its task will be to organize the struggle against the counterrevolutionary intrigues seeking to reconquer "Paradise Lost," on the road to completely crushing the resistance of the reactionaries who are nostalgic for the past. Therein lies the need for and the role of the CDRs as the base of operations for the popular masses as they storm the citadels of reaction and counterrevolution.

For an accurate understanding of the nature, role, and functioning of the CDRs

Building a popular democratic state, which is the ultimate goal of the August revolution, cannot and will not be done in a single day. It is an arduous task that will demand enormous sacrifices of us. The democratic character of this revolution requires us to decentralize and spread out administrative power and draw the administration closer to the people, in order to make public matters the concern of everyone. In this immense and long-term endeavor, we have set about revising the administrative map of the country for greater efficiency.

We have also set about replacing those managing administrative services, to guide this in a more revolutionary direction. At the same time, we have dismissed government officials and military officers who, for various reasons, cannot keep pace with the revolution today. Much remains for us to do, and we are aware of that.

The National Council of the Revolution—which, in the revolutionary process launched on August 4, is the power that plans, leads, and oversees political, economic, and social life on a national level—must have local bodies in the various sectors of national life. Therein lies the profound significance of the creation of the CDRs, which are the representatives of revolutionary power in the villages, the urban neighborhoods, and the workplaces.

The CDRs are the authentic organization of the people for wielding revolutionary power. This is the instrument the people have forged in order to take genuine command of their destiny and thereby extend their control into all areas of society. The people's arms, the people's power, the people's wealth—it will be the people who manage these. The CDRs exist for that purpose.

The CDRs' functions are enormous and varied. Their main task is to organize the Voltaic people as a whole and involve them in the revolutionary struggle. Organized into CDRs, the people acquire not only the right to have a say on the problems of their future, but also to participate in making and carrying out decisions on their future. The revolution, as an accurate theory for destroying the old order and building a new type of society in its place, can be led only by those who have a stake in it.

The CDRs are therefore the shock troops who will attack all the strongholds of resistance. They are the builders of revolutionary Upper Volta. They are the seeds that must carry the revolution into all the provinces, all our villages, all public and private workplaces, all homes, and all milieus. In order to do that, the revolutionary militants within the CDRs must zealously outdo each other in carrying out the following vital tasks:

1. Action directed toward CDR members. Revolutionary militants bear responsibility for politically educating their comrades. The CDRs must be schools of political education. The CDRs are the appropriate framework in which militants discuss decisions of the higher bodies of the revolution, the CNR, and the government.

2. Action directed toward the popular masses, aimed at creating overwhelming support among them for the CNR's goals through bold and constant propaganda and agitation. The CDRs must be able to counter the propaganda and lying slanders of reaction with appropriate revolutionary propaganda and explanations, based on the principle that only the truth is revolutionary.

The CDRs must listen to the masses so that they

understand their moods and needs, in order to inform the CNR in a timely way and make corresponding concrete proposals. They are urged to look at questions concerning the improvement of the situation of the popular masses by supporting the initiatives taken by the masses themselves.

It is vitally necessary for the CDRs to maintain direct contact with the popular masses by periodically organizing public meetings at which questions of interest to them are discussed. This is essential if the CDRs wish to help apply the CNR's directives correctly. The CNR's decisions will be explained in this way to the masses through propaganda activities. All measures aimed at improving their living conditions will also be explained. The CDRs must fight together with the popular masses of the cities and countryside against their enemies, against the adversities of nature, and for the transformation of their material and moral existence.

3. The CDRs must work in a rational manner, thereby illustrating one of the features of our revolution: its rigor. Consequently, they should equip themselves with coherent and ambitious plans of action that all their members must follow.

Since August 4—a date that has now become historic for our people—in response to the appeal of the National Council of the Revolution, Voltaics have taken initiatives to equip themselves with CDRs. CDRs have thus been established in the villages, in urban neighborhoods, and will soon be in workplaces, in public services, in factories, and within the army. All this is the result of spontaneous action by the masses. Work must now be done to structure them internally on a clear basis and to organize them on a national scale. The National General Secretariat of the CDRs is currently taking up this task. While waiting for definitive results from studies currently under way based on accumulated experiences, we will limit ourselves to outlining the plan and the general guiding principles for the functioning of the CDRs.

The main idea behind the creation of the CDRs is to democratize power. The CDRs will become organs through which the people exercise local power derived from the central power, which is vested in the National Council of the Revolution. The CNR is the supreme power except during sessions of the national congress. It is the leading organ of this entire structure, whose guiding principle is democratic centralism.

On the one hand, democratic centralism is based on the subordination of lower bodies to higher ones, of which the CNR is the highest and to which all organizations are subordinate. On the other hand, this centralism remains democratic, since the principle of elections is the rule at all levels, and the autonomy of the local bodies is recognized regarding all questions under their jurisdiction, but within the limits and in accordance with the general directives drawn up by the higher body.

On revolutionary morality within the CDRs

The revolution aims to transform all aspects of society—economic, social, and cultural. It aims to create a new Voltaic man, with exemplary morality and social behavior that inspires the admiration and confidence of the masses. Neocolonial domination led to such a state of deterioration of our society that it will take us years to cleanse it.

Nevertheless, CDR members must forge a new consciousness and a new behavior with the aim of setting a good example for the masses. While making the revolution, we must pay attention to our own qualitative transformation. Without a qualitative transformation of the very people who are supposed to be the architects of the revolution, it is practically impossible to create a new society rid of corruption, theft, lies, and individualism in general.

We must strive to have our actions match our words and watch our social behavior so as not to open ourselves up to attack by the counterrevolutionaries who lie in wait. If we always keep in mind that the interests of the popular masses take precedence over personal gain, then we will avoid going off course.

The activities of some militants who harbor the counterrevolutionary dream of amassing property and profits through the CDRs must be denounced and combated. The prima donna mentality must be eliminated. The sooner these inadequacies are combated, the better it will be for the revolution.

From our point of view, a revolutionary is someone who knows how to be modest, while at the same time being among the most resolute in carrying out the tasks entrusted to him. He fulfills them without boasting and expects no reward.

We have noticed lately certain individuals who actively participated in the revolution and who expected that this would entitle them to privileged treatment, honors, and important positions. Out of vexation, these persons devote themselves to undermining the revolution because they did not get what they wanted. This proves that they participated in the revolution without ever understanding its real objectives.

One does not make a revolution simply to take the place of the despots who have been deposed. One does not participate in the revolution for vindictive reasons, driven by the desire for a privileged position: "Get out of the way and make room for me!" This kind of motive is alien to the ideals of the August revolution. Those with this motivation demonstrate their petty-bourgeois careerist flaws, if not their dangerous counterrevolutionary opportunism.

The image of the revolutionary that the CNR seeks to impress on everyone's consciousness is that of an activist who is one with the masses, who has faith in them, and who respects them. He rids himself of any contemptuous attitude toward them. He does not see himself as a schoolmaster to whom the masses owe obedience and submission. To the contrary, he learns from them, listens to them carefully, and pays attention to their opinions. He drops all authoritarian methods worthy of reactionary bureaucrats.

The revolution is not destructive anarchy. It demands an exemplary conduct and discipline. Acts of vandalism and adventurist actions of all sorts, rather than strengthening the revolution by winning the masses' support, weaken it and repel countless masses. That is why CDR members must increase their sense of responsibility toward the people and seek to inspire respect and admiration.

Inadequacies such as these most often reflect ignorance on the character and objectives of the revolution. To guard against that, we must immerse ourselves in the study of revolutionary theory. Theoretical study deepens our understanding of phenomena, clarifies our actions, and protects us against a good many assumptions. From now on we must give special importance to this aspect of the question and strive to set examples that inspire others to follow us.

For revolutionizing all sectors of Voltaic society

All the previous political regimes, one after the other, until now have strived to introduce measures to better run neocolonial society. The changes introduced by these regimes amounted to installing new teams within the continuity of neocolonial power. None of these regimes wished nor was able to question the socioeconomic foundations of Voltaic society. That is why they all failed.

The August revolution does not aim to establish one more regime in Upper Volta. It represents a break with all previously known regimes. Its ultimate goal is to build a new Voltaic society, within which the Voltaic citizen, driven by revolutionary consciousness, will be the architect of his own happiness, a happiness equal to the efforts he will have made.

To do this, the revolution—whether the conservative and backward forces like it or not—will be a deep and total upheaval that will spare no domain, no sector of economic, social, and cultural activity.

Revolutionizing all domains and all sectors of activity is the slogan of the day. Strengthened by the guiding principles laid out here, each citizen should work to revolutionize his sector of activity, wherever he finds himself.

The philosophy of revolutionary transformations is already affecting the following sectors: (1) the national army; (2) policies concerning women; and (3) economic development.

(1) The national army: its place
in the democratic and popular revolution

According to the defense doctrine of revolutionary Upper Volta, a conscious people cannot leave their homeland's defense to one group of men, however competent they may be. Conscious people take charge themselves of their homeland's defense. To this end, our armed forces constitute simply a detachment that is more specialized than the rest of the population for Upper Volta's internal and external security requirements. Similarly, even though the health of the Voltaic people is the business of the people and of each individual Voltaic, there exists and will continue to exist a more specialized medical corps that devotes more time to the question of public health.

The revolution imposes three missions on the national armed forces:

1. To be capable of combating all internal and external enemies and to participate in the military training of the rest of the people. This presupposes an increased operational capacity, making each soldier a competent fighter, unlike the old army, which was merely a mass of employees.

2. To participate in national production. Indeed, the new soldier must live and suffer among the people to which he belongs. The days of the free-spending army are over. From now on, besides handling arms, the army will work in the fields and raise cattle, sheep, and poultry. It will build schools and health clinics and ensure their functioning. It will maintain roads and will transport mail, the sick, and agricultural products between regions by air.

3. To train each soldier as a revolutionary militant. Gone are the days when the army was declared to be neutral and apolitical, while in fact serving as the bastion of reaction and the guardian of imperialist interests. Gone are the days when our national army conducted itself like a corps of foreign mercenaries in conquered territory. Those days are gone forever. Armed with political and ideological training, our soldiers, noncommissioned officers, and officers engaged in the revolutionary process will no longer be potential criminals, but will instead become conscious revolutionaries, at home among the people like a fish in water.

As an army at the service of the revolution, the National Popular Army will have no place for any soldier who looks down on, scorns, or brutalizes his people. An army of the people at the service of the people—such is the new army we are building in place of the neocolonial army, which was utilized to rule over the people as a veritable instrument of oppression and repression in the hands of the reactionary bourgeoisie. Such an army, even in terms of its internal organization and its principles of functioning, will be fundamentally different from the old army. Thus, instead of blind obedience of soldiers toward their officers, of subordinates toward their superiors, a healthy discipline will be developed that, while strict, will be based on its conscious acceptance by the men and the troops.

Contrary to the opinions of reactionary officers fostered by a colonial attitude, the politicization of the army, its revolutionization, does not signal the end of discipline. Discipline in a politicized army will have a new content. It will be a revolutionary discipline. That is, a discipline that derives its strength from the fact that the human dignity of the officer and the soldier, of the commissioned and noncommissioned personnel, is worth the same, and that they differ from one another only with regard to their concrete tasks and respective responsibilities. Armed with this understanding of the relations between men, military cadres must respect their men, love them, and treat them as equals.

Here too the Committees for the Defense of the Revolution have a fundamental role to play. CDR militants within the army must be tireless pioneers in building the National Popular Army of the democratic and popular state, whose essential tasks internally will be to defend the rights and interests of the people, maintain revolutionary order, and safeguard the democratic and popular power; its task externally will be to defend our territorial integrity.

(2) The Voltaic woman: her role
in the democratic and popular revolution

The weight of age-old traditions in our society has relegated women to the rank of beasts of burden. Women suffer doubly from all the scourges of neocolonial society. First, they experience the same suffering as men. Second, they are subjected to additional suffering by men.

Our revolution is in the interests of all the oppressed and all those who are exploited in today's society. It is therefore in the interests of women, since the basis of their domination by men lies in the system through which society's political and economic life is organized. By changing the social order that oppresses women, the revolution creates the conditions for their genuine emancipation.

The women and men of our society are all victims of imperialist oppression and domination. That is why they wage the same battle. The revolution and women's liberation go together. We do not talk of women's emancipation as an act of charity or out of a surge of human compassion. It is a basic necessity for the revolution to triumph. Women hold up the other half of the sky.

Forging a new mentality among Voltaic women that allows them to take responsibility for the country's destiny alongside men is one of the essential tasks of the revolution. The same is true of the transformation to be made in men's attitudes toward women.

Until now, women have been excluded from the realm of decision making. The revolution, by entrusting women with responsibilities, is creating the conditions for unleashing women's fighting initiative. As part of its revolutionary policy, the CNR will work to mobilize, organize, and unite all the dynamic forces of the nation, and women will not be left behind. They will be involved in all the battles we will have to wage against the various shackles of neocolonial society in order to build a new society. They will be involved at all levels in conceiving projects, making decisions, and implementing them—in organizing the life of the nation as a whole. The final goal of this great undertaking is to build a free and prosperous society in which women will be equal to men in all spheres.

However, we must have a correct understanding of the question of women's emancipation. It is not a mechanical equality between men and women, acquiring habits recognized as male—drinking, smoking, and wearing pants. That's not the emancipation of women. Nor will acquiring diplomas make women equal to men or more emancipated. A diploma is not a free pass to emancipation.

The genuine emancipation of women is one that entrusts responsibilities to women, that involves them in productive activity and in the different fights the people face. The genuine emancipation of women is one that compels men to give their respect and consideration. Emancipation, like freedom, is not granted, it is conquered. It is for women themselves to put forward their demands and mobilize to win them.

For that, the democratic and popular revolution will create the necessary conditions to allow Voltaic women to achieve total and complete fulfillment. For could it be possible to eliminate the system of exploitation while maintaining the exploitation of women, who make up more than half our society?

(3) The national economy: independent, self-sufficient, and planned at the service of a democratic and popular society

The process of revolutionary transformations undertaken since August 4 places major democratic and popular reforms on the agenda. The National Council of the Revolution is therefore aware that the construction of an independent, self-sufficient, and planned national economy requires the radical transformation of present society, a transformation that itself requires the following major reforms:

- Agrarian reform.
- Administrative reform.
- Educational reform.
- Reform of the structures of production and distribution in the modern sector.

The agrarian reform will aim to:

- Increase labor productivity through better organization of the peasants and the introduction of modern agricultural techniques in the countryside.
- Develop a diversified agriculture, together with regional specialization.
- Abolish all the fetters that are part of the traditional socioeconomic structures that oppress the peasants.
- Finally, make agriculture the basis for the development of industry.

All this is possible by giving real meaning to the slogan of food self-sufficiency, a slogan that now seems dated for having been proclaimed so often without conviction. First, this will be a bitter struggle against nature, which, by the way, is no more thankless for us than for other peoples who have conquered it magnificently on the agricultural level. The CNR will harbor no illusions in gigantic, sophisticated projects. To the contrary, numerous small accomplishments in the agricultural system will allow us to transform our territory into one vast field, an endless series of farms.

Second, this will be a struggle against those who starve the people, the agricultural speculators and capitalists of all types. Finally, it will mean protecting our agriculture against domination by imperialism—with regard to its orientation, the plunder of our resources, and unfair competition from imports against our local products, imports whose only advantage is their packaging aimed at bourgeois afflicted with snobbishness. As for the peasants, sufficiently high prices and industrial food-processing facilities will guarantee them markets for their produce in any season.

The administrative reform aims to make operational the administration inherited from colonialism. To do that, it must be rid of all the evils that characterize it—namely, the unwieldy and nitpicking bureaucracy and its consequences—and a complete revamping of the civil service statutes must be undertaken. The reform should result in a less costly, more effective, and more flexible administration.

The educational reform aims to promote a new orientation for education and culture. It should result in transforming the schools into instruments at the service of the revolution. Graduates of the system should not serve their own interests and the exploiting classes, but rather the popular masses. The revolutionary education that will be taught in the new schools must imbue everyone with a Voltaic ideology, a Voltaic personality that rids the individual of blind mimicry. One of the jobs of education in a democratic and popular society will be to teach students to assimilate the ideas and experiences of other peoples in a critical and positive manner.

To end illiteracy and obscurantism, emphasis will have to be placed on mobilizing all energies, with the idea of organizing the masses, to increase their awareness and induce in them a thirst for knowledge by showing them the drawbacks of ignorance. Any policy of fighting illiteracy without the participation of those most concerned is doomed to failure.

Culture in a democratic and popular society, should

have a three-fold character: national, revolutionary, and popular. Everything that is antinational, antirevolutionary, and antipopular must be banished. To the contrary, our culture extols dignity, courage, nationalism, and the great human virtues.

The democratic and popular revolution will create favorable conditions for the blossoming of a new culture. Our artists will have a free hand to go boldly forward. They should seize the opportunity before them to raise our culture to a world level. Let writers put their pens at the service of the revolution. Let musicians sing not only of our people's glorious past, but also of their radiant and promising future.

The revolution expects our artists to be able to describe reality, portray it in living images, and express them in melodious tunes while showing our people the true way forward to a better future. It expects them to place their creative genius at the service of a national, revolutionary, and popular Voltaic culture.

We must be able to draw on what is positive from the past—that is, from our traditions, and what is positive in foreign cultures—in order to give a new dimension to our culture. The inexhaustible source for the masses' creative inspiration lies within the popular masses. Knowing how to live with the masses, becoming involved in the popular movement, sharing the joys and sufferings of the people, and working and struggling with them—all these should be the major concerns of our artists. Before producing, they should ask themselves: for whom is our creation intended? If we are convinced that we are creating for the people, then we must understand clearly who the people are, what their different components are, and what their deepest aspirations are.

The reform of our economy's structures of production

and distribution seek to increasingly establish effective control by the Voltaic people over the channels of production and distribution. For without genuine control over these channels, it is practically impossible to build an independent economy at the service of the people.

People of Upper Volta;

Comrade militants of the revolution:

The needs of our people are immense. Satisfaction of these needs requires that revolutionary transformations be undertaken in all fields.

In the field of health care and social assistance for the popular masses, the goals to be achieved can be summed up as follows:

- Making health care available to everyone.
- Setting up maternal and infant assistance and care.
- A policy of immunization against communicable diseases by increasing the number of vaccination campaigns.
- Raising the masses' awareness of the need to acquire good habits of hygiene.

All these goals can be attained only with the conscious involvement of the popular masses themselves in this fight, under the revolutionary guidance of the health services.

In the field of housing—a field of crucial importance—we must undertake a vigorous policy to end real estate speculation and the exploitation of workers through rent-gouging. Important measures in this field must be taken:

- Setting reasonable rents.
- Rapidly dividing neighborhoods into lots.
- Undertaking large-scale construction of modern residential homes, in sufficient numbers and accessible for workers.

One of the CNR's essential concerns is to unite the different nationalities that exist in Upper Volta in the common struggle against our revolution's enemies. There are indeed in our country a multitude of ethnic groups that differ from each other in language and customs. The Voltaic nation consists of the totality of these nationalities. Imperialism, through its policy of divide and rule, strove to exacerbate the contradictions among them, to set one against the other.

The CNR's policy aims to unite these different nationalities so that they live on an equal basis and enjoy equal opportunities for success. To do that, special emphasis will be placed on:

- Promoting economic development of the different regions.
- Encouraging economic exchanges between them.
- Combating prejudices between the ethnic groups, resolving in a spirit of unity the differences that divide them.
- Punishing those who foment divisions.

In view of all the problems that our country faces, the revolution can be described as a challenge that we must rise to. We do so driven by the will to victory, and together with the active participation of the popular masses mobilized through the CDRs.

In the near future, with the elaboration of programs for the various sectors, the entire territory of Upper Volta will be one vast construction site. The participation of all Voltaics able and old enough to work will be needed in the ruthless fight we will be waging to transform this country into a prosperous and radiant country, a country where the people will be the only masters of the nation's material and spiritual wealth.

Finally, we must define the place of the Voltaic revolution in the world revolutionary process. Our revolution is an integral part of the world movement for peace and democracy, against imperialism and all forms of hegemonism. That is why we will strive to establish diplomatic relations with other countries, regardless of their political and economic systems, on the basis of the following principles:

- Respect for each other's independence, territorial integrity, and national sovereignty.
- Mutual nonaggression.
- Noninterference in domestic affairs.
- Trade with all countries on an equal footing and on the basis of mutual benefit.

We will give active solidarity and support to national liberation movements fighting for the independence of their countries and the liberation of their peoples. This support is directed in particular:

- To the Namibian people, under the leadership of SWAPO.
- To the Saharawi people, in their struggle to recover their national territory.
- To the Palestinian people, for their national rights.

Objectively, the anti-imperialist African countries are allies in our struggle. The neocolonial alliances operating on our continent make closer ties with these countries necessary.

Long live the democratic and popular revolution!

Long live the National Council of the Revolution!

Homeland or death, we will win!

The People's Revolutionary Courts

Speech to inaugural session
January 3, 1984

On January 3, 1984, the new People's Revolutionary Courts (TPRs) held their first session at the House of the People in Ouagadougou. Under indictment was former president Sangoulé Lamizana, overthrown in a 1980 military coup, who was accused of misappropriating public funds. Lamizana was later found not guilty. The following speech given at the opening session was published as a pamphlet by the Ministry of Justice.

Comrade presidents of institutions;
Comrade members of the National Council of the Revolution;
Comrade members of the revolutionary government;
Comrade members of the People's Revolutionary Courts;
Comrade militants of the democratic and popular revolution;
Excellencies, ladies and gentlemen:
    It was exactly seventeen years to the day[1] that the Voltaic people took to the streets in a revolutionary out-

---

1. Actually eighteen years. See the chronology.

pouring, shouting slogans such as "Down with the embezzlers of public funds!" and "Down with those who starve the people!" at those who had always gagged, exploited, and oppressed them. Seventeen years ago today the Voltaic people took to the streets to demand "bread, water, and democracy!"

On January 3, 1966, in a collective burst of energy the Voltaic people put the reactionary and corrupt bourgeoisie of our country in the dock. After having used the people as a springboard to attain power, the bourgeoisie had turned its back on them in a frenetic race to accumulate ill-gotten wealth. Today, the Voltaic people again accuse. The Voltaic people accuse and demand that the people's verdict be carried out.

Today, to achieve its deepest long-standing aspirations, the Voltaic people themselves have forged an appropriate instrument—the People's Revolutionary Courts. We have made our choice, and from now on, nothing can prevent the people from rendering their verdict. From now on, nothing will be able to prevent the people from meting out exemplary punishment to all the political scum who have fed off famine, and to all the criminals who have always scorned and humiliated the people by inflicting a thousand and one indignities.

The Voltaic people accuse and the world trembles.

The world of the exploiters, the plunderers, and all those who profit from the neocolonial system are trembling because the Voltaic people have now become masters of their destiny and want to render their own justice.

Comrade members of the People's Revolutionary Courts:

By choosing January 3, 1984, as the date for the solemn opening of your deliberations, you are thus simply reviving a recent past, which constituted a decisive moment in the development of our people's conscious opposition to rule and exploitation by reactionary social layers and classes, who are genuine local supporters of imperialism.

The creation of the People's Revolutionary Courts is justified by the fact that, in place of the traditional courts, from now on the Voltaic people intend to put into practice the principle of real participation by the toiling and exploited classes in the administration and management of state affairs in all spheres and in all sectors of society.

The judges of the People's Revolutionary Courts have been chosen from among workers and by workers only, with the mission of carrying out the people's will. For this, there is no need for them to know the old laws. Having been born among the people, they only need to let themselves be guided by their sense of popular justice.

In the absence of codified texts, they need only base themselves on revolutionary law, rejecting the laws of neocolonial society. By establishing as its goal the destruction of the bureaucratic state apparatus, and by making it much easier for the people to have access to their representatives, our revolution, the August revolution, is proving—if proof were still needed—that the regime we have established is more democratic than the most democratic of bourgeois republics.

However, we must expect the establishment of the People's Revolutionary Courts to be subjected to attack by our enemies both inside and outside the country. Without a shadow of a doubt they will see in these courts an instrument of repression, if not of political inquisition. They will surely scream that human rights are being violated. But let them scream.

Our popular justice system is different from the system of justice in a society where the exploiters and oppressors control the state apparatus, in that it will strive to bring to light and publicly expose all the hidden social and political sides to the crimes perpetrated against the people, and to help them understand the consequences of these in order to draw lessons of social morality and practical politics. The decisions of the People's Revolutionary Courts will allow the wounds of the neocolonial regime to be revealed for the world to see by supplying material for critical analysis and by bringing out the elements needed for constructing a new society.

Consequently, by issuing verdicts against socioeconomic and moral crimes, these are in fact political trials, which call into question the political system of neocolonial society. Through the men on trial, it is society that is at stake here. That's why the judicial proceedings should take on an educational character through the explanations given to the popular masses, both at the trial and in the press. The verdicts rendered should be sufficiently thought-provoking. The hypocrisy of reactionary, bourgeois morality is expressed through fits of indignation over the guilty verdicts against a few individuals, and through silent complicity in the wholesale genocide of a people dying of poverty, starvation, and obscurantism.

We are judging one man in order to give rights to millions. We are therefore fervent defenders of the rights of man and not the rights of one man. To the immoral "morality" of the exploiting, corrupt minority, we counterpose the revolutionary morality of an entire people acting in the interests of social justice.

Armed with this revolutionary legitimacy, the National Council of the Revolution urges you, comrade judges of the TPRs, to act cooly and with revolutionary consciousness, to act firmly yet without excess, clear-headedly rather than from passion, and with discernment but without leniency, so as to protect the gains of our revolution.

We have chosen between two forms of law—the

revolutionary law of the people on the one hand, and the old reactionary law of the bourgeois minority on the other. The justice you are called upon to render is inspired by the democratic principles of our revolution. A democracy for the people and against the exploiters and oppressors—that is the foundation for the work of the People's Revolutionary Courts.

You should be proud. Proud to have been chosen and to have been called upon to be the architects of an undertaking that is innovative from every point of view.

Let us leave the supporters of so-called pure democracy to their whining and procrastination. Let the jurists and other scholars wax indignant and be scandalized. They're all formalists, obsessed by procedures and protocol, which they have not yet understood are aimed at tricking the people, turning the judge—draped in his robe, decked out with his sash, and sometimes even a wig—into a clown for whom we revolutionaries feel compassion, especially when we feel him so close to the people that he wants to abandon his profession.

Indeed, reactionary regimes beget reactionary justice. We understand the distress of a progressive or even revolutionary judge when forced to apply laws that make a mockery of his innermost political convictions. We have observed such dilemmas in other professions—in the army, to cite just one example. But fortunately the revolution of August 4, the democratic and popular revolution, came to liberate and mobilize the conscience of all those who have consciously chosen the people's camp.

The popular masses of Upper Volta ceased being the dupes of reactionary politicians the day they understood that in a society where exploiters exert their rule over the majority of the people, justice unquestionably means justice for the exploiters. Since one of the goals of our popular revolution is to institute a democratic state, this state must be fundamentally different from the state of the exploiters.

The system of justice in a democratic state is therefore different from the system of justice of the exploiters. The reactionary political regimes buried in our country—and those like them fossilizing elsewhere—have never dared and do not dare to put these political gangsters on trial, precisely because they've understood that under their reactionary system they cannot institute People's Revolutionary Courts, in which the people would speak out, without being swept away themselves. Just as they cannot leave the matter to the traditional courts, whose verdicts would only provoke the legitimate wrath of the voiceless, of the voice of the people.

This was the reason for the rough-and-ready solutions, such as administrative detentions, for example, which the philistines of the Military Committee for Redressment and National Progress administered under the learned tutelage of the inventor-historian-inquisitor-reactionary, Joseph Ki-Zerbo.

Elsewhere, there is life imprisonment and permanent house arrest, where the authorities count on the passage of time to make people forget that the leaders were faced with political problems that they should have solved— namely, the problem of the people and their right to justice.

By establishing the People's Revolutionary Courts, the CNR, the revolutionary government, and the militant people of the democratic and popular revolution know that popular justice will have to be meted out in all its severity, even if it involves degenerate elements found within their own ranks. At the same time, every militant knows that the open character of his political work, his daily conduct, and his social activity will ensure that he doesn't do by night or in the shadows, what he can do with a clear conscience in broad daylight. In truth, there is no virtue other than that imposed by, and genuinely under the control of, society and the people.

In a society such as ours, where the population is 95 percent illiterate and held in obscurantism and ignorance by the ruling classes, bourgeois law, defying all common sense, dares assert that "ignorance of the law is no excuse." With the help of such tricks, the idle propertied classes oppress the broad popular masses—the peasants of our countryside and the workers of our towns.

The same thing is true when, in the name of this same legal system, it is asserted that "the law alone may employ force." Since the law was enacted to defend and uphold the interests of the ruling classes, this argument on force is dredged up every time the interests of the minority are threatened. "The law alone may employ force" is a hallowed expression of the expropriators to rule out any idea of popular justice.

Thus, anything is permissible, except not having enough money to buy a lawyer and judges, who are the only ones responsible for interpreting purposely confusing texts that use esoteric and elitist language.

Actually, in the final analysis, the law alone does employ force, meaning that the law of the richest, the laws belonging to the highest bidder, and the oratorical talents sold to the highest bidder, always win out over the "common rights" of the people, those who remain forever guilty of being poor, of being unable to buy the services of renowned lawyers, or who simply show themselves to be ignorant and illiterate.

Every day, under our very eyes, we see thieves pursued by a crowd who seek refuge in a police station, convinced that "the law alone may employ force," and that their protection will be assured. By contrast, a peasant passing through Ouagadougou, facing charges for the slightest trifle, will have to avoid both his pursuers and the police station. Because he has no hope of finding justice anywhere in the world of the big city. Indeed, he believes that the police station is a place where he will be punished in the name of the law. And he naively believes that all citizens are equal before the law, a law that is implacable and inescapable.

The democratic and popular revolution must smash the antidemocratic, antipopular judicial system. Exactly as our people smashed the verdict of the rigged elections of December 1965, in which the reactionary megalomaniac Maurice Yaméogo claimed to have "democratically" won 99.99 percent of the vote. A few days later, on January 3, 1966, our people—outside the ballot boxes and against the ballots—imposed their own implacable, revolutionary verdict by deposing the impostor. No interpreter of the texts of Roman law, no judge, no lawyer, no court dared stand in the way of this powerful, implacable, and truly popular democracy. And for good reason!

More recently, after the counterrevolutionary coup of May 17, 1983, when Comrade Blaise Compaoré joined his troops and the revolutionary people of the town of Pô in order to prepare the revolutionary counterattack against the usurpers, no one dared challenge the legitimacy of such a response. Obviously legality, the law books, and the military regulations of the neocolonial army were totally called into question on that occasion. Comrade Compaoré knew that the commandos and the people of Pô truly personified the most profound feelings of justice, honor, and dignity of all our people. From this point of view, his action was democratic and legal a thousand times over. No military regulation, no law of the neocolonial Voltaic judicial system could support such an attitude.

And yet, this attitude was just and legitimate in the eyes of the great majority of our revolutionary people, who had been humiliated and insulted by the reactionary betrayal of May 17, 1983.

The actions of our people in these two examples teach us that there's no point in conforming to the bourgeois legality of the minority if we're not in total agreement with the uncodified morality of our people.

The Voltaic people offer to share their experience with the other peoples of the world. No arsenal of juridical-political scheming, no corrupting wizardry of financial feudalism, no violation of conscience, and no electoralist circus will be able to prevent the people's justice from emerging triumphant.

Comrades, as long as oppression and exploitation exist, there will always be two systems of justice and two systems of democracy: that of the oppressors and that of the oppressed, that of the exploiters and that of the exploited. Justice under the democratic and popular revolution will always be justice for the oppressed and exploited, as opposed to the neocolonial justice of yesterday, which was that of the oppressors and exploiters. Comrades, the people must apply justice themselves, their justice.

Whining and crocodile tears must not influence you in any way when it comes to dealing weighty blows against those who show themselves incapable of any feelings other than the most feudal contempt for the people and their interests. However, if there happen to be some who convince you of their gratitude toward the people because, by being severely punished, they have been given the opportunity to comprehend their crimes, then hold out a helping hand to them.

Have them get to know us. After having made them pay every last penny legitimately demanded from them by the people, we will create the conditions for them to understand that, once stripped of their immense, ill-gotten wealth, they can succeed in finding true happiness. This happiness, in our revolutionary society, will be nothing other than honest labor that brings an honest wage. This honest wage brings with it dignity and freedom that can be calculated neither in terms of secret bank accounts in Switzerland or elsewhere, nor in speculative securities on the most reputable stock exchanges, nor in parading aggressive and traumatic luxury before a people dying of hunger, disease, and ignorance. This happiness, in which we invite any possible penitents to share, will lie in the satisfaction of having proven your usefulness to society and in enjoying your right to participate in defining and actually achieving the aspirations of the people who accept you and include you.

Comrades, the People's Revolutionary Courts are sounding the death knell of old Roman law. It is the swan song of foreign, Napoleonic social law that has marginalized so many of our people and that had consecrated the illegitimate and scandalous privileges of a minority class. May the very next sessions in Ouagadougou open up a brightly lit path, at the end of which, in the skies of the universal revolution, will shine the great sun of justice, shooting its powerful rays into the hearts of all those who hope, but do not dare; of all those who dare, but do not understand; and of all those who understand, but do not dare.

Homeland or death, we will win!

There is only one color—
that of African unity

On return from Africa tour
August 1984

In the summer of 1984 Sankara went to Ethiopia, Angola, Congo (Brazzaville), Mozambique, Gabon, and Madagascar. Upon his return, he held a press conference in Ouagadougou, which took place after the celebration of the revolution's first anniversary, at which Upper Volta was renamed Burkina Faso. Below are major excerpts, which were published in the August 10, 1984, issue of *Carrefour africain.*

QUESTION: What is the state of relations with your conservative, relatively wealthier neighbor, the Ivory Coast?

THOMAS SANKARA: What is the Ivory Coast conserving? I know what you meant, but I'd like to know more precisely what ideology the Ivory Coast conserves, in order to better judge the contrast, if there is one, between our ideology and theirs.

Our relations are good, since Upper Volta had relations with the Ivory Coast. Burkina Faso states, as I said in my first anniversary message, that we will be open toward everyone and we will reach out to everyone. In this context, in this spirit, I believe our relations are good. Naturally, there's always something that can be done to improve relations. But as far as we are concerned, the current situation is fine with us. And if our brothers in the Ivory Coast wish, we can continue like this and even do better. But I'm not aware of any particular problems between the Ivory Coast and Burkina Faso.

Of course, we have opponents in the Ivory Coast, many opponents. But as revolutionaries—as soon as we began to consider ourselves revolutionaries—we knew very well that the world we live in is not revolutionary. We have to live with realities that are not always to our liking. We have to be ready to live with governments that are not making a revolution at all, or perhaps that even attack our revolution. This is a very big responsibility for revolutionaries. Perhaps those who come after us—the revolutionaries—will live in a better world and will have a much easier task.

For us, anyway, as soon as we accept this reality—that the Ivory Coast is not making a revolution, whereas we are—then everything becomes simple. The difficulties, complications, and concerns are only in the minds of those who are revolutionaries, but who, in a romantic way, hope or think that everyone should act like revolutionaries. But we're not surprised. So we're not bothered. It's a reality we were prepared for.

QUESTION: Historic ties exist between Burkina Faso and the Ivory Coast. We can see this by the periodic visits you make within the framework of regional and subregional organizations. But concretely, Comrade President, since the National Council of the Revolution has come to power, how is the Abidjan-Ouagadougou axis doing? Because some people speak of a certain coolness, and it's even claimed that your absence at the last summit of the Entente Council in Yamoussoukro[1] and the cancellation of a working visit to the Ivory Coast are significant.

SANKARA: You ask how the Abidjan-Ouagadougou axis is doing. The axis is straight, when run by Air Ivoire and Air Volta (soon to be Air Burkina). The axis is twisting and winding, when represented by the Abidjan-Ouagadougou railway. The axis is chaotic, very difficult, with ups and downs, when it corresponds to the Abidjan-Ouagadougou road—an axis that passes through dark regions, forest regions, and savanna, that stretches from the ocean to the heart of the parched Sahel. So it's a set of complex realities that each of us must grasp. There you have that axis. You wanted a description, there you are.

You asked me a second question. Some say a coolness exists. You don't specify who says that, which doesn't make our task easy. Be that as it may, you say that some people or some papers speak of a certain coolness between Abidjan and Ouagadougou.

Here we live in the warmth of the revolution, and those who are shivering should just protect themselves and take the necessary precautions. Between the Ivory Coast and Burkina Faso there are all kinds of relations—geographical, historical, economic, social, and others. These are relations we can't just erase by ringing a bell, relations that the Ivorians can't deny either.

Today Burkina Faso is embarked on a revolutionary road to transform its society, to fight a certain number of ills and scourges that we are familiar with here, and we think only Burkina Faso's enemies are complaining about that. Every Ivorian who loves the Burkinabè people should applaud the Burkinabè Revolution. Every Ivorian who does not

---

1. In 1983 Yamoussoukro replaced Abidjan as the capital of Côte d'Ivoire (Ivory Coast), although Abidjan remained the de facto capital.

love the Burkinabè Revolution does not love the Burkinabè people. That's where you must start from in figuring out where it's cold and who's getting cold.

Does this mean that the Ivory Coast, which had excellent relations with reactionary Upper Volta, is suddenly cooling off because Upper Volta has become revolutionary? That's a question that can only be asked of Ivorians. We are living in the warmth of the revolution, warmth that we gladly share with anyone who is willing to accept it. But we can't impose it on anyone, and it would really be a shame if fraternal peoples, neighboring peoples, were not to share in the same joy, or to benefit from the same warmth.

QUESTION: In contrast to the Ivory Coast, Ghana and its president are welcome in Burkina Faso. We even saw Ghanaian troops on parade during the commemoration of the revolution. Where does support end and interference begin? In a word, can Ghana become a liability for your young country?

SANKARA: Support to whom? Interference in the affairs of whom? Interference begins when a people feels treachery is being committed against it. As long as this is not the case, there will never be enough support.

Ghana comes to Burkina Faso, shows up here whenever an occasion warrants it, on happy occasions and also on not-so-happy occasions. Because—we have no doubt about it, and I think you have no doubt either—Burkinabè and Ghanaians share a deep affinity. As long as this affinity lasts, we can only deplore the fact that we have not done enough to increase the amount of support.

We don't have a chauvinist view of things, and we condemn sectarianism. For those reasons we see borders as administrative lines, perhaps necessary in order to limit each country's sphere of activity and enable it to see things clearly. But the spirit of liberty and dignity, of counting on one's own resources, of independence, and of consistent anti-imperialist struggle should blow from north to south and from south to north, crossing borders with ease. We're happy to say that's the case between Burkina Faso and Ghana, and it must continue to be the case.

Do you think our country would have any problems or difficulties in its relations if that wind were to blow through our country and all the other countries? Do you think countries would have gotten to the point of threatening each other with the apocalypse today if this same wind were blowing through all the countries of the world? Currently we're talking about Iran and Iraq—don't you think it would be good if Iranians could go visit Iraqis in the same way that Ghanaians go visit Burkinabè and vice versa?[2]

We believe it's an example we'd like to see repeated. We think it's in the interests of the peoples of the world. Those who lose out may be the people who would like to set Ghana against Burkina Faso for their own ulterior motives.

QUESTION: What does Burkina Faso think of the current crisis within the Organization of African Unity [OAU]?

SANKARA: We think that it's a completely normal and welcome crisis, because there's a revolutionary process going on that requires calling into question and redefining the goals of the OAU.

The OAU cannot continue to exist as it has. The desire to engage in unity-mongering won out too quickly over

---

2. In September 1980, with the support of Washington, London, Paris, and Tokyo, the Iraqi government of Saddam Hussein invaded Iran. Hussein sought control of Iran's oil fields and to push back the 1979 revolution in which millions of urban and rural working people and youth had overthrown the pro-U.S. monarchy. The Iran-Iraq war lasted eight years and resulted in hundreds of thousands of deaths.

the desire to realize unity. Many things were sacrificed in the name of unity and through unity-mongering. The peoples of Africa are increasingly hard to please today. And because they are, they're saying no to meetings and conferences whose function is to adopt resolutions that are never acted on, or whose function is to not adopt long-awaited resolutions that could be acted on.

Africa stands face to face with its problems—problems the OAU always succeeds in avoiding by putting off their solution until tomorrow. That tomorrow is today. We can no longer put all these questions off until tomorrow. That's why we find this crisis to be quite normal. It may even be a little late in coming.

QUESTION: Could you tell us Burkina Faso's position on the conflict in Western Sahara?

SANKARA: We have recognized the Saharawi Arab Democratic Republic [SADR] and we feel there's no reason to hesitate on the question—when a people has decided to choose an organization, it's a duty to recognize it. So we feel there can be no OAU summit without the SADR. Someone would be missing. If someone is missing and the reasons for that absence aren't legitimate, Burkina Faso won't play along.[3]

QUESTION: You've spoken several times about aid and cooperation, whether African or non-African, but not just of any kind of aid. What do you mean by that?

SANKARA: Aid must go in the direction of strengthening our sovereignty, not undermining it. Aid should go in the

---

3. See glossary, Saharawi Arab Democratic Republic. At the Organization of African Unity's November 1984 summit, the SADR was admitted as a full member, with the active support of the Burkinabè delegation, led by Thomas Sankara. Morocco then withdrew from the OAU in protest.

direction of destroying aid. All aid that kills aid is welcome in Burkina Faso. But we will be compelled to abandon all aid that creates a welfare mentality. That's why we're very careful and very exacting whenever someone promises or proposes aid to us, or even when we're the ones taking the initiative to request it.

You cannot make a revolution or gain your independence without a certain amount of stoicism and sacrifice. The people of Burkina demand such stoicism of themselves, precisely so as to avoid temptation, to avoid taking the easy way out, as some aid would encourage us to do. These mirages have done a lot of harm to our country and to others. We want to put a stop to them.

QUESTION: Comrade President, during your retreat in Koupéla[4] you received a member of the International Court of Justice. He must have talked to you about the Burkina Faso–Mali problem. So how are the deliberations coming along? Are you optimistic about the outcome?

SANKARA: Forty-five days after we took power in Burkina Faso, we expressed to the Malian people our utmost willingness to work on finding a fair solution to this problem. We lifted all the vetoes, all the bans, and all the obstacles that prevented a frank, constructive dialogue around this question.[5] I should say that spontaneous gestures are generally the most sincere.

We consider it important to assure the Malian people of our will, our sincerity, and our profound desire to live in

4. Koupéla is located in eastern-central Burkina Faso.

5. Based on a long-standing border dispute with Mali, successive governments in Upper Volta had vetoed Mali's admission to the West African Monetary Union. In October 1983 Upper Volta's new revolutionary government lifted this veto and referred the dispute to the International Court of Justice.

peace with them. That's why we got rid of this ball, which was in Burkina's court. That issue for us is over with. We're looking to the other partners, whether they be the International Court of Justice or Mali. We're giving them time to act or react. We're not worried about it.

QUESTION: Your counterpart from Zaire recently requested that a league of Black African states be set up. Were you consulted, and what do you think of this initiative by President Mobutu? Specifically, do you think that such a league could resolve the problems Black Africa is facing? And do you think the conflicts in Western Sahara and Chad[6] are the causes of the OAU's current situation?

SANKARA: Your question disturbs me a great deal because you seem to be saying once again that the heads of state consulted one another around this famous proposal for a league of Black African states. That's what your question seems to imply. At any rate I wasn't consulted, luckily for me! Perhaps only those who had something to "contribute" were consulted.

We're not opposed to Black Africans getting together, since the reality is that there are Black Africans and white Africans, but we don't know exactly what this would accomplish. We don't know what purpose it would serve to keep repeating that we are Blacks, as if the problems facing the OAU are due to the fact that there's a two-color OAU, and that we should be thinking of forming a single-color OAU. This is surrealism, which produces a certain kind of painting that we don't find appealing.

---

6. A former French colony in Central Africa, Chad was gripped by a recurrent civil war between factions supported by France in the south and Libya in the north. Paris intervened militarily in 1968–72, 1977–79, 1983–84, and 1986 to the present. Libyan troops occupied the north from 1983 to 1987.

You and *Jeune Afrique* seem to be saying that the conflict in Western Sahara—we call it the conflict between the SADR and Morocco, just so we understand each other—and to a lesser extent the conflict in Chad, could explain why the OAU is beginning to come apart. It's a little as if these two questions, Chad and the SADR, were ones that involve non-Black Africans and that by tossing them out of the OAU, we could harmoniously find ourselves back among Black Africans. I'm not sure relations between the SADR, which is African and mostly white, and certain Black African countries are worse than between some Black African countries and other Black African countries. So it's not a question of color. With regard to how we conceive of the OAU, there is no room for the color-sensitive. There is only one color—that of African unity.

QUESTION: What is your view of the evolution, particularly the failure, of the Brazzaville conference?[7]

SANKARA: As you know very well, we supported the efforts in Brazzaville. We said the Brazzaville conference should not be a boxing ring from which a heavyweight champion would emerge. We gave full support to [Congolese] President Sassou Nguesso in his efforts to establish conditions for a dialogue allowing the Chadians to sort things out among themselves. But we also said that in order for the conference to be of use, it would have to recognize the Chadian people's success over its enemies.

QUESTION: Concerning your relations with Libya, could you mention an example of aid from that country to Burkina Faso?

SANKARA: You're asking me a very delicate, very difficult

---

7. Several African governments took part in a conference in Brazzaville in the Republic of the Congo aimed at negotiating an end to the civil war in Chad and the withdrawal of French and Libyan troops.

question. There are so many examples. We could spend hours and hours, if not days and days, telling you about that aid. We have very good relations, which have only deepened as each country has asserted its own personality, as each country has asserted its own independence. We're very satisfied, very pleased that Libya respects our independence.

We visit Libya often. Not long ago, I met Colonel Qaddafi. We discussed many questions and made some mutual criticisms. We're also ready to engage in self-criticism when we feel the criticism is well-founded and should prompt us to change our position. Just as we invite Libya to do the same. Among revolutionaries we should engage in criticism and self-criticism. This doesn't mean Libya is perfect, because nothing is perfect in any country of the world. And this gives rise to discussions. So our relations continue to be as they have been, and have even taken on a new aspect with this form of mutual criticism and fruitful debate.

QUESTION: During a tour of Africa you visited Mozambique and Angola. However, we know these countries have signed pacts with South Africa that seem, at first sight, to be unnatural.[8] What is the position of Burkina Faso on those accords?

---

8. In February 1984 the governments of Angola and South Africa signed the Lusaka Accord whereby the apartheid government said it would withdraw its invasion force from southern Angola and the Angolan government promised to restrict the activities on its territory of SWAPO (South West Africa People's Organisation), which was leading the independence struggle in Namibia, ruled by South Africa from 1915 to 1990. This accord was followed in March 1984 by the Nkomati Accord between Mozambique and South Africa, whereby the apartheid government said it would withdraw its support for the proimperialist Renamo forces in Mozambique while the Mozambican government promised to no longer allow the African National Congress of South Africa to operate from its territory.

SANKARA: We've already expressed our position. There's a basic question involved here. Racist South Africa will never cease being a poison, a thorn in the side of all Africans. As long as this thorn, this barbaric, backward, and anachronistic ideology—apartheid—has not been removed, racism will not cease. So there's no room to hem and haw, to change positions on that question.

The ways and means to resolve this problem are tactical questions for each country. But fundamentally, the fight against racism must continue. Furthermore, tactics and strategy should not be confused with one another. That's why, while avoiding giving lessons or criticizing our Angolan and Mozambican comrades, we do remind them of their duty to struggle against racism, and that whatever tactics they use, they must wage a permanent fight against that racism. Any other position would be a negation of the sacrifices made by the African martyrs. It would also be a negation of everything being done today and everything done yesterday.

At the same time, we don't hesitate to criticize the other African states for having failed to offer effective, genuine, and concrete support to these countries at the front, who have watched over everyone's security with regard to racism. It's because Mozambique dared to support other struggles that what used to be Rhodesia is living a different reality today.[9] It's because Angola stands guard against South Africa that the rest of us, as far away as western or North Africa, can escape the direct threat of racism. But if those two countries should fall, if the Frontline States

---

9. In 1980 the racist white minority regime of Rhodesia, faced with an intensifying war of national liberation and growing international isolation, was forced to give up its effort to prevent majority rule. The country became the republic of Zimbabwe.

were to collapse,[10] it would mean a steady, dangerous, and incursionary advance of the racists' real borders.

So we can only encourage both countries to continue their fierce struggle against racism, against racist South Africa. And while we're at it, we can only hope that they exercise all the necessary vigilance. When you deal with the devil, you must take care to have a spoon with a very long handle—long enough, at any rate.

QUESTION: What does Burkina Faso think of the precondition raised by South Africa for the independence of Namibia—the withdrawal of Cuban troops from Angola?[11]

SANKARA: The precondition South Africa raises is a red herring, because it has dealings with countries, including African countries, that have foreign troops on their soil. Why is there no problem in these cases? Why do they want to prevent Angola from calling on troops that it feels make a useful contribution, and give useful support? It's their right. Calling on Cuban troops is a question that involves Angola's sovereignty. It's to the Cubans' credit that they agree to go die for another country when they too have dangers on their doorstep and on their coastlines.

As far as the question of the presence of foreign troops in this or that country is concerned, we think there are countries that have the right to raise the question and others that don't have the right, especially when they have

---

10. See glossary, Frontline States.

11. From November 1975 to May 1991, more than 375,000 Cuban volunteers responded to the Angolan government's appeal for solidarity to repel invasions by the South African armed forces backed by Washington and in alliance with the proimperialist regime in Zaire. This internationalist effort culminated in 1988 with the defeat of the racist forces at the battle of Cuito Cuanavale, leading to South Africa's withdrawal from Angola and the independence of Namibia.

foreign troops in their own countries. Cuban troops are no less legitimate than those seeking to extend their policy of domination.

QUESTION: You made reference in your speech to countries that greet you with the kiss of Judas, or those that support the enemies of your people. Do you count France among those countries, and how do you envision relations between France and Burkina Faso?

SANKARA: Perhaps at the time only Jesus spotted Judas. I'm not sure the other eleven disciples did. Let's not get ahead of ourselves. We don't put words in anyone's mouth. But we're also aware that the Judases know who they are and perhaps, having been caught red-handed plotting against us, they'll betray themselves one way or another.

Since we're on the subject, a person can deny everything, but their deepest intentions will come out in the end. The first of the twelve disciples, Peter, was caught himself. When Peter pretended he wasn't with the person who was the subject of popular condemnation, he was told, "Your accent betrayed you." Well, you've read the Holy Scriptures like everyone, so I won't go on.

France has relations with us that some may find surprising. We think these relations could be better. We do want to improve them. We've repeated this many times. But for those relations to improve, France has to learn to deal with the African countries, at least with us, on a new basis. We deeply regret the fact that if May 1981 made it possible to transform France, you're the only ones who know it. As far as France's relations with Africa are concerned, at any rate, May 1981 changed nothing.[12]

The France of May 1981 is following practically the

12. In May 1981 François Mitterrand of the Socialist Party was elected president of France.

same course as the preceding governments. It is also dealing with the same spokespeople representing the various
African groups. The France of today is no different from
the France of yesterday. That's why we, who are expressing, who are conveying a new African reality, are not understood. Perhaps we're even stirring up the tranquil pond
of Franco-African relations a bit.

We turn up using the language of truth, a truthfulness that is perhaps direct and somewhat forthright, but
a truthfulness coupled with sincerity not found elsewhere.
For too long France has been accustomed to the kind of
language used by—I wouldn't quite call them sycophants,
but. . . . France was often used to the language of the local
lackeys of neocolonialism. In such conditions it can't understand that there are some who don't want to get in line.

If France were to make the effort to understand this
new reality—which is viewed in Burkina Faso as a reality
largely shared by many other African countries—if the
effort were made to accept this as is, many things would
change. But unfortunately, they want to dismiss Burkina
Faso as a minor glitch, a fluke, perhaps a temporary one.
No, that's the reality in Africa, and so relations between
Africa and its other partners must evolve accordingly.

QUESTION: You said you were open to countries with different ideologies. In May 1981 the Socialists took power
in France. Yet your country's ideology is opposed to that
of France. Would it be right to say that there should be
a friendship between the two countries, one that might
be characterized as conditional? If so, what would be the
conditions?

SANKARA: I think there's no such thing as unconditional
friendship. Even love at first sight has, I believe, certain
conditions, which, when they wear off, bring human beings back to earth and to surprisingly cold realities.

Friendship between Burkina Faso and any other country is a friendship conditional on respect for our sovereignty and our interests, which in turn compels us to respect the other partner. These conditions are not a one-way street. We think that the dialogue with France must be frank. Truthfulness, as long as both partners are really willing to abide by it, could lead us to a program of friendship.

France's representative, its ambassador, has calculated that from August 4, 1983, until today the balance of diplomatic exchanges between France and the former Upper Volta has shown a big deficit to our disadvantage. That says a lot. France continues to believe that the positions of Burkina Faso can be guessed at, interpreted through, or expressed by this or that big shot. Which means that on this level France has not considered Burkina Faso to be something new—something new that reflects a certain reality in Africa.

QUESTION: Upper Volta decided not to participate in the [1984 Los Angeles Summer] Olympic Games. Why? How do you explain the fact that other African countries decided to go?

SANKARA: Upper Volta decided not to participate, and Burkina Faso upholds that decision. Not because there wasn't much hope of us bringing home medals, no! But out of principle. We should use these games, like any platform, to denounce our enemies and the racism of South Africa. We cannot participate in such games alongside supporters of South Africa's racist policies. Nor alongside those who reject the warnings and condemnations that Africans have issued in order to weaken racist South Africa. We do not agree and chose not to go, even if it means never going to the Olympic Games.

Our position was not dictated to us by anyone. Each country that refused to go has its reasons. Ours have to do with the relations between British sports authorities and South Africa. Great Britain has never accepted the various warnings and numerous protests. Great Britain has not budged and neither have we. We will not stand at its side to celebrate. We can't go to that celebration! We don't feel like celebrating.

QUESTION: You know that what often scares the West, Europe, and France, is the term "revolution." In your speech, you said that "revolution cannot be exported." Is this a way of reassuring the countries that are a little afraid? Is it possible to not export revolution, when borders are merely administrative lines?

SANKARA: Revolution cannot be exported. An ideological choice cannot be imposed on any people. Exporting revolution would also mean that we Burkinabè think we can go teach others what they have to do to solve their problems. This is a counterrevolutionary view. This is what pseudorevolutionaries, the bookish, dogmatic petty bourgeoisie, proclaim. It would be saying that we imported our revolution, and that being true, we're now supposed to continue the chain.

This is not the case.

We've said that our revolution is not unaware of the experiences of other peoples, their struggles, their successes, and their setbacks. This means the revolution in Burkina Faso therefore takes into account all the revolutions of the world, whatever they may be. The revolution of 1917 teaches us many things, for example; and the revolution of 1789 provides us with many lessons. Monroe's theory of "America for the Americans" teaches us a lot. We're interested in all that.[13]

---

13. A reference to the Russian Revolution of 1917 and the French Revolution of 1789. The Monroe Doctrine of 1823, issued by U.S. presi-

We also think that having borders that are simply administrative lines does not mean our ideology can invade other countries. Because if they don't accept it, if they reject it, it won't make much headway. For these borders not to be a barrier to ideas, as well, they have to be understood on both sides of the line as merely administrative. If Burkina Faso sees this or that border as being only an administrative line, whereas on the other side it's seen as a protective rampart, the result will not be what happens between Ghana and Burkina Faso.

The better the revolution is known, the better will it be understood that it's not dangerous—that it's good for the peoples of the world. Many men fear revolution because they're not familiar with it, or because they're only familiar with the excesses as reported by columnists and newspaper correspondents looking for something sensational.

Let's be clear. Although our revolution is not made for export, we don't intend to go out of our way to shut the Burkinabè Revolution up inside an impenetrable fortress. Our revolution is an ideology that blows freely and is at the disposal of all those who feel the need to take advantage of it.

---

dent James Monroe, declared that the young U.S. republic would act to prevent any interference in the Americas by the reactionary European monarchies and colonizers.

Top: Sankara receiving the Order of José Martí from Cuban
president Fidel Castro in Havana, Cuba, September 25, 1984.
Bottom: Castro and Sankara at ceremony, surrounded by Burkinabè
children's chorus that traveled with Sankara.

Our struggle draws strength from Cuba's example and support

Receiving Order of José Martí, Havana
September 25, 1984

Sankara headed an official delegation to Cuba from September 25 to 30, 1984. He met with President Fidel Castro and other leaders of the revolutionary government. On the day of Sankara's arrival, Cuba's Council of State awarded him the Order of José Martí, the highest honor bestowed by the Cuban government. Armando Hart, a member of the Cuban Communist Party's Political Bureau and minister of culture, spoke at the ceremony. The following are Hart's remarks and Sankara's response, which was given in Spanish. The English-language text was first published in the October 7, 1984, issue of *Granma Weekly Review*, published in Havana.

ARMANDO HART

Comrade Fidel;
Dear Comrade Captain Thomas Sankara, president of the National Council of the Revolution and head of state and government in Burkina Faso;

Dear comrades of the visiting delegation;
Comrades:

We have the honor this evening of carrying out the resolution of our Council of State, which confers on you, dear President Sankara, a high and distinguished decoration: the Order of José Martí. Our revolution reserves it, very selectively, as a well-deserved recognition of those who have rendered outstanding service to the cause of their people, to international relations between our countries; to dignity and honor; or to the struggle against imperialism, colonial and neocolonial domination, and for genuine national liberation. You, Comrade Thomas Sankara, display all these merits simultaneously.

First we should underscore the deep feelings of friendship and solidarity with which the leadership of our party, our government, and the entire Cuban people have been following the revolutionary events unfolding in the former Republic of Upper Volta, today known by its new name, Burkina Faso.

Revolutionary peoples, those who have experienced the hard struggle for independence, dignity, and development, have no difficulty understanding the efforts and battles of other fraternal peoples. They feel the need to immediately extend political support and solidarity—both of which are so important at all times, but even more so at the outset of a revolution. This is how we feel toward the people of Burkina Faso, toward the process of renewal and transformation taking place in their country and toward their outstanding leader, Captain Thomas Sankara.

President Sankara is a shining example of the role that patriotic youth in the military can and are playing in the struggle for the liberation and development of their countries, with their advanced ideas and deep commitments to the people. Comrade Captain Sankara has led the progressive forces of the army, the workers, and the young people of his country with admirable tenacity, intelligence, and courage. He has managed to frustrate reactionary maneuvers aimed at stemming the revolutionary process. Together with your people, you have prevented the neocolonial order from being reestablished, with all its accompanying poverty, oppression, and corruption—problems that the new leadership of Burkina Faso is combating.

We deeply identify with these objectives and with Burkina Faso's active foreign policy—a policy of solidarity with the African peoples confronting apartheid, the aggression of the South African racists, and domination by the forces of reaction and imperialism; a policy of support for national liberation movements and of adherence to the principles of the Nonaligned Movement; in conclusion, a policy of anti-imperialist unity and of struggle for peace.

We are confident, dear Comrade Sankara, that this visit by you and your delegation, and your conversations with Comrade Fidel and other leaders of the Cuban Revolution, will help further strengthen our fraternal bonds and will mark a higher stage of friendship and cooperation between our countries, which have been developing so satisfactorily.

Burkina Faso and Cuba established relations very recently. Imperialism and colonialism separated us for a long time. In fact, however, our ties go back centuries and it is only now, in this era of revolution, that we can do them justice. In the past, countless sons and daughters of your country were uprooted from their native land and brought to Cuba in chains, as slaves for unscrupulous exploiters. They contributed to forging a new nation with the sweat of their brows and with their lives, a nation for whose independence they would later fight with admirable heroism. José Martí, the extraordinary Cuban who epitomizes revolutionary thought and action in Cuba and the Americas during the last century, and after whom this cherished award has been named, witnessed the terrible spectacle of African slavery as a child and expressed his unforgettable impression in heart-felt lines. It made him tremble with passion for those who cried out in pain, and he pledged to vindicate that crime with his blood. Today Fidel is completing the work Martí was unable to finish. In both Cuba and Burkina Faso, revolution has made those dreams a reality.

Today, men who come to our two countries no longer wear the chains of slavery, they wear the star of liberty instead. In this spirit, as an expression of friendship, admiration, and respect, dear Comrade Sankara, please receive from the hands of Commander in Chief Fidel Castro the medal of the Order of José Martí.

THOMAS SANKARA

Comrades:

Revolutionaries do not waste time hypocritically praising one another, a common practice among reactionaries.

The tribute that the people of Cuba have paid to my people, by conferring the highest distinction of the Cuban Revolution on me, is more than a symbolic gesture. It is a pledge of political support to my country, Burkina Faso, and its democratic and popular revolution. It is a firm pledge based on the memory of one of the greatest patriots not only of Cuba and Latin America, but of all corners of the world where peoples are fighting for freedom and independence.

This distinction demonstrates the Cuban people's deep feelings of love for the Burkinabè people. Did not José Martí himself entitle his unforgettable work, "Love Is Repaid with Love"? José Martí, who at the early age of sixteen was deported from his country because of his revolutionary political ideas, felt the reality of militant solidarity among the peoples of the world in his blood and bones.

Peoples of the world love one another, and they know how to love. For nine years, Martí lived in the United States, Mexico, and Guatemala, where he became part of the people and earned their love. Without that profound love, when he was deported—it happened twice in his short life, in 1869 and 1879—he could have been discouraged and his morale might have flagged. But in 1895 José Martí returned to his country and took up arms against the colonial oppressors. The man who died at Dos Ríos did so for the freedom of all the world's peoples. He belongs to us all, to Cuba and to Burkina Faso.

The precious blood of heroes like him nurtures the peoples of the world and gives them the strength to wage ever more important battles. Comrade Fidel Castro and his comrades in the Sierra Maestra in 1956 were simply carrying forward the same revolutionary battle by the Cuban people for their full freedom.[1] The revolutionaries and the Burkinabè people, who spent years combating reactionary and proimperialist regimes in Burkina Faso, were following in the footsteps of the battle waged by José Martí and they continue to do so today.

Cuba and Burkina Faso are so far and yet so near, so different and yet so similar, that only revolutionaries can understand the sincere love that pushes us irresistibly toward one another.

My country is small. It covers 274,000 square kilometers

---

1. The revolutionary war in Cuba against the U.S.-backed Batista dictatorship began in December 1956.

and has a population of seven million—seven million peasant men and women, who for centuries lived under conditions identical to, if not worse than, those endured by your people under the fascist Batista dictatorship. Safe drinking water, three meals a day, a clinic, a school, and a simple plow are still elements of an ideal in life that millions of Burkinabè have not yet achieved after a year of revolutionary power. I must explain that the National Council of the Revolution and the people of Burkina Faso conquered state power and wield it today under the weight of a heavy legacy from the past.

But there are positive examples such as yours that revive the morale of the less-determined, strengthen the revolutionary convictions of others, and spur people on to struggle against the centers of hunger, disease, and ignorance that still exist in our country.

We have been fighting, we fight, and we will continue to fight to create, with our own hands, the material foundations for our happiness. At all times in this fight, we know we can count on the firm support of the revolutionary people of Cuba and of all who have embraced José Martí's ideals.

May José Martí hear me!

May this medal guide me and my comrades in leading our revolution to victory at the service of the people who demand their share of happiness!

It is no accident at all that our national slogan is captured in one you know so well:

Homeland or death, we will win![2]

---

2. This is also the slogan of the Cuban Revolution.

Asserting our identity, asserting our culture

At Burkinabè art exhibit in Harlem
October 2, 1984

While visiting New York City to address the United Nations General Assembly, Sankara inaugurated an exhibition of Burkinabè art at the Third World Trade Center in Harlem.

Dear friends, thank you.

Thank you for giving us the opportunity to present Burkina Faso. As our brother just explained so brilliantly, we have decided to change names. This comes at a time of rebirth for us. We wanted to kill off Upper Volta in order to allow Burkina Faso to be reborn. For us, the name of Upper Volta symbolizes colonization. We feel that we are no more interested in Upper Volta than we are in Lower Volta, Western Volta, or Eastern Volta. This exhibition allows us to present here to the world the real name we have chosen—Burkina Faso. This is a very big opportunity for us.

You may ask why we chose to start our exhibition off in Harlem. It's because we feel that the fight we're waging in Africa, principally in Burkina Faso, is the same fight

Kwame Brathwaite

At Burkinabè art exhibit at Third World Trade Center in Harlem,
October 2, 1984.

you're waging in Harlem. We feel that we in Africa must give our brothers in Harlem all the support they need so that their fight too becomes known. When people the world over learn that Harlem has become a living heart beating to the rhythm of Africa, then everyone will respect Harlem. Every African head of state who comes to New York should first stop in Harlem. Because we consider our White House to be in Black Harlem.

The exhibition you've come to see this evening has deep meaning for us. It conveys our entire past, and also our present. At the same time, this exhibition opens a door to our future. It constitutes a living link between us and our ancestors, us and our children. Every object you will see here expresses the pain of the African. In addition, every object expresses the struggle we are waging not only against natural scourges, but also against the enemies who have come to subjugate us.

Every object here expresses the sources of energy on which we rely in the fight we're waging. Whether they are in the style of our ancestors or in a modern style, we think our future is also portrayed and embodied in these objects of art.

The magic concealed in these objects, in these masks, is perhaps the same magic that allowed others to have confidence in the future, to explore the heavens, and to send rockets to the moon. We want to be left free, free to give our culture and our magic their full meaning. It is, after all, a magical phenomenon to simply flip a switch and see light appear suddenly. If Jules Verne had been stopped in his tracks, certainly there would not be all these developments in space today.

Our ancestors in Africa began a certain form of development. We don't want those great African wise men to be denigrated. That's why we've decided to create a research center on the Black man in Burkina Faso.[1] In this center we'll be studying the origins of the Black man. We'll also be studying the evolution of his culture, African music throughout the entire world, the art of dress throughout the entire world, African culinary art throughout the entire world, and African languages throughout the entire world. In short, everything that enables us to assert our identity will be studied in this center.

The research center will not be a closed place. We call on all Africans to come study at it. We call on Africans from Africa, we call on Africans from outside Africa, and we call on Africans from Harlem. Let everyone come participate on their own level for the development and fulfillment of the African. We hope this exhibition constitutes a kind of prelude to the gigantic task before us.

Let's see to it, dear brothers and comrades, that the coming generations don't accuse us of sacrificing or silencing the Black man.

I don't want to take more of your time. Other objects of art are expected to complete this exhibition—specifically, bronze objects, I believe—and I also hope to have the opportunity, perhaps tomorrow or the day after, to stop back here in Harlem and discuss this exhibition with you.

I thank you for having allowed an African country, Burkina Faso, to make itself known. In the name of the people of Burkina Faso, and in the name of our brothers who are here in Harlem, I would like to declare this exhibition open.

Thank you.

---

1. The Institute of Black Peoples opened in 1990, after the overthrow of the revolution.

Our White House
is in Black Harlem

At rally in Harlem
October 3, 1984

During his trip to New York, Sankara spoke to a rally of more than 500 at the Harriet Tubman School in Harlem. The event was organized by the Patrice Lumumba Coalition.

Imperialism!
[*Shouts of "Down with it!"*]
Imperialism!
[*Shouts of "Down with it!"*]
Neocolonialism!
[*Shouts of "Down with it!"*]
Racism!
[*Shouts of "Down with it!"*]
Puppet regimes!
[*Shouts of "Down with them!"*]
Glory!
[*Shouts of "To the people!"*]
Dignity!

At rally in Harlem, New York City, October 3, 1984.

[*Shouts of "To the people!"*]
Power!
[*Shouts of "To the people!"*]
Homeland or death, we will win!
Homeland or death, we will win!
Thank you comrades. [*Prolonged applause*]

I'm not going to be long, because those who spoke before me have said what the revolution should be. The comrade who is a member of the Central Committee [of the All-African Peoples Revolutionary Party] did a good job explaining what the revolution should be and what our commitment should be. The comrade reverend said in very ironical terms what the revolution should be. The comrades from the other regions of the continent and outside the continent also explained what the revolution should be. The singers, dancers, and musicians said what the revolution should be.

What is left for us to do is make the revolution! [*Applause*]

A moment ago, as I watched the ballet, I really thought we were in Africa. [*Applause*] That's why I've always said— and I'll say it again—our White House is in Black Harlem. [*Prolonged applause*]

There are many who think Harlem is a dump. There are many who think Harlem is a place to suffocate in. But there are also many of us who believe that Harlem will give the African soul its true dimension. [*Applause*] There are many of us Africans—very many in fact—who have to understand that our existence must be devoted to the struggle to rehabilitate the name of the African. We must wage the fight to free ourselves from domination by other men and from oppression.

Some Blacks are afraid and prefer to swear allegiance to whites. They must be denounced. They must be fought. We must be proud to be Black. [*Prolonged applause*] Remember, many of these politicians think of Blacks only on election eve. We must be Black with other Blacks, night and day. [*Prolonged applause*]

We understand that our struggle is a call to build. We don't ask that the world be built for Blacks alone and against other men. As Blacks, we want to teach others how to love each other. Despite their meanness toward us, we will be capable of resisting and then teaching them the meaning of solidarity. We also know that we must be organized and determined. [*Applause*] Our brothers are in South Africa. They must be freed. [*Prolonged applause*]

Last year I met [Grenada's Prime Minister] Maurice Bishop. We had a lengthy discussion. We gave each other mutual advice. When I returned to my country, imperialism had me arrested. I thought about Maurice Bishop. Some time later I was freed from prison thanks to the mobilization of the population. Again, I thought about Maurice Bishop. I wrote him a letter. I never had the opportunity to send it to him. Once again, because of imperialism. So we have learned that from now on imperialism must be fought relentlessly. If we don't want other Maurice Bishops to be assassinated tomorrow, we have to start mobilizing as of today. [*Applause*]

That's why I want to show you I'm ready for imperialism. [*Unbuckles belt and brandishes pistol in its holster. Cheers and prolonged applause*] Please believe me, this is not a toy. These bullets are real. And when we fire these bullets, it will be against imperialism. It will be on behalf of all Black people. It will be on behalf of all those who suffer domination. It will also be on behalf of those whites who are genuine brothers to Blacks. And it will also be on behalf of Ghana, because Ghana is a brother country.

Do you know why we organized the Bold Union maneuvers

with Ghana?[1] It was to show imperialism what we are capable of in Africa. Many other African countries prefer to organize their military maneuvers jointly with foreign powers. When we hold our next maneuvers, there should be fighters from Harlem who come to participate with us. [*Cheers and prolonged applause*]

Our revolution is symbolized by our flag. It's our country's new flag. Our country has also changed names. As you can see, this flag resembles the flag of your party. It's because we too are in that party. It's because we're working for the same cause as that party. That is why, quite naturally, the colors of the two flags resemble each other. And these colors have the same meaning. We didn't use the color black because we're already in Africa. [*Applause, cheers, shouts of "Down with imperialism!"*] But you can consider the two flags to be equivalent.[2]

You know, it's important that every day each of you remember one thing. While we are here discussing, while we are here talking to each other as Africans, there are spies who are here in order to make a report tomorrow morning. We say to them that they don't need to bring secret microphones because even if television cameras came here, we'd be repeating exactly the same thing. [*Applause*]

So I have to tell you that we have the strength and the capacity within ourselves to fight imperialism. The only

---

1. Burkina Faso and Ghana held joint military maneuvers in Ghana, November 4–8, 1983.

2. The flag of Burkina Faso is red and green with a yellow star. The red represents the revolutionary struggle; the green agriculture, abundance and hope; and the yellow the country's riches. The Black liberation flag, adopted in 1920 by the Universal Negro Improvement Association and other organizations, is red, black, and green.

thing you need to remember is that when the people stand up, imperialism trembles. [*Applause*]

I admired very much the ballets that were performed. That's why I'd like to invite you to the next National Week of Culture taking place in Burkina Faso in December. Even if you can send only one person, you must send someone. [*Applause*] I also invite you to the next pan-African film festival in Ouagadougou in February. All the African countries will be represented. South Africa will be represented by the African liberation movement. Harlem should be represented. [*Applause*]

We will do everything we can to send troupes from Burkina Faso to you here in Harlem to perform on behalf of our African brothers and sisters who are here. I ask you to encourage and support them and to allow them to go to other American cities to meet other Africans who are in those cities.

I've noticed that you hold Comrade Jerry John Rawlings in high esteem, so we'll send you some African wraparound clothing printed with his picture. And we've also printed on this clothing, "Ghana-Burkina Faso: same fight." These clothes should be worn everywhere—to work, in the street, while shopping, everywhere. Be proud of them, show that you are Africans. Never be ashamed of being African. [*Applause*]

I said I wouldn't take long. Before ending I'd like to ask you to stand up, because tomorrow, when I address the United Nations, I will speak about the ghettos. I will speak about Nelson Mandela, who must be freed. [*Applause*] I will speak about injustice. I will speak about racism. And I will speak about the hypocrisy of the leaders around the world. I will tell them that we and you, all of us, are waging our struggles and that they would do well to pay attention. [*Applause*] Because you represent the people.

Wherever you stand up, imperialism trembles. That is why I ask you to repeat:

When the people stand up, imperialism trembles!

[*Shouts of "When the people stand up, imperialism trembles!"*]

Again!

[*Shouts of "When the people stand up, imperialism trembles!"*]

Again!

[*Shouts of "When the people stand up, imperialism trembles!"*] [*Applause*]

Imperialism!

[*Shouts of "Down with it!"*]

Imperialism!

[*Shouts of "Down with it!"*]

Puppet regimes!

[*Shouts of "Down with them!"*]

Racism!

[*Shouts of "Down with it!"*]

Zionism!

[*Shouts of "Down with it!"*]

Neocolonialism!

[*Shouts of "Down with it!"*]

Glory!

[*Shouts of "To the people!"*]

Dignity!

[*Shouts of "To the people!"*]

Music!

[*Shouts of "To the people!"*]

Health!

[*Shouts of "To the people!"*]

Education!

[*Shouts of "To the people!"*]

Power!

[*Shouts of "To the people!"*]

All the power!

[*Shouts of "To the people!"*]
Homeland or death, we will win!
Homeland or death, we will win!
Thank you, comrades.
[*Prolonged applause*]

Freedom must be conquered

At United Nations General Assembly
October 4, 1984

Sankara delivered this address to the Thirty-ninth Session of the United Nations General Assembly in New York. His speech was published as a pamphlet by the Permanent Mission of Burkina Faso to the United Nations.

Mr. President;
Mr. Secretary General;
Honorable representatives of the international community:

I come here to bring you fraternal greetings from a country of 274,000 square kilometers whose seven million children, women, and men refuse to die of ignorance, hunger, and thirst any longer. In their quarter century of existence as a sovereign state seated at the UN, they have been unable to really live.

I come to address you at this Thirty-ninth Session on behalf of a people who, in the land of their ancestors, have decided to henceforth assert themselves and accept their history—both its positive and negative aspects—without the slightest complex.

I come here, finally, mandated by the National Council of the Revolution of Burkina Faso, to express the views of my people concerning the problems on the agenda—consisting of the tragic web of events that are painfully cracking the foundations of our world at the end of the twentieth century. A world in which humanity has been transformed into a circus, torn apart by struggles between the great and the semi-great, attacked by armed bands, and subjected to violence and pillage. A world in which nations, eluding international law, command groups of outlaws who, guns in hand, live by plunder and organize sordid trafficking.

Mr. President:

I make no claim to lay out any doctrines here. I am neither a messiah nor a prophet. I possess no truths. My only aspiration is twofold: first, to be able to speak on behalf of my people, the people of Burkina Faso, in simple words, words that are clear and factual. And second, in my own way to also speak on behalf of the "great disinherited people of the world," those who belong to the world so ironically christened the Third World. And to state, though I may not succeed in making them understood, the reasons for our revolt.

All this indicates our interest in the United Nations. We understand that demanding our rights requires from us a vigorous and rigorous awareness of our duties.

No one will be surprised to see us associate the former Upper Volta, today Burkina Faso, with that hodgepodge held in such contempt—the Third World—invented by the other worlds as many countries became formally independent in order to better ensure our intellectual, cultural, economic, and political alienation.

We want to place ourselves within this world, without

lending any credence to that gigantic fraud of history, and certainly without accepting the status of "hinterland of a satiated West." Rather, we want to assert our awareness of belonging to a tricontinental whole and, with the force of deeply felt convictions, acknowledge, as a Nonaligned country, that there is a special relationship of solidarity uniting the three continents of Asia, Latin America, and Africa in a single struggle against the same political traffickers, the same economic exploiters.

Therefore, recognizing that we are part of the Third World means, to paraphrase José Martí, "asserting that our cheek feels the blow struck against any man in the world." Up to now we have turned the other cheek. The blows increased. But the wicked-hearted were not moved. They trampled the truth of the righteous. The word of Christ was betrayed. His cross was transformed into a club. And after they put on his robe, they slashed our bodies and souls. They obscured his message. They Westernized it, whereas we had understood it as one of universal liberation. Then our eyes opened to the class struggle. There will be no more blows.

It must be proclaimed that there can be no salvation for our peoples unless we decisively turn our backs on all the models that all the charlatans, cut from the same cloth, have tried to sell us for the past twenty years. There can be no salvation without saying no to that. No development without breaking with that.

Moreover, all the new "intellectual leaders" emerging from their slumber, awakened by the dizzying rise of billions of men in rags, aghast at the threat that this famished multitude presents to their digestion, are beginning to revamp their speeches. In an anxious quest, they are looking in our direction once again, for miracle concepts and new forms of development for our countries. It's enough to read the numerous proceedings of innumerable symposiums and seminars to be convinced of this.

Far be it from me to ridicule the patient efforts of those honest intellectuals who, because they have eyes to see, are discovering the terrible consequences of the devastation imposed by the so-called specialists in Third World development. The fear haunting me is that the fruit of so much effort may be commandeered by Prosperos of all kinds to make a magic wand, designed to return us to a world of slavery redone in the fashion of the day.[1]

This fear is even more justified by the fact that the educated petty bourgeoisie of Africa—if not the Third World—is not prepared to give up its privileges, either due to intellectual laziness or simply because it has tasted the Western way of life. So it forgets that any genuine political struggle requires rigorous, theoretical debate, and it refuses to make the effort to think out and invent new concepts equal to the murderous fight awaiting us. A passive and pathetic consumer, the petty bourgeoisie abounds in terminology fetishized by the West, just as it abounds in Western whiskey and champagne, enjoyed in lounges of dubious taste.

We would search in vain for genuinely new ideas that have emanated from the minds of our "great" intellectuals since the emergence of the now-dated concepts of Negritude and African Personality.[2] The vocabulary and

---

1. In William Shakespeare's play *The Tempest*, Prospero is a sorcerer who uses his power to control the fate of others. In the eyes of many anticolonial fighters in the twentieth century, Prospero came to symbolize the oppressors.

2. Negritude was a literary movement that began among French-speaking African and Caribbean writers living in Paris in the 1930s. Formed as a protest against French rule and its policy of cultural as-

ideas come to us from elsewhere. Our professors, engineers, and economists content themselves with simply adding color—because often the only things they've brought back from the European universities of which they are the products are their degrees and their velvety adjectives and superlatives!

It is both necessary and urgent that our trained personnel and scribes learn that there is no such thing as unbiased writing. In these stormy times we cannot leave our enemies of yesterday and today with an exclusive monopoly over thought, imagination, and creativity.

Before it's too late—because it's already late—these elites, these men of Africa and the Third World, must come back to who they are—that is, to their societies and to the misery we have inherited. They must understand that the battle for a system of thought at the service of the disinherited masses is not in vain. They must understand too that they can only become credible on an international level by being genuinely inventive, that is, by painting a faithful picture of their people. This picture must allow the people to achieve fundamental changes in the political and social situation, changes that allow us to break from the foreign domination and exploitation that leave our states no perspective other than bankruptcy.

This is what we glimpsed—we, the Burkinabè people—during the evening of August 4, 1983, when the first stars began to sparkle in the skies of our homeland. We had to take the leadership of the peasant revolts, signs of which were visible in a countryside that is panic-stricken by the advancing desert, exhausted by hunger and thirst, and

---

similation, it stressed the value of African cultural traditions. African Personality was a concept that attributed unique qualities to African culture predisposing Africans toward socialism.

abandoned. We had to give meaning to the brewing revolt of the idle urban masses, frustrated and weary of seeing limousines driving the elites around, elites that were
out of touch, succeeding one another at the helm of state
while offering the urban masses nothing but false solutions elaborated and conceived by the minds of others. We
had to give an ideological soul to the just struggles of our
popular masses as they mobilized against the monster of
imperialism. The passing revolt, the simple brushfire, had
to be replaced forever with the revolution, the permanent
struggle against all forms of domination.

Others have explained before me, and others will explain after me, the extent to which the chasm has wid-
ened between the affluent peoples and those who aspire
only to eat their fill, quench their thirst, survive, and preserve their dignity. But no one can imagine to what extent
"the poor man's grain" in our countries "has fattened the
rich man's cow"!

In the case of the former Upper Volta, the process was
even more striking. We represented a wondrous conden-
sation, the epitome of all the calamities that have ever
befallen the so-called developing countries. The example
of foreign aid, presented as a panacea and often heralded
without rhyme or reason, bears eloquent witness to this
fact. Very few countries have been inundated like mine
with all kinds of aid. Theoretically, this aid is supposed to
work in the interests of our development. In the case of
what was formerly Upper Volta, one searches in vain for
a sign of anything having to do with development. The
men in power, either out of naiveté or class selfishness,
could not or would not take control of this influx from
abroad, understand its significance, or raise demands in
the interests of our people.

In his book, *Le Sahel demain* [The Sahel of tomorrow],

Jacques Giri, with a good deal of common sense, analyzes a table published in 1983 by the Sahel Club, and draws the conclusion that because of its nature and the mechanisms in place, aid to the Sahel helps only with bare survival. Thirty percent of this aid, he stresses, serves simply to keep the Sahel alive. According to Jacques Giri, the only goal of this foreign aid is to continue developing nonproductive sectors, saddling our meager budgets with unbearably heavy expenditures, disorganizing our countryside, widening our balance of trade deficit, and accelerating our indebtedness.

Just a few images to describe the former Upper Volta: 7 million inhabitants, with over 6 million peasants; an infant mortality rate estimated at 180 per 1,000; an average life expectancy limited to 40 years; an illiteracy rate of up to 98 percent, if we define as literate anyone who can read, write, and speak a language; 1 doctor for 50,000 inhabitants; 16 percent of school-age youth attending school; and, finally, a per capita Gross Domestic Product of 53,356 CFA francs, or barely more than 100 U.S. dollars.

The diagnosis was clearly somber. The root of the disease was political. The treatment could only be political.

Of course, we encourage aid that aids us in doing away with aid. But in general, welfare and aid policies have only ended up disorganizing us, subjugating us, and robbing us of a sense of responsibility for our own economic, political, and cultural affairs.

We chose to risk new paths to achieve greater well-being. We chose to apply new techniques. We chose to look for forms of organization better suited to our civilization, flatly and definitively rejecting all forms of outside diktats, in order to lay the foundations for achieving a level of dignity equal to our ambitions. Refusing to accept a state of survival, easing the pressures, liberating our countryside from medieval stagnation or even regression, democratizing our society, opening minds to a world of collective responsibility in order to dare to invent the future. Shattering the administrative apparatus, then rebuilding it with a new kind of government employee, immersing our army in the people through productive labor and reminding it constantly that without patriotic political education, a soldier is only a potential criminal. Such is our political program.

On the level of economic management, we're learning to live modestly, to accept and impose austerity on ourselves in order to be able to carry out ambitious projects.

Thanks to the example of the National Solidarity Fund, which is financed by voluntary contributions, we're already beginning to find answers to the harsh questions posed by the drought. We have supported and applied the Alma Ata principles by widening the range of primary health-care services. We've adopted the GOBI FFF Strategy recommended by UNICEF as our own, making it government policy.[3]

Through the United Nations Sahel Office (UNSO), we believe the UN should enable the countries affected by the drought to set up a medium- and long-term plan to achieve food self-sufficiency.

To prepare for the twenty-first century, we have launched a huge campaign to educate and train our children in a

----

3. The Alma Ata principles of the World Health Organization (WHO) and the United Nations International Children's Emergency Fund (UNICEF) emphasized proper nutrition, safe water, sanitation systems, maternal and child health care, immunization, and a reserve of basic medicine. UNICEF's GOBI FFF Strategy, focused on women and children, includes treating diarrhea-caused dehydration with an inexpensive solution of clean water, glucose, and salts; breastfeeding; immunization against six major communicable diseases; and education.

new kind of school, financed by the creation of a special "Teach our children" raffle. Through the salutary action of the Committees for the Defense of the Revolution, we have launched a vast program to build public housing (500 units in three months), roads, small reservoirs, and so on. Our economic aspiration is to create a situation where every Burkinabè can at least use his brain and hands to invent and create enough to ensure him two meals a day and drinking water.

We swear, we proclaim, that from now on nothing in Burkina Faso will be done without the participation of the Burkinabè. Nothing that we have not first decided and worked out ourselves. There will be no further assaults on our sense of decency and our dignity.

Armed with this conviction, we would like our words to embrace all who suffer in the flesh and all whose dignity is flouted by a handful of men or by a system that is crushing them. To all of you listening to me, allow me to say: I speak not only on behalf of my beloved Burkina Faso, but also on behalf of all those who are in pain somewhere.

I speak on behalf of the millions of human beings who are in ghettos because they have black skin or because they come from different cultures, and who enjoy a status barely above that of an animal.

I suffer on behalf of the Indians who have been massacred, crushed, humiliated, and confined for centuries on reservations in order to prevent them from aspiring to any rights and to prevent them from enriching their culture through joyful union with other cultures, including the culture of the invader.

I cry out on behalf of those thrown out of work by a system that is structurally unjust and periodically unhinged, who are reduced to only glimpsing in life a reflection of the lives of the affluent.

I speak on behalf of women the world over, who suffer from a male-imposed system of exploitation. As far as we're concerned, we are ready to welcome suggestions from anywhere in the world that enable us to achieve the total fulfillment of Burkinabè women. In exchange, we offer to share with all countries the positive experience we have begun, with women now present at every level of the state apparatus and social life in Burkina Faso. Women who struggle and who proclaim with us that the slave who is not able to take charge of his own revolt deserves no pity for his lot. This slave alone will be responsible for his own misfortune if he harbors illusions in the dubious generosity of a master pretending to set him free. Freedom can be won only through struggle, and we call on all our sisters of all races to go on the offensive to conquer their rights.

I speak on behalf of the mothers of our destitute countries who watch their children die of malaria or diarrhea, unaware that simple means to save them exist. The science of the multinationals does not offer them these means, preferring to invest in cosmetics laboratories and plastic surgery to satisfy the whims of a few women or men whose smart appearance is threatened by too many calories in their overly rich meals, the regularity of which would make you—or rather us from the Sahel—dizzy. We have decided to adopt and popularize these simple means, recommended by the WHO and UNICEF.

I speak, too, on behalf of the child. The child of a poor man who is hungry and who furtively eyes the accumulation of abundance in a store for the rich. The store protected by a thick plate glass window. The window protected by impregnable shutters. The shutters guarded by a policeman with a helmet, gloves, and armed with a billy club. The policeman posted there by the father of another child, who will come and serve himself—or rather be served—because he offers guarantees of representing the capitalistic norms of the system, which he corresponds to.

I speak on behalf of artists—poets, painters, sculptors, musicians, and actors—good men who see their art prostituted by the alchemy of show-business tricks.

I cry out on behalf of journalists who are either reduced to silence or to lies in order not to suffer the harsh law of unemployment.

I protest on behalf of the athletes of the entire world whose muscles are exploited by political systems or by modern-day slave merchants.

My country is brimming with all the misfortunes of the peoples of the world, a painful synthesis of all humanity's suffering, but also—and above all—of the promise of our struggles. This is why my heart beats naturally on behalf of the sick who anxiously scan the horizons of a science monopolized by arms merchants.

My thoughts go out to all those affected by the destruction of nature and to those 30 million who will die as they do each year, struck down by the formidable weapon of hunger. As a military man, I cannot forget the soldier who is obeying orders, his finger on the trigger, who knows the bullet being fired bears only the message of death.

Finally, it fills me with indignation to think of the Palestinians, who an inhuman humanity has decided to replace with another people—a people martyred only yesterday. I think of this valiant Palestinian people, that is, these shattered families wandering across the world in search of refuge. Courageous, determined, stoic, and untiring, the Palestinians remind every human conscience of the moral necessity and obligation to respect the rights of a people. Along with their Jewish brothers, they are anti-Zionists.

At the side of my brother soldiers of Iran and Iraq who

are dying in a fratricidal and suicidal war, I wish also to feel close to my comrades of Nicaragua, whose harbors are mined, whose villages are bombed, and who, despite everything, face their destiny with courage and clear-headedness. I suffer with all those in Latin America who suffer from the stranglehold of imperialism.

I wish to stand on the side of the Afghan and Irish peoples, on the side of the peoples of Grenada and East Timor, each of whom is searching for happiness based on their dignity and the laws of their own culture.[4]

I protest here on behalf of all those who vainly seek a forum in this world where they can make their voice heard and have it genuinely taken into consideration. Many have preceded me at this podium and others will follow. But only a few will make the decisions. Yet we are officially presented as being equals. Well, I am acting as spokesperson for all those who vainly seek a forum in this world where they can make themselves heard. So yes, I wish to speak on behalf of all "those left behind," for "I am human, nothing that is human is alien to me."

Our revolution in Burkina Faso embraces the misfortunes of all peoples. It also draws inspiration from all of man's experiences since his first breath. We wish to be the heirs of all the world's revolutions and all the liberation struggles of the peoples of the Third World. Our eyes are on the profound upheavals that have transformed the world. We draw the lessons of the American Revolution,

---

4. These were all countries under military occupation when this speech was given. Afghanistan had been occupied since 1979 by troops from the Soviet Union; northern Ireland remained a British colony brutally repressed by London; the Caribbean island of Grenada had been invaded by the U.S. army in October 1983; and the former Portuguese colony of East Timor in the Pacific had been invaded by Indonesia in 1975 and forcibly annexed.

the lessons of its victory over colonial domination and the consequences of that victory. We adopt as our own the affirmation of the Doctrine whereby Europeans must not intervene in American affairs, nor Americans in European affairs. Just as Monroe proclaimed "America to the Americans" in 1823, we echo this today by saying "Africa to the Africans," "Burkina to the Burkinabè."

The French Revolution of 1789, which overturned the foundations of absolutism, taught us the connection between the rights of man and the rights of peoples to liberty. The great revolution of October 1917 [in Russia] transformed the world, brought victory to the proletariat, shook the foundations of capitalism, and made possible the Paris Commune's dreams of justice.[5]

Open to all the winds of the will of the peoples of the world and their revolutions, having also learned from some terrible failures that led to tragic violations of human rights, we wish to retain only the core of purity from each revolution. This prevents us from becoming subservient to the realities of others, even when we share common ground because of our ideas.

Mr. President:

It is no longer possible to keep up the deception. The new international economic order for which we fight and will continue to fight can be achieved only if we succeed in destroying the old order that has ignored us; if we impose our rightful place in the political organization of the world; and if, conscious of our importance in the world, we obtain the right to participate in discussions and decisions on the mechanisms governing trade, the economy,

---

5. In 1871 the insurgent workers and craftsmen of Paris established the first workers government in history, the Paris Commune. It was crushed in blood by the troops of the French bourgeoisie.

and currencies on a global scale.

The new international economic order should simply be inscribed alongside all the other rights of the people—the right to independence, to the free choice of governmental forms and structures—like the right to development. And like all the peoples' rights, it is conquered in struggle and by the struggle of the people. It will never be the result of an act of generosity from the powers that be.

I personally maintain unshakable confidence—a confidence shared by the immense community of Nonaligned countries—that, under the pounding blows of the howling anguish of our peoples, our group will maintain its cohesion, strengthen its collective bargaining power, find allies among all nations, and begin, together with those who can still hear us, to organize a genuinely new international system of economic relations.

Mr. President:

I agreed to come before this illustrious assembly to speak because, despite all the criticism made of it by some of its big contributors, the United Nations remains the ideal forum for our demands—the place where countries without voices must appear to be considered legitimate.

This is what our secretary general [Javier Pérez de Cuéllar] so correctly expressed when he wrote:

"The United Nations is unique in that it reflects the aspirations and frustrations of numerous countries and groupings around the world. One of its great merits is that all nations, including those that are weak, oppressed, and victims of injustice"—he's talking about us—"can, even when they are facing the harsh reality of power, come and find a tribune to be heard. Though a just cause may meet with misfortune or indifference, it can nevertheless find an echo in the United Nations. This characteristic of our organization has not always been appreciated, but it is nonetheless essential."

There can be no better definition of the meaning and significance of our organization.

This is why it is a pressing need for each of us to consolidate the foundations of our organization, to give it the means to act. We therefore approve the proposals made along these lines by the secretary general to extricate the organization from numerous dead ends, which have been carefully fostered by big-power maneuvering to discredit the UN in the eyes of public opinion.

Mr. President:

Recognizing the merits, however limited, of our organization, I can only rejoice to see it welcome new members. This is why the Burkinabè delegation salutes the admission of the 159th member of our organization: the state of Brunei Darussalam.

Due to the folly of those into whose hands the leadership of the world has fallen by quirk of fate, the Movement of Nonaligned Countries—of which I hope Brunei Darussalam will soon become a member—is compelled to consider the fight for disarmament to be one of the permanent goals of its struggle. This is an essential aspect and a basic condition of our right to development.

In our opinion, we need serious studies that take into account all the elements that have led to the calamities that have befallen the world. In this regard, President Fidel Castro expressed our point of view admirably in 1979 at the opening of the Sixth Summit Conference of Nonaligned Countries when he declared:

"Three hundred billion dollars is enough to build 600,000 schools a year with a capacity of 400 million children; or 60 million comfortable homes with a capacity of 300 million people; or 50,000 hospitals with 18 million beds; or 20,000 factories to provide employment for more than

20 million workers; or make possible the irrigation of 150 million hectares of land, which with an adequate technical level could provide food for a billion people."[6]

Multiplying these figures today by ten—and I'm sure this would fall short of reality—we realize what humanity squanders every year in the military field, that is, against peace.

One easily sees why the masses' indignation is rapidly transformed into revolt and revolution at the sight of the crumbs thrown their way in the degrading form of a little aid, sometimes tied to frankly despicable conditions. So it is clear why in the fight for development we refer to ourselves as tireless militants for peace.

We pledge to fight to ease tensions, to introduce principles of civilized life into international relations, and to extend them to all regions of the world. This means that we can no longer passively watch various concepts being bandied about. We reiterate our determination to be active proponents of peace; to take our place in the fight for disarmament; and finally to act as a decisive factor in international politics, completely unfettered by any of the major powers, whatever their plans may be.

But the quest for peace goes hand in hand with the firm application of the right of countries to independence, of peoples to liberty, and of nations to an autonomous existence. On this score the most pitiful and appalling—yes, the most appalling—record in terms of arrogance, insolence, and incredible stubbornness, is held by a small country in the Middle East, Israel. With the complicity of its powerful protector, the United States—which words cannot

---

6. Fidel Castro's speech to the Nonaligned summit meeting on September 3, 1979, can be found in *Fidel Castro Speeches: Cuba's Internationalist Foreign Policy 1975–80* (New York: Pathfinder, 1981).

"The democratic and popular revolution needs a convinced people, not a conquered people, not a people simply enduring their fate."

Peasant rally in Pibaoré, October 1987. Banner says in the Mooré language, "Peasants of Burkina Faso, yesterday the hoe, today the hoe, tomorrow the machine."

Ernest Harsch

"For the popular masses, independence was a victory over foreign oppression and exploitation."

❶ Illustration of French troops seizing town of Abomey in Benin, 1892. ❷ Workers at cocoa bean plantation in French colony of Cameroon, 1941.

❸ Sétif, Algeria, May 8, 1945. On day of end of World War II in Europe, French troops brutally repress Algerian demonstration for independence, slaughtering up to 45,000 over the next six weeks.
❹ Dien Bien Phu, Vietnam, May 1954. Vietnamese liberation fighters escorting captured French soldiers. French defeat in this battle hastened collapse of its colonial regime and strengthened independence movements in other French colonies.

"The most incredible acts of daring enabled men to stand up against the barbarity of colonialism and emerge victorious."

❶ Egyptians celebrating nationalization of Suez Canal, July 1956. At center is President Gamal Abdel Nasser. ❷ Patrice Lumumba, prime minister of Congo, which had just won independence from Belgium, at United Nations, July 1960. ❸ Colonial revolution helped inspire fight against racist Jim Crow segregation in the United States. In photo, civil rights protest in Canton, Mississippi, 1966.

❹ Celebration of Algeria's independence, July 1962. Triumphant workers and peasants brought to power a revolutionary government. **❺** Entrance of Rebel Army led by Fidel Castro (at right, waving) into Havana, Cuba, January 8, 1959. Victory over U.S.-backed Batista tyranny opened the first socialist revolution in the Americas.

"Sankara's stay in Madagascar had a deep impact on him. A popular uprising toppled the government, and he met with students who had been part of the May 1968 prerevolutionary uprising in France."

—from Introduction

❷

Dany Be

Courtesy Paul Sankara

❶

❶ Sankara as a young cadet in Madagascar, where he served from 1969 to 1973. ❷ Antananarivo, Madagascar, May 14, 1972. Workers and youth accompany soldiers who joined rebellion against proimperialist regime, on their way to attack police station.

Flax Hermes/Militant

❸ Paris, May 29, 1968. High school students occupying their school shout support to workers' demonstration. ❹ In Madagascar and France, Sankara had his first contact with revolutionary ideas. "Thanks to reading, but above all thanks to discussions with Marxists on the reality of our country, I came to Marxism," Sankara later explained.

"Safe drinking water, three meals a day, a clinic, a school, and a simple plow. These are still elements of an ideal in life that millions of Burkinabè have not yet achieved."

❶ Traditional peasant dwellings, Ouagadougou region, October 1987. **❷** Woman preparing a meal, Upper Volta, 1979. **❸** Peasants plowing land for planting, Upper Volta, mid-1970s.

Margaret Manwaring/Militant

United Nations

❹ Shoemakers at Ouagadougou market, October 1987. ❺ Peasant drawing water to irrigate his land near Dori, in Sahel desert area in north, Upper Volta, mid-1970s.

"On August 4, 1983, we took the leadership of the peasant revolts, the brewing revolt of the urban masses, and the just struggles of our popular masses as they mobilized against imperialism and its domestic allies."

Coumbite

HAUTE VOLTA: UN CAPITAINE «ANTI-IMPERIALISTE» DE 33 ANS PREND LE POUVOIR ❸

❶ (background) and ❷ Scenes from revolutionary upsurge in 1983 that toppled pro-imperialist regime, Ouagadougou, May and August, respectively. ❸ Headline from newspaper in France reads: "Upper Volta: a 33-year-old 'anti-imperialist' captain takes power."

❹ Three leaders of August 1983 uprising: Sankara (front); Blaise Compaoré (far left); Etienne Zongo (far right). ❺ Guy Penne, adviser on Africa to French president François Mitterrand, who was in Ouagadougou during May 17, 1983, coup and arrest of Sankara. ❻ Jean-Baptiste Ouédraogo, president of Council of Popular Salvation, which was overturned by the August 1983 uprising.

"We have built schools, clinics, roads, dams, enlarged our fields, done reforestation, and provided housing. Each Burkinabè feels that wielding power is now his business."

❶ Meeting of a Committee for Defense of the Revolution in Ouagadougou neighborhood, August 1985. The CDRs aimed to mobilize workers, farmers, and youth to work together to build a new society.

❷ A literacy class in Kamboincé, March 1986. To combat 92 percent illiteracy rate, the revolution initiated campaign to teach reading and writing in main languages spoken in country. ❸ Ceremony on August 4, 1986, in Bobo-Dioulasso, Houet province, celebrating third anniversary of revolution. Banner says, "Vaccinated children," part of the revolution's primary health campaigns. ❹ Construction of apartment building in center of Ouagadougou, 1985.

Margaret A. Novicki/Africa Report

Augusta Conchiglia/Afrique Asie

Charafi El/La documentation française

> "We will give active solidarity to national liberation movements fighting for independence and the liberation of their peoples."

Jacques Pavlovsky/Sygma/Corbis

1

Courtesy Balozi R. Harvey

3

At every international forum, Sankara championed the struggles of peoples fighting for national liberation. ❶ Western Sahara, December 1975–January 1976. In refugee camp, Polisario Front combatants receive arms training to resist occupation by Morocco and Mauritania. ❷ Palestine Liberation Organization fighters leaving Lebanon, August 1982, following their heroic resistance to Israeli invasion.

Sankara traveled around the world to forge ties of solidarity. ❸ In Harlem, New York City, October 2, 1984. ❹ Cuban president Fidel Castro welcomes Sankara to Havana, September 25, 1984.

"I bring you fraternal greetings from a country whose seven million children, women, and men refuse to die of ignorance, hunger, and thirst any longer."

New York, October 4, 1984. Addressing United Nations General Assembly.

describe—Israel has continued to defy the international community for more than twenty years.

Scorning history, which only yesterday condemned each Jew to the horror of the gas chamber, Israel has now ended up inflicting on others an ordeal that was once its own. In any case, Israel, whose people we love for their courage and sacrifices of yesterday, must be made aware that conditions for its own tranquility cannot be achieved through military might financed from abroad. Israel must begin to learn how to become a nation like others and among others.

For the present, from up here at this rostrum, we want to assert our militant and active solidarity toward the combatants—women and men—of the wonderful people of Palestine, because we know that no suffering lasts forever.

Mr. President:

In analyzing the prevailing economic and political situation in Africa, we cannot fail to emphasize the deep concerns we harbor regarding the dangerous challenges made to the rights of peoples by certain nations which, secure in their alliances, openly scorn international moral standards.

Of course, we have the right to be delighted by the decision to withdraw foreign troops from Chad, so that without intermediaries Chadians can seek among themselves the means to end this fratricidal war and finally give their people, who have wept through so many winters, the means to dry their tears.[7]

Despite some progress registered here and there by the African peoples in their struggle for economic emancipation, however, our continent continues to reflect the basic reality of the conflicts between the major powers. We continue to bear the intolerable difficulties of the

---

7. See footnote on page 132.

contemporary world.

This is why we hold the fate meted out to the people of Western Sahara by the Kingdom of Morocco to be unacceptable, and we unconditionally condemn it. Morocco is using delaying tactics to postpone a decision that, in any case, will be imposed on it by the will of the Saharawi people. Having personally visited the regions liberated by the Saharawi people, I am convinced that nothing will be able to impede any longer their march toward the total liberation of their country, under the militant and enlightened leadership of the Polisario Front.

Mr. President:

I do not wish to dwell too much on the question of Mayotte and the islands of the Malagasy archipelago. When things are clear, when principles are obvious, there is no need to elaborate. Mayotte belongs to the Comoros. The islands of the archipelago belong to Madagascar.[8]

In Latin America, we salute the initiative by the Contadora Group, which marks a positive stage in the search for a just solution to the prevailing explosive situation. On behalf of the revolutionary people of Nicaragua, Commander Daniel Ortega has made concrete proposals here and asked fundamental questions of the appropriate people. We expect to see peace take hold in his country and in Central America October 15 and thereafter, and we call on world public opinion to bear witness to what happens.[9]

---

8. Three of the four islands making up the Comoros archipelago in the Indian Ocean near Mozambique gained independence from France in 1975. The fourth, Mayotte, remains a French colony.

The French-controlled islands off Madagascar include Europa, Bassas da India, Juan de Nova, the Iles Glorieuses, and Tromelin.

9. Addressing the UN General Assembly on October 2, 1984, Daniel Ortega had warned that the U.S. government planned to escalate

Just as we condemned foreign aggression against the island of Grenada, we also denounce all foreign interventions. Therefore we cannot remain silent about foreign military intervention in Afghanistan.

There is, however, one particular question of such gravity that it demands a frank and decisive answer from each of us. As you might imagine, this question can be none other than that of South Africa. The incredible arrogance of that country toward all the nations of the world—even toward those who support the terrorism it has built into a system designed to physically liquidate the country's Black majority—and the contempt with which it treats all our resolutions, are among the weightiest concerns of today's world.

But the most tragic thing is not that South Africa has placed itself outside the international community because of the despicable character of its apartheid laws. Even less that it continues to illegally keep Namibia under the boot of colonialism and racism. Or that it behaves toward its neighbors with the impunity of a gangster. No, the most despicable, the most humiliating thing for the human conscience, is that it has managed to make "ordinary" the misfortune of millions of human beings who have nothing but their chests and the heroism of their bare hands with which to defend themselves. Secure in the complicity of the major powers, knowing that some will even actively intervene on its behalf, counting too on the criminal collaboration of a few wretched leaders of African countries, the white minority makes no bones about mocking the feelings of all peoples everywhere across the world, who

---

its attacks against Nicaragua to disrupt the November 4 presidential elections there. According to information obtained by the Nicaraguan government, the escalation was to begin around October 15.

consider intolerable the savagery of the methods employed.

There was a time when international brigades were formed to defend the honor of nations whose dignity had been assaulted. Today, despite the festering wounds we all bear, we are going to vote for resolutions whose only purpose, we will be told, is to bring to its senses this nation of pirates, which "destroys a smile like hail kills flowers."

Mr. President:

We will soon be celebrating the 150th anniversary of the emancipation of slaves by the British Empire. My delegation supports the proposal made by the countries of Antigua and Barbados to commemorate this event in a major way, an event whose meaning has taken on very great importance for the African countries and for the Black world. In our opinion, everything that is done, said, or organized around the world as part of the commemorative ceremonies should stress the terrible price paid by Africa and the Black world for the development of human civilization. A price paid without receiving anything in return, and which no doubt explains the reasons for the current tragedy on our continent.

It is our blood that fed the rapid development of capitalism, that made possible our current state of dependence, and that consolidated our underdevelopment. The truth can no longer be avoided, the numbers can no longer be doctored. For every Black person who made it to the plantations, at least five others suffered death or mutilation. I purposely leave aside the devastation of our continent and its consequences.

Mr. President:

If, thanks to you and with the help of the secretary general, the entire world can be convinced of that truth on the occasion of this anniversary, then it will understand why we desire peace between nations with every fiber of our being. And why we demand and lay claim to our right to development on the basis of total equality, through the organization and redistribution of human resources.

Of all the human races, we belong to those who have suffered most. That's why we Burkinabè have solemnly promised ourselves never again to accept the slightest denial of justice on the slightest bit of this earth. It is the memory of this suffering that places us at the side of the PLO against the armed bands of Israel. It is the memory of this suffering that leads us, on the one hand, to support the ANC and SWAPO, and makes it intolerable to us on the other that South Africa harbors men who torch the world in the name of being white. Finally, it is this same memory that leads us to place in the United Nations all our faith regarding shared duty, shared effort, and shared hope.

We call for intensifying throughout the world the campaign to free Nelson Mandela and guarantee his actual presence at the next session of the UN General Assembly. This will be a victory we can be proud of together. In memory of our sufferings and as a collective pardon, an International Prize for Human Reconciliation should be created, to be awarded to all those whose research has contributed to defending human rights. All the space research budgets should be cut by 1 percent, and the funds devoted to research in health and the restoration of the environment, which has been disturbed by all these fireworks harmful to the ecosystem.

We also propose that the structures of the UN be rethought and that we put a stop to that scandal known as the right of veto. It is true that the pernicious effects of its misuse have been mitigated by the vigilance of some of those who hold a veto. However, nothing justifies such a right—neither the size of the countries that hold it nor their wealth.

There are those who justify such iniquity by citing the price paid during the last world war. The nations that have granted themselves these rights should know that each of us, too, has an uncle or a father who, like thousands of other innocent people, was torn from the Third World to defend rights flouted by Hitler's hordes. Our flesh, too, bears the scars of Nazi bullets. So the arrogance of the big powers should cease—the powers that miss no opportunity to challenge the rights of the peoples of the world. Africa's absence from the club of those holding the right of veto is unjust and must cease.

Finally, my delegation would not be fulfilling all its duties if it failed to demand the suspension of Israel and the outright expulsion of South Africa from our organization. With the benefit of time, when these countries have carried out the transformation that returns them to the international community, each of us, starting with my country, should welcome them with kindness and guide their first steps.

We want to reaffirm our confidence in the United Nations. We are indebted to it for the work carried out by its agencies in Burkina Faso and for their presence at our side in the difficult times we are going through. We are grateful to the members of the Security Council for having allowed us to preside over the work of the council twice this year. We would simply hope to see the council adopt and apply the principle of fighting against the extermination of 30 million human beings every year by the hunger weapon, which today wreaks more devastation than the nuclear weapon.

This confidence and faith in the organization compels me to thank the secretary general, Mr. Javier Pérez de Cuéllar, for the much appreciated visit he made to us to see firsthand the harsh realities of our existence and obtain an accurate picture of the aridness of the Sahel, and the tragedy of the conquering desert.

I could not end without paying tribute to the eminent qualities of our president [Paul Lusaka of Zambia], who, with the perceptiveness for which we know him, will ably lead the work of this Thirty-ninth Session.

Mr. President:

I have traveled thousands of kilometers. I have come here to ask each of you to put our efforts together so that the arrogance of those who are wrong ceases, so that the sad spectacle of children dying of hunger vanishes, so that ignorance disappears, so that the legitimate revolt of the people triumphs, so that the sound of weapons falls silent, and so that finally, as we fight for the survival of humanity, united by a single will, we are able to sing to-gether with the great poet Novalis:

"Soon the stars will revisit the earth they left during the age of obscurity. The sun will lay down its harsh specter and once again will become one star among many. All the races of the world will come together anew, after a long separation. Orphaned families of yore will be reunited and each day will be a day of reunification and renewed embraces. Then the inhabitants of olden times will return to the earth, in every tomb the extinguished cinders will be rekindled, and everywhere the flames of life will burn again. Old dwelling places will be rebuilt, the olden times will be born again, and history will be the dream of the present stretching to infinity."

Homeland or death, we will win!

Thank you.

We must fight imperialism together

Interview with 'Intercontinental Press'
March 17, 1985

The following interview was given in Ouagadougou to *Inter-continental Press*, a sister publication of the *Militant*, a socialist newsweekly published in New York. A translation of the interview, conducted by Ernest Harsch, appeared in the April 29, 1985, issue of the magazine.

INTERCONTINENTAL PRESS: The revolution came to power a year and a half ago. What do you see as its greatest accomplishments?

THOMAS SANKARA: Today, after a year and a half of revolution, what we see is that we have not succeeded in—at least we have not completed—carrying out the material transformations. But we can pride ourselves on having built schools, clinics, roads, dams, on having enlarged our fields, and on having done some reforestation. We can also pride ourselves on having provided some housing for the people. It's not enough. Much more remains to be done.

The most important thing for us, however, is not that.

Most important is the transformation of people's attitudes that we've tried to bring about. This transformation of attitudes means that each of us feels that wielding power is now his business, that the destiny of Burkina Faso is the business of all Burkinabè, not just some, and that everyone has something to say. Each one of us demands an accounting from the other. Never again will things be done as before. Never again will the wealth of our country belong to a minority. It belongs to the majority, a majority that speaks its mind.

Perhaps there are ways of doing things that are not very pleasant. But that's natural. When people have been subjected to domination for many years, for many decades, and then one fine day they have the freedom to express themselves, naturally they go to extremes. We should understand that and view it with a little leniency. That's natural.

So the most important aspect of our revolution is this transformation. The rest will follow.

INTERCONTINENTAL PRESS: In your view, what have been the greatest problems and difficulties you've faced?

SANKARA: The greatest difficulty we've faced is the neocolonial way of thinking that exists in this country. We were colonized by a country, France, that left us with certain habits. For us, being successful in life, being happy, meant trying to live as they do in France, like the richest of the French. So much so that the transformations we want to carry out run into some obstacles and brakes, namely, those people who won't accept even a minimum of social justice, who want to preserve all their privileges at the expense of others. Naturally, this forces us into a struggle.

Our first fight was against the bourgeoisie. Then, and above all, against the petty bourgeoisie, which is very dangerous, which is very much inclined toward the bourgeoisie while at the same time also admiring the prestige of the revolutionaries. It is a petty bourgeoisie that wavers. We think that so long as the petty bourgeoisie is not massively involved in the revolution, we will have difficulties. It's the petty bourgeoisie that screams, poisons minds, and defames. Numerically it represents nothing. But since our society is a neocolonial society where the intellectual has the preponderant role, these people have the preponderant role and shape opinion. The other difficulties, natural and otherwise, are not serious.

The other big difficulty is imperialism. Imperialism tries to dominate us from both inside and outside our country. Through its multinationals, its big capital, its economic power, imperialism tries to control us by influencing our discussions, influencing national life, and creating difficulties. It tries to strangle us with an economic blockade. At the same time, it tries to plot against us, against our internal security. To fight imperialism, we still have many battles to wage.

INTERCONTINENTAL PRESS: Has imperialism's opposition been as severe as you expected? How well do you think you've been able to resist it?

SANKARA: I must tell you in all honesty that as a revolutionary I understood what imperialism was in theoretical terms. But once in power, I discovered other aspects of imperialism that I hadn't known. I have learned, and I think there are still other aspects of imperialism to discover. There is quite a difference between theory and practice. It's in practice that I've seen that imperialism is a monster—a monster with claws, horns, and fangs—that bites, that has venom, and is merciless. A speech is not enough to make it tremble. No. Imperialism is determined, it has no conscience, it has no heart.

Fortunately the more we've discovered how dangerous

an enemy imperialism is, the more determined we've become to fight and defeat it. And each time we find fresh forces ready to stand up to it.

INTERCONTINENTAL PRESS: How has the organization and training of the militia and the Committees for the Defense of the Revolution been going?

SANKARA: We're satisfied with them. Of course, at the beginning there were many people who became involved without knowing what sacrifices would be demanded of them. When they understood that it would be a little difficult, they began to pull back. But we think this is natural. The revolution advances like a bus, with its difficulties. When it changes speed, there are people who fall off. That's natural. But now raising consciousness has overtaken euphoria. Raising consciousness has allowed us to make a great leap forward.

INTERCONTINENTAL PRESS: It's obvious that the youth are on the side of the revolution. What success have you had in drawing the older members of society behind what you're trying to do?

SANKARA: We've scored some successes with the others too, because they recognize that the revolution has brought them things they never dared dream of. To be sure, they often take fright at the methods and language of the revolution and think they no longer have the energy and strength to keep up with it. But we've set up a framework for those elders who want to participate in the revolution, in their own way and at their own pace, while still entrusting the political and ideological leadership to us. We're in the process of establishing an organization of elders, which will be very useful to us. In fact there are elders, older people, who are already doing important work.

INTERCONTINENTAL PRESS: Last week there was a women's week here, culminating in International Women's Day,

March 8. What did that indicate about women's involvement in the revolutionary process?

SANKARA: Under previous regimes women here were organized into folkloric groups. They sewed uniforms, sang, and danced. But they did not really know where they were going. Right after August 4, 1983, we faced problems in mobilizing women because of their subjectivity. The women were very subjective and did not always see what the revolution could bring them and what role they themselves could play in it.

We have given them the time to think about their revolutionary role. This time was beneficial, because now women use a different language in their meetings, their gatherings. They feel that women aren't there just to make demands. Women should above all explain clearly and objectively the basis of their oppression and domination.

They are managing to do this better and better. They are becoming capable of defining who their enemies are. Enemies within the country—men, males—but also enemies such as imperialism and the cultural system it brought with it. There is also the feudal system of yesterday, which existed here even before the arrival of colonialism. Women have now managed to understand all these things and will be able to fight them.

A positive thing we have noted with women is this: they are now ready to liberate themselves. You cannot free slaves who are not conscious of being slaves, of their situation of slavery. We have noticed now that women have become conscious. The work that will be done will be for their own liberation, and will be their contribution to the revolution. They have understood that the revolution, and only the revolution, can liberate them. It was this qualitative change that was lacking. Without it, bringing together thousands and thousands of women was easy, something we could do at any time. But we understood at a certain point that this was not productive, was not useful, and we stopped doing it. We have now come back to basics in a very modest way, and this is why we were able to organize the women's week, a week that was very positive.

INTERCONTINENTAL PRESS: How will the agrarian reform and the formation of CDRs change social relations in the countryside, including the role of the traditional chiefs?

SANKARA: The traditional form of organization in the country is being attacked and that's natural. It's a feudal system that does not allow for development and that denies the masses even a minimum of social justice or space in which to grow and blossom. This feudal system functioned so that some men, simply through circumstances of birth, could control considerable amounts of land—many hectares, many square kilometers of land. They distributed it as they saw fit. Others could only cultivate the land and had to pay them. Their reign is coming to an end. In some regions, I might add, it's already over.

We know that this breakdown of the feudal system in our countryside will be beneficial, since from now on the peasant who is on a piece of land will be able to work it with the security of knowing the land is entrusted to him. The land today belongs to the Burkinabè state. It no longer belongs to an individual. But the Burkinabè state can entrust the use, management, and cultivation of the land to one who works it.[1]

The peasant will be encouraged to improve the land he cultivates, rather than being condemned, as under the old system, to a situation where he could have a piece of land

---

1. The National Council of the Revolution decreed the nationalization of all land and mineral wealth on August 4, 1984, the first anniversary of the revolution.

and use organic fertilizer or manure to enrich the soil; but then a year or two later, just when the land was starting to become fertile, the owner would say, "You must leave." The development of our agriculture requires security for the toilers who cultivate it. The feudal form of organization is giving way to new forms of organization through which the people find expression.

INTERCONTINENTAL PRESS: A few weeks ago, *Le Monde* and *Jeune Afrique*, both published in Paris, reported on a statement by several trade union leaders criticizing the government's policies. They presented it as a major split between the National Council of the Revolution and the working class. Is that the case? Is the conflict with the workers, or is it just with these trade union officials?

SANKARA: It's basically a problem with the leadership of these organizations. These leaderships are petty bourgeois. As petty bourgeois, they thought the revolution had swept aside the reactionary and bourgeois classes in order to place them in power. So naturally we have conflicts.

The worker, however, is completely satisfied with the decisions we are making. When we say rents no longer have to be paid, the worker benefits.[2] But the union leaders had houses that they rented out, so they could not be happy. It's very important that you understand this.

You posed the question very well. Is this a conflict with the workers, the working class, or with the leadership? It's a conflict with the leadership, not with the workers. The proof: have you seen any strikes here? There are no strikes. The workers are in both the CDRs and the unions. But the

---

2. On December 31, 1984, the government announced that no rent for housing would have to be paid the following year, and it established a national organization to ensure compliance with this measure. Commercial and industrial rents continued to be paid directly to the state.

leaderships are not at all pleased. That's natural. It's because of their petty-bourgeois outlook.

The revolution in Africa faces a big danger, since it is
initiated every time by the petty bourgeoisie. The petty
bourgeoisie is generally made up of intellectuals. At the
beginning of the revolution the big bourgeoisie is attacked.
That's easy. They are the very wealthy, the big capitalists—big, fat, gross—who have big cars, big houses, many
women, and so on. People know who they are and go after them. But after one, two, or three years, it's necessary
to take on the petty bourgeoisie. And when we take on
the petty bourgeoisie, we take on the very leadership of
the revolution.

The unions have contributed a great deal to the revolution here. They have contributed to our country's popular struggles. But they did so as petty bourgeois who were
dreaming of sweeping away the bourgeois in order to
take their places. Now that the revolution has happened,
they're afraid of it.

You see, that's what happens in certain African countries where people talk of "revolution, revolution, revolution!" But they have gold chains and fine ties. They are
always in France buying expensive clothes and big cars.
They have bank accounts. Yet they talk about "revolution."

Why is this? When they've finished attacking the big
bourgeoisie and want to go after the petty bourgeoisie,
the petty bourgeoisie bares its claws and they take fright.
What do they do? They give big salaries to the military, to
government ministers, or to the praetorian guard. They
appoint all the top union leaders, and so on, to big positions. They make them ministers, prime ministers, big co-
ordinators of this or that. They're happy, they keep quiet.
The ministers themselves begin to become businessmen—
traffickers. They send their children to school in Europe

or the United States. If you take the situation under Sékou Touré, the former president of Guinea who talked about revolution, the largest number of French-speakers in the United States were Guineans. At Harvard, at Cambridge in Great Britain, everywhere. That's the petty bourgeoisie.

Every revolution that starts out with the petty bourgeoisie comes to a crossroads where it must choose what road to take. To take on the petty bourgeoisie means keeping the revolution radical, and there you will face many difficulties. Or you can go easy on the petty bourgeoisie. You won't have any difficulties. But then it won't be a revolution either—it will be a pseudorevolution.

That's why the petty bourgeois here is against our reducing their salaries. But they're in favor of our taxing the peasants in the countryside. They make 200,000 CFA francs a month. They think their salaries should be increased by 5,000, 10,000, 15,000, or 20,000 francs. If we raise their salaries, they organize support marches. If we cut them, they protest. But they don't see the peasants and how they benefit. They can't see that. We say the petty bourgeoisie is constantly torn between two interests. They have two books: Karl Marx's *Capital* and a checkbook. They waver: Che Guevara or Onassis? They have to choose.

INTERCONTINENTAL PRESS: This problem you've just discussed is also reflected in the conflicts involving the different left-wing political organizations here. How do you see this problem being overcome?

SANKARA: Each organization struggles and maintains itself through its influence and importance among the masses. Organizations must be allowed to continue like this and differentiate themselves in the eyes of the masses. When the masses get to know all of them, they will choose and will join some organizations and fight others. That's why a revolution can never be made with a handful of people who lock themselves in an office and declare: "I am from such-and-such organization. You should accord me such-and-such importance."

This is the problem we find in some countries. Take Chad, for example, with its political tendencies. When the leaders gather in an office for discussions, each one says he represents a tendency. "I represent a tendency." "Me too! Me too!" But if you leave them to the masses, the masses will eliminate those who should be eliminated and retain those who should be retained.

Our problem here is that this petty bourgeoisie, thanks to its connections with the press abroad, tries to create a lot of noise. You will see that here, inside the country, there's no problem. But when you read *Le Monde* or *Jeune Afrique* or listen to the Voice of America or Radio France Internationale, you hear "Things are not going well in Burkina Faso," and so on. Yet things *are* going well here. Abroad, it's "things are not going well." They give you this impression because the petty bourgeoisie here has connections. They are intellectuals. They have traveled. They have connections in all countries and they can draw on that. But here they've been exposed and there's no longer a problem. They are even ready to discuss with us. You've seen that Arba Diallo, the former minister of foreign affairs, who was in prison, has been released. They're ready to discuss with us, but it's because they no longer have any influence. The only thing that keeps them afloat is support from abroad—the foreign press that writes articles against us every day, messages in all the papers. If we had a lot of money we could give it to a newspaper, and then they would write articles supporting us. But we don't have money for that.

INTERCONTINENTAL PRESS: Are there prospects for unifying the various groups that support the revolution?

SANKARA: It's possible. We're confident it's possible. Of course, such unity will be built at the expense of individuals, not organizations. Because in an anti-imperialist struggle, a revolutionary struggle, it is organizations that adopt platforms. Individuals may say, "No, there's nothing in it for me." There are individuals who prefer to be number one in a village rather than number two in the city. And since they don't wish to be number two in the city, they prefer to keep their organizations for themselves. They reject unification even though the organization is for it. Such individuals will be eliminated one by one to make way for the organizations.

INTERCONTINENTAL PRESS: When you visited the United States last October, you made a stop in Cuba. In Cuba you received the Order of José Martí. What do you think is the significance of the Cuban Revolution?

SANKARA: I consider the Cuban Revolution a symbol of courage and determination. It's a great lesson.

Cuba—a small agricultural country, without vast resources, except for some very limited ones—has been able to stand fast, despite direct and indirect pressure by the big United States next door. It's a great lesson. We know Cuba did not resist alone. It needed the internationalist support of the Soviet Union to support it and help it out. But we also know that support is not enough. That's why we look at the Cubans with admiration.

When I saw Fidel Castro, I told him, "It's been twenty-five years, but you still look like a revolutionary who's just come down from the Sierra Maestra." We have a very, very great admiration for the Cuban Revolution.

Of course, our two revolutions are not the same. The conditions are not the same either. But in terms of courage, determination, and the constant involvement of the people—the people, always the people—in what is done,

Cuba provides very interesting lessons.

INTERCONTINENTAL PRESS: It's important for the working class in the United States to learn more about revolutionary struggles in other countries, such as Burkina Faso. That's a first step toward solidarity. We have the same enemy—U.S. imperialism. The forms of our struggles may be different, but the enemy is the same. If workers become conscious of that, they will naturally feel solidarity with your struggle against imperialism here. Developing internationalist consciousness is also important for working people in the United States to understand who their enemy is at home. Do you have any comment on this?

SANKARA: It's a problem of communication. The imperialism we're fighting is not an isolated thing. It's a system. As revolutionaries, from a dialectical point of view, we should understand that we too should have a system. You have to counter a system with a system, an organization with an organization, not simply individuals full of goodwill, good sentiments, honesty, courage, and generosity.

The imperialist system, which is worldwide and not located simply in this or that country, has to be fought with an entire system that we will forge together. Consequently, we should get to know each other, understand each other, establish a platform, an area of understanding between us so as to be able to fight imperialism seriously, with a good chance of success.

That's why I agree with you on the need for communication, for getting to know each other. You're a journalist, that's your job, and I'll help you in that. That's why—even though I'm very busy today and have many files on my table—I am duty-bound to give you at least five minutes to explain to you what we're doing. As revolutionaries, we don't have the right to say we're tired of explaining. We should always explain. Because we also know that when people understand, they cannot but follow us. In any case, we, the people, have no enemies when it comes to countries or peoples. Our only enemies are the imperialist regimes and organizations.

INTERCONTINENTAL PRESS: If you had a few minutes to address the working people of the United States, what would you say?

SANKARA: First of all, we want the American working people, and the American people in general, to understand that the people of Burkina Faso are not the enemies of Americans.

The people of Burkina Faso are a people who are proud of their identity, who are proud of their independence, who jealously guard their independence, just as you Americans did when you fought for your independence. You said, "America for the Americans." You certainly did not want any intervention by Europe. You fought Great Britain, you fought England for your independence. I think that's natural and it's only just that we should have the same elementary right.

You should know that we are in solidarity with Americans in their suffering. Even if you have greater material wealth than we do, you have misery in your hearts, and we know, as you do, what the causes of this misery are. By misery I mean, for example, the ghettos of Harlem. It's also a fact that an American, whatever his wealth, lives like a pawn on a chessboard, a pawn who is moved around, who is manipulated. This misery is also the life of aggression and barbarism, the inhuman life created in the United States because of the power of money, because of the power of capital.

We know, as you do, that imperialism organizes and lies behind all this. We should fight it together. We appeal to the American people to understand us, to aid us in our struggle, just as we will also aid them. But let it never be said that we are the enemy of the American people. It's not true. We wish total success to the American people. All their struggles are our struggles.

Unfortunately, they are not told even one-tenth of the truth, of the realities of the world. We hope the American people will not be a people subjected to insults around the world, by slogans on the walls of "Yankee go home. Yankee go home." The American people can't be proud of that. A country, a people, can't be proud of the fact that, wherever they go, other people look at them and see behind them the CIA, see behind them the attacks, the weapons, and so forth. The American people are also a people capable of love, of solidarity, and of sincere friendship.

We want to correct all this. We want to help you take your place tomorrow—whether through your leaders or through yourselves, the people—on condition that one accepts our denunciation of the evils and causes of this generalized, worldwide distrust toward the American people.

Dare to invent the future

Interview with Jean-Philippe Rapp
1985

In 1985 Swiss journalist Jean-Philippe Rapp conducted a number of interviews with Sankara in Ouagadougou, which were published as *Sankara: Un nouveau pouvoir africain* [Sankara: a new African power] by Jean Ziegler, excerpted below. Footnotes have been added.

JEAN-PHILIPPE RAPP: Isn't the decision to become head of state a decision taken under a very definite set of circumstances?

THOMAS SANKARA: There are events, moments in life, that are like an encounter, a rendezvous, with the people. To understand them you have to go back a long way into the past, the background, of each individual. You don't decide to become a head of state. You decide to put an end to this or that form of bullying or humiliation, this or that type of exploitation or domination. That's all.

It's a bit like someone who has suffered from a serious illness, malaria say, and then decides to devote all his energies to vaccine research—even if it means along the way that he becomes an eminent scientist in charge of a laboratory or the head of a cutting-edge medical team.

In any event, I started out with a very clear conviction. You can fight effectively only against things you understand well, and you can't win unless you're convinced your fight is just. You can't wage a struggle as a pretext, a lever, to acquire power, because generally the mask cracks very fast. You don't get involved in a struggle alongside the popular masses in order to become head of state. You fight. Then the need to organize means that someone is required for a given post.

RAPP: But why you?

SANKARA: You have to convince yourself that you're capable of fighting, that you're courageous enough to fight for yourself, but above all that you have sufficient will to fight for others. You'll find men who are determined to wage a fight, and who know how to go about it. But they're doing it only for themselves and don't get very far.

RAPP: You think this is because of their origins?

SANKARA: Yes. There are leaders who have natural roots, and there are those who have artificially created roots. By artificial I mean those leaders who were created by erecting a wall around themselves. Such people are definitely cut off from the popular masses. They can be generous up to a point, but that doesn't make them revolutionaries. You'll run into officials at various levels who are unhappy because no one understands them, even though they've proven their commitment. Though they're making honest sacrifices, no one understands what they're doing.

It's a little like some of the international aid volunteers who come here from Europe. They too are very sincere, but their ignorance about Africa leads them to make mistakes, blunders, that are sometimes insignificant, but that become decisive as time goes on. So after a stay of several years they go home completely disgusted with Africa. Yet it's not for lack of noble purpose. It's just that they came here with a patronizing attitude. They were lesson-givers.

RAPP: As far as you're concerned, one has to have lived the reality?

SANKARA: Other leaders have had the chance to immerse themselves in the daily lives of the people. That's where they find the necessary reserves of energy. They know that by making such-and-such a decision they'll be able to solve such-and-such a problem, and that the solution they've found is going to help thousands, even millions of people. They have a perfect grasp of the question without having studied it in a sociology department. This changes your perception of things.

RAPP: But what concrete personal experiences led you to discover these realities yourself?

SANKARA: There were several. For example, I remember a man I knew well. We were right in the middle of a period of drought. To avoid starvation, several families from his village collected the little money they had left and gave him the job of going to Ouagadougou to buy food. He traveled to the capital by bicycle. On arrival, he had a brutal and painful encounter with the town. He stood in line to get what he needed, without success. He watched a good many people jump ahead of him to buy their millet because they knew how to speak French. Then, to make a bad situation worse, the man's bike was stolen along with all the money the villagers had entrusted to him.

In despair, he committed suicide. The people of Ouagadougou didn't lose any sleep over him. He was just another dead body. They dug a hole and threw in the body like a useless weight they had to get rid of. The city went merrily about its business—indifferent to, and even ignorant of, this drama. In the meantime, far away, dozens of people, whole families, awaited the happy return of this man who was to give them another lease on life, but who never came back. We have to ask ourselves: Do we have the right to turn our backs on people like this?

RAPP: This shocked you?

SANKARA: Yes. I think about it often, even today.

RAPP: But have you experienced inequality firsthand yourself or have you just observed its impact on other people?

SANKARA: No, I've experienced it personally. When I was little I went to primary school in Gaoua. The principal there was a European and his children had a bicycle. The other children dreamed about this bicycle for months and months. We woke up thinking about it; we drew pictures of it; we tried to suppress the longing that kept welling up inside of us. We did just about everything to try to convince them to lend it to us. If the principal's children wanted sand to build sand castles, we brought them sand. If it was some other favor they wanted, we rushed to do it. And all that just in the hope of having a ride—going for a spin, as we say here. We were all the same age, but there was nothing to be done.

One day, I realized all our efforts were in vain. I grabbed the bike and said to myself: "Too bad, I'm going to treat myself to this pleasure no matter what the consequences."

RAPP: And what were the consequences?

SANKARA: They arrested my father and threw him in prison. I was expelled from school. My brothers and sisters did not dare go back. It was terrifying. How could this possibly fail to create profound feelings of injustice among children of the same age?

They put my father in prison another time too, because one of my sisters had gathered some wild fruit by throwing stones up at it. Some of the stones fell on the roof of the principal's house. This disturbed his wife's nap. I understood that after a wonderful, refreshing meal, she wanted to rest, and it was irritating to be disturbed like this. But we wanted to eat. And they didn't stop at putting my father in prison. They issued a notice forbidding anyone to pick this fruit.

RAPP: Today, when you're with your father and he can see what's become of you and what you've embarked upon, what does he have to say to you?

SANKARA: My father is a former soldier. He fought in the Second World War and was taken prisoner by the Germans. As a former soldier, it's his view that we haven't seen anything yet, that it was much worse for them. Let's say our discussions are more like confrontations. [*Laughter*]

RAPP: This brings us to the question of the elders, who play an important role in traditional society and who must have enormous difficulty understanding, and above all accepting, what is happening today.

SANKARA: There are a lot of them, and we always need to acknowledge them with a word or two. They're surprised we mention them in different speeches. These older people have the feeling they're being excluded. This is all the more frustrating given that, when they were our age, they displayed admirable courage. Today, they're resting on their laurels. But we should still be fair by recognizing their past achievements, in order to draw from the dynamic energy they can inspire with just a simple word.

RAPP: But how are you thinking of integrating them?

SANKARA: We've decided to set up an organization for this. It does not have a name yet, but we know who will be in charge. Provisional committees are being formed in all the provinces, and a national convention will be held soon where the elders will establish a national office. Different committees and leadership bodies will lay out ways of participating.[1]

RAPP: There is a real willingness to be open-minded?

SANKARA: We are in Africa, a society where feudalism, in the broadest sense of the word, is very powerful. When the elder, the patriarch, has spoken, everyone follows. So we say, "Just as young revolutionaries must combat young reactionaries, old reactionaries will be fought by old revolutionaries." I'm sure there are ideological limits to this. But we can accept those limits as long as the elders combat those who must be combated in their sector.

RAPP: Let's come back to your childhood. Do you have other memories that could help shed light on your character and explain certain aspects of your conduct?

SANKARA: I went to high school in Bobo-Dioulasso. My family lived in Gaoua and I knew no one when I arrived. As it happened, the day classes were supposed to begin, we were told that, for management reasons, the school would not open until the following day. The boarding facilities were closed too, so we had to fend for ourselves for a place to sleep.

With my suitcase on my head—I was too small to carry it any other way—I wandered through the town, which was far too big for me. I got more and more tired, until finally I found myself in front of a bourgeois house. There were cars and a big dog in the yard. I rang the bell. A gentleman came to the door and eyed me disdainfully. "What's a little boy like you doing at my door?" he asked. "I saw this house and said to myself: this is where I'm going to spend the night," I told him. He let out a big sigh—he couldn't believe his ears—and then took me in. He settled me in, gave me something to eat, and then explained he

---

1. The National Union of Elders of Burkina (UNAB) was established in February 1986.

had to go out because his wife was waiting in the maternity hospital. The next day I took my things, said goodbye, and left.

One day, when I had become a government minister, I named someone to the post of general secretary in the Ministry of Information. I asked him, "Don't you remember me?" He said no. A month later, same question, same answer. The day he was leaving his post I called him. "You used to work at the radio station in Bobo. You lived in such-and-such a neighborhood and you had an Ami 6 car. You opened your door to me and fed me when I was just a little boy in high school."

"So that was you?" he asked.

"Yes, it was me."

His name was Pierre Barry. When I left his house, I swore to myself that one day I would do something for this man so that he'd know his kindness had not been in vain. I searched for him. Fate was kind. We met each other. Today he's retired.

RAPP: Burkina Faso was a member of the United Nations Security Council. You yourself have addressed the General Assembly. What are your thoughts on this?

SANKARA: If I hadn't gone there, I would never have had that experience, so as they say, every cloud has a silver lining. But to tell you the truth, you have to avoid becoming one of the rats in the UN corridors. Because you can very quickly fall into international complicity, a kind of acquiescence that reduces the problems people face to sterile sparring matches between theoreticians.

When you see the people there, you get the impression they're serious, but I don't enjoy being with them much. It was only at the beginning that I felt it necessary to go there.

But as you say, we were members of the Security Council. Our view was that if our role in the United Nations was not to be limited simply to filling our slot, we should have the courage to speak out on behalf of the peoples who had put their confidence in us. Burkina Faso was elected with the votes of more than 104 countries. We had to represent their interests, in particular those of the Nonaligned countries. Their interests, as well as those of other peoples in revolt, should be defended every day, constantly and courageously. Otherwise the UN would become an echo chamber manipulated by a few powerful drummers.

RAPP: Under these circumstances, have you been pressured? Have there been threats to cut off certain aid?

SANKARA: At the time, the U.S. ambassador, for example, tried to pressure us in this way. It was in relation to Puerto Rico, Nicaragua, Grenada, and several other questions. We explained to him the sincere friendship we feel for the American people, but we told him it was not in their interests to cause suffering in other countries. We were so sincere in our friendship, we added, that we could not solidarize with anyone who made empty, unfounded attacks on the United States.

I should add, for the sake of intellectual honesty, that the American ambassador backpedaled after our conversation and explained our position to his government.

RAPP: Were these pressures because you were a member of the Security Council?

SANKARA: In reality there were all kinds of different pressures, in different forms, by different groups of people. But could we keep quiet when a big power assaults a small country, or when one nation invades another? Our view was that we had a battle to wage there on behalf of all those who had put their trust in us and, equally important, all those who hadn't because they didn't yet know us well enough.

RAPP: Are you satisfied with the results?

SANKARA: We took the positions we had to take. We got ourselves known by a good many people this way. We also made ourselves a good many enemies. We attacked to the left and to the right, to the East and to the West. Everyone took a bit of a beating. Was it worth making so many enemies? Should we have opened so many fronts at once? I don't know.

RAPP: Given your situation, if a big power withdraws its aid, this could cause you serious problems. This would be true, for example, in the case of France, the United States, the Soviet Union, and other Western countries.

SANKARA: It's precisely for this reason that we must fight imperialism and everything connected with it. From imperialism's point of view, it's more important to dominate us culturally than militarily. Cultural domination is more flexible, more effective, less costly. This is why we say that to overturn the Burkinabè regime you don't need to bring in heavily armed mercenaries. You just need to forbid the import of champagne, lipstick, and nail polish.

RAPP: Yet these are not products often used by Burkinabè.

SANKARA: Only the bourgeoisie is convinced they cannot live without them. We have to work at decolonizing our mentality and achieving happiness within the limits of sacrifices we should be willing to accept. We have to recondition our people to accept themselves as they are, to not be ashamed of their real situation, to be satisfied with it, to glory in it, even.

We must be consistent. We did not hesitate to turn down aid from the Soviet Union that, in our opinion, did not meet our expectations.[2] We had a frank discussion with

---

2. In 1984, when the country faced a major drought and a 150,000-ton food shortage, the government of Burkina Faso refused, "for reasons of dignity," an offer of 5,000 tons of food from the Soviet Union.

the Soviets, and I think we understand each other. We have our dignity to protect.

RAPP: When you have a budget of 58 billion CFA francs and 12 billion are earmarked for the debt, can you really have a financial plan or strategy?

SANKARA: Yes, by simply and very starkly posing the choice between champagne and water. We make every effort to reject unequal allocations. So what do we find? Out of a budget of 58 billion, 30,000 government employees monopolize 30 billion, and that leaves nothing for everyone else. This is not normal. If we want greater justice, each of us must recognize the real situation of the people and accept the sacrifices that each individual must make for justice to be done. Who are these 30,000 government employees? People like me.

Take my case. Out of 1,000 children born the same year I was, half died in the first three months. I had the great fortune to escape death, just as I had the great fortune to not die later from one of the diseases here in Africa that killed more of those born that same year.

I am one of the 16 children out of 100 who were able to go to school. That's another extraordinary piece of luck. I'm one of 18 out of 100 who managed to obtain a high school degree, and one of the 300 from the entire country who were able to go abroad and continue their education and who, on coming home, were assured of a job. I'm one of those 2 soldiers out of 100 who, on the social level, have a stable, well-paid position, because I'm an officer in an army where this rank represents something.

The number of people whose lives have been touched by even part of this luck amount to only 30,000 in a country of 7 million inhabitants. And we alone soak up more than 30 billion! This can't go on.

RAPP: Not to mention other advantages!

SANKARA: In fact, it's those of us in town who set the tone, who explain to world public opinion what's running smoothly and what's not and how to interpret the situation here. We're the ones who talk about human rights, the drop in buying power, a climate of terror. We forget that we condemned thousands of children to death because we wouldn't agree to cutting our salaries just a tiny bit so that a little clinic could be built. And we didn't stir up international public opinion against the scandal such deaths represent. We're part of the international complicity of men of good conscience: "I'll forgive you your mistakes if you forgive me mine. I'll keep quiet about your dirty deeds if you keep quiet about mine, and we'll all be clean together." It's a veritable "gentlemen's agreement" among men of good conscience.

RAPP: Being indignant about this is one thing. But what can be done about it?

SANKARA: You have to dare to look reality in the face and dare to strike hammerblows at some of the long-standing privileges—so long-standing in fact that they seem to have become normal, unquestionable. Of course, you run the risk of being violently attacked in the media. But then no one will ever ask seven million voiceless peasants if they're happy or not with a road, a little school, a clinic, or a well.

RAPP: But what would you do without international aid and structural adjustment loans?[3]

SANKARA: In 1983, when we came to power, the state coffers were empty. The regime we overturned had negotiated and obtained a structural adjustment loan from France of 3 billion CFA francs. After a certain amount of pushing

---

3. Short-term loans by the World Bank and International Monetary Fund to colonial and semicolonial countries, granted under extremely disadvantageous conditions.

and pulling, this loan was reassigned to our government. That wasn't an easy task and I can assure you that since then no one has lent us anything at all, not France nor any other country. We receive no financial aid.

RAPP: Under these circumstances, how do you avoid a budget deficit?

SANKARA: We fill the hole by preventing it from appearing—that is, we don't allow a deficit. We've lowered salaries. State officials have lost up to one month's income. Government employees have had to give up some of their benefits, which, as you can imagine, is never welcomed by anyone. These are the kinds of sacrifices we impose on members of the government, of whom we demand an extremely modest lifestyle. A minister who is a schoolteacher receives a schoolteacher's salary. The president who is a captain receives a captain's salary, nothing more.

RAPP: The power of example?

SANKARA: Yes. Can you believe that in the past, in this country, they were talking about introducing a thirteenth and even a fourteenth month of salary? At the same time, people were dying for lack of money to buy a tiny capsule of quinine.[4]

We shouldn't be surprised, then, that Cartierism appeared in France aimed against those black kings who buy themselves cars and build mansions with means supplied by their taxpayers. Cartierism was very much a product of our own mistakes and errors.[5]

Did you know too that there were Burkinabè who got foreign-service benefits—in their own country—extra compensation for the hot sun! Others had salaries of between

---

4. A medication against malaria.

5. See glossary, Cartierism.

200,000 and 300,000 CFA francs just for heading unions. And they demanded salary raises despite the colossal sums they were already receiving! We've had to demand sacrifices. That's what changing people's mentality means. And we're nowhere near the limit of our possibilities. This is just one of many steps to come.

RAPP: Given such a situation, is it possible to foresee any kind of investment?

SANKARA: By lowering salaries, by adopting more modest lifestyles, but also through better management of the funds we have, and by preventing their misappropriation, we've been able to generate some surplus that allows for modest investment. But this only bears witness to the need to continue along these lines. We draw up our budget once a year, then every quarter we see where we are and compare that with where we should be. This will tell you how carefully we watch our pennies.

I'll give you a few numbers, if you like. In the first quarter of 1983, the budget—in which we had already been involved as CSP members, but did not have final say—showed a deficit of 695 million CFA francs. By the first quarter of 1984 we had reduced this to 1 million CFA francs, since we were able to direct and implement the budget ourselves. In the first quarter of 1985 we no longer had a deficit but instead a surplus of 1.0985 billion CFA francs, and this is how it will continue.

RAPP: Yes, but at what price?

SANKARA: We've tightened up in all areas. You're not allowed to write on only one side of a sheet of paper here. Our ministers travel economy-class and have an expense allowance of only 15,000 CFA francs per day. It's the same for me, except that as head of state I have the advantage of being provided for when I am received abroad.

Our minister of labor went to Geneva a little while ago

for an international conference. You're in a good position to know that with his daily allowance of 15,000 CFA francs, there's no way he could expect to find a room in Geneva. He had to go to neighboring France and share a modest hotel room with his colleagues. This is nothing to be ashamed of. Perhaps his living conditions enabled him to carry out his assignment even better than had he been staying in a palace. This is just one example among many.

RAPP: A few months ago, *Sidwaya* carried a headline that read: "Had Lenin known what we are doing, he would have helped us." Does this reflect a certain disappointment with the Soviet Union and other countries?

SANKARA: Given the risks we are taking—for we are leading a genuine revolution here—and maybe we lack modesty, but given what we think we could represent for Africa, we don't understand this wait-and-see policy, this lack of interest, this lack of urgency to help us on the part of those who should most logically do so. From the point of view of ideological leanings, they're in the same camp as we are.

We have even greater difficulty understanding it given that we can be choked to death for lack of 5 million CFA francs. Several times we've almost had to close normal operations and put people out of a job for lack of this kind of a sum. The consequences would have been strikes, protests, and maybe even the complete downfall of our government, if the situation had been exploited by more cunning people. And as they say, "Once bitten, twice shy!" Horrendous measures would have been taken to make sure there would never be another government like ours.

RAPP: So it really was a case of disappointment?

SANKARA: The article in *Sidwaya* did express that, yes. But on the other hand, I don't think you can ask others to sacrifice for you to the point of ignoring their own problems, even if theirs are not comparable. The unhappiness of the person in your country who finds the quality of the wine poor is as valid as the sadness of someone here who has no water to drink.

Elsewhere in the world, the population is unhappy with the government because it hasn't created a third or a fourth, or a twenty-fifth, television channel. There's no reason for us to ask you to mark time, to wait for us, for those of us who only have one, and sometimes not even one. Other countries have their own burdens to carry.

We should also add that we are the ones who are making our revolution. So much the better or worse for us, we must accept the consequences. After all, no one asked us to make it! We could have mortgaged off our country and put it up for rent—someone would have paid. We are the ones who decided that all forms of outside control should be rejected. We are the ones who should pay the price.

RAPP: Learn how to shed the welfare mentality?

SANKARA: Yes. We should get rid of this mentality. Had we not been colonized and therefore not had relations with France to begin with, how could we possibly think we had a right to expect something of France? Why? In Corrèze and Larzac, there are those who still aren't happy.[6] So we must do away with this mentality, even if, in the name of some form of internationalism, we would have liked the aid to go where it should.

But even there, we should not forget that, unless you're a masochist or have suicidal tendencies, you don't help your enemy. You don't provide him with arms so he can survive and make his influence felt and convince those around him to follow his example. There are many, many

---

6. Corrèze and Larzac are two low-income agricultural areas in central France.

people who are afraid we will succeed. They come after us with all kinds of challenges.

RAPP: Isn't time working against you?

SANKARA: Well, they give us less than a year, for example, before our coffers are empty—before we're no longer able to pay government employees and have to run to the International Monetary Fund or some other organization for help. But struggling along, for better or for worse, we'll get through this storm and emerge on the other side with our heads high. Then they'll set another deadline by which time, it seems obvious to them, we'll fail. But we'll hold our own through thick and thin. We're proving over the long run and in real life that there are other game plans that can make it possible to bypass the classical methods of filling the coffers.

RAPP: But what more can the Burkinabè people do? Won't it backfire on you if you demand too many sacrifices?

SANKARA: Not if you know how to set an example. We've set up a Revolutionary Solidarity Fund to which thousands of Burkinabè contribute. Their contributions, though small individually, represent a considerable effort aimed at relieving our people of the need to beg for food aid. The fund has allowed us to ward off the most urgent problems, in particular the problem of survival faced by the population of the Sahel region.

RAPP: A related question is that of the foreign debt. At the conference of the Organization of African Unity (OAU) in Addis Ababa, the participants were quite divided on how to deal with the question of paying back this debt.

SANKARA: As far as we're concerned, we say very clearly: the foreign debt should not be repaid. It's unjust. It's like paying war reparations twice over. Where does this debt come from, anyhow? It comes from needs imposed on us by other countries. Did we need to build mansions or to tell doctors they would receive a fabulous salary at the end of the month? Or foster the mentality of overpaid men among our officers? We were coerced into running up very heavy debts, and the economic enterprises made possible by these loans have not always run smoothly. We entered into weighty financial commitments on their account—often suggested, proposed, organized, and set in place by the same people who lent us the money.

They have quite a system. First come the members of the assault squad, who know exactly what they are going to propose. Then they bring out the heavy artillery, and the price keeps going up. These are wonderful investments for the investors. They don't put their money in their own banks because at home the returns aren't good. They have to create the need for capital elsewhere and make others pay.

Do we really need to smoke this or that brand of cigarette? They've convinced us, "If you smoke such-and-such brand you'll be the most powerful man on earth, capable of seducing any woman." So we took up smoking, and got cancer as a bonus. The most privileged among us have gone to Europe to be treated. And all to give a second wind to your tobacco market.

RAPP: But does refusing to pay the debt make any sense if only one or two countries do it?

SANKARA: The pressure to pay the debt does not come from the isolated usury of a single banker. It comes from an entire organized system, so that in the event of non-payment, they can detain your planes at an airport or refuse to send you an absolutely indispensable spare part. So deciding not to pay the debt requires we form a united front. All the countries should act together—on the condition, of course, that each one of us is open to looking critically at the way we ourselves manage these funds.

People who have contracted huge debts because of their own lavish personal expenses don't deserve our support. We said this clearly in the message we delivered to the OAU: "Either we resist collectively and refuse categorically to repay the debt or, if we don't, we'll have to go off to die alone, one by one."[7]

RAPP: But this point of view was not unanimous?

SANKARA: Though everyone understands the logic behind such a legitimate refusal to pay, each of us thinks he's smarter, more cunning than the other. A particular government will skirt the need for collective action to go and see the moneylenders. This country is then immediately portrayed as the best organized, the most modern, the most respectful of written agreements. They're given more loans, so further conditions can be imposed. When the discontent spills out into the streets, they suggest sending in the "heavies" to break those who won't fall into line—and to put someone of their choice on the throne.

RAPP: Aren't you afraid of a violent public reaction against your internal economic measures?

SANKARA: The general support we're finding as we impose measures that are not in themselves very popular shows the nature of our revolution. It's a revolution directed not against any people or any country, but rather one that's aimed at restoring the dignity of the Burkinabè people, at allowing them to achieve happiness as they define it.

In other countries happiness and development are defined by ratios—so many hundred pounds of steel per inhabitant, so many tons of cement, so many telephone lines. We have different values. We're not the least bit embarrassed to say we are a poor country. Within international

---

7. A reference to the OAU's summit of November 12–15, 1984, in Addis Ababa.

organizations we're not at all afraid to get up and speak and to block discussions in order to gain a reduction of a dollar or two in the dues or contributions countries must pay. We know this irritates a good many delegations that are capable of throwing thousands, if not millions, of dollars out the window.

When we receive a foreign ambassador who has come to present his credentials, we no longer do so in this presidential office. We take him out into the bush, with the peasants. He travels on our chaotic roads and endures dust and thirst. After that we can receive him, explaining, "Mr. Ambassador, your Excellency, you have just seen Burkina Faso as it really is. This is the country you must deal with, not those of us who work in comfortable offices."

We have a wise and experienced people capable of shaping a certain way of life. While elsewhere people die from being too well-fed, here we die from not having enough food. Between these two extremes there is a way of life to be discovered if each of us meets the other halfway.

RAPP: One other economic factor that should be taken into account is the growth of nongovernmental organizations (NGOs). There are an estimated 600 such organizations in Burkina, 400 of French origin. How do you explain this growth?

SANKARA: I think the nongovernmental organizations have both a good and a bad side. Above all they reflect the failure of state-to-state relations, so that people are obliged to find other channels for contact and dialogue. Even though you'll find in other countries a Ministry of Cooperation, a Ministry of Foreign Relations, or a Ministry of External Affairs, they look to other means. This indicates politically that these ministries are nonfunctional.

Of course we know there are nongovernmental organizations that serve as spy agencies for imperialism. If we thought otherwise, we'd either be totally naive or be blinding ourselves to reality. But that's not the case with all of them. Many are organizations of men and women who think this is the ideal way for them to express themselves and make a contribution. They've heard talk of suffering in different countries and feel ill at ease under the burden of their calories and luxury. They feel the need to do something about it, and that's good.

RAPP: But couldn't this create problems that can't be set straight simply by good will?

SANKARA: We've said to ourselves, "The NGOs have come, we have to organize them." If we don't, it could get very dangerous. Before, these organizations were established according to the country's electoral map. If there was a man of political importance in a certain fiefdom, that's where the wells would be dug, even if it meant digging a well every twenty-five centimeters. While elsewhere, where there was a real need, nothing would be done because in these parts there was no citizen of our country in the public eye.

The work of the NGOs is also hampered in that the wells are built in the English, German, or French style, while the water is drunk Burkinabè-style. The NGOs refuse to share the necessary information, preferring to let each one repeat the same mistakes just so they can say, "You see, these people really don't understand anything."

RAPP: But aren't these organizations in a rather difficult and delicate position?

SANKARA: The fact is, they've often made the mistake of not daring to assert themselves and tell local leaders, "Look, gentlemen, we've come for such-and-such a precise reason. If you agree, we're in business. If not, we'll pack our bags and go elsewhere."

Their willingness to please has at times become complicity.

For some, the most important thing is to get some good press clippings to circulate in Europe so they can say, "You see, my good people, we are over there saving souls. Give us your pennies, God will repay you." While in reality they're just backing the policies of this or that deputy or senator who uses their work as proof of his growing influence.

RAPP: Do you think they upset the local political scene?

SANKARA: The main thing is that they haven't had the courage to confront those who act incorrectly. The result is that they arrive here and are told, "You've come from Europe, very good. You have money and you wish to help the country, bravo, that's what needs to be done because people are starving here. But you're going to need an office, so why not rent mine. You'll need a national director since we very much want to assure some continuity—I have a cousin who is ready to do that. For receptionist, I have a cousin. And as janitor there's my nephew." To make a long story short, they bring the whole village into it, and provide everything right down to the assistant janitor. You, of course, are quite satisfied since your work is talked about in France or Switzerland. He's happy because he can go to his village and say, "If you are smart and vote for me, I'll bring you powdered milk." The milk arrives and everyone is in ecstasy over the sterling performance that produces such miracles.

RAPP: But how do you guard against such situations?

SANKARA: You have to wage a battle around this also. That's why we've created an "Office for Overseeing Nongovernmental Organizations." We don't intend to stop them from existing or functioning normally. They need a certain flexibility given the nature of their funding and their particular work methods. But we should make sure they all learn from the experiences of those who came before them. We must also indicate the areas where they can be most effective and useful, as well as how to go about their work.

RAPP: Under what conditions does your government accept international aid?

SANKARA: We do so when the aid offered respects our independence and our dignity. We reject aid that buys off consciences and that provides benefits only for the leaders. If you offer us aid to facilitate our purchase of your products, or to enable certain of us to open up bank accounts in your country, we'll turn it down.

RAPP: Food is a dramatic problem in your country. Malnutrition affects more than 50 percent of the children. The average caloric intake is 1,875 per day, or only 79 percent of the recommended caloric intake. What can be done about this?

SANKARA: Hunger has been, in fact, a cyclical problem in Burkina Faso for many years now. This is a reflection of our lack of organization, as well as the scant attention paid to the rural population. The problem also stems from a level of production that's inadequate because our soil is less and less fertile; from population growth; but also rainfall that's unpredictable and rare. We should add speculation to this list.

We confront a combination of physical, social, and political problems that must be resolved simultaneously. We expect to take a number of technical and political measures to transform our agricultural production from a random enterprise into a source of wealth. We aim to go from food stability to self-sufficiency, and one day to become a food-producing power.

RAPP: An ambitious program. How do you intend to carry it out?

SANKARA: First we have to figure out how to interest the rural population, how to organize it for production, as we provide technical and organizational assistance. I'll give you an example. The complete anarchy of our grain distribution was a joy for the speculators and a misery for the consumers. We know of thousands and thousands of peasants who were compelled to give up their land to usurers and all types of capitalists during difficult times between harvests. The capitalists could then use this land for speculation at a later time. So we took measures to prevent this by nationalizing the land.

RAPP: More than 90 percent of the population lives on the land. Given the extremely difficult conditions—poor soil, shortage of agricultural land, lack of watering places—what is your plan for rural development?

SANKARA: Development requires solving a series of different problems. First, we must master the water problem. We're currently building a number of small dams to retain water. But we must also master the different aspects of production. We need to create sales outlets as an incentive, as well as an agro-food industry capable of absorbing and preserving the crops produced. We also need better distribution countrywide so that seasonal and geographic shortages can be avoided. And finally, we see no reason why we shouldn't increase our exports to other markets.

We don't favor big industrial installations since automation eliminates jobs and requires the use of substantial amounts of capital, which we do not have. There is also the problem of maintaining this technology. A single broken part can mean dispatching a plane to Europe because the replacement can be obtained only there.

RAPP: So you anticipate an increase in food production?

SANKARA: In terms of citrus, market farming, and stock raising, our country has possibilities that could bring very good results if we apply the know-how of those who have already done this kind of work elsewhere. We're not opposed to private enterprise as long as it doesn't infringe upon our honor, our dignity, and our sovereignty. We see no reason why people from overseas shouldn't come and join with Burkinabè in developing the country, either in the private or public sector.

RAPP: At what pace?

SANKARA: At our pace. We much prefer small installations, part way between industrial and craft production—workshops that employ labor with little training. Given their small size, they can be set up close to production zones. We prefer old clunkers to high-technology machinery.

RAPP: You cultivate green beans, even though this is an export crop very much at the whim of the international market.

SANKARA: Every cloud has a silver lining. Green beans do cause us problems, it's true. But this has the merit of laying bare the reality of the capitalist world and exposing how those abroad view our revolution. It has enabled us to show clearly who these different pressure groups are that have decided to keep Burkina Faso in the clutches of dependency, tied to a certain type of export.

RAPP: Can you give us some concrete examples?

SANKARA: The green bean is grown in the Kougassi region and has been for a long time. It grows well and has been shipped out steadily to Europe, to France in particular. This has always been done, of course, in collaboration with the airline companies: the Union de Transport Aérien, a French-owned company, and Air Afrique, an African multinational essentially controlled by France. In 1984 we noticed that despite a mediocre rainy season it had, oddly enough, been a splendid season for the green bean. Well, these same airline companies refused to ship them.

The green bean is fragile. Every day roughly 30 tons of beans arrived in Ouagadougou yet only a maximum of

20 tons were shipped out. As a result, tons of beans began to rot at the airport, since we had no facilities for storing and preserving produce. The airline companies told us their services had been purchased for other flights. We think that if cooperation is to exist between ourselves and these companies, especially with Air Afrique, in which we participate as a sovereign state, some sacrifices should be made. For example, some of the pleasure flights could have been canceled to safeguard the income of the poor peasants who sweated blood to produce the beans, and demonstrated their capacities in the process.

And another thing. When our beans arrive in Europe they're immediately classified as second-grade produce. But we know they are later repackaged and put back on the market under a different label. This is low-level extortion. We can't bring them home again, so we have to sell them off at any price.

RAPP: Do you think there are political reasons behind this kind of thing?

SANKARA: Yes, there is this too. A systematic boycott of exports from Burkina is organized in order to strangle us economically and cause problems between us and the growers.

RAPP: Is this the only example?

SANKARA: Not by any means. Take the example of cattle. Our country is a big exporter of livestock, yet we're currently having problems. They're refusing to buy our livestock, or else they place such unacceptable conditions on us that there's no way we can export it.

But the boycott is carried out in the area of imports too, especially with regard to products we need urgently. Pressure is exerted to prevent us from importing the quantity of cement we need for general construction work. They know that by depriving us of such materials, we'll have a lot of workers on our construction sites who will end up turning against us, thinking we're nothing but demagogues. We've sent out information and goodwill delegations to explain to as many people as possible that our revolution is not aimed against other peoples, and that they have no reason to attack us. In the future, however, we'll be forced to consider this kind of provocative gesture as grounds for war.

RAPP: Are these kinds of blockades in retaliation for some of your international positions?

SANKARA: You're right. The positions we take don't always make people happy. But we face a dilemma: We either remain silent on positions we believe to be correct, consciously lying in order to enjoy the good graces of those who can help us, to please our delicate and powerful partners. Or we tell the truth in the firm conviction that we are helping our own people and others.

When a strike is under way in Europe, we're not the ones who incited the workers to act in this way against a particular industrialist. No. But we know the workers are striking to defend their legitimate interests. We have to know how to express solidarity, even without a formal link between us.

RAPP: Another concern in Burkina Faso is the slow and seemingly inescapable deterioration of the environment. What can you do to stop the damage?

SANKARA: African societies are living through an abrupt rupture with their own culture, and we're adapting very badly to our new situation. Completely new economic approaches are required. Our populations are growing as well as our needs. In addition, our natural universe, and the spontaneous development of it to which we're accustomed—the expansion of forests, food-gathering, and so on—exists less and less.

We've become great predators. Take the annual consumption of firewood in Burkina, for example. If we were to place end to end the carts traditionally used to transport wood here, they would form a convoy the equivalent of 4.5 times the length of Africa from north to south. Can we allow people to continue such devastation? But likewise, can we forbid people to do it, knowing that wood is the main source of energy here?

We face new needs, new demographic and sociological pressures, for which we have not yet found corresponding solutions. Deforestation has taken its toll elsewhere, too, but reforestation was possible and, above all, it proved possible to find wood substitutes. In Burkina, wood is our only source of energy. We have to constantly remind every individual of his duty to maintain and regenerate nature. The galloping and catastrophic spread of the desert, whose impact our people can see concretely, helps us in this.

RAPP: Explaining this, trying to convince people of it, is one thing. But what concrete measures can be applied?

SANKARA: After a detailed analysis of this phenomenon, its causes and manifestations, we have come to the conclusion that we have only one solution: to take draconian measures. And I mean draconian, since they affect what people consider to be their most basic and immediate rights. However, we think that in the end our collective liberty will be preserved through these measures. So we've launched what we call the three battles.

First, we've forbidden the unplanned, anarchic cutting of wood. It must be cut within certain limits defined by specialists so that we can control it to some extent. Just because you have wood a few meters from your house doesn't mean you can cut it. No. You'll go five kilometers away if you have to, if that's where there's enough wood for you. To get the situation under control, we've forbidden the transport of wood except in specially whitewashed vehicles that are clearly identifiable. This way, those who work in this trade are limited in number and can be regulated, allowing us to back them up more easily with technical assistance.

Second battle: We've outlawed the practice of letting livestock roam free, the second major cause, after man, of uncontrolled destruction. Here too, I consider the measures we've had to take to be truly draconian, but we won't be able to solve the problem without imposing rigorous changes in people's mentalities. We've decided that any animal discovered grazing on crops may be slaughtered on the spot without any form of trial. This is to force our livestock raisers to adopt more rational methods. At the moment, our method of stock raising is purely contemplative. Stock raisers are quite content to have 5,000 head of cattle without worrying about how to feed them, to the point of allowing them to destroy other people's crops and devastate the forest, right down to its youngest shoots. Everyone is selfishly proud of his large number of cattle. In reality, despite their numbers, these animals don't produce much wealth, either in terms of weight, milk, or capacity for work. They're puny. Livestock raisers must be made to ask themselves, "What are my rearing costs and what is the optimal number of livestock for me to get the best return for the least expenditure?"

RAPP: But couldn't this solution entail a number of abuses?

SANKARA: I must admit that there have been some very painful instances of livestock raisers who are unhappy because farmers have killed their animals. They have the impression they've been tricked, because there are some cunning and wily farmers who purposely go and farm right next to the animals and wait for them with a club. That's the stage we're going through. I know I don't have the perfect solution. But even if this decision were only 60 percent right, I would stick by it. As I see it, we're well above that percentage.

RAPP: So there are bans and constraints, but what about constructive measures?

SANKARA: We have a program of reforestation, a positive act to regenerate nature. We've decreed that every village and town must have a grove of trees. As part of its socioeconomic system, African tradition included a form of preservation of nature called the sacred woods. A certain number of rituals, in particular initiation rituals, were carried out there. According to myth and animism, these woods supposedly possessed certain powers that protected them. As these values gave way to more modern ones, to a certain Cartesianism as well as to other forms of religion, the protection failed and the woods disappeared. The protective shield afforded by the forest was destroyed, and the spread of the desert naturally proceeded at an even more rapid pace.

This is one of the reasons we've established groves. And though we haven't succeeded in investing them with the religious content of olden times, we try to give them an equivalent sentimental value. This is why all happy events are marked by the planting of a tree, whether it be a baptism, a marriage, or some other ceremony.

On August 3 there was an awards ceremony. Those who received awards, after having been congratulated, went to plant trees with family and friends. We'll do the same thing every year. Even if only 15 percent of these trees survive, it'll be a good start.

RAPP: The improved cookstoves are another means of cutting down on wood consumption?[8]

---

8. These were devices that required less wood and had the capacity to heat as many as three pots on a single fire.

SANKARA: Over the past few years we've talked a great deal about these improved cookstoves. We've been subsidized by the hundreds of millions—billions—to promote and popularize their use. First, we did basic research, then we applied our research, then, finally, came the stage of popularizing them. But we only began to make real progress once wood became scarce. Faced with an emergency, solutions had to be found to preserve this precious resource. Then the women finally became interested.

We've said that agricultural development in Burkina Faso can be carried out only by a harmonious marriage between stock raising and cultivation techniques. But it's impossible to integrate stock raising as long as the breeder himself does not take the same approach as the farmer. Today, he has to take a cost-effective approach. It's not only the milk, meat, manure, and bones that must be sold, but also, since they're present all year round, the animals' capacity for work. Out of necessity, we're establishing a positive rhythm of production.

RAPP: You use symbols often in your speeches, and in this interview too.

SANKARA: This is a pedagogic style, the product of our reality. As you will have noticed, we not only speak a great deal, we also give very long answers and, as you say, we're fond of symbols. This is because the speeches are directed to listeners who are accustomed to the oral tradition of African civilization, where speech progresses with many twists and turns.

I most often speak to peasants, so I let my spirit flow in this form of dialogue, debate, and exchange of views, though I very much admire the brilliance of those who adopt other styles. They give short, concise, and well-structured answers even without a written text. Their skill is a product of the kind of audiences they are used to addressing. When you speak to the university milieu you don't have to develop your point for hours on end as we need to do here. Ultimately, in Africa, we mistrust those who give journalistic answers. These are professional politicians, not men of the people.

RAPP: It seems that the period of grace following August 4, 1983, has come to an end. In your opinion, at what stage are you today?

SANKARA: Interestingly enough, there's less exuberance today and yet it's easier to convince people. The phenomenon has lost some of its novelty and, up to a certain point, its sparkle, its alluring glow. The revolution has become our normal rhythm. When I saw you in May 1984, I told you I was convinced that after the euphoric mobilization we'd have to think in terms of a conscious mobilization of the masses. We've reached that point.

RAPP: Without any difficulties or period of transition?

SANKARA: There was a short transition period between the two phases, a period of drifting and doubts, despair even. During this period many people said, "You see, now that they've finished with their pompous and demagogic speeches, these people are proving incapable of leading our country forward." At the time every decision we tried to take ran up against hostility, whether organized and conscious or not. But fortunately for us, this period passed quite quickly and we've been able to carry through from start to finish on a number of decisions that had seemed rash.

The benefits and accomplishments were recognized. Today there is no self-satisfied euphoria, but there is a conscious enthusiasm. It's less exuberant, but it's our best source of support and allows us to make further decisions. One example: when you invite all a country's government employees to take up sports and you say that this will be taken into account for everyone's promotions, you have to have the courage of your convictions. It's all well and good to be convinced of the beneficial effects of physical exercise, but it's not easy to accept. Yet people did it.

RAPP: Everyone?

SANKARA: No. Here and there people refused or said, "They shouldn't have done that." It was above all a handful of petty bourgeois who dreaded having to make the effort. But overall it is accepted. People don't make it into a point of contention. They believe we know where we're going. Today, taking part in organized sports activity has become a real part of our lives.

RAPP: But some people talk about a drop in the level of enthusiasm and mobilization.

SANKARA: The seductive side, the fascination of such a new phenomenon, has worn off. People are already familiar with our general orientation—some can even guess in advance more or less what will be said and done. People continue to like the revolution, but the period of proselytizing ended some time ago.

Unfortunately, badly informed observers have claimed this reflects a drop in enthusiasm, a demobilization, and so on. But this is not so.

RAPP: Does Thomas Sankara still know what is happening in the country—the attitude of certain government employees who abuse their power, or the actions of one or another CDR that is terrorizing a neighborhood?

SANKARA: It's 10:00 p.m. now. Once we've finished this interview, around midnight, I'll be leaving for a small village, where I'll stay until 5:00 a.m. You have to take the time to listen to people and make a real effort to enter into every milieu, including those with little to recommend them. You have to maintain relations of all kinds—with the young, the elderly, athletes, workers, the great intellectuals, and the illiterate. In this way, you get a mountain of information and ideas.

When a leader addresses an audience, I think he should do it in a way that makes every single person feel included. When congratulations are in order, everyone should have the feeling that he, personally, is being congratulated. When it's a question of criticism, everyone must recognize that his own actions are being judged as well—everyone must know that he has done such a thing himself, have the feeling of standing naked, of being ashamed, and determined to not make the same mistakes again in the future.

In this way, we can become aware of our errors collectively and retrace our steps together. I must take steps to inform myself. I must break with protocol and everything that boxes us in. At times, too, I must say what I've discovered and denounce specific situations. This shakes things up.

Of course, I'm not informed about everything, especially since there are those who are hesitant to speak to me, who believe I'm not accessible. Efforts should be constantly made to bring us closer together. Every week I answer fifty private letters, at the very least, asking me the most unimaginable and unanswerable questions. But we keep the lines of communication open. I'm extremely pleased when people present their proposals to me in response to the problems I've laid out, even if we don't always accept their particular solutions.

RAPP: How do you foresee a more systematic way of handling this? It's hard to believe you're not completely overwhelmed.

SANKARA: The National Council of the Revolution will soon be setting up a body to deal with this. But the important thing is to convince everyone that each individual has the right to make a complaint, and that maybe his complaint will be taken up, and in any case it will be studied with the same consideration and importance no matter what powers have been conferred on the person who is the source of his problem. We have to set some examples, even if it's our own relatives.

RAPP: With the course you have taken, do you foresee the creation of a single party and when?

SANKARA: The future is leading us toward an organization much more developed than the current mass mobilization, which is by necessity much less selective. So a party could come into existence in the future, but we don't intend to focus our thought and concerns on the notion of a party. That could be dangerous. We'd be creating a party in order to conform to revolutionary dictums—"A revolution without a party has no future"—or to belong to an International for which this would be an indispensable precondition for membership.

If leaders create a party just by an act of will, you open the door to all kinds of opportunism. A party has to have structures, leaderships, people who take responsibility. Who would you ask to do this other than those who are there already and who are not necessarily the most combative of revolutionaries? All kinds of people would profess allegiance to this party in order to be sure of a post, a little bit like the way the carving up of government ministries is viewed. Certain people would suggest we divide it this way so that they too can have a post. We must at all costs avoid the opportunist temptation to create a tailor-made party. The creation of a party after the seizure of power is truly a tricky undertaking.

A party can also have its disadvantages. It can become too restrictive, overly selective in relation to the masses who are mobilized. From the moment you begin to base yourself on no more than a minority, the masses become disconnected from the struggle you are waging.

To avoid this, the party must play its role as leader, guide, and vanguard. It must lead the whole revolution. It must be an integral part of the masses. For that, its members must be the most serious people, those who are moving forward and who are succeeding in convincing others by their own example. But first the masses must be allowed to struggle without a party and fashion their weapons without a party. Otherwise you fall into using a *nomenklatura*.[9]

RAPP: We are fifteen years away from the third millennium. In your opinion, are we going to see a rebirth of a continental united front? Or are we going to find ourselves in the same situation as in Havana in 1966?[10] That is, will each revolutionary nationalist grouping continue to act on its own, with no cohesion, no unity beyond national borders?

SANKARA: This is a difficult question, one that really calls for speculation. But I think we're heading toward greater cohesion. We must be optimistic even though it's natural and human, at a time when sovereign states are mushrooming, that each one should be more preoccupied with enjoying their new powers than with understanding the evolution of the world. As they say, "There are as many shades of opinion as there are people writing books." But this will change.

Of course, our predecessors were more or less obliged

---

9. Beginning with the Stalin regime in the former Soviet Union, this was the list used by top echelons of the Communist Party and state apparatus to dole out privileged appointments to high government and administrative posts.

10. The First Solidarity Conference of the Peoples of Africa, Asia, and Latin America—also known as the Tricontinental Conference—was held in Havana January 3–15, 1966. Among the 512 delegates attending were 150 from 28 African countries.

to act that way in order to show the way forward, even if sometimes they fell into acting like messiahs. But just as we talk more and more in terms of a universal civilization, we'll talk of a universal revolution. Imperialism has been organizing an International of domination and exploitation on a world scale for a long time, yet we have no International of the revolution, no International of resistance to oppression. Of course there have been some attempts—the three Internationals—and there's even talk of a fourth.[11]

Step by step, leaders as such will be superseded by the organized masses, especially as the means of communication break through barriers and reduce distances. At the same time, the leveling out of different cultures allows us to feel things in more or less the same way. So the current leaders will be superseded.

RAPP: How will you solve the problem of illiteracy?

SANKARA: With regard to education we intend to attack both the container and its content. When the colonial masters opened schools, they had no benevolent or humanitarian intentions in mind. Their concern was to produce clerks capable of performing work useful to their system of exploitation. Our task today is to inject new values into our schools, so that they can produce a new

---

11. A reference to four international working-class organizations: the First International (International Workingmen's Association), led by Karl Marx and Frederick Engels, founded in 1864 and dissolved in 1876; the Second International, founded in 1889, the majority of whose leaders abandoned a revolutionary course at the opening of World War I in 1914; the Third International (Communist International), founded under V.I. Lenin's leadership in 1919; and the Fourth International, founded in 1938 under the leadership of Leon Trotsky in response to Joseph Stalin's reversal of the Communist International's course under Lenin.

man who understands ideas, who absorbs them, and who functions in total harmony with the dynamic evolution of his people.

RAPP: But isn't your main concern to democratize education?

SANKARA: Precisely. Until now only the privileged have had access to schools. Democratizing education means building classrooms everywhere. Today, people are mobilized to do that—and with such enthusiasm, in fact, that they have outstripped the government's capacity to back them up technically. They're going a little too fast for us, but we're certainly not going to stop something that's going so well.

RAPP: In 1984, 1,500 teachers who were members of the National Union of African Teachers of Upper Volta were fired.[12] Can you really afford the luxury of such a decision when more than 90 percent of your population is illiterate?

SANKARA: They were fired for waging a strike that was, in reality, a subversive movement against Burkina Faso. At the time we told them very clearly, "Don't go ahead with this strike because it's part of a destabilization plan aimed against both Ghana and our country." The date had been set for a joint action. There was supposed to be a coup attempt in neighboring Ghana, and simultaneously a series of strikes here. We had been informed of this and took the necessary measures.

You know that in Burkina Faso strikes have always been used to make and break governments. We made public a certain amount of proof in this instance, but not all of it for fear of exposing certain sources of information. We invited the teachers to renounce their action. On the same day, Friday, March 23, a French television network

---

12. See chronology, March 1984.

broadcast a program devoted entirely to a Burkinabè dissident. The maneuver was transparent. They were aiming to build this man up, to give him a certain credibility. It was a double maneuver aimed both at putting this kind of individual back in the saddle and destabilizing the situation inside the country.

We arrested the main leaders, who had received $250,000 to hand out in order to buy support for the action. As part of the same operation, security agents also arrested a unionist who, according to our information, was not involved in the plan. We released him for the simple reason that he was protesting legitimately as a unionist and had no hand in the plot.

RAPP: But why take it out on the teachers?

SANKARA: We aren't against the teachers but against the plot that was using the teachers. Because the party that instigated the plot is made up predominantly of primary, secondary, and even university teachers.[13] It launched its shock troops against our regime—a regime it's condemned ever since August 4, 1983, since the day our regime was born. We carried out our threat because it seemed extremely serious to us that these teachers, who have enormous responsibilities and yet cannot make decisions for themselves, would allow themselves to be led off like Panurge's sheep.[14]

RAPP: Given the urgency, people find it hard to understand

---

13. This is a reference to the social-democratic Voltaic Progressive Front. Its best-known leader was Joseph Ki-Zerbo.

14. In one of his series of novels on the adventures of Gargantua and Pantagruel, François Rabelais tells of how Pantagruel takes revenge against a merchant who had robbed him by throwing one of the merchant's sheep overboard into the sea. The rest of the herd jump in as well.

why you don't modify your position now.

SANKARA: We're taking the time to examine one by one the cases of those who have written to us in repentance. But there can be no question of entrusting the education of Burkinabè children to people who are irresponsible. The door is not closed, however. We're rehiring little by little, depending on our evaluation of the individual's concrete conduct, whether or not they show a sincere capacity to change character and become more responsible. Many are in the process of being rehired or are well on the way.

RAPP: In the meantime, with whom have they been replaced?

SANKARA: With others of the same level—people we called on and to whom we've given a minimum of training, especially ideological training. We simply cannot submit to the wholesale blackmailing of our people. The education of Burkinabè children was taken hostage to force us to resign.

RAPP: But when only 16 percent of the budget goes to education, and only 20 percent of your children finish their education, what measures can you take to get better results?

SANKARA: Even 100 percent of our budget would not be enough to educate all of our children. So we have to call on other forms of education that have nothing in common with classical teaching models. We'll be launching a campaign soon in which everyone who knows how to read will have the duty of teaching a certain number of others. Those who don't participate will lose the possibility of continuing themselves.

RAPP: But how will you do this? Through a kind of obligatory period of public service?

SANKARA: We'll launch a vast national campaign. We'll have to go everywhere. What's more, I'm convinced that all problems between men are problems of communication.

When you speak and people don't quite understand what you're trying to say, misunderstandings are always possible. We need a good dose of nonconformity. You'll see.

RAPP: Does this mean you're thinking more generally about setting up an obligatory period of public service?

SANKARA: We do want to completely reorganize our military service. Right now military service is obligatory and lasts eighteen months. But with the means at our disposal we're reaching only 2 percent of those eligible.

Here the army represents an opportunity, a stable job. The stampede to get into recruitment offices is the complete opposite of the situation in Europe. I remember when I was in training with French officers, we were given courses to prepare us to convince young people to agree to a military life. In my country we have to learn how to turn away as many as possible.

RAPP: But what will you change, and with what goal?

SANKARA: We're going to make military service longer. It will be two years instead of eighteen months. During this period people will obviously learn how to use weapons. But three-quarters of their time will be devoted to production. That's because we believe the defense of a people is the task of the people themselves. They must be able to mobilize themselves and have access to the necessary weapons, for we have many enemies. We think, too, that it's out of the question to entrust the defense of a country to a minority, no matter how specialized it may be. The people must defend themselves. They must decide to make peace when they cannot—or don't wish to—pursue a war. They must decide, too, what the army should be.

RAPP: What does this mean concretely?

SANKARA: We don't want a caste sitting on top of others. We want to break with this kind of thinking and make a number of changes. Our stripes, for example; we want to change these so the army fuses with the people.

RAPP: What do you mean by "working on production"?

SANKARA: Those doing their national service will work in agriculture, some of them. Others will teach or be health-care workers. We're not talking about them becoming doctors, but gaining a certain knowledge of hygiene and first aid so they in turn can teach others lifesaving techniques. That's all. It'll be much more valuable than multiplying the number of doctors by ten. We're not thinking of any innovations on that score. We're considering a system that would mobilize people from different social layers and different ages, somewhat similar to the Swiss system.

RAPP: But what qualifications will these people have?

SANKARA: They'll be quite heterogeneous. Doctors, before entering into public service, should take it upon themselves to practice in the armed forces. In this way they'll discover or rediscover the Burkinabè people. We'll call up both high-ranking academics and simple peasants alike. For a small number it would even be possible to do an apprenticeship, or at least to learn the rudiments of a trade: agriculture, stock raising, construction.

RAPP: And what about those who are currently enlisted?

SANKARA: Similarly, we believe the army to be an arm of the people, and that it can't live in tranquility and opulence that clash with the chronic poverty of our people. Our soldiers must constantly experience what the people experience. It's not right for military men to be paid regularly while the civilian population as a whole doesn't have the same possibilities. So to bring military personnel into contact with reality, we put them in touch with the needs of the day. We've decided that in addition to their purely military, professional, and tactical activities, they should participate in economic life. We've instructed them to build chicken coops and start working in stock raising.

RAPP: What was the slogan?

SANKARA: One-quarter of a chicken per soldier per week. This way, not only will the quality of food improve, but in addition, this particular layer of people with regular salaries will not be in the business of buying chickens, and this will surely lower the price for the civilian population. With this kind of training, the soldier who has gotten into the habit of acting like this, either under orders from his officer or on his own initiative, will do the same at home. So the movement will be generalized. Some say we have already gone over our goal. That's all we ask, because the revolution is not only the means to a better life, but to a better life and greater happiness for all.

RAPP: You're not immune to imminent physical elimination. What image would you like to leave of yourself and your role if this happens?

SANKARA: I would simply hope that my contribution had served to convince the most disbelieving that there exists a force, called the people, and that we must fight for and with the people. I would like to leave behind me the conviction that, having taken a few precautions and having organized ourselves to some extent, we will see victory—a sure and durable victory. I would like this same conviction to take hold of all others so that what seems to them today to be a sacrifice will seem tomorrow to be normal and simple activities.

Maybe in our lifetime it will seem like we're tilting at windmills. But perhaps we're blazing the trail along which, tomorrow, others will surge forward cheerfully, without even thinking—as we do when we walk. We place one foot in front of the other without ever questioning, though all our movements are subject to a complex set of laws having to do with the balance of our bodies, speed, pace, and rhythm. It will be a real consolation to me and my comrades if we've been able to be useful in some regard, if we've been able to be pioneers. Provided, of course, we're able to get that consolation where we're going.

RAPP: If someone does not share your views, are you prepared to use violence and constraint and, in doing so, go against the convictions you hold?

SANKARA: Given a choice between two solutions, I'm not prepared to say I'd choose violence, but I do know that the logic of some situations at times leaves you no choice. This is a decision you must make alone. It's distressing, painful. Agonizing. The following day you come face to face with those against whom you've had to order violent measures, and all the time, up to the very last minute, you were hoping there would be some other way to avoid resorting to violence, a way to save these men. Sometimes you don't find such a solution.

RAPP: Against whom have you had to use violence?

SANKARA: There are those who naively think they can get away with anything. This is not a serious problem. We can exercise restraint in our use of force against these people.

Then there are those who for their own ends devise elaborate, cynical, and Machiavellian means to provoke an escalation of violence in the country. They send people to plot against us. If you show weakness toward them and they succeed, everything you have accomplished, all your commitment to the service of the people as a whole will be reduced to nothing. These people are totally cynical. They care nothing for the lives of those they enlist for their plots. We can catch ten, twenty, thirty. They won't shed a single tear. They'll simply go find others to send against us.

And should you fight against these actions with violence, they'll resort to powerful, even terrifying, means to try to give you a bad conscience. "There's a man with blood on his hands." But the point is, should you sacrifice the majority in order to preserve a minority—which sometimes amounts to no more than a single individual? Somebody must decide these questions, alone.

RAPP: A difficult task that can lead to arbitrary decisions?

SANKARA: It's extremely difficult for the individual with regard to himself. Outwardly, one can refuse to listen, or to hear everything that's being said. There are those elsewhere who have bathed in blood without feeling the slightest remorse. But inwardly, if one has a minimum of conviction and faith in man, it's deeply upsetting.

I'm a military man. I can be called to the battlefield at any moment. On the battlefield, I hope to be able to help my enemy and spare him senseless suffering, even though the logic of the battlefield demands that I use my weapon against him and kill him as quickly as possible in order not to be killed myself.

RAPP: But how far are you willing to allow your enemies to go before resorting to violence?

SANKARA: I hope to be able to give my enemy the opportunity to comprehend me, because from that moment on he'll understand one fundamental thing: we can disagree on a certain number of questions without my necessarily being against him. The goals I'm striving for are noble. Does he think my methods are bad, inadequate? If that's what he thinks, we should discuss it.

RAPP: But when his position is more radical?

SANKARA: We've set a number of prisoners free, including the one who betrayed me and had me imprisoned.[15] I'm still alive not because he took pity on me, and not because he didn't try to kill me. I was fired at. I'm not dead. I was lucky.

---

15. A reference to former president Jean-Baptiste Ouédraogo.

We set him free. Some people say we acted for sentimental reasons, out of weakness. But my concern is that
this man understand he is at our mercy, that he always
has been, and that even today we could still condemn him
to death, shoot him, but that something higher than revenge prevents us from harming him.

RAPP: Why didn't you do it?

SANKARA: We weren't after his life. It's true we could have
had him executed the day we took power.

RAPP: Your attitude was, perhaps, simply a good political move?

SANKARA: That's what he probably thinks, that I declared him a free man today to give myself a good image.
He may be thinking, "We're definitely enemies, but since
he's the stronger at this moment I'll play dead and take my
revenge as soon as the opportunity arises." I don't know,
but it would sadden me to think he sees anything in this
act other than a profound conviction that we must lead
all men to understand each other and work together. This
is a very long and painstaking task.

RAPP: Executions have been ordered, however.[16] Were
these souls that couldn't be saved?

SANKARA: Any soul can be saved. I believe the best of a
man is always ahead of him. But we were in a particular
situation that did not allow me to respond favorably to
requests to pardon those condemned. Justice had to take
its course.

RAPP: Aren't you ever afraid—tomorrow it could all be
over?

SANKARA: No, that kind of fear I don't have. I've told

16. On June 11, 1984, seven people, arrested May 26 and 27, were executed for plotting a coup. They included former military officers, the
head of security at Ouagadougou airport, and a former mayor of the city.

myself: either I'll finish up an old man somewhere in a library reading books, or I'll meet with a violent end, since we have so many enemies. Once you've accepted that reality, it's just a question of time. It will happen when it happens.

RAPP: Do you know other kinds of fear?

SANKARA: Yes, the fear of failure, the fear of not having done enough. You can fail because of a disagreement, but not because of laziness, because you should have done something that you had the means to do but didn't. That I do fear, and I'm prepared to fight to the end against such a thing.

Imagine what it would be like if tomorrow someone said you'd stolen money and it were true; or if you let people die of hunger because you didn't have the courage to punish the person responsible for bringing them food and who failed to do so; that you knew this man and you knew he was guilty as charged. I should have, and I didn't. If I'm shot for having that kind of attitude, fine. But if I'm not, this would be a cross I'd have to bear for the rest of my days—the cross of my own incapacity, of my own escape from responsibility. Every day of my life, having to explain myself to everyone—that would really drive you out of your mind. Imagine you're out there in the street, on the sidewalk, a man talking to himself, trying to tell everyone: "I'm innocent, believe me, save me." No, this would be impossible.

RAPP: But doesn't a kind of Sankara madness already exist in a certain way?

SANKARA: Yes. You cannot carry out fundamental change without a certain amount of madness. In this case, it comes from nonconformity, the courage to turn your back on the old formulas, the courage to invent the future. Besides, it took the madmen of yesterday for us to be able to act with extreme clarity today. I want to be one of those madmen.

RAPP: To invent the future?

SANKARA: Yes. We must dare to invent the future. In the speech I gave launching the five-year plan, I said, "Everything man is capable of imagining, he can create." I'm convinced that's true.

There are attempts to unleash an unjust war against us

Speech at mass rally in Ouagadougou
September 11, 1985

To protest the growing hostility of a number of regimes in the region toward the Burkinabè Revolution, Sankara left an emergency meeting of the Entente Council in Yamoussoukro, Côte d'Ivoire (Ivory Coast). On his return, he reported on the meeting to a mass rally in Ouagadougou. His remarks were published in the September 13, 1985, issue of *Sidwaya*, a French-language daily published in Ouagadougou.

Comrades:

We had to respond to international imperialism, we had to respond to its local lackeys. As soon as we stood up, they began to tremble. [*Applause*] There are no speeches to give, other than to simply state and remind you that as we speak here, imperialist radios are all tuned to Ouagadougou. [*Applause*]

We know that the imperialist agencies will try to dissect what is said here. Above all, they will try to figure out how far the Burkinabè people will succeed in pushing

247

back the enemy. I say to you that we will keep pushing back the enemy until we've drowned him in the ocean! [*Applause*]

We know that right now there are attempts to cook up all kinds of plots against our people. In particular, attempts are being made to have the sound of saber-rattling resonate at our borders. Attempts are being made to create, to unleash an unjust, many-sided war against our Burkinabè people. Attempts are being made to pit the Burkinabè people against other peoples. Attempts are being made to manipulate those who can be manipulated. But as for us, we maintain the serenity, the calm, and the tranquility of those who have confidence in their strength, who know that the limits of their struggle will be dictated not by the enemy, but by themselves.

What I mean to say is that once the Burkinabè people have decided to march ahead, only Burkina Faso, only the Burkinabè people, will be able to draw the line where we stop. [*Applause*]

On behalf of all of you, I issue a very firm warning to those who confuse Burkina Faso with Upper Volta. [*Applause*] I issue a firm warning to all those who would dare disturb the tranquility of a single Burkinabè, either inside the country or abroad. [*Applause*]

For our part, we have no need to call on foreign troops or foreign advisers. A short while ago, the comrade commander in chief [Jean-Baptiste Lingani] addressed you in very clear language, in the language of combat. He explained that you are the attack troops that will seize the citadels from which certain lackeys are now conspiring against us. Very well! I will complete his presentation by telling you that even if we don't have enough weapons because there are so many of us, we'll go take those weapons from the enemy. [*Applause*] So all the equipment, the arsenal of war and death from which they're right now supplying themselves, constitutes our very own supply! [*Applause*]

Comrades, it's obvious that a demonstration of this kind is not to everyone's liking. But I'd like to insist above all on the feelings of friendship and internationalist duty that must be with us at all times. The struggle of the Burkinabè people is not in any way a chauvinist struggle. In no way will our struggle be one of limited, narrow nationalism. Our struggle is that of the peoples who aspire to peace and freedom. This is why we must never lose sight of the good qualities of the peoples that surround us and of their legitimate aspirations of peace—a just peace—of dignity, and of genuine independence.

Of course, it is up to them to carry out their historic duty. It is up to them to rid themselves of all the snakes who infest their territory, of all the monsters who prevent them from being happy. We have faced up to our responsibilities at home. It's up to the other peoples—their youth, their patriotic and democratic forces, their civilians, their military personnel, their men, their women—to face up to their responsibilities.

We want to build an Entente Council, a revolutionary Entente Council. [*Applause*] And we'll fight to our last breath to ensure that our just perspective is the one that triumphs. We can count on the peoples of Benin, Niger, Togo, and the Ivory Coast because we know that these peoples need freedom, dignity, peace, and security; and because we know that these peoples have understood that only revolution will enable them to rid themselves of all those inside and outside their countries who stand in the way of achieving this noble goal.

This is why we say that today it's the Entente Council. Tomorrow, thanks to the people of Togo, thanks to the people of Benin, thanks to the people of Niger, thanks to the people of the Ivory Coast, and together with the people of Burkina Faso, with or without any individual's goodwill, the revolution will take hold. [*Applause*] The revolution is already under way.

We are well-informed of their plots, their attempts to divide, to create opposition, their attempts at assassination. In this we see that these out-and-out reactionaries don't understand, that they confuse the forward march of a people with the evolution of an individual. This is why we say—as we've said before: attacking this or that leader will never suffice to put a stop to the revolution. This is why we say that their plots will never be able to stop the revolution. The revolution is indeed under way and it will triumph. It will liberate all the peoples.

Since we spoke about security at Yamoussoukro, it's natural that we sought the ways and means to concretely ensure this security. But it will never happen. We will never obtain this security as long as the revolution has not liberated the peoples. Our struggle will not be limited to the Entente Council. The other peoples on our borders are also peoples in need of revolution. Of course, I'm not talking here about Ghana. But I am talking about Mali. [*Applause and cheers*]

Our sister republic of Mali can understand, must understand, that its happiness will be our happiness; its misfortune will be our misfortune. The concerns of the people of Mali are the concerns of the Burkinabè people. The preoccupations of the people of Mali are the preoccupations of the Burkinabè people. The revolution of the Burkinabè people is at the disposal of the people of Mali, who need it. [*Applause*] Because only revolution will allow them to fight against hunger, thirst, disease, ignorance, and above all, against the neocolonial and imperialist forces of domination. Only revolution will allow them to free themselves.

Revolution cannot be the monopoly of any one people. We have the duty to recognize that all peoples aspire to revolution. The peoples are on the move, so the revolution is advancing. We thus salute the just struggles that all these peoples wage every day, and we will be present with them at the appointed time to celebrate the joyful days when they will have destroyed all their enemies, inside and outside the country. [*Applause*]

Of course—and this must be repeated and stressed—it's up to them to face up to their historic responsibility for their own liberation. There's absolutely no question of waiting for the saving grace of another people or of a messiah. That would be an error, a gross error, a monumental error, a counterrevolutionary error.

Will the revolutionary Entente Council be created or will it not? [*Shouts of "It will!"*]

The security of our people depends on each militant. The security of our people depends on each combatant, both inside and outside the country. We must call on our combatants who are abroad to increase their vigilance, their fervor in unmasking the plots that are being fomented, so they can point out the vermin's lairs to us. So that, thanks to our invincible flamethrowers, we can incinerate our enemies once and for all, spewing out fire to burn them to cinders, reducing them to dust. [*Applause*]

This evening we simply needed to reaffirm something we have become permanently convinced of. We needed to reaffirm the mobilization and determination of the Burkinabè people. We also needed to say and stress that we are in solidarity with our neighbors. This very evening I will send a message on behalf of you all to Félix

Houphouët-Boigny, [*Applause*] a message to Eyadéma, a
message to Seyni Kountché, a message to Moussa Traoré,
a message to Mathieu Kérékou, and one to Rawlings.[1]
[*Applause*] To tell them that you affirm your solidarity
with their peoples, to tell them that all the just struggles
of their peoples will be our struggles. [*Applause*] I hope
these messages will be read in their capitals.

Whatever the case, we will send these messages because they are messages of friendship, a friendship that
has no need whatsoever of a legal agreement. [*Applause*]
We will tell them, too, that we think the Entente Council itself already provides a legal and moral framework for
the permanent defense of our various interests. We don't
think other documents, other legal provisions, need to
be added to the Entente Council. After all, what has been
done since 1958? What has been done since the creation
of the Entente Council if agreements only became necessary in 1985? This is disturbing.

Comrades, thank you. Thank you for coming out in
such numbers, in such great numbers, for having shown
that the mobilization is permanent, that the enthusiasm
is permanent, and that the struggle here will be victorious.

Comrades:

Long live the people of Ghana!

Long live the people of Benin!

Long live the people of the Ivory Coast!

Long live the people of Niger!

Long live the people of Togo!

Long live the people of Mali!

---

1. Félix Houphouët-Boigny, Gnassingbe Eyadéma, Seyni Kountché,
Moussa Traoré, and Mathieu Kérékou were presidents, respectively,
of Côte d'Ivoire, Togo, Niger, Mali, and Benin. Jerry Rawlings was
Ghana's head of state and government.

Revolution for all!
Revolution for all!
Revolution for all the peoples!
Homeland or death, we will win!
Homeland or death, we will win!
Thank you.

On Africa

Interview with Mongo Beti
November 3, 1985

The following are major excerpts of a never-before published written interview conducted by Mongo Beti, a writer from Cameroon and author of *Main basse sur le Cameroun, autopsie d'une décolonisation* (Grabbing up Cameroon: autopsy of a decolonization). The book was banned in France and Cameroon at the time of its publication in 1972. The interview was prepared for the magazine *Peuples noirs Peuples africains*, edited by Mongo Beti, but never published.

MONGO BETI: The first question concerns the security of the president and the future of the ipso facto regime. In the face of the insidious campaign being waged in the French press, many Africans think it's the warning sign of an all-out offensive, and they recall with apprehension Lumumba and Nkrumah. They fear a strategy of physical elimination.

Are you aware of this danger and especially this apprehension on the part of Africans? Are you aware of the existence of this strategy and in particular this campaign in the press?

THOMAS SANKARA: You have given me an opportunity to repeat something that perhaps you already know. Indeed, quite a few people are not pleased with us and our revolution. I was going to say that it's quite natural given the class interests we defend. It's thus logical and normal that we have enemies, class enemies, since we are determined to defend our class interests to the detriment of theirs and we're fully justified in doing so. From this standpoint, it's not surprising that everywhere our enemies are organizing to confront the revolution, to use the press to smear and defame all our actions in an insidious and dishonest way. This is the case with newspapers that are well financed, radio programs that obey orders, and all kinds of actions organized in a despicable way to totally distort the image of the revolution.

This strategy is well known. It was used on a number of occasions by imperialism to destabilize many firmly revolutionary regimes such as Nkrumah, Lumumba— whom you mentioned—Allende in Chile, and so on. We are conscious of this. It is a real danger to the extent that powerful measures are being undertaken day and night to poison international opinion against the peoples' struggles for emancipation.

Nkrumah, Lumumba, and so many others were victims of imperialism, of this neocolonial strategy. Moreover, the worthy sons of Africa acknowledged them as genuine patriots, political men who had a true and great love for Africa and for Africans. Today we can only admire them, and it's an honor for us to show that they were the precursors, guides, pioneers on the path of Africa's dignity.

Everywhere today, in the four corners of the continent, there are Nkrumahs, Lumumbas, Mondlanes, etc. Should

Sankara be physically eliminated today, there will be thousands of Sankaras to take up the challenge to imperialism. With regards to our Faso, the determination of our people, of our youth removes any worry as to the pursuit of the struggle for the dignity of Burkina and our continent. Nevertheless, for a thousand and one reasons, our people and the revolutionary African youth remain attached to Sankara and wish that he never be harmed in the slightest way.

BETI: I'm wondering about the nature of the corruption in African societies. Is it a curse inherited from colonization? Is it one of our traditions? (After all, everyone knows about the petty black kings who handed over their brothers to the slave merchants for a handful of glass beads.) The question is posed because it seems to me that the fight against corruption is conducted differently depending on the way the question is answered. What do you think?

SANKARA: Without being a well-informed sociologist, or a historian of precapitalist African societies, I cannot state that corruption is a peculiarity of African societies. It is a phenomenon linked above all to the capitalist system, a socioeconomic system that cannot really advance without developing corruption. It is thus unquestionably a curse inherited from colonization. Therefore, it is logical that to effectively fight colonization, colonialism, and even neocolonialism, corruption must also be combated.

Regarding the feudal kings used by the colonizers, the handfuls of glass beads, from the African standpoint, were not the same as corruption to the extent that the mode of exchange was built on barter. The petty kings sold their "brothers" for one or another object of value that we consider in hindsight to be trinkets. The value of each thing is based only on its practical usefulness and the milieu in which its use meets a need. A king who had never seen himself in a mirror would not hesitate to obtain it in exchange for a man, that is, for one of his subjects. Based on this fact, he is giving the corresponding value in exchange for this thing. He cannot be considered corrupt even if the colonizer or the explorer, given the economic system their society had attained, approached him on the basis of corruption.

BETI: Does this not pose the general problem of tradition? Isn't there an incompatibility between revolution, which aims in part to modernize our societies, and tradition, which is very often a brake on progress? More precisely, if women are to be liberated, isn't it necessary to fight against female circumcision, against polygamy?

SANKARA: In general, African traditions are the product of a backward ideology. Nevertheless in every thing and every phenomenon there is a progressive and a regressive aspect. In our traditions, it's the progressive aspect that we must learn to single out in order to allow society to evolve much more rapidly toward progress, toward the modernism you speak of. Revolutions are not made to regress in time. The aim is to constantly move forward. The revolution will inevitably suppress the negative aspects of our traditions. Such is our fight against all the backward forces, all the forms of obscurantism, a legitimate fight that is essential to freeing society of all old and decaying influences and prejudices, including those that marginalize women or turn them into objects.

It's my opinion that in order to liberate women, we must fight against female circumcision and polygamy. Above all we must know how to undertake the struggle. Banning by laws or other means is not the best solution. We are fighting for the equality of men and women—not a mechanical, mathematical equality but making women the equal of men before the law and especially in relation to wage labor. The emancipation of women requires their education and their gaining economic power. In this way, labor on an equal footing with men on all levels, having the same responsibilities and the same rights and obligations, are weapons against circumcision and polygamy, weapons that women will not hesitate to use to gain liberation by themselves and not by someone else.

BETI: There was some good in African traditions, it's true! For example, the *palabre* [communal assembly] reflects the constant need for consensus. Nevertheless, is it not true that African traditions in general, or what remains of them, are fundamentally backward? Isn't the logical outcome of the revolutionary process a cultural revolution?

SANKARA: Inasmuch as social revolution is the radical transformation of society at all levels, every revolutionary process must result in a cultural revolution. Culture is totally linked with society in the sense that there is no human society without culture, and no culture without a correspondence to society.

BETI: An example: the veneration of age. Isn't this one of those values that is most easily manipulated by neocolonialism? Thus the French press regularly contrasts the age of Houphouët-Boigny to the young generations from the Ivory Coast who are questioning their president.

SANKARA: The veneration of age is an aspect of African culture. No one can deny this, insofar as the gerontocracy appeared in our societies as a system of power that was always adopted and applied. Neocolonialism naturally uses our own systems, our own vision of the world in order to manipulate them to its advantage. The image of the elder, a symbol of wisdom, experience, and merit, is still very much accepted in Africa in contrast to the image of youth, a symbol of inexperience, uncertainty, and a departure from normality. These are aspects of our traditions that neocolonialism knows well and intends to exploit to manipulate public opinion in Africa. To this end the French and Western press block debates between African generations in order to cover up the sharp class contradictions in certain African societies, believing they can kill the enthusiasm of the young people who want to put an end to the old and decaying past that paralyzes their country each day.

BETI: With regard to cooperation. Can maintaining special relations with the power that colonized us be justified? If not, why do you continue to participate in summit conferences with leaders of French-speaking states whom the educated African youth view so negatively?

SANKARA: From a dialectical standpoint, all things or all actions can be explained. Therefore, the relations with this or that country, even a colonizing power, have an explanation, even if it's only a historical one as in the case of the colonizing power. Everything is on that level, beyond the ideological differences that may come up. And there are state-to-state relations.

To fight for one's independence against colonialism does not mean that one is preparing to leave earth and isolate oneself in a corner of outer space after independence is achieved. As for the summit conferences with leaders of French-speaking states, whenever we have a chance to participate, we use these as a platform, a springboard for our revolution, to make it known, to say openly what it thinks of these conferences or political bodies. Participating in order to denounce what goes against the interests of African peoples is a much more profitable strategy than throwing in sarcastic remarks from the outside. That's the way we see things in the framework of our revolutionary process.[*]

---

[*] This section could leave the impression that we will seize the opportunity of the very next summit to go speak, and therefore to attend.

BETI: As regards the domination of our peoples, has the French left in power acted differently from the right? Can you disclose to the magazine *Peuples noirs Peuples africains* at least a part of your personal experience? For example, in what way was Guy Penne the instigator of the coup against you?

SANKARA: In relation to the expectations of the African peoples, the French left generally disappointed many people, particularly the African youth. Since the independence of our countries from 1960 to 1981, we had known only the right. With May 1981 a new and promising experience for Africans presented itself. Simply comparing the two was already something, in and of itself. Very soon, however, everyone realized that things had not fundamentally shifted. In short, it was Tweedledum and Tweedledee. My personal experience, which is also the experience of the African peoples, is that the approach to defending French interests in the ex-colonies (Chad, Central African Republic) and the colonies (Kanaky, the Comoro Islands . . .) was a strange reminder of the operating principles of Foccart.[1]

Guy Penne's coup has been sufficiently denounced and brought to the attention of international opinion that I needn't take the time to come back to it.

BETI: Concerning the franc zone. The most common justification for keeping our countries in the franc zone is the convertibility of the CFA franc. But is that an advantage for the poor, who are 90 percent of our society? What need does the African peasant in his village have for a convertible currency? In short, isn't the CFA franc a

---

However, I don't believe that it's opportune to go. (Note by Sankara) [This is a reference to the First Francophone Summit, which Sankara did not attend but sent a message to. See page 285.]

1. See glossary, Foccart, Jacques.

weapon for the domination of Africans? Does revolutionary Burkina plan to continue dragging this ball and chain?

SANKARA: Whether the currency was convertible or nonconvertible was never a preoccupation of the African peasant. He has been unwillingly thrust into an economic system against which he is powerless. I think it is necessary to organize him to defend himself against the ravages of such a system. Therein lies the problem, inasmuch as the currency is not isolated from the economic system.

In this framework I will say that the CFA franc, which is tied to the French monetary system, is a weapon of French domination. The French economy, and consequently the French commercial capitalists, amass their fortune on the backs of our peoples on the basis of this link, of this monetary monopoly. That is why Burkina is struggling to put an end to this situation through our people's struggle to build an independent, self-sufficient economy. How long this will take, I can't say.

BETI: Concerning technical assistance: personally I have always considered it as primarily a question of time. How long do you think it will take before Burkina Faso no longer needs non-African technical assistance? Do you have a strategy for recruiting African technical advisors? What is it?

SANKARA: That is very difficult to determine because it's a complex area where enormous technical and financial resources are necessary. But the shortest possible time period would be the best. There is no better strategy than increasing South-South cooperation in technical aid. All those who would like to discuss with us their aid to Burkina are welcome. The land of Burkina is a free land of fraternity and friendship among peoples. The Burkinabè people are therefore ready to welcome anyone who wants to come work with us to build a new society. That is our strategy for the moment.

BETI: Regarding Pan-Africanism: These days, no one talks about it anymore, or hardly at all. African youth are therefore very frustrated today because Pan-Africanism for them had a mystique, an uplifting effect, an extraordinary force. Are you thinking of taking up the torch of Nkrumah? How? Perhaps by regional rapprochements?

SANKARA: Yes, Pan-Africanism, in its purest form, inspired great hopes not only for Africans but for Blacks of the diaspora as well. Much has been written and continues to be written in many circles about this political phenomenon. I won't elaborate on that. But I think it's a problem, a serious question for Africans, if they really want to free themselves of all foreign domination.

Faced with the ravages and other abuses of imperialism, Nkrumah had every reason to place all his hopes in the unity of the continent, as everyone today notes with bitterness. Nevertheless the idea remains, and it falls to us, to African patriots, to struggle everywhere and at all times for its realization. It falls to all Pan-Africanist people to give Africa hope by taking up the torch of Nkrumah.

BETI: Concerning the French language and the French-speaking world. Personally I think these are two different problems: the position of the French language is a fact whose origin is in history. The idea of the French-speaking world is a strategy to control our creativity and even our future. Do you accept this distinction? Do you plan to replace French, the current official language, by the national languages of Burkina? Or do you think that French must continue to play this role (for a long time? permanently?).

SANKARA: I agree with you completely on this distinction. There is the historical fact and there is also the neocolonial strategy. The concept of the French-speaking world is nothing other than that. Unfortunately it's the "Africans" who defend it more than the French themselves. It's a paradox, but one that can be thoroughly explained by the acculturation and the complete cultural alienation of those Africans.

As for Burkina, we are carrying out a total reform of education, where the question of the national languages and the French language is at the center of the debates. The question is not yet settled, but things seem to be evolving toward using French as the unifying language of all our numerous nationalities; and doing so from the standpoint of efficiency and the best way to solve the problem we face. That doesn't mean that our national languages will be rejected, far from it.

As language in general is above classes, it's up to us as revolutionaries to know how to put French to use in the defense of our class interests. It's in this framework that we are called upon to create our own institutions, for a cultural apparatus that serves our people. Otherwise our struggle cannot succeed given the harmful influence of the cultural invasion we experience basically from France. The revolution, in our present context, is above all a mental liberation. To score any victories we must do this as soon as possible.

BETI: Concerning unplanned urbanization: I have observed two African cities: Algiers and Brazzaville. Especially Algiers. No sooner have the inhabitants of a shantytown been moved to government-subsidized housing than they are replaced by the battalions of the rural exodus. The government leaders run a desperate race against this insane development of the capital. Ultimately the African capitals will absorb all of the various national budgets. Are you already confronting this in Ouagadougou? Without adopting the extreme approach of a Pol Pot,[2] don't you think it is necessary to put an end to this legacy that jeopardizes our development? The colonial city was created for the colonizer not for the African.

SANKARA: In comparison, Ouagadougou is not as populous as Brazzaville or Algiers. But this phenomenon can be seen. We are solving it with a vigorous policy of large-scale housing development. All the shantytowns are being torn down in order to build decent housing in their place. The Year II Housing Project, the Year III Project, the SOGOGIB housing, the August 4 Projects, the popular housing developments are all responses to this question.

In this framework we are attempting to reduce as much as possible the difference between city and country by developing in the countryside all the infrastructures to make rural life more pleasant and thus to slow down the rural exodus. We are establishing in the countryside sociocultural centers, popular recreation centers, movie theaters, dance halls, and modern musical groups. In the case of some colonial legacies, all we can do is be aware of them, while taking care to eliminate their harmful effects. Such is the case of the city.

BETI: And now in a more personal and colorful vein, which unfortunately fascinates the masses! Are you a Marxist? For how long now? As a result of what evolution? You're accused (in a despicable way, to be sure, and you can legitimately object that it doesn't deserve to be answered) of carrying out a policy based on a feeling of personal

---

2. Immediately after taking power in Cambodia in 1975 under the leadership of Pol Pot, the Khmer Rouge ordered the forcible evacuation of the capital Phnom Penh. This was the first of many repressive anti-working-class measures that led to the death of at least 1.5 million people in four years.

vengeance and not on an ideological choice. Perhaps it's time for you to make things clear.

SANKARA: For now, I am anti-imperialist. Speaking as your comrade president, this also is the case. We think that this is the product of a specific ideology. That's enough for us—to be useful to our people, especially when they don't trouble themselves with labeling their leaders but judge them above all by their revolutionary action. Later we'll see.

The Malian troops are no longer prisoners, they are our brothers

At Burkina-Mali solidarity rally
January 3, 1986

In December 1985 the government of Mali, armed by France, used a border dispute as the pretext to launch an attack on the Burkinabè Revolution. Backed by tanks, armored vehicles, and jet fighters, Malian soldiers invaded Burkina Faso, starting a five-day conflict known as the "Christmas war." The following is excerpted from a speech given to a Burkina-Mali solidarity rally in Ouagadougou after the signing of a cease-fire between the two countries. It was published in the January 6, 1986, issue of *Sidwaya*.

Comrade militants of the democratic and popular revolution:
On December 25, 1985, with the year drawing to a close, our populations were bombed. They were bombed by planes, they were wounded and killed by tanks and troops coming from the other side. We then counterattacked. Confronting material superiority, confronting an abundance of weapons, we countered with collective political and revolutionary determination, we unleashed the creative

267

genius. Our strategists have written deeds of great prowess into the pages of African military history. We protected our people. We protected them because we were victims of aggression, because we owe them liberty and tranquility day and night. We protected them, thus fulfilling a revolutionary duty.

War is nothing other than an extension of politics. Their politics were extended and transformed into war. Our politics were extended and transformed into a generalized popular defense. Two political courses confronted each other, and one political course triumphed.

Dear comrades, on this day, January 3, 1986, I would like us to think of all those who fell on the field of honor—Malians and Burkinabè—of all those who were wounded, of all the tearful families, of these two peoples, and of other peoples from Africa and elsewhere who have been touched by these painful confrontations. I would like each of us to make an effort to surmount feelings of hate, rejection, and hostility toward the Malian people. I would like each of us to achieve the most important victory: to kill inside ourselves the seeds of hostility and enmity toward anyone. We have an important victory to win: planting the seeds of genuine friendship in our hearts, capable of withstanding even the murderous assault of cannons, planes, and tanks. This kind of friendship is only built on the revolutionary basis of sincere love for other peoples.

I know you are capable of this, capable of loving the Malian people and demonstrating it. We will demonstrate it. In their speech, the brothers from Mali said they favor developing relations. First of all, we answer: yes! But in addition, we are going to follow these words with deeds. For this reason, comrades, I want to tell you that as far as we're concerned, there has never been anything but friendship and love between the Malian and Burkinabè peoples.

Comrades! Are you or are you not for friendship between our two peoples? [*Shouts of "Yes!"*] The popular masses, who hold power in Burkina Faso, have spoken. On their behalf I say directly to the entire world that there are no longer any Malian prisoners in Burkina Faso. The Malian military personnel who are here are no longer prisoners. They are our brothers. They can return to Bamako[1] when and as they wish, in total freedom.

We did not fight in order to take prisoners, but to repel the enemy. We have repelled him. Every Malian in Burkina Faso is a brother. The Malians who are here are our brothers. Starting today, arrangements will be made for them to live in complete freedom, for them to taste the joy of freedom in Burkina Faso, especially in Ouagadougou. Their families in Mali should know that they can come and get them, just as they can wait for them at Bamako airport, whatever they wish.

Comrades, let us avoid being diverted, dragged into fights that are not the people's fights. Let us avoid being dragged into concerns that are not the people's concerns, into the mad race toward confrontation and stockpiling of weapons. We know that in certain minds the temptation will be great, come what may, to seek military arsenals, and in so doing justify bellicose actions and thus find easy and convenient pretexts for holding the masses for ransom. This will not happen in Burkina Faso.

The Western media, the imperialist press, has often said that Burkina Faso is a country with a massive stockpile of weapons. You have often read in the papers that our country has received tons and tons of military equipment. Fortunately, this same press has admitted its error, has reversed judgment, and has recognized that Burkina

---

1. Bamako is the capital of Mali.

Faso was militarily underequipped. We are not the ones who said this; they are the ones who wrote it. It's true, we are underequipped. All the talk they spread about us was nothing but slanders. Today they are faced with their own slanders, faced with their own lies. We now know which country has stockpiled weapons, and which country has military scrap at its disposal. We now know which country imposes sacrifices on its people in the interests of social, political, and economic development rather than for excessive militarization.

The events of these five days have allowed Burkina Faso to wash away the shame, to reestablish the truth. They have allowed the entire world to see us as we really are. Only those who detest the revolution—and there are many—will continue trying to spread confusion through their maneuvers. Battles await us, and we must win them.

For 1986, which is beginning, I would like to wish all of you happiness—a happiness in keeping with the intentions we are expressing and with the efforts we are ready to make. In wishing you all a good and happy year, I would like to ask you all to pull yourselves together and look on what has just occurred as an episode, an unfortunate one, of course, but rich in lessons.

I would like us to analyze this experience. We revolutionaries know that every day that goes by is a day of confrontation. On March 26, 1983, in this very square, we proclaimed, "When the people stand up, imperialism trembles." Ever since that day, we've known that we are face to face with imperialism and its lackeys.[2]

---

2. After the hostilities, the governments of Burkina Faso and Mali asked the International Court of Justice in The Hague to resume its efforts to arrange a settlement. In a decision the following year, the court divided the contested territory between the two countries.

Imperialism is the arsonist of our forests and savannas

At International Conference
on Trees and Forests, Paris
February 5, 1986

This speech was given at the first International Silva Conference for the Protection of the Trees and Forests in Paris. It was
published in the February 14, 1986, issue of *Carrefour africain.*

My homeland, Burkina Faso, is without question one of
the rare countries on this planet justified in calling itself
and viewing itself as a distillation of all the natural evils
from which mankind still suffers at the end of this twentieth century.

Eight million Burkinabè have painfully internalized
this reality for twenty-three years. They have watched
their mothers, fathers, daughters, and sons die, with hunger, famine, disease, and ignorance decimating them by
the hundreds. With tears in their eyes, they have watched
ponds and rivers dry up. Since 1973 they have seen the
environment deteriorate, trees die, and the desert invade
with giant strides. It is estimated that the desert in the
Sahel advances at the rate of seven kilometers per year.

Only by looking at these realities can one understand and accept the legitimate revolt that was born, that matured over a long period of time, and that finally erupted in an organized way the night of August 4, 1983, in the form of a democratic and popular revolution in Burkina Faso.

Here I am merely the humble spokesperson of a people who, having passively watched their natural environment die, refuse to watch themselves die. Since August 4, 1983, water, trees, and lives—if not survival itself—have been fundamental and sacred elements in all action taken by the National Council of the Revolution, which leads Burkina Faso.

In this regard, I am also compelled to pay tribute to the French people, to their government, and in particular to their president, Mr. François Mitterrand, for this initiative, which expresses the political genius and clear-sightedness of a people always open to the world and sensitive to its misery. Burkina Faso, situated in the heart of the Sahel, will always fully appreciate initiatives that are in perfect harmony with the most vital concerns of its people. The country will be present at them whenever it is necessary, in contrast to useless pleasure trips.

For nearly three years now, my people, the Burkinabè people, have been fighting a battle against the encroachment of the desert. So it was their duty to be here on this platform to talk about their experience, and also to benefit from the experience of other peoples from around the world. For nearly three years in Burkina Faso, every happy event—marriages, baptisms, award presentations, and visits by prominent individuals and others—is celebrated with a tree-planting ceremony.

To greet the new year 1986, all the schoolchildren and students of our capital, Ouagadougou, built more than 3,500 improved cookstoves with their own hands, offering them to their mothers. This was in addition to the 80,000 cookstoves made by the women themselves over the course of two years. This was their contribution to the national effort to reduce the consumption of firewood and to protect trees and life.

The ability to buy or simply rent one of the hundreds of the public dwellings built since August 4, 1983, is strictly conditional on the beneficiary promising to plant a minimum number of trees and to nurture them like the apple of his eye. Those who received these dwellings but were mindless of their commitment have already been evicted, thanks to the vigilance of our Committees for the Defense of the Revolution, committees that poisonous tongues take pleasure in systematically and unilaterally denigrating.

After having vaccinated throughout the national territory, in two weeks, 2.5 million children between the ages of nine months and fourteen years—children from Burkina Faso and from neighboring countries—against measles, meningitis, and yellow fever; after having sunk more than 150 wells assuring drinking water to the 20 or so districts in our capital that lacked this vital necessity until now; after having raised the literacy rate from 12 to 22 percent in two years—the Burkinabè people victoriously continue their struggle for a green Burkina.

Ten million trees were planted under the auspices of a fifteen-month People's Development Program, our first venture while awaiting the five-year plan. In the villages and in the developed river valleys, families must each plant one hundred trees per year.

The cutting and selling of firewood has been completely reorganized and is now strictly regulated. These measures range from the requirement to hold a lumber merchant's card, through respecting the zones designated for wood cutting, to the requirement to ensure reforestation of deforested areas. Today every Burkinabè town and village owns a wood grove, thus reviving an ancestral tradition.

Thanks to the effort to make the popular masses aware of their responsibilities, our urban centers are free of the plague of roaming livestock. In our countryside, our efforts focus on settling livestock in one place as a means of promoting intensive stockbreeding in order to fight against unrestrained nomadism.

All criminal acts of arson by those who burn the forest are subject to trial and sanctioning by the Popular Courts of Conciliation in the villages. The requirement of planting a certain number of trees is one of the sanctions issued by these courts.

From February 10 to March 20, more than 35,000 peasants—officials of the cooperative village groups—will take intensive, basic courses on the subjects of economic management and environmental organization and maintenance.

Since January 15 a vast operation called the "Popular Harvest of Forest Seeds" has been under way in Burkina for the purpose of supplying the 7,000 village nurseries. We sum up all of these activities under the label "the three battles."

Ladies and gentlemen:

My intention is not to heap unrestrained and inordinate praise on the modest revolutionary experience of my people with regard to the defense of the trees and forests. My intention is to speak as explicitly as possible about the profound changes occurring in the relationship between men and trees in Burkina Faso. My intention is to bear witness as accurately as possible to the birth and development of a deep and sincere love between Burkinabè men and trees in my homeland.

In doing this, we believe we are applying our theoretical conceptions on this, based on the specific ways and means of our Sahel reality, in the search for solutions to present and future dangers attacking trees all over the planet.

Our efforts and those of the entire community gathered here, your cumulative experience and ours, will surely guarantee us victory after victory in the struggle to save our trees, our environment, and, in short, our lives.

Excellencies, ladies and gentlemen:

I come to you in the hope that you are taking up a battle from which we cannot be absent, we who are attacked daily and who are waiting for the miracle of greenery to rise up from the courage to say what must be said. I have come to join with you in deploring the harshness of nature. But I have also come to denounce the ones whose selfishness is the source of his fellow man's misfortune. Colonial plunder has decimated our forests without the slightest thought of replenishing them for our tomorrows.

The unpunished disruption of the biosphere by savage and murderous forays on the land and in the air continues. One cannot say too much about the extent to which all these machines that spew fumes spread carnage. Those who have the technological means to find the culprits have no interest in doing so, and those who have an interest in doing so lack the technological means. They have only their intuition and their innermost conviction.

We are not against progress, but we do not want progress that is anarchic and criminally neglects the rights of others. We therefore wish to affirm that the battle against the encroachment of the desert is a battle to establish a balance between man, nature, and society. As such it is a political battle above all, and not an act of fate.

The creation of a Ministry of Water as a complement to the Ministry of the Environment and Tourism in my country demonstrates our desire to clearly formulate the problems in order to be able to resolve them. We must fight to find the financial means to exploit our existing water resources—drilling operations, reservoirs, and dams. This is the place to denounce the one-sided contracts and draconian conditions imposed by banks and other financial institutions that doom our projects in this field. It is these prohibitive conditions that lead to our countries' traumatizing debt and eliminate any meaningful maneuvering room.

Neither fallacious Malthusian arguments—and I assert that Africa remains an underpopulated continent—nor the vacation resorts pompously and demagogically christened "reforestation operations" provide an answer. We and our misery are spurned like bald and mangy dogs whose lamentations and cries disturb the peace and quiet of the manufacturers and merchants of misery.

That is why Burkina has proposed and continues to propose that at least 1 percent of the colossal sums of money sacrificed to the search for cohabitation with other stars and planets be used, by way of compensation, to finance projects to save trees and lives. We have not abandoned hope that a dialogue with the Martians might lead to the reconquest of Eden. But in the meantime, earthlings that we are, we also have the right to reject a choice limited simply to the alternatives of hell or purgatory.

Explained in this way, our struggle for the trees and forests is first and foremost a democratic and popular struggle. Because a handful of forestry engineers and experts getting themselves all worked up in a sterile and costly manner will never accomplish anything! Nor can the worked-up consciences of a multitude of forums and institutions— sincere and praiseworthy though they may be—make the Sahel green again, when we lack the funds to drill wells for drinking water a hundred meters deep, while money abounds to drill oil wells three thousand meters deep!

As Karl Marx said, those who live in a palace do not think about the same things, nor in the same way, as those who live in a hut. This struggle to defend the trees and forests is above all a struggle against imperialism. Because imperialism is the arsonist setting fire to our forests and our savannas.

Excellencies, ladies and gentlemen:

We rely on these revolutionary principles of struggle so that the green of abundance, joy, and happiness may take its rightful place. We believe in the power of the revolution to stop the death of our Faso and usher in a bright future for it.

Yes, the problem posed by the trees and forests is exclusively the problem of balance and harmony between the individual, society, and nature. This fight can be waged. We must not retreat in face of the immensity of the task. We must not turn away from the suffering of others, for the spread of the desert no longer knows any borders.

We can win this struggle if we choose to be architects and not simply bees.[1] It will be the victory of consciousness over instinct. The bee and the architect, yes! If the author of these lines will allow me, I will extend this twofold analogy to a threefold one: the bee, the architect, and the revolutionary architect.

Homeland or death, we will win!

Thank you.

---

1. Sankara is referring here to François Mitterrand's book, *L'abeille et l'architecte* (The bee and the architect).

On books and reading

Interview with 'Jeune Afrique'
February 1986

Jeune Afrique, a weekly magazine published in Paris, carried this interview by Elisabeth Nicolini in its March 12, 1986, issue.

JEUNE AFRIQUE: You came to France recently to participate in the Silva conference on the trees and forests where the problem of the advancing desert was raised—a problem of great concern to your country. Have you read any books on this topic?

THOMAS SANKARA: [*smiling*] No, they're too dry.

JEUNE AFRIQUE: What was the last book you read?

SANKARA: *La gauche la plus bête du monde* [The most stupid left in the world] by Jean Dutourd. There are some amusing things in it. It's relaxing.

JEUNE AFRIQUE: That's a book on the upcoming legislative elections in France, written by a right-wing journalist. Does the election campaign in France interest you that much?

SANKARA: No. It amuses me.

JEUNE AFRIQUE: But you read political books?

SANKARA: Of course. Without giving myself away, I can nonetheless admit to being familiar with the classics of Marxism-Leninism.

JEUNE AFRIQUE: You've surely read *Capital* by Karl Marx.

SANKARA: No, not all of it. But I have read all of Lenin.

JEUNE AFRIQUE: Would you take these works with you if you were to find yourself on a desert island?

SANKARA: Certainly *State and Revolution* [by Lenin]. This is a book I take refuge in, that I reread often. Depending on whether I'm in a good or a bad mood, I interpret the words and sentences in different ways. But on an island, I would also take the Bible and the Koran.

JEUNE AFRIQUE: You find that Lenin, Jesus, and Muhammad go well together?

SANKARA: Yes. There are many references to the Bible and the Koran in my speeches. I believe these three works form the three most powerful currents of thought in our world, except perhaps for Asia.

State and Revolution provides an answer to problems that require a revolutionary solution. On the other hand, the Bible and the Koran allow us to synthesize what peoples thought in the past and what they continue to think, in time and space.

JEUNE AFRIQUE: Who, according to you, is the most revolutionary of the three?

SANKARA: That depends on the period. In modern times, it goes without saying that Lenin is the most revolutionary. But it's undeniable that Muhammad was a revolutionary who turned a society upside down. Jesus was too, but his revolution remained unfinished. He ends up being abstract, while Muhammad was able to be more materialist. We received the word of Christ as a message capable of saving us from the real misery we lived in, as a philosophy of qualitative transformation of the world.

But we were disappointed by the use to which it was put. When we had to look for something else, we found the class struggle.

JEUNE AFRIQUE: Among political writers today, are there some whose writings you appreciate more than others?

SANKARA: In general, I find them all interesting. Whether it's military books, books on tactics, or on the organization of labor. De Gaulle, for example, I've read most of his books. Mitterrand too—*L'abeille et l'architecte* [The bee and the architect]. He writes well but not just for the pleasure of writing. You understand through his writings that he wanted to become president, and he succeeded.

JEUNE AFRIQUE: You have a library, I suppose?

SANKARA: No, absolutely not. My books are in trunks. A library is dangerous, it betrays. As a matter of fact, I don't like saying what I read, either. I never make notes in a book or underline passages. Because that's where you reveal the most about yourself. It can be a true personal diary.

JEUNE AFRIQUE: Apart from official speeches, do you yourself write?

SANKARA: Yes, I have for a long time. Since 1966. I was still in high school. Every night. There was a short interruption starting in 1982. But I've taken it up again since then. I write down thoughts.

JEUNE AFRIQUE: Do you intend to publish them?

SANKARA: No, I don't think so.

JEUNE AFRIQUE: What book would you like to have written?

SANKARA: A book on organizing and building for the happiness of the peoples.

JEUNE AFRIQUE: Don't you like books as relaxation?

SANKARA: No, I don't read to pass the time nor to discover a fine narrative.

JEUNE AFRIQUE: How do you choose your books?

SANKARA: Well, first I should say that I buy them. And

it's the title more than the author that catches my eye. I don't read to discover the literary journey of a writer. I like to look ahead to new men, new situations.

JEUNE AFRIQUE: Let's talk a bit about African literature, about Burkinabè writers. Which of them has made an impression on you?

SANKARA: I don't like African novels. Any more than the films, as a matter of fact. Those I've read have disappointed me. It's always the same story: the young African goes to Paris, suffers, and when he returns he's out of touch with tradition.

JEUNE AFRIQUE: You're referring to *L'aventure ambiguë* [Ambiguous adventure] by Cheikh Hamidou Kane!

SANKARA: Yes, and I don't like this way of describing people. In African literature it's not really Blacks who are speaking. You have the impression you're dealing with Blacks who want to speak French at all costs. That bothers me. The authors should write like we speak today.

JEUNE AFRIQUE: You'd rather they speak pidgin French?

SANKARA: To a certain extent, I'd prefer that. Anyhow, the African writers I prefer are those who deal with concrete problems, even if I don't agree with their positions. I don't like those who seek to write for literary effect.

JEUNE AFRIQUE: In your office in Ouagadougou you have the complete works of Lenin in a really fine edition.

SANKARA: Yes, but I've read Lenin in a more practical edition, a little like those paperback series that I found when I went to get my supply of books in Paris at 1 Paul-Painlevé Place, at the Herbes-Sauvages bookstore.

JEUNE AFRIQUE: Are you familiar with Arabic literature?

SANKARA: Yes, I've read a few Algerian and Tunisian books. A book about Oum Kalsoum, the Egyptian singer. The author? I don't remember names. I've also read a book called *L'Autogestion en Algérie* [Self-management in Algeria] written by a member of the National Liberation Front.

JEUNE AFRIQUE: So you don't read novels?

SANKARA: No, almost never. I recently read a novel by chance, *L'Amour en vogue* [Love in fashion], a simple story. It was a book on sale. I went into a bookstore and bought it.

JEUNE AFRIQUE: No detective stories either? What about the *SAS* book by Gérard de Villiers, for example, that takes place in Ouagadougou?

SANKARA: No, I'm not interested in it. It's a similar literary genre. Apparently Gerard de Villiers came to Ouagadougou before writing the book in his SAS series. He never asked to see me.

JEUNE AFRIQUE: Would you have met with him?

SANKARA: Why not? In the spy genre, I'm reading *The Devil's Alternative* by Frederick Forsyth at the moment. It sheds a lot of light on the duplicity of the great powers.

JEUNE AFRIQUE: There's a Burkinabè author who you obviously know well and who lives in exile: Ki-Zerbo. Have you read his books?

SANKARA: Yes, his studies are very interesting. But he's still an African with a complex—he came to France, he learned, then he returned home to write so that his African brothers might recognize and see in him what wasn't seen or recognized in France. Nothing is more frustrating for an African than to reach the top without having been crowned in France. He says to himself that at home, at least, he will be recognized as one of the greats.

JEUNE AFRIQUE: What has become of him?

SANKARA: When the revolution called, he fled. I've asked him to come back twice, but he wants to hide his continual failures. He never succeeded in Burkina, neither by the electoral route nor the putschist route. That's why he left. I met with him twice before he left. We were happy he left because we sensed he was really very scared, and we didn't want him to die from that, to die on us, which would have brought us terrible accusations. Once he left, he went over to active opposition. But he can come back whenever he wants. The door is open for him.

French enables us
to communicate with
other peoples in struggle

Message to First Francophone Summit
February 17, 1986

The First Francophone Summit was held in Paris February 17–19, 1986, attended by numerous heads of state of French-speaking countries. Burkina Faso was represented by Henri Zongo, minister of economic development. The following is the message to the conference that Sankara sent, which was published in *Sidwaya.*

As a result of colonialism, we have become part of the French-speaking world, even though only 10 percent of Burkinabè speak the language. When we proclaim ourselves part of the French-speaking world, we do so with two preconditions: First, the French language is simply a means of expressing our reality. And second, like any language, French must open itself up to experiencing the sociological and historical realities of its own evolution.

Initially, for us, French was the language of the colonizer, the ultimate cultural and ideological vehicle of foreign and imperialist domination. But subsequently it was with this language that we were able to master the dialectical method of analyzing imperialism, putting us in a position to organize ourselves politically to fight and win.

Today in Burkina the Burkinabè people and their political leadership, the National Council of the Revolution, no longer use the French language as a vehicle of cultural alienation, but as a means of communication with other peoples.

Our presence at this conference is justified by the fact that from the point of view of the National Council of the Revolution, there are two French languages—the French spoken by those in metropolitan France, and the French spoken on the five continents.

In order to contribute to the enrichment of this universalized French, we intend to participate in this gathering and assess how the French language brings us closer to others. That's why I wish to thank the French authorities very sincerely for this welcome initiative.

It is through the intermediary of the French language that we, with our other African brothers, analyze our respective situations and seek to join efforts in common struggle.

It is through the intermediary of the French language that we shared the struggle of the Vietnamese people, and that we are reaching a better understanding of the cry of the Caledonian people.[1]

It is through the French language that we discover the richness of European culture, and defend the rights of our workers who have emigrated.

It is through the intermediary of the French language

---

1. In the mid-1980s, the archipelago of New Caledonia, a French colony in the South Pacific, was the scene of widespread anticolonial mobilizations by the Kanaks, its native population.

that we read the great educators of the proletariat and all those who, in a utopian or scientific manner, have put their pens at the service of the class struggle.

Finally, it is in French that we sing the *Internationale*, the hymn of the oppressed, of "the wretched of the earth."

We, for our part, interpret the universality of the French language to mean that we should use this language in conformity with our militant internationalism. We firmly believe in unity between the peoples. This unity will emerge from shared convictions, because we all suffer the same exploitation and the same oppression, no matter the social forms or how it may be dressed up over the course of time.

That is why, in our view, the French language, if it wishes to serve the ideals of 1789 more than those of the colonial expeditions, must accept other languages as expressions of the sensibilities of other peoples. In accepting other peoples, the French language must accept idioms and concepts that the realities of France have not permitted the French to get to know.

Who could, out of vanity or false pride, entangle themselves in circuitous formulations to convey in French, for example, the words *Islam* or *baraka*, when the Arabic language expresses these realities better than any other? Or the word *pianissimo*, the sweet musical expression from the other side of the Piedmont? Or the word *apartheid*—exported to France from Albion—without perfidiousness[2]—with all its Shakespearean richness.

To refuse to integrate the languages of others into French is to erect barriers of cultural chauvinism. Let us not forget that other languages have accepted terms from the French language that are untranslatable in their own. For example, English with its "fair play," adopted from

---

2. "Perfidious Albion," an epithet of French origin, refers to Britain.

French the aristocratic and bourgeois term *champagne*. The German language, in its realpolitik, squarely admits, without beating around the bush, the French word *arrangement*. Finally, Peul, Mooré, Bantu, Wolof, and many other African languages have assimilated, with suppressed anger, the oppressive and exploitative terms *impôts* [taxes], *corvée*, and *prison*.

This diversity [*diversité*] brings us together in the French-speaking family. We make it rhyme with friendship [*amitié*] and fraternity [*fraternité*].

To refuse to integrate other languages is to be unaware of the roots and history of one's own. Every language is the product of several others, today more so than in the past, because of the cultural permeability created in these modern times by the powerful means of communication. To reject other languages is to adopt a rigid attitude against progress, and that approach stems from an ideology inspired by reaction.

Burkina Faso opens itself to other peoples and counts heavily on the culture of others to grow richer. For we are convinced that we are headed toward a universal civilization that will lead us to a universal language. This is the framework for our use of French.

For the genuine progress of humanity! Forward!

Homeland or death, we will win!

The CDRs' job is to
raise consciousness, act, produce

At First National Conference of CDRs
April 4, 1986

The First National Conference of the Committees for the Defense of the Revolution (CDRs) was held in Ouagadougou from March 31 to April 4, 1986, attended by more than 1,300 delegates. This speech was published as a pamphlet by the National Secretariat of the CDRs.

After the show we've just seen, after what we've just heard, my task is easy. It's easy because I will have only a few things to say to you.

Dear comrades;

Dear invited guests:

Here we are after some hard work. Here we are after a special kind of test, the first of its kind, in the course of which the Committees for the Defense of the Revolution voluntarily and consciously agreed to take a critical look at themselves. They have been in session nonstop day and night, in the spirit of criticism and self-criticism, in order to examine the work they've done over the two and a half years of revolution in Burkina Faso. This principle is a victory in itself. Victory in the sense that only revolutions are willing to question themselves, only revolutions are willing to draw critical balance sheets of their struggle. By contrast, the forces of reaction spend their time singing their own praises and blowing their own trumpet, only to end in inevitable failure. [*Applause*]

Comrades, I first want to ask all the foreign delegations who could not be represented here to please understand and excuse this procedure. The fact that we felt that this First National Conference of the CDRs should be conducted largely in closed session, that is, exclusively among Burkinabè, does not mean that we undervalue the internationalism that binds us to other struggles. I'm convinced they will grant us their indulgence and their understanding.

Indeed, around the world messages had been prepared to be sent to us. Delegations were to be sent, too. We ask all the fraternal countries, all the sister revolutions that were understanding and refrained from sending their delegations, we ask them to transmit to their members the internationalist greetings of the Committees for the Defense of the Revolution of Burkina Faso. [*Applause*]

I would like to thank the Pioneers who were present here and who enlivened this first national conference from beginning to end. For us, the Pioneers constitute hope, the hope of tomorrow. They symbolize and represent the future within the present. But at the same time they show each of us our daily task. What these young revolutionaries become, their evolution, directly depends on how conscious we are about the way we carry out our responsibilities toward them. As revolutionaries we have no right to think that the Pioneers should be kept on the sidelines of revolutionary activity, to be included in our activity only once they reach the age of eighteen.

Wherever revolutionaries are directly concerned with the lives of these Pioneers, they should assume their responsibilities—to guide, to educate, to raise the consciousness of these young children so they grow up as revolutionaries, live as revolutionaries, and die as revolutionaries. [*Applause*]

So how could we fail to congratulate and admire these young children—the Voice of the Pioneers orchestra from Bobo-Dioulasso; the Little Singers with Raised Fists from Ouagadougou; the Little Dancers from District 27 in Ouagadougou and from District 6 in Banfora, who performed earlier.

How could we fail to be heartened! The minute we see them perform and express themselves, we know that our culture is in good hands. If only each one of us had learned both music and the mastery of our culture when we were these children's age, then Mozart would be a measly celebrity today compared with us. Alas, we grew up with flaws. [*Applause*]

I also thank the National Union of Elders of Burkina for its participation in this First National Conference of the CDRs of Burkina Faso. [*Applause*]

The National Union of Elders of Burkina Faso makes an important contribution. It is very important, on a tactical level, because we know that if we don't mobilize the elders, our enemies will mobilize them against us. [*Applause*] All the reactionaries, all the counterrevolutionaries, encourage us to leave the elders on the sidelines so they can mobilize them against us. [*Sustained applause*] Well, comrades, let's not for one moment play into the hands of the forces of reaction and counterrevolution. Let's not for one moment play the game of populism. On the contrary, let's tell ourselves that there mustn't be one human being in Burkina Faso, no matter what their age, who has not been mobilized. We need them.

I must nevertheless also say to our dear comrade elders that, while it's true that snow on the roof doesn't mean it's not warm inside, it's important to understand that even among the elders there are tortoises with double shells. [*Applause*] Among the elders are owls with shady looks in their eyes, [*Applause*] that is, a certain number of fence-sitting chameleons who think and who calculate that, as in a game of checkers, the revolution has just given them a dangerous opening that they will take advantage of to position themselves to resume their favorite sport—intrigues, plots, settling of scores, defamation, scheming, and I don't know what else!

It is first and foremost up to the elders to unmask and combat these bad elders. [*Applause*] If after crossing swords with these bad elders—who are generally tenacious because they have tough hides [*Laughter*]—the good elders haven't succeeded, they should call on the CDRs. They should let us go ahead. We will know what to do. Isn't that so, comrades, isn't that so? [*Shouts of "Yes!" and applause*] So let's be vigilant.

We also thank the Women's Union of Burkina [*Applause*] whose silence at the beginning of the First National Conference of the CDRs was particularly "deafening" and was noted.[1] [*Applause*] A mass organization, a latecomer compared with others, it is nevertheless far from marginal to our victorious march. We are relying on the UFB to mobilize all women—all our women, every woman, and all the women of the entire world. So the task is a hard one.

I congratulate the National General Secretariat of the CDRs for the important organizational work that has just

1. At the opening of the conference, the Women's Union of Burkina did not have its own delegation.

been accomplished. [*Applause*] I congratulate it all the more since it wasn't certain that we could organize such an important meeting in such a meticulous manner and on such short notice. In an impertinent lapse, our daily paper, *Sidwaya*, even dared to speak ill of the National General Secretariat of the CDRs. The General Secretariat of the CDRs will reply to this meddling by *Sidwaya* at the appropriate time. [*Applause*]

So I congratulate all the organizers, all those who came from all the provinces for this impressive demonstration, because once again we have just chalked up a victory for ourselves.

Do you recall August 4, 1984, after the celebration of the first anniversary of the popular and democratic revolution? Remember how the forces of reaction and counterrevolution, singing in unison, said that we had spent billions and billions to organize that celebration—that's how magnificent and beautiful it had been. Appalled, these gentlemen could not imagine that the resourcefulness of revolutionaries could compensate for—and even overcompensate for—the lack of resources! Since then they no longer talk about the billions spent. On the contrary, when they hear that we're organizing an event, they're panic-stricken and try to sabotage it as best they can.

The last summit conference of the heads of state of the West African Economic Community [CEAO] was a resounding success for the democratic and popular revolution.[2] [*Sustained applause*] It was a success not because it brought us a lot of resources, but because revolutionaries outdo themselves when they are attacked. And we were attacked, as you well know! [*Applause*] We even commanded the admiration of those who didn't want to come. But they came

2. This summit was held in Ouagadougou in March 1986.

despite themselves, right here to Ouagadougou. [*Applause*]

The last People's Revolutionary Court [TPR], the fif-teenth of its kind, also bestowed an international stamp on this revolutionary authority. [*Applause*] We tried and convicted international crooks![3] [*Applause*] We dared to do what many dared not do. So we have gloriously estab-lished the TPR among the forms of jurisdiction genuinely needed by the peoples of the world. We are pleased to note that in some parts of the world attempts have been made to imitate our example. [*Applause*]

Elsewhere, too, there is a desire to put on trial and con-vict, and we know that individuals can be put on trial and convicted. But the difference will always be between the truth—the whole truth that one dares to utter—and the half-truths that one is compelled to proclaim because . . . perhaps the person is himself involved, or at any rate heads a reactionary and corrupt regime. [*Applause*] Have you ever seen a cat ask for a certificate of good behavior for its son! [*Laughter, applause*] He is a thief himself. After all, we know that even cats try to look like serious people. We warn those who imitate. They follow us, they imitate us. But there remains a secret, a single secret, which allows us to overcome great obstacles. This is something they do not possess, and it will lead to their downfall. [*Applause*]

Comrades, there was a lot of talk here and there when this national CDR conference was called. It was said that

---

3. Sankara is alluding to the trial of Mohamed Diawara, Moussa Ngom, and Moussa Diakité by the People's Revolutionary Courts in April 1986. These three high-ranking administrators known throughout West Africa had stolen over 6 billion CFA francs (about US$17 million in 1986) from the West African Economic Commission. Diawara and Diakité were each sentenced to fifteen years in prison without parole; Ngom to fifteen years with the right to parole after ten years. They were also ordered to repay the stolen money.

the conference would be an opportunity to tell all. By "tell all" certain people understood that it would be an opportunity for them to settle certain accounts with certain individuals. Others also said that this national CDR conference would be a mere masquerade to give the appearance of letting the people speak, but that in reality it would prevent the truth from being aired. Even as I speak to you now, some participants at this conference think it was nothing but a masquerade because they weren't called on to speak.

There were more than 1,310 delegates and just by giving ten minutes to each delegate—do the arithmetic, math whizzes!—it would have amounted to more than ten days in a row listening to nothing but delegates' remarks. This would obviously have been impossible. So we had to go with summaries. But I must admit that the summary of the summaries occasionally distorted certain ideas. Some remarks, some points of view are no longer fully or adequately expressed in what is presented in the final analysis, in the final draft. Unfortunately, these are the normal rules of procedure in an endeavor that seeks to address the greatest number of people, and not simply limit itself to a minority.

That is why, from now on, I urge the CDR National General Secretariat to take all necessary steps so that, periodically—for example every three months—sessions are held around the country between the CDR National General Secretariat and the main representatives of the CDRs. This will allow what each person is thinking to be better heard, and will ensure that, when we're forced to summarize ideas, we don't end up distorting them despite ourselves. [*Applause*]

Some thought that this First National Conference of the CDRs had been called to definitively lay the CDRs to

rest. It's true, some people came here to present their condolences to the National General Secretariat of the CDRs.
Condolences that, as is often the case, would merely be
forms of hypocrisy, since in reality many came to celebrate
the disappearance of these famous CDRs.

Why the CDRs?

You know that, historically, nothing could be more erroneous than to say that the CDRs were created the day
after August 4, 1983. The CDRs were born with the first
bullets that were fired here. The CDRs were created precisely on August 4, 1983. [*Applause*] The CDRs were born
dialectically at the same time as the revolution in Burkina
Faso [*Applause*] because the very moment we pronounced
the word "revolution" in this country, the need to defend
it was felt. And he who speaks of revolution without taking
the necessary measures to protect that revolution commits
a serious error and misunderstands the fighting capacities,
the destructive capacities, of the forces of reaction.

As for us, we called on the people on the evening of
August 4 to organize themselves everywhere into Committees
for the Defense of the Revolution because we had no illusions—the revolution would be attacked. The revolution
was attacked, it is being attacked, and it will be attacked.
Therefore, the Committees for the Defense of the Revolution were attacked, are being attacked, and will be attacked.
[*Applause*] Not one of the positive accomplishments of the
revolution could have been carried out without the CDRs.

We know that we, the CDRs, are not perfect. We know
this, but we continue to look for examples of perfection
in this world. As the CDRs, we have been called upon
to exercise popular power. On the political level, on the
economic level, on the military level, on all levels of national life, on all levels of the lives of the Burkinabè, we,
as the CDRs, are directly involved. So it's important that

we understand that the correct functioning of the CDRs has beneficial and favorable consequences for each of us. To turn your back on the CDRs is to do harm to yourself, unless you're in a position to leave Burkina Faso. We need the CDRs and we will always need the CDRs, no matter what form they may take in the future.

In Burkina Faso we notice that when certain foreigners arrive, they think the country is divided in two. There is the normal Burkina Faso with a flag, an anthem, offices, an administration, organizational structures—that is to say, the Burkina Faso that knows the right rules, that wears white gloves, nice ties, and who knows what else! And then there's the Burkina Faso of the CDRs. Oh, those CDRs! [*Applause*] They tell us: "What a magnificent country you have! And what colossal work you have accomplished! Too bad about your CDRs." [*Applause*] But what do you want us to do with our CDRs? Put them in bottles? There are so many of them that if we put them in bottles, they'll be in all the bars! [*Applause*]

Even citizens, Burkinabè, say to us, "Ah! Comrade President, we really are very satisfied. What has been accomplished is magnificent. But couldn't you do something about the CDRs, [*Laughter*] because those children . . ." I listen with great interest to their remarks and their advice, with all the respect due to the white beard that speaks in this manner. Then I ask them: What, in fact, is the difference in age between these CDRs and myself? [*Applause*]

No, we could never agree to eliminate the CDRs. There are not two Burkina Fasos. There is one single Burkina Faso—the Burkina Faso of the CDRs. It begins with the CDRs and ends with the CDRs. [*Applause*] That is why wherever CDRs do not yet exist, they must rapidly be formed. Wherever there are Burkinabè, their first reflex must be to form a Committee for the Defense of the Revolution because they owe their existence to the revolution. And if they do not do this, they are going against the revolution and there's no reason for them to benefit from the revolution's accomplishments.

In this regard, it's important I tell you of some problems we have encountered with regard to international organizations. Claiming not to be political, the international organizations forbid and oppose the formation of CDRs in their midst. Well, we say that Burkinabè who work in international organizations must remain connected to the revolution by means of the CDRs. [*Applause*] So there must be CDRs everywhere. [*Applause*] I'll not name any of these international bodies, but they know who they are.

When we put on trial the thieves from the West African Economic Community—those bandits, those gangsters, those manipulators—if there had been a single Burkinabè from the CEAO involved, do you think the Committees for the Defense of the Revolution would have drawn up a motion to congratulate that thief? So you see, the CDRs—the inspiration behind the People's Revolutionary Courts—is a guarantee for the CEAO. Against thieves, for example! It is because we have the CDRs that we dare to go after the bad guys, the thieves. They've been making billions for a long time. [*Applause*]

Let it be said once and for all: every international organization that accepts us must likewise accept our CDRs. Of course, we will respect the rules and statutes of conduct of these international organizations. We will organize ourselves within them to the extent possible. It's not a matter of going to ask the UN secretary general for permission to hold a general assembly of the CDRs in the glass house in New York—which, by the way, wouldn't be so bad!

This First National Conference of the CDRs must contribute to greater cohesion, to greater unanimity, to greater organic unity within the CDRs. This is very important.

As a leading member of the CDRs, I cannot escape the duty of criticizing our CDRs profoundly and thoroughly. But at the same time, I don't hesitate to give them all the support and all the reinforcement they require to continue to advance. [*Sustained applause*] That's why we must have the courage to look ourselves in the face. There are bad CDR members among us! Let's make no secret of this.

You well know that at the beginning of the revolution very few people wanted to join the CDRs. But as soon as it became clear that the CDRs could be instrumental in resolving a certain number of problems, the old tricksters returned to their old ways in order to get themselves elected in the CDRs. [*Applause*]

You saw them driving around in their cars during the Battle for the Railroad.[4] They asked, "Will the television be coming?" [*Laughter, applause*] As soon as they were sure the television would come, they went there and waited, coolers and cold beer in the car. They drove around, they went back and forth in front of the cameraman, who didn't seem to understand. [*Laughter*] They ended up gesturing to the cameraman and to the crowd, "Working hard, guys! We've been here for hours! Oh, yes!" And all the journalists would end up asking them, "Your impressions?" Ahh, this was the moment they'd been waiting for! [*Applause*] "Yes, very impressed! My impressions are very good. In any event, we're standing together as one!"

The old refrains, you know them! We sang the same thing in Revolution Square, formerly January 3 Square:

---

4. On February 1, 1985, the National Council of the Revolution issued an appeal to government-employed workers to volunteer to help build a rail line linking Ouagadougou to Tambao, a Burkina mining town near the border with Mali.

"We're standing together as one." Meanwhile some were going off to the left and others to the right. [*Applause*] Ah, yes! These opportunists have understood which way the wind is blowing, the wind of power, and there they are in the CDRs. They can also be seen doing everything to get elected and to become officials.

I want to say something that may be a double-edged sword. But I'll say it anyhow because it's the truth. With regard to the Revolutionary Solidarity Fund, we often see this: "Comrade such-and-such donates one-tenth of his salary for three months and requests to remain anonymous." Well! Do you know what form this anonymity takes?

The good comrade, the valiant militant, this great militant, first goes to see the minister he is working under and tells him, "Comrade minister, I've donated a part of my salary. But I ask to remain anonymous because, personally, I prefer to be discreet." [*Applause*] He goes to the National General Secretariat of the CDRs and he repeats, "I'm contributing, but I want to remain anonymous. I want to be discreet." He goes to his sector and he says the same thing. He writes a long letter to the comrade president, to show how, ever since the historic night of August 4, he [*Laughter*] and his entire checkbook quiver just for the revolution, but he is requesting anonymity. He signs, he prints his last name, his first name, his sector number, his date of birth, the name of his wife and his children. [*Laughter*] He writes to the comrade minister of family development and requests anonymity. Now he waits. A Council of Ministers announces that the comrade is donating one-tenth of his salary for three months and has asked to remain anonymous. Meanwhile, the entire town and especially "his constituents" knows who this generous, anonymous person is. All these are ploys to get oneself elected.

Of course, no one should say that as of today it's no

longer worth sending anything to the Solidarity Fund. We must continue to contribute to this fund, as well as to the other funds that need a lot of money to help those who criticize the funds, and who nonetheless take advantage of them. [*Applause*]

Political power is used in this way for ulterior motives. There are bad elements. They must be removed. These neo-feudal elements in our ranks must be rooted out, combated, and defeated. They set themselves up as veritable despots in the local districts, in the villages, and in the provinces. They are also very dangerous. Their method of functioning is anarchistic. Reigning and holding sway like warlords, they are fascists. In the final analysis, they're anarcho-fascists. We're dealing with a new race. [*Sustained applause*]

It is also in this regard that the CDRs, particularly the service CDRs,[5] really terrorize the directors. Right now, there are service directors who can no longer even sign a dispatch note, they are so afraid of their CDR. [*Applause*] There are some service directors who call a general assembly before deciding on which paint to choose for their car, because, comrades, the people will decide. They are afraid. They are afraid because they have been terrorized. They have been truly mistreated—they have been threatened with suspension, firing, and dismissal. We must admit that there has been some settling of accounts in this regard that we must straighten out today. [*Applause*]

Or sometimes you have the case of directors who secured their posts through wheeling and dealing. They go door-to-door every night in order to become director. As a

---

5. A reference to CDRs in the workplaces, regardless of the type of work done. Members frequently belonged to a neighborhood CDR and a service CDR at the same time. But they could hold elected office in only one of the two.

result, they are at the mercy of those who appointed them.

On the political level, we have seen cowardly CDRs that do not dare to assume their responsibilities. Suspensions, for example. Such-and-such comrade is suspended for such-and-such gross misconduct. The comrade is in the street complaining, ranting and issuing threats. The very same people who proposed his suspension come and say, "Well, you know, we didn't know ourselves." [*Applause*] This kind of cowardice must be combated. Some CDRs, when they are threatened, run to the National General Secretariat of the CDRs and say, "We're under attack by a group of fascists, by populists, by counterrevolutionaries, by reactionaries." No! It is up to them to face their enemies where they are. [*Applause*]

Let's go on. We are forced to resolve problems in Ouagadougou that involve confrontations thousands of kilometers away between our CDRs and counterrevolutionaries. This indicates a poor understanding of the role of the National General Secretariat of the CDRs. There are some who do not hesitate to cross the Mediterranean, the Caspian Sea, even the Sahara, to come all the way to Ouagadougou to raise their problems. No! It's over there in Trocadero or in the Nineteenth District [of Paris] that you must fight and triumph. It's not here. The fight in [CDR] Sector 26 is not the fight of comrades who may be in Leningrad or in Bouaké [in the Ivory Coast].

On the military level, the CDRs have often been riddled with incompetent people. Competence does not boil down to taking up arms and being able to handle them well. Because if it were merely a question of dexterity, of finesse with weapons, it would be enough to go down to the Ouagadougou jail—there are many very skillful people to be found there. If it were just a question of know-how and intelligence, we could simply ask Moussa Ngom to be the CDR's economic affairs representative. Because Moussa Ngom, as you know, is very smart. His boss, [Mohamed] Diawara, could be national general secretary of the CDRs. [Moussa] Diakité could take care of social issues. [*Sustained applause*]

Now, we have had a lot of accidents. These accidents are not the result of inadequate training, because, I insist on pointing this out right away, we have not had more accidents with weapons in the CDRs than among regular troops, here in Burkina or abroad. Every year in all the armies of the world, accidents happen. They are not talked about. There are people who die, parachutists, pilots. When the French plane went down in Bangui [in the Central African Republic], how many deaths did that cause? A lot, anyway. Was that a CDR? You see, there are accidents everywhere. When the *Challenger* exploded, people died. These are accidents, they even happen to NASA. Accidents happen everywhere.

What must be condemned, rather, are the bad elements, and we have some in our ranks. We must fight them. Because in order to show off, they sport a whole arsenal of weapons, as if they needed them, as if they were Himmler's deputies. No! These are the people who must be pushed aside. They are very often the cause of accidents. "If you do that, I'll blast you." That's what must be condemned. That's the kind of person you must make it your business to punish severely from now on. So be it. The person who is not sure of himself should put down his weapons.

Militarily, we know too that during patrols, some CDRs have committed atrocities, unspeakable things. But since unspeakable is not a revolutionary concept, we must speak of everything. In fact, some CDRs took advantage of the patrol to engage in looting. Well, we will pursue them like thieves from now on and we'll shoot them down, pure and simple. Let this be clear: if we have arms, it's to defend the people. All those who steal from the people and loot will be shot down.

There have even been cases—this too should be said—where scores were settled during the curfew period. This must be condemned. There have been comrades who, because they are CDR members in charge of security, armed with a big gun—without even being sure it would fire—thought they could do anything. When curfew was to begin at 7:00 p.m., they would show up at a female comrade's house at 6:50 p.m. and start saying to their rivals, to the other suitors, "It's almost time! You have to leave! If you don't leave, you'll be locked up." Oh, yes! Some asked that the curfew be maintained permanently so they might continue to reign supreme. Well, we lifted the curfew so that we could all be on an equal footing in this regard. And those destined to fail because of their incompetence will fail.

Again with regard to military matters, we've seen CDR militants poorly dressed. Of course, the problem of uniforms is a real one. There aren't enough, it's true. But the few you have, you must take care of. These militants are badly dressed, negligent, and slovenly. No! From now on, all those in charge of the CDRs should not hesitate to immediately undress militants who show up poorly dressed. These are outward signs of an inability to organize oneself.

We have seen CDRs arrest someone, lock them up, and then say, "That's it. Those are the rules, that's justice. We'll deal with you." No! Every Burkinabè has the right to the CDR's protection. The CDR office must not be a locale of torturers but the complete opposite: an office where you find people in charge who lead, who organize, who mobilize, who educate, and who struggle as revolutionaries. But you can have occasion to educate with a firm hand. In that case you need to be clear while being firm. However, abuse of power must be considered alien to our struggle.

On the economic and social level, too, there are many militants, very many, who schedule construction work, for example, but who themselves sit on the sidelines. They make the masses work! Their own laziness stands out so clearly that the masses themselves become demoralized and demobilized. We must fight against this.

In addition, the funds entrusted to the CDRs are often managed in an anarchic, fraudulent, wasteful, and thievish fashion. This is why it's right to create structures to monitor the funds. From now on, how much is in the fund and what has been done with it must be disclosed. And this is not enough. Many people have grown rich off the backs of CDR militants by declaring themselves to be CDR militants. This is a new category of thieves.

Don't think that in the National Council of the Revolution we are unaware of these numerous shortcomings and failings that continue to undermine our CDRs. We're aware of them and we have firmly resolved to combat all these negative practices that are harmful to the revolution. That, in fact, is one of the reasons for this conference. CDR militants should everywhere and at all times set a good example. This is why, in saluting the small children who performed for us earlier, we're also saluting their coaches who made their performance possible.

But at the same time, we're pointing out that in the provinces there are those who are lagging behind. There are high commissioners acting like circle commandants and regional governors, who think they're still in the era of the Voulet-Chanoine column. Others think they're in the era of rural collectives.[6] All of this is bad. We must

---

6. Circle commandants, regional governors, and rural collectives were institutions of the French colonial administration. Paul Voulet and

denounce them and fight them. As high commissioners we should lead our provinces on every level. We should be energetic and full of initiative, supporting innovation and organizing its implementation.

If our thirty provinces organized thirty shows like the ones we've seen, that would be good! We'd be making good progress. But this is not yet the case.

At the workplace level, the CDRs still function very poorly. They function very poorly because, far from seeking to offer good quality service, far from seeking to qualitatively and quantitatively increase the production of social and economic wealth, our workers organized in Committees for the Defense of the Revolution are·instead busy pursuing honors, titles, and power. This bulimic taste for power must be combated. [*Applause*] If we continue in this way, this is how bureaucracy can take root in our workplaces and in our administration. Because for any given document, twenty-five people want to sign "seen and passed on," "seen and passed on." This adds absolutely nothing to the quality of the document, but everyone wants to be sure to add their two cents. [*Applause*] We are held up simply because the CDR militant in charge wants people in town to say, "Ah, yes, really comrade, thank you! Really, thanks to you . . . !" [*Laughter*] If you haven't thanked him and haven't been to see him to bow down, well, he delays, he holds up your document as much as he wants until you've understood that might is right.

We want nothing to do with these kinds of methods. Because bureaucratism and bureaucrats are the worst

---

Charles Chanoine were French military officers who led a colonial expedition in 1896 and 1897 with the aim of conquering the region of West Africa that is today Burkina Faso. They used extremely brutal methods to subdue the local populations.

enemies of our cause. And as such, we must fight against them in all their forms relentlessly and doggedly.

Our workplaces are dirty and badly maintained despite the revolutionary days, despite the revolutionary weeks, and soon the revolutionary months, the revolutionary years, and the revolutionary decades and centuries. We will continue to have badly organized, badly maintained workplaces as long as we don't face up to our responsibilities by denouncing what must be denounced.

I have always held up certain workplaces as examples. There are some that are very well maintained and deserve congratulations, and everyone should look to their example. I won't list them all. I don't want to make people jealous. I'll limit myself to mentioning the presidential offices. [*Applause*] This is what should be done! How can you enter a revolutionary office and find chairs that wobble, not because they weren't bought new, but because they've been used improperly? There are officials, dirty managers, badly dressed, grubby just like their own documents, [*Laughter*] lazy typists, and absent-minded telephone operators. [*Laughter*] This is not worthy of the CDRs and we must mend our ways. Quality begins with accepting the truth. Let's look at our weaknesses, let's become aware of them, and let's pledge to improve ourselves. Even better, as revolutionaries we should always distinguish ourselves.

A lot could be said against the elders who say they are mobilized within the UNAB, or that they're in the revolution now, but who forbid their children to go to CDR meetings. A lot could be said against the husbands who prevent their wives from going to CDR meetings or who terrorize them. This must also be denounced. [*Applause*]

We must now move on to a much more conscious level of organization. During the first days of the revolution our mobilization was enthusiastic, euphoric—a festival. But increasingly we must organize ourselves a lot more scientifically, a lot more methodically, and we must correct ourselves at every step in order to advance. We have examples in other places of the failures of certain organizations similar to CDRs—revolutionary committees. Wherever such failures have occurred, it's been because the forces of reaction successfully laid traps for these other organizations in some countries. We must be conscious of our weaknesses.

That's why we must struggle unceasingly. We must struggle and we must keep in mind that the Committees for the Defense of the Revolution signify courage, political courage, and above all courage in face of our responsibilities. We are not the CDRs just to shout slogans. We are the CDRs to raise consciousness, to act, to produce. This is why we should banish empty slogans—tedious, uselessly repetitive, and ultimately irritating slogans— from our demonstrations. You arrive at a demonstration, someone shouts at you twenty-five times: "Homeland or death, we will win!" It begins to be a bit much, [*Laughter*] especially when there's not even a good militant explanation along with it. It's just repetition. No! Tape-recorder CDRs, move aside! [*Applause*] We improvise slogans to fill up time. So down with "Down with thieves! Down with liars!" [*Laughter*] It's not good. We should differentiate ourselves from folkloric theater troupes.

In some shows there are crude scenes where comrades perform occasionally obscene dances. That is not revolutionary either. The revolution should have a sense of dignity. [*Applause*] We need to criticize the lack of organization in our public events. While we have scored victories in some areas, this is not the case in others. No! Some ceremonies are tedious. And, without approving of the ambassadors who are often absent from our ceremonies, I nevertheless understand why they might not want to come.

This is very important. We must put a stop to forms of praise that are expressions of inadequately suppressed, inadequately extinguished reflexes on our part. That song, for example: "O CNR, Thomas Sankara, may he forever be president!" is not good. [*Applause*] Because when you're president, you're president. Either you're president or you're not. [*Applause*] We must be clear. This song is not good. At this rate, in one year, or in two years, we'll find ourselves in some festivals with some troupes that will have practiced this a lot more and that may also have nothing else to do than this.

The Committees for the Defense of the Revolution are there to produce. Of course, if we need themes to mobilize around, if we need slogans, okay, we need slogans! If we need images and symbols of the revolution in order to understand, okay, we need them! We won't hesitate! But we must not value form over content. The revolution will not be measured by the number of slogans and by the number of tenors and basses doing the chanting. It will be measured by something else, it will be measured by the level of production. We must produce, we must produce. That's why I welcome the slogan, "Two million tons of grain."

Our country produces enough food to feed ourselves. We can even exceed our level of production. Unfortunately, due to lack of organization, we're still forced to hold out our hand to ask for food aid. Through massive production, we must do away with this food aid, which is an obstacle in our path, creating and instilling this habit in our minds, these instincts of beggars and welfare recipients. We must succeed in producing more—producing more, because it's natural that he who feeds you also imposes his will.

At the Tabaski festival,[7] at Easter, at Christmas, at family gatherings, when we slaughter the cocks, the turkeys, and the sheep, it's done, knowing that we have fed the cock, the turkey, and the sheep. They can be slaughtered whenever we want. At Christmas, at Easter, during the Pentecost, or even during Lent. We are free. He who does not feed you can demand nothing of you. Here, however, we are being fed every day, every year, and we say, "Down with imperialism!" Well, your stomach knows what's what. [*Laughter, applause*] Even though as revolutionaries we don't want to express gratitude, or at any rate, we want to do away with all forms of domination, our stomachs will make themselves heard and may well take the road to the right, the road of reaction, and of peaceful coexistence [*Applause*] with all those who oppress us by means of the grain they dump here.

Let us consume only what we control! There are those who ask, "But where is imperialism?" Look at your plates when you eat—the imported grains of rice, corn, millet—that is imperialism. Go no further. [*Applause*] So comrades, we must organize ourselves to produce here, and we can produce more than we need.

They say that the drought has caused our production to fall. The Ministry of Agriculture is there to bear witness that even during the drought, cotton production simply continued to increase. Why is this? Well, because SOFITEX[8] pays. Well, we'll change methods. Yes, we must change methods.

But production is not only limited to grain. We must

---

7. Tabaski is used in a number of West African countries to refer to the Muslim lamb festival known in Arabic-speaking countries as Eid al-Adha.

8. The Burkinabè Society of Textile Fibers.

produce in all areas—in the factories, in the offices—and I invite everyone to participate in intellectual production. The national CDR conference congratulated—and correctly so—all those who wrote, who produced something in the realm of literature and art, and in all other realms. This is production, we are revolutionaries!

I read in a telex, in an agency dispatch, that Burkina Faso was beaten by Nigeria and by Liberia in a table tennis tournament. I thought this was very good. We should be beaten again. If we are beaten now, it's the fault of those who failed to organize us in past years. On the other hand, if we are beaten in the years to come, comrades, it will be our fault. [*Sustained applause*] So we must produce, produce, and produce some more.

On the intellectual level, many positive things are said but not written down. Let's take the example of the People's Revolutionary Courts. Who can name for us a book written by a Burkinabè on the People's Revolutionary Courts, the TPRs? The little that has been written has been written by foreigners—students, university professors, and researchers. And yet the TPRs are teaching us great lessons that we would do well to write down carefully in books. Ask our broadcasting station if they still have the tape recording of the fourteenth TPR. They will tell you that the tape, the cassette, has been used to record the latest hit song of I don't know which star.

This is not right. We haven't developed the instinct of safeguarding our intellectual capital. We must produce more. After all, we hold the record in the matter of underground literature. It's in Burkina Faso, after all, that there are the most leaflets, as you well know! This proves that we know how to read and write. Mamadou and Bineta grew up a very long time ago. They're beginning to grow old.[9] [*Laughter and applause*]

Comrades, it's important that we come back on other occasions to what has not been done, to what must be done: unity, unity in our ranks! Unity, criticism, self-criticism, unity. Let's banish all maneuvering from our ranks; the insidious plots, visible and invisible, that are brewing; the directives masterminded from afar and by remote control. Fortunately, this conference has allowed us to see that unity has been strengthened. This proves that healthy elements from all over have been at work consciously and loyally to consolidate unity. This is a victory. [*Applause*]

Comrades, I congratulate you all for the efforts made. I particularly congratulate you on the efforts you made before this conference. Everything we have accomplished in Burkina Faso in the revolution has been accomplished above all thanks to the CDRs. We have built houses, schools, clinics, roads, bridges, and dams. We have carried out intellectual and artistic production. In short, we have made progress. On the economic, financial, and budgetary levels, we have made sacrifices and efforts. And each one of us has paid the price that had to be paid. I know that no one likes pay deductions. Who in this lowly world is ready to give up part of their wages except when necessity demands it?

The universe in which we evolve and the forces that surround us are not conducive to independent development such as ours. On the contrary, all possible traps will be laid to compel us to prostitute ourselves in order to achieve a semblance of development. "Rely above all

---

9. Mamadou and Bineta were characters in elementary school primers used in former French colonies in West Africa. They aged a year with each new school year.

on our own resources!" must cease to be a slogan, it must possess us. And we must know that it's a principle for us to always rely on our own resources. Sometimes this is difficult and we hear defeatist sirens here and there singing to us the praises of aid. Aid, no! Cooperation, yes! We need the cooperation of all the peoples of the entire world. But we really do not want aid that creates a welfare mentality in us. [*Applause*]

This is why we have made and are making an effort. These efforts have been opposed and distorted. There are people who said, "There, you see, with the revolution, salaries are low, purchasing power is low, there are people who only have 20 francs per month. Why? Because of the one-twelfth of the wages, because of the 12 percent, because of deductions." Come on, comrades, this is a crude insult! We cannot fall into this trap. When someone has 20 francs per month because we have withheld one-twelfth of their wages, 12 percent of their wages, what does this mean? Those who have only 20 francs per month because we deducted 12 percent will be reimbursed 100 percent of their salary. So they will have 22.40 francs at the end of the month. Mathematically, that's what it is!

Don't tell us that people's wages have disappeared because of the Popular Investment Effort [EPI] or other deductions. Wages have disappeared because of beer, kebabs, offensive luxury, and habits of consumption. [*Applause*] Those who drive around in cars bought on credit, the schemers, those who go to witch doctors to increase their money—they are the ones who no longer have their purchasing power.

But the revolution is made for us, and our efforts are meant for us all. This is why I'm telling you that we must mobilize right away for the upcoming budget meetings. We must widely inform our militants that these meetings will continue along the same lines as what has been done to date. And in particular, that the purpose of these budget meetings will be to underline the successful efforts made for the benefit of the people. This is why, starting with the next budget, there will be no more EPI. [*Applause*]

I see you're not happy that full wages are to be restored. I know. But I understand how you feel, isn't that right, comrades? [*Shouts of "Yes!"*] Sincerity has eluded you. The courage of your opinions has failed you. Well, we are restoring wages because the efforts we've made allow us to do so. We want to be frank with our people—never promise them anything we cannot give them. [*Applause*] There are countries where wage increases are promised and wages are not paid. We promised to make wage deductions. Did we make the deductions, yes or no? [*Shouts of "Yes!"*] So we kept our word! [*Applause*]

That's the difference. When we say we're going to make wage deductions, we make the deductions. And that can be verified. If there is a single person among you whose wages, by mistake, were not deducted, he should indicate this to the Budget Ministry. [*Laughter*] The National Council of the Revolution intends to channel these efforts into improving our country's development. This is possible. It can be done because of our unity, because we stand shoulder to shoulder. But after this First National Conference of the CDRs we must learn to fight our enemies without fear, without pity, without weakness, without useless sentimentality. Every time we let ourselves be moved by their tears, we are the ones who lose.

Moussa Ngom shed tears and he made other people cry. But when children died at the hospital here for lack of a mere 1,000 francs-worth of medicine with which to be treated, everyone understood that 6 billion francs equaled 6 million times that we could have bought medicine for children's care. Moussa Ngom's tears cannot move us. [*Applause*] And if there is anyone among you with a sensitive heart—pointlessly sensitive, sensitive to the impact of the bourgeoisie, of reactionary forces, of counterrevolutionary forces—they should make an effort to stand firm.

Comrades, I congratulate all those who have come from far away, in particular from abroad, from outside Burkina Faso, to participate in this conference. I wish them a safe return journey to the countries where the search for knowledge—or at any rate the search for the ability to produce more for their country, may have taken them. I would like them to communicate to their comrades over there the message from the National Council of the Revolution and the resolutions of this First National Conference of the CDRs in which they themselves have taken part.

To those who came from our provinces near or far, I wish a safe return journey. Have a safe journey home. May they return safely to their provinces to pass on the message from the National Council of the Revolution and the Committees for the Defense of the Revolution. I wish them a safe journey home, and urge them to be careful so that the accidents we've been experiencing don't recur anymore, so that these accidents don't cause us to lose militants, so that these accidents don't cause us to lose equipment.

We should take the opportunity to say that we, the Committees for the Defense of the Revolution, have maintained equipment badly up to now. We have broken vehicles, pumps, generators, typewriters, loudspeakers, microphones, and even weapons. This is not normal. From now on, better management of our equipment must be implemented as a form of respect for our people, because this material was acquired by our people, it belongs to the people. We must take care of it well. Those who damage vehicles must know that they are damaging the vehicles of the people, that they are showing contempt for and insulting the people.

I reiterate my congratulations to the National General Secretariat of the Committees for the Defense of the Revolution for the great efforts made. The National General Secretariat of the CDRs, which—despite adversity, ingratitude, and disparagement—is evolving efficiently. An efficiency that improves every day. [*Applause*]

Our First National Conference of the CDRs is drawing to a close. But at the same time, it opens the door to other national conferences, to other congresses, to a deepening of our revolution, to a radicalization of our revolution. So I encourage you right now to think hard about future battles. I encourage you, too, to genuinely engage in solid militant activity, real militant activity, conscious and consistent militant activity.

I declare the First National Conference of the CDRs of Burkina closed.

Homeland or death, we will win!

Thank you.

[*Applause and chants*]

At Nicaragua's side

Remarks greeting Daniel Ortega
August 27, 1986

President Daniel Ortega of Nicaragua headed a delegation to Burkina Faso in August 1986. At an official dinner on August 27, Sankara presented him with the Gold Star of Nahouri, the country's highest decoration. Sankara's remarks were published in the August 29, 1986, edition of *Sidwaya*.

This visit by the leader of the Nicaraguan Revolution to Burkina Faso is an honor and an event of great political significance. As you know, Nicaragua is very far from our country—both geographically and historically. And yet despite the thousands of kilometers that separate us, despite the language barrier, and despite the cultural differences, Comrade Daniel Ortega, president of the revolutionary Republic of Nicaragua, is here with us. Let us salute Comrade Ortega.

Comrade President:

Allow me first of all, on behalf of myself and the Burkinabè people, to welcome both you and the delegation accompanying you to the free African territory of Burkina Faso. It is with feelings of pride and joy that I and the Burkinabè people welcome you today.

Comrade Ortega:

To those who wonder what interests Nicaragua and Burkina might have in common, I would answer that across oceans, across seas and continents, our two countries share the same ideals of peace, justice, and freedom for the peoples of the world. We intend to join forces to safeguard and defend this ideal at a time when imperialism is arrogantly spreading its tentacles. Furthermore, a whole network of ties and interests unites us, be it as developing countries, because of our membership in the Group of 77 and the Nonaligned Movement, or as nations having chosen the path of freedom and dignity.

Comrade President:

Neither Burkina nor Nicaragua can allow themselves to accept the simplistic division of the world, a division whereby those who do not pledge allegiance to the West are working for the East. We Nonaligned countries are of the opinion that the politics of blocs are harmful to world peace. We refuse to be either backyards of the West or beachheads of the East. Though we are willing to cooperate with both, we demand the right to be different.

But let no one expect us to be indifferent spectators at a game played by the big powers, in which our most essential interests constitute the football. We too are players in international life. We have the right to choose the political and economic system most in keeping with our aspirations. And we have the duty to work for a more just and more peaceful world—even though our states possess neither large industrial cartels nor nuclear arsenals.

It is for this reason, Comrade President, that you and I, together with our peoples, have chosen to condemn colonialism, neocolonialism, apartheid, racism, Zionism, and all forms of aggression, occupation, domination, and outside interference, wherever they come from.

We condemn and fight apartheid in South Africa as we do Zionism in Palestine. We protest the aggression against Nicaragua as we protest that perpetrated against Libya and the Frontline States.[1] We denounce the invasion of Grenada as we do the occupation of Namibia. We will not cease doing so until these peoples obtain justice.

What is Nicaragua for us? To say that it is a country of the Americas is not enough. It would even amount to hiding the truth through an unforgivable oversight. First of all, Nicaragua means four centuries of the harshest colonial rule, one hundred years of infighting by rival gangs to divide the spoils, and fifty years of a bloody, greedy dictatorship. Nicaragua is the struggle against domination, exploitation, and oppression. It is the struggle against foreign control. It is the direct and open confrontation with imperialism and its local henchmen.

The men, women, and children of Nicaragua are fighting against this slavery, as they always have and always will. There are almost three million of them. Marxists, intellectuals, peasants, believers, nonbelievers, bourgeois and rich people who love their homeland—fighting against humiliation. And there are also the poor. They are all *compañeros*—combatants. They are fighting and dying for the same ideal, writing the most beautiful and noble pages in the great book of Latin American history.

Thousands of children have perished in combat. Women have fallen after being tortured and raped. Combatants have been mowed down. Priests have interrupted mass in order to repel the enemies of the people with the help

---

1. See chronology, April 15, 1986; May 19, 1986.

of their Kalashnikov, making it spit fire in the name of a progressive gospel.

Comrades, how difficult it is to be free!

Dear Nicaraguan brothers, we understand the suffering of your flesh and your soul. Yes, there are countries that luck does not smile upon. Poor Nicaragua, so far from God and so close to the United States.[2] Yes, under such conditions it is difficult to be born and live free.

But heroes die on their feet. They never say they are dying for their homeland. They simply die. And their blood fertilizes the soil of the revolution. Thus Sandino shed his blood, and the Sandinista revolution triumphed one summer day in 1979. The Sandinista National Liberation Front led the struggle of the Nicaraguan people to victory. On July 19, 1979, God passed through Nicaragua. This new dawn was hailed the world over. Including by the United States. It was not enough to be born. Nicaragua had to live. How difficult it is to live free!

Was it necessary for the Nicaraguan people's celebration to be disrupted, a shadow cast over it by so many hostilities?

With Nicaragua, an explosive situation developed in Latin America. The plots began. First there was talk of appeals to reason, then rumors of negotiations that were smothered by threats and abuse. North American public opinion was troubled and divided. The Nicaraguan regime was denounced as Marxist-Leninist, and called another Cuba. The campaign to discredit Nicaragua unfolded. It was called a dictatorship. They invented destabilization efforts against its neighbors that Nicaragua was supposed to be carrying out, claiming, to justify the hatred, that the

---

2. A paraphrase of an expression attributed to Mexican president Porfirio Díaz, whose corrupt rule helped precipitate the revolution of 1910: "Poor Mexico, so far from God and so close to the United States."

"The revolution has become our normal rhythm. Conscious mobilization of the masses is replacing euphoria."

Ouagadougou, August 4, 1985. Parade of women celebrates revolution's second anniversary.

Pat Hunt/Militant

"Burkina Faso is a construction project, one vast construction project."

❶ Revolutionary government launched "Battle for the Railroad" in early 1985, aiming to link Ouagadougou with north. Here, volunteer government employees lay track, March 1985.

John Vink/Magnum Photos

❷

Sequence: Didier Mauro/Orchidées

❷ 200 volunteers build irrigation dam near Ouahigouya, September 1984, with women carrying stones over half a mile to men working at site. Between 1983 and 1987, 32 dams were built, compared to 20 in previous 23 years. **❸** Textile mill in Koudougou, August 1985. **❹** Construction of housing complex, Ouagadougou, 1987. **❺** CDR members build housing there, 1984.

Marla Puziss/Militant

Ernest Harsch

Augusta Conchiglia/Afrique Asie

"The battle against the encroaching desert is a battle for balance between man, nature, and society. It is a political battle."

❶ April 1986. Women building terrace to prevent spread of desert in Sahel.

Margaret Manwaring/Militant (photo 2)

Charafíf El/La documentation française (photo 3)

Augusta Conchiglia/Afrique Asie (photo 4)

United Nations (photo 5)

Mobilizing to prevent deforestation and soil erosion was a central goal of the revolution. ❷ Delegates at international antiapartheid conference participating in a tree-planting ceremony at housing complex, Ouagadougou, October 1987. ❸ Traditional wood gathering. ❹ Truck displays wood saved by improved cookstoves at parade celebrating revolution's second anniversary, Ouagadougou, August 4, 1985. ❺ An example of these new ovens. Manufactured from easy-to-find materials, they use up to 40 percent less wood than traditional open-hearth ovens.

"The revolution gives birth to a new peasant—serious, aware of his responsibilities, turning to the future by arming himself with new technology."

❶ Tomato harvest, Sourou valley, 1986. Shortly after taking power, the revolutionary government mobilized people in this northern valley to channel the river, creating a dam and irrigation system.

❶

❷ Upper Volta, 1979.
A peasant cultivates millet using back-breaking short-handled hoe. ❸ Peasant rally in Pibaoré, October 1987.
❹ Agricultural cooperative near Ouahigouya, April 1986.

❸

United Nations

❹

Ernest Harsch

"Our revolution has worked to eliminate prostitution, vagrancy, forced marriages, female circumcision, and the particularly difficult conditions for women."

❶ Village woman grinds millet, May 1983.

❷ Members of
Committees for
the Defense of
the Revolution
staffing booth
at agricultural
fair promoting
improved
cookstoves,
Bobo-Dioulasso,
August 1985.
❸ Women
militia members,
Ouagadougou,
August 1985. **❹**
Germaine Pitroïpa,
Kouritenga
province high
commissioner,
reviews tank
squadron
graduates, August
4, 1985. Of thirty
province high
commissioners,
ten were women.
❺ *Sidwaya*, August
5, 1985, the day
after revolution's
second anniversary
celebration.
Front page photo
pictures women
combatants on
parade. Headline
reads "The women
were magnificent!"

Marla Puziss/Militant

Augusta Conchiglia/Afrique Asie

Courtesy Germaine Pitroïpa

SIDWAYA

QUOTIDIEN BURKINABÈ D'INFORMATION ET DE MOBILISATION DU PEUPLE

LES FEMMES ONT ÉTÉ MAGNIFIQUES !

POUR UN BURKINA VERT

"Imperialism is a monster with claws, horns, and fangs. It bites, it is poisonous, and shows no mercy. It is determined, it has no conscience, it has no heart."

1

Tony Savino

DEBT

Nuez

Françoise de Mulder/Corbis

❶ France intervened repeatedly in Chad to back proimperialist regime. Here French troops from Biltine base located in capital, N'Djamena, September 1984. ❷ Children near lake of sewage, Cité Soleil slum in Port-au-Prince, Haiti, 1988. ❸ Cuban cartoon from 1985 depicts onerous weight and explosiveness of foreign debt imposed on Third World by imperialist banks. Sankara championed Cuban president Fidel Castro's call for a cancellation of the debt and a moratorium on all interest payments. ❹ Iraqi tanks cross bridge into Iran, October 1980. In collusion with Washington and Paris, Saddam Hussein's regime invaded Iran, aiming to seize oilfields and push back 1979 revolution.

"We protest the aggression against Nicaragua as we denounce the invasion of Grenada."

Barricada

1

❶ Managua, Nicaragua, November 8, 1986. Sankara addresses crowd of 200,000 on behalf of international delegations to 25th anniversary of Sandinista National Liberation Front, and 10th anniversary of death in combat of its founder, Carlos Fonseca.

In July 1979, popular uprising overthrew U.S.-backed dictatorship in Nicaragua and brought to power workers and peasants government. ❷ Rally supporting agrarian reform, December 1983. ❸ Nicaraguan president Daniel Ortega with Sankara during visit to Burkina, Ouagadougou, August 1986. Scoreboard says, "A people, however small, can conquer the most powerful imperialism in the world." ❹ Maurice Bishop, prime minister of workers and farmers government in Grenada, 1979–83. Washington invaded Grenada in wake of counterrevolutionary coup in October 1983.

Prensa Latina

Michael Baumann/Militant

Barricada

> "Our foreign policy is one of solidarity with the African peoples confronting apartheid, support to national liberation movements, and anti-imperialist unity."

❶ Middleburg, South Africa, March 1986. Demonstration against apartheid regime demanding freedom for political prisoners.
❷ Logo of antiapartheid conference in Ouagadougou in October 1987. Poster reads: "Apartheid is a crime against humanity! To condemn it is good, to overthrow it is best!" ❸ Mark Shope, African National Congres (ANC) leader, and Sankara at conference.

❹ Rally in Burkina Faso in solidarity with struggle in Namibia against South African colonial rule, mid-1980s. ❺ Cuban combatants in Angola, May 1991. From 1975 to 1991, more than 375,000 Cuban volunteers helped defeat U.S.-backed South African invasion of Angola. That victory forced apartheid regime to withdraw troops from Angola, recognize Namibian independence, and free ANC leader Nelson Mandela.

"The Burkinabè Revolution is at the disposal of the people of Africa. Only revolution will allow them to free themselves from neocolonial and imperialist domination."

Rally in Orodara during revolution.

country was being manipulated from the outside.

So the Somozaists and their guards woke up—over there they're called *las bestias, los perros,* that is, beasts and dogs. They were greatly aided with dollars. Sister and neighboring countries sheltered them, trained them, and equipped them. The counterrevolution was institutionalized. And there you have the *contras*—a new race of carnivores of terror.

And then, from time to time there was a lull. There were hopes it would last. But the fire continued to smolder, then flared up anew.

To live free, simply to hope for a better future—not easy when you're Nicaraguan. This is why the Burkinabè people sing this poem with you—a poem born not of poetic inspiration but of their revolutionary commitment to say what they think.

The imperialists are on the prowl

From the depths of fiery earth,
Arise the protests of a determined people.
For each day is a day of struggle,
Of combat proclaiming the enemy's downfall.

But the price to pay is heavy—
What rivers of blood are spilled daily.
Mothers have mourned their children dead at the front.
Children have buried their fathers as best they could.

In this darkness wrought by the *contras,*
Babies have lost their bottles.
They have grasped the Kalashnikov instead,
And have found themselves grown up.

White bridal veils have been stained with blood,
Wherein patriotic priests have recognized a sign of
the times.

How hard it is to live free and be Nicaraguan.
How sweet it is to die for one's fellow man.

Nicaragua will triumph. Already the people know
how to read.
They write, and fend for themselves, cultivate their
fields, and rediscover how to smile.

The revolution will triumph.
As for the *contras, no pasarán*![3]
Your land, our land, will know true bounty
Thanks to our genius.

Next to Nicaragua, Burkina will stand.
For the revolution is invincible and the people will
reign.
And so from the depths of the calm and fragrant
earth
Will rise the fraternal clamor of a perfect symphony.

It is for all these reasons, comrades, that I have the honor
and the pleasure of presenting you, in the name of the
Burkinabè people, with a symbol of their pride in you.
Free homeland or death!
Homeland or death, we will win!

----

3. "They shall not pass!" a slogan of the Republican government
during the Spanish Civil War (1936–39) adopted by the Nicaraguan
government during the revolution's war against the U.S.-organized
contra army.

What is the Nonaligned Movement doing?

At Nonaligned Summit, Harare
September 3, 1986

The Eighth Summit Conference of the Movement of Nonaligned Countries was held in Harare, Zimbabwe, September 1–7, 1986. Sankara's address was published in the September 12, 1986, issue of *Carrefour africain*.

As a result of being in Harare, our Eighth Conference must live up to the expectations of the liberation movements. That is why this summit conference must take place under the pressing theme of the close relationship between Nonalignment and the concrete demands of liberation struggles, especially with regard to alliances and support.

The experience of the struggles of peoples throughout the world demonstrates every day that we can and must be nonaligned, even if by necessity we have received heavy backing in struggle from powerful countries and states. To succeed in this, you must be armed with an ideology guaranteeing the correct leadership of the struggle with a consistent and fundamentally accurate political line. The three dimensions of this freedom struggle are: the anti-colonial dimension, the anti-imperialist dimension, and the class-struggle dimension.

Those who won their independence were successful thanks to the anticolonial struggle. This independence only became real when they understood that other battles against neocolonialism and imperialism would have to ensue.

We believe the world is divided into two antagonistic camps: the camp of the exploiters and the camp of the exploited. In principle, every national liberation struggle is part of the camp of the exploited, is in the interest of the peoples of the world. An automatic alliance is naturally established between all countries and governments in the people's camp. But this is not sufficient to protect countries from new bondage. We must be able to see further and keep up a permanent struggle. We can receive help without becoming subjugated. We can forge alliances and remain independent and nonaligned. We can proclaim ourselves part of the same school of thought as others while preserving our autonomy. Such is our deep conviction.

Comrade President;

Excellencies;

Comrades;

Ladies and gentlemen:

I would like to salute the memory of Mrs. Indira Gandhi, who gave me an exceptional opportunity to speak about my conception of Nonalignment and, above all, to receive valuable advice from her. Today, I miss her.

Being among the youngest here in age and seniority, I feel duty-bound to explain to you the feelings of a youth of this world, a Third World youth, an African youth, a youth of Burkina Faso. I would like to describe the thoughts of all those like me, who heard about the Nonaligned Movement in their childhood; who, in their adolescence, proclaimed fanatically that the Nonaligned Movement is a force against colonialism, neocolonialism, imperialism, and racism. And that the Nonaligned Movement is a force that roars and will, like a volcano, soon set the earth on fire to create a new international order.

It is now 1986 and my eighteenth birthday was a long time ago. My country's history has placed me among the leaders of the Nonaligned Movement. Nonalignment is already twenty-five years old. Today, a feeling more of disappointment, of failure, and of frustration has taken the place of certainty, of the enthusiastic promise of victory, and of hopeful satisfaction. Perhaps this is called reality and realism. If so, how sad realism is! In that case, I prefer the dream! For this dream made possible the wildest acts of daring of that time. And it was this wildness that enabled men to stand up against the barbarity of colonialism, trust in their victory, and, indeed, emerge victorious.

Of course, not all anticolonial victories were won after the formation of the Nonaligned Movement. Many obtained their independence—in whatever form—well before the birth of the Nonaligned Movement. But fundamentally the philosophy of the struggles that took many forms and led to independence was nothing other than the application of the general principles of the Nonaligned Movement.

The dream that animated the Nonaligned Movement was the morally just and scientifically logical undertaking that gave birth to our economic projects: the United Nations Conference on Trade and Development, the New International Economic Order. And even though these contacts were congenitally limited by certain reformist characteristics, it was true nevertheless that the utopia of some, combined with the great pragmatic caution of others, produced beneficial results. The combination of these two currents resulted in a force capable of giving impetus to an order where economic relations would cease to be invariably unfavorable to our peoples.

The bold dream we prefer is that seething antiracist, antiapartheid, anti-Zionist fervor that led us to believe at one time that the death knell had sounded for the ethno-fascism that relegated our brothers in the diaspora to the status of beasts of burden on every continent. This same ethno-fascism that established the most iniquitous denial of justice in the Middle East, to the misfortune of the Palestinian people. This same ethno-fascism which, not far from here preserves the Nazism of our time, with Pieter Botha and his superstructure in the role of Hitler; and, in the role of non-Aryans, the Blacks—them again!

The Nonaligned Movement signifies this awakening and this refusal to be the grass that fighting elephants trample with impunity. It is the force that must be respected and must be reckoned with. The Nonaligned Movement is dignity reclaimed.

But today we find ourselves wanting to shout out: "Tito, Nehru, Nasser, Kwame Nkrumah, wake up! The Nonaligned Movement is dying!" We would like to call to them with all the strength of our lungs and faith: "Help! Namibia is still occupied, the Palestinian people are still searching for a home, the foreign debt torments us." Who would dare deny it?

Can't we see that the Palestinians are increasingly dispersed, and that they are now being attacked and bombed even in the sovereign states that were ready to welcome them thousands of miles away from the high risk zones around their territory?[1] The Nonaligned Movement has

---

1. On October 1, 1985, the Israeli air force bombed the Palestine Liberation Organization headquarters in Tunis, Tunisia, killing some

not yet restored the rights of the Palestinians. The PLO's admission to the Nonaligned Movement no longer has the same soothing effect for these brothers, who have been wandering for decades and who can tell us only where they spent the last night, never where they will spend the next! And this has been going on for a long time. They too expect definitive protection from the Nonaligned Movement.

In South Africa, in Namibia, Blacks continue to be treated as slaves in reservations. An expression used the world over says there's no place like home. For our brothers in South Africa, this is false. Blacks are not at home in their country. It is the only homeland in the world that also serves as a collective prison. If you are born Black, you must flee South Africa in order to breathe the air of freedom. They too had faith in the Nonaligned Movement. The Nonaligned Movement's support, along with that of others, spurred them on. They came out of their townships and confronted the racists. Alas, they are dying in ever-greater numbers. After the clubs and police dogs of the whites, came the tear gas and exploding bullets of guns that have become the basic tools of racist repression.[2] So where is the Nonaligned Movement? What is the Nonaligned Movement doing?

We are in Harare, just an hour's flight from Pieter Botha's bunker, the headquarters of Nazism. We're not very far from the townships where mothers bury their children, mowed down by the bullets of whites, and where coffins are lowered into the ground every day because of the

---

sixty people. Tunis is over 1,500 miles (approximately 2,300 kilometers) from the borders of Israel.

2. South Africa's Black townships at the time were in the midst of a rebellion that had began at the end of 1984. Attempting to crush it, the army of the apartheid state killed hundreds of youth and workers.

repression. Yes, outside the walls of this august and reassuring conference hall, death is the fate of all those who are not white. Moral suffering is the lot of all those who, without being Black, hold ideals opposed to categorizing men according to the color of their skin. Yes, in leaving here, just a few steps away, we find a world where death is the supreme deliverance, the only remaining road to freedom.

And what are we doing? Will we continue to whip up our Black brothers in South Africa with fiery speeches and deceive them as to our determination, thus rashly throwing them up against the racist hordes? Knowing full well that we have done nothing to create a relationship of forces favorable to Blacks? Are we not criminal to exacerbate struggles in which we do not participate?

And what about our duty toward the Frontline States—the living rampart that protects us from the wild beasts of South Africa? Have we done our duty as Nonaligned members? This country [Zimbabwe] has been bombed and other Frontline States are also regularly subjected to military and economic attack, either directly or indirectly by bandits acting as intermediaries. What is the Nonaligned Movement doing?

By meeting in Harare we are, of course, expressing our solidarity with all those struggling in South Africa and in the Frontline States. Let's not forget that we are hereby enraging the racists who will focus their vindictive anger on those whom we will soon abandon. What will we do? Send messages of support, of compassion, of condemnation? No! That will not return to their mothers the children who have been killed. That will not restore the country's sabotaged economy.

What will we do if, as soon as we leave and because of our very menacing speeches, Pieter Botha sends his bombers against Zimbabwe, a country guilty of impertinence by hosting such a unanimously antiapartheid summit? It's useless to congratulate and praise Robert Mugabe. It's more important to protect him and all the others of the Frontline.

The Nonaligned Movement is also the struggle for our development. Today our economies are battered by the terrible problem of indebtedness. On this question, threatened daily by our creditors, we have looked to the Nonaligned Movement in vain. So each one of us has tried to ease his plight in his own way. Some talk about paying back the debt but ask for a moratorium. Others figure they'll declare their moratorium unilaterally. Still others figure that the debt is not to be repaid. In fact, we're all making repayments in whatever way the capitalists wish, because we're disunited.

But we must be able to say no. Because paying back the debt is not a moral choice based on supposed respect for obligations incurred. It's a concrete question to be resolved concretely. Objectively, we cannot continue to repay it. Elementary arithmetic demonstrates this. So let's stop paying individually for our docility. Let's stop negotiating with our creditors by betraying our brothers, in the secret hope of receiving a bonus or two for this. These favors are rewards for indignity, shame, and betrayal. On the moral level, as far as logic is concerned, they express our meager understanding of economic questions. They are futile sacrifices. We must resist together, collectively. What is the Nonaligned Movement doing?

All these questions should lead us to ask ourselves what strength the Nonaligned Movement has today, now that the Titos, Nehrus, Nassers, and Kwame Nkrumahs are gone.

I won't make the list any longer by citing the fratricidal conflicts between member states of the Nonaligned

Movement that we still have not been able to resolve; the punitive expeditions against Grenada, Libya, and the Frontline States; the drought that is ruining the weak economies of some among us; the migrating locusts that lead us to wonder which is preferable—drought without locusts or rain with locusts. Then there are the cyclones every year that inevitably devastate the coastal regions of some countries present here.

For all this, we are tempted to call on the founding fathers for help. Yet that is not a solution. First, because I want to drop messianism. Yes, there is neither a prophet nor a messiah to wait for. This must be faced. Secondly, because I have faith that the historical laws of humanity's development produce contradictions that themselves generate radical solutions. This is why, while not hiding the disappointment I spoke of earlier, I am pleased to note the confidence in the struggle that an accurate assessment of the situation generates.

Yes, the Nonaligned Movement faces increasing difficulties. Our united front has been cracked. Our combativity has ebbed. No one fears our movement anymore. But while ridding ourselves of the enthusiasm, romanticism, and lyricism of the founding fathers—attitudes that were understandable given the reality of the time—we must give our movement a new boost.

Comrade President;
Excellencies;
Ladies and gentlemen;
Comrades:

Burkina Faso is a small, landlocked country in West Africa. A member of the Nonaligned Movement, Burkina maintains its membership because it is in our interests to do so, and because the principles of the movement conform to our revolutionary beliefs. My country, Burkina

Faso, has come to Harare to seek solutions to the problems of security, of peace, of good neighborliness, of economic cooperation, of foreign debt, and, finally, in the hope of escaping from the humiliation of small countries at the hands of large ones that are contemptuous of the wisdom of nations refusing to accept that might is right. Can the Nonaligned Movement help me on this today, or must we wait another twenty-five years?

Burkina Faso is a country that refuses to continue to be classified among the poorest of the poor. One of the obstacles to my country's development is this famous question of the foreign debt. My country knows that this debt was contracted on the advice of—was imposed by means of an infernal trap by—those who today exhibit such intransigence and cynicism toward us, which only their pocketbooks understand. Burkina Faso knows that the foreign debt is a vicious circle they want to lock us into—to go into debt to pay one's debt, and go into debt even further. Yet Burkina Faso wants to put an end to this situation. The country knows, however, that alone it can do nothing or practically nothing. It needs at least fifteen other countries in order to resist together and win.

The Nonaligned Movement has more than one hundred members. When the poor mobilize, as OPEC did, they will impose their law on the rich. You can be sure that this will simply be the law of justice. The world economy will then be reorganized. We have been speaking of a New International Economic Order for twenty-five years. Are we to go through another twenty-five years of vain pleading?

Disarmament, peace, and development are closely interrelated concepts for the Nonaligned. One cannot sincerely want one without fighting for the others.

An end to famine, ignorance, and disease is a prerequisite for development. We therefore hope that International

Literacy Day, celebrated on September 8 every year, will be an occasion for profound reflection by all sincere members of the Movement. Illiteracy must figure among the ills to be eliminated as soon as possible from the face of our planet in order to foster better days for our peoples. This is why UNESCO's action is and will remain irreplaceable.

The objective weaknesses of the Movement explain why we are incapable of sticking to our principles. They trigger our instability, which is linked to the current international relationship of forces and to real pressures from imperialist powers that determine the positions of theoretically independent Nonaligned states. These same weaknesses make the choice of host country for the Ninth Summit a nightmare for those who reject Nonalignment and who fall in behind the powers mining the territorial waters of others, bombing cities, invading territories that don't belong to them, imposing certain governments and overthrowing others, and financing movements they create, organize, and train simply because they are the strongest.

Burkina Faso could have been a candidate to host our Ninth Summit. It's not concern for the lack of reception facilities that holds us back. It's not the unwritten rule of alternating continents that preoccupies us. It's simply because we believe there is another people that has suffered more than we have, and is therefore more deserving than we are to host the summit. Nicaragua, more than any other country today, knows the price of Nonalignment. It pays daily in blood and sweat for its courageous choices.

If it's possible for the Nonaligned Conference to help pave the way to victory for the country that hosts it, then we will undoubtedly go to Managua in order to support Nicaragua, to bring aid and comfort to its struggle, and allow it once and for all to guarantee peaceful agricultural labor to its farmers; a walk to school by its children without dread of counterrevolutionary attacks; and peaceful nights to all its inhabitants.[3]

The Nonaligned Movement must survive and win. Thousands of men and women are investing their hopes in it. Yesterday, generations of Third World youth watched the birth of the Nonaligned Movement with euphoria and passion. Disappointment came only later. Let us see to it that future generations who know less about our Movement discover it through the victories it accumulates.

Homeland or death, we will win!

Thank you.

---

3. The Ninth Summit of the Movement of Nonaligned Countries in 1989 took place in Belgrade, Yugoslavia.

A death that must enlighten
and strengthen us

Speech on death of Samora Machel
October 1986

Samora Machel, president of Mozambique and leader of Frelimo (Mozambique Liberation Front), was killed on October 19, 1986, when his plane crashed in South Africa. Many supporters of the African freedom struggle expressed suspicion that the apartheid regime was responsible for the crash. The following speech given in Ouagadougou was published in the October 31, 1986, issue of *Carrefour africain*.

Comrade militants:

Our task today is not to weep, but to adopt a revolutionary attitude as we face the tragic situation caused by Samora Machel's disappearance. To avoid falling into sentimentalism, we must not weep. With sentimentalism one cannot understand death. Sentimentalism belongs to the messianic vision of the world, which, since it expects a single man to transform the universe, inspires lamentation, discouragement, and despondency as soon as this man disappears.

Another reason we should not weep is to avoid being

Sankara with Mozambique's President Samora Machel, Maputo, Mozambique, June 28, 1984.

confused with all the hypocrites here and elsewhere—those crocodiles, those dogs—who make believe that Samora Machel's death saddens them. We know very well who is saddened and who is delighted by the disappearance of this fighter. We do not want to join in the competition among cynics who decree here and there this-and-that many days of mourning, each one trying to establish and advertise his distress with tears that we revolutionaries should recognize for what they are.

Samora Machel is dead. This death must serve to enlighten and strengthen us as revolutionaries, because the enemies of our revolution, the enemies of the peoples of the world, have once again revealed one of their tactics, one of their traps. We have discovered that the enemy knows how to strike down combatants even when they're in the air. We know that the enemy can take advantage of a moment's inattention on our part to commit its odious crimes.

Let us draw the lessons from this direct and barbaric aggression, together with the brothers of Mozambique. Its only purpose is to disorganize the political leadership of Frelimo and definitively jeopardize the Mozambican people's struggle, thus putting an end to the hopes of an entire people—of more than one people, of all peoples.

We say to imperialism and to all our enemies that every time they carry out such actions, it will be yet another lesson we have learned. Certainly these are not free lessons, but they're ones we deserve all the more. Yesterday, when Eduardo Mondlane was killed in cowardly, barbaric, and treacherous fashion by the enemies of the peoples of the world, the enemies of freedom for the people, they thought they had done well, that they had been successful.[1] They

1. Eduardo Mondlane, founder of Frelimo, was assassinated by agents of Portuguese colonialism in 1969. He was succeeded by Samora Machel.

hoped that in this way the flag of liberation would fall in the mud and that the people would take fright and give up the fight forever.

But they did not reckon with the people's determination, with their desire for freedom. They did not reckon with the special force men have within them that makes them say no despite the bullets and the traps. They did not reckon with the fearless combatants of Frelimo.

These were the conditions in which Samora Machel dared to pick up the flag carried by Eduardo Mondlane, whose memory is still with us. Machel immediately established himself as a leader, a force, a star that guides and lights the way. He knew how to put his internationalism at the service of others. He fought not only in Mozambique, but elsewhere too, and for others.

Let's ask ourselves a question today: who killed Samora Machel? We're told that investigations are being conducted, and experts are meeting to determine the cause of Machel's death. With the help of imperialist radio stations, South Africa is already trying to peddle the theory of an accident. They would have us believe that lightning struck the plane. They would have us believe that pilot error led the plane where it should not have gone.

Without being pilots or aeronautical experts, there is one question we can logically ask ourselves: How could a plane flying at such a high altitude suddenly graze the trees and flip over, that is, come within 200 meters of the ground?

We're told that the number of survivors is proof this was an accident and not an assassination. But comrades, how can a plane's passengers—awakened brutally by the impact—say how and why their plane flipped over and crashed?

In our opinion, this event is purely and simply the

continuation of the racist policies of South African whites. It is another manifestation of imperialism. To discover who killed Samora Machel, let us ask ourselves who is rejoicing, and who has an interest in having Machel killed. We find, side by side and hand in hand, first the racist whites of South Africa, whom we have never stopped denouncing. At their side we find those puppets, the armed bandits of the MNR, the so-called National Resistance Movement.[2] Resistance to what? To the liberation of the Mozambican people, to the march to freedom of the Mozambican people and others, and to the internationalist aid that Mozambique provided, via Frelimo, to other peoples.

We also find the Jonas Savimbis. He is planning to go to Europe. We protested against this. We told the Europeans, in particular France, that if they were to issue an entry visa in order to fight terrorism, if they're looking for terrorists, they've found one: Jonas Savimbi. By their side we find the African traitors who allow arms for use against the peoples of Africa to pass through their countries. We also find those people who cry "peace" here and there, yet who deploy their knowledge and energies every day to help and support traitors to the African cause.

These are the ones who assassinated Samora Machel. Alas, we Africans also delivered Samora Machel to his enemies by not providing him with the necessary support. When Mozambique answered the call by the Organization of African Unity (OAU) and completely severed relations with South Africa, who in the OAU supported it? Yet Mozambique—economically tied to South Africa—was

---

2. A reference to the Mozambican National Resistance, or Renamo. This was an organization closely tied to the South African apartheid regime, which was waging a terrorist war against Mozambique's government and people that killed thousands.

experiencing enormous difficulties. The Mozambicans fought against and resisted South Africa alone. This is why we Africans within the OAU bear a heavy responsibility for Samora Machel's disappearance.

Today's speeches will never count for anything if we don't try to be more consistent with our resolutions in the future. Burkina Faso put forward the same position in Harare [at the Eighth Summit of the Movement of Nonaligned Countries]. It's not enough to applaud Robert Mugabe, and put him forward as the Nonaligned Movement's worthy son if, a few hours after our departure, South Africa starts bombing Zimbabwe, and each of us stays snugly at home in his capital, doing nothing more than sending messages of support. Some states applauded us. Others thought we were going too far. But history has proven us right. Shortly after the Nonaligned Summit, South Africa did its dirty deed. And here we are, simply issuing verbal condemnations.

It is imperialism that organizes and orchestrates all these misfortunes. That's who armed and trained the racists. That's who sold them the radar equipment and the fighter planes to track and bring down Samora Machel's plane. That's also who placed their puppets in Africa to communicate the information as to the plane's takeoff time, and when it would pass over their territory. That's who is now trying to take advantage of the situation, and that's who is already trying to figure out who will succeed Samora Machel. That's also who is trying to divide the Mozambican combatants by categorizing them as moderates or extremists.

Samora Machel was a great friend of our revolution, a great backer of our revolution. He said so everywhere and demonstrated it in his attitude toward Burkinabè delegations. We made contact with him for the first time through his writings on revolution. We read and studied Machel's works and we were intellectually close to him. The second time we met him was in New Delhi at the [1983] Nonaligned summit. He told us he was following the situation in our country, but was worried by imperialism's desire to dominate.

After that, we met him twice in Addis Ababa. We had discussions together. We admired this man who never bowed his head, not even after the Nkomati Accords, the tactical character of which he understood—and that certain opportunist elements tried to use against him, making him out to be a coward.[3] The Burkinabè delegation took the floor to say that those who were attacking Mozambique had no right to speak as long as they had not taken up arms to go fight in South Africa.

We supported him a great deal, but he too supported us. At the last OAU summit, when Burkina's position was under attack by certain states, Machel took the floor and said, "If they didn't have the gratitude and courage to applaud Burkina Faso, they should at least have some shame and keep quiet."

We met up with him again in his homeland in Maputo. He helped us a lot to understand the extremely difficult internal and external situation in which he found himself. Everyone knows the role Samora Machel played among the Frontline States.

Finally, we met him again at the last Nonaligned summit in Harare where we had numerous exchanges. Samora Machel knew he was being targeted by imperialism. He also made a commitment to visit Burkina Faso in 1987. We agreed to exchange delegations from our CDRs, from the army, from our ministries, and so on.

---

3. See note on page 134.

We must learn from all this. We must stand firm, hand in hand with other revolutionaries, because there are other plots lying in wait for us, other crimes in preparation.

Comrades, we are taking this medal, this distinction of honor, to Mozambique to confer on Samora Machel, and I would ask you all to send your thoughts with it. We will send him the highest distinction of Burkina Faso, of our revolution, because we think that his work contributed and contributes to the progress of our revolution. He therefore deserves the award of the Gold Star of Nahouri.

At the same time, I ask you to name streets, buildings, and so on, after Samora Machel over the whole expanse of our territories, because he deserves it. Posterity must remember this man and all that he did for his people and for other peoples. We will thus shape his memory in our country, so that other men remember him forever.

Comrades, we are gathered here today to think about the loss of Samora Machel. Tomorrow we must go forward, we must win.

Homeland or death, we will win!

We must make
Nicaragua's struggle known
throughout the world

At mass rally in Managua
November 8, 1986

Sankara delivered this speech on behalf of 180 foreign delegations invited to Nicaragua by the Sandinista National Liberation
Front, to participate in events marking the twenty-fifth anniversary of its founding and the tenth anniversary of the death in
combat of FSLN founder Carlos Fonseca. The speech was given
to a crowd of 200,000 people in Managua. It appeared in English in the November 28, 1986, issue of the *Militant*.

Comrade members of the leadership of the Sandinista National Liberation Front;
Comrade members of foreign delegations;
Comrade militants:
    First of all, I would like to thank you for the warm wel-
come we have received here in Managua. I also want to
express the pride we feel in speaking on behalf of all the
foreign delegations.
    We have come from far away, from very far away—in
some cases thousands of miles away. What, you may ask,

unites us with Nicaraguans, whose skin color is so different from ours? What, you may ask, unites us with Nicaraguans, who are geographically so far away from us? We are united by the struggle for the people's freedom and well-being. We are united by the desire to seek justice for our people. We are united because we stand together against imperialism and the enemies of the people.

All the delegations present here understand the importance of the Nicaraguan people's struggle. Throughout the world we salute your struggle. Throughout the world we support your struggle. Your struggle is a just one. It is a just one because it is anti-imperialist. It is a just one because it is against the oppressors and the enemies of the people. Your struggle is just because it is against the bandits. Your struggle is just because it joins with the struggles of all the peoples of the world.

The Palestinian people fight for their freedom and well-being. The Namibian people fight for their independence. Many other peoples around the world are fighting for their freedom. In Africa we are directly confronting colonialism, neocolonialism, and imperialism. The fascists, the Nazis who exist in South Africa, created apartheid against Blacks. The struggle against apartheid is not only the struggle of Blacks. Rather, it is the struggle of all peoples who want to live free and united. This struggle belongs to all the peoples of the world, and we Africans call on everyone to participate.

The peoples of the world and the leaders who do not participate in the struggle against apartheid are ungrateful, traitorous leaders. They are traitorous and ungrateful because they forget that yesterday Africans shed their blood fighting Nazism for the peoples of Europe and elsewhere. Today, blood must be shed against apartheid and for the well-being of other peoples.

Comrades, I would like to ask you to observe a minute of silence in remembrance of Samora Machel, that great fighter for African freedom. [*Twenty second pause*] Thank you.

We say that throughout the world each one of us must support the struggle of the Nicaraguan people. We must support Nicaragua because if Nicaragua were to be crushed, it would mar the happiness of other peoples all over the world.

This is why we must fight to support Nicaragua politically and diplomatically. We must also support Nicaragua economically. We must make Nicaragua's struggle known throughout the world. And here we want to congratulate all those throughout the world who support Nicaragua wholeheartedly, whether they be the countries of the Contadora Group or the countries of the Contadora Support Group, whether they be parties and organizations, or international organizations that have agreed to recognize Nicaragua's just cause. They all deserve to be congratulated, because imperialism has maneuvered in many and varied ways to stop them from supporting the Nicaraguans.

Nicaraguan comrades:

Today we celebrate together the twenty-fifth anniversary of the Sandinista Front. Today we also salute the memory of Carlos Fonseca. The only way and the best way for each of you to honor the memory of Carlos Fonseca is to see to it that every square inch becomes a square inch of freedom and dignity.

The *contras* must be crushed. The *contras* are vultures that must be crushed. The *contras* are jackals that do not deserve respect. The *contras* are people who have sold their hearts to obtain money from imperialism. But you, you must resist the bombers, the mining of your ports, and the economic blockade. Each Nicaraguan has the duty to firmly repel imperialism's puppets and marionettes, which is what the *contras* are.

We simply want to thank you on behalf of revolutionary Burkina Faso. We want to thank you on behalf of all the progressive and revolutionary countries that are here. Likewise, we want to thank you on behalf of all the fraternal parties that are here.

Together with you, we say: Down with imperialism! Down with colonialism! Down with neocolonialism! Down with the exploiters of the people! Down with the enemies of Nicaragua!

Long live the Sandinista National Liberation Front!

Eternal glory to the land of Carlos Fonseca!

Eternal glory to the revolutionary friendship between the peoples!

No pasarán!

No pasarán!

No pasarán!

Muchas gracias.

Against those who exploit and oppress us—here and in France

At official reception for François Mitterrand
November 17, 1986

Sankara presented these remarks at an official reception for François Mitterrand during a one-day stopover by the French president as part of a tour of Africa.

Allow me to address our illustrious guest, Mr. François Mitterrand, and his wife, Mrs. Danielle Mitterrand.
Mr. President:

When you came through here a few years go, this country was called Upper Volta. Since then many things have changed and we have proclaimed ourselves Burkina Faso. That's an entire program, which includes a code of honor and of hospitality. That is the reason we have come out to welcome you here in Burkina Faso upon the occasion of your brief stopover in Ouagadougou.

Cursed is the person at whose door no one ever knocks and whose home no hungry and thirsty traveler ever visits or enters. To the contrary—and this is our case—the traveler has stopped at our home and, regaining strength

347

after a mouthful of refreshing water, has engaged us in conversation in order to get to know us better, to understand us better, and to take back with him, to his home, memories of our home.

Mr. President:

It is hard to separate the statesman you are from the man himself. But I would like to insist on the fact that here we are welcoming François Mitterrand. It is for this reason that everyone here has shown to you, in their own way, their satisfaction and joy in being able to greet the person who came to see and to attest in good faith and in all objectivity to the fact that something is happening somewhere under the African sun, in Burkina Faso.

Burkina Faso is a construction project, one vast construction project. Time has not allowed us to visit and pay tribute to the many workers in different places who persist in transforming the world each day, in transforming an arid, difficult world. The victories they have just achieved already allow us to say that we are far from the myth of the labors of Sisyphus.[1] Indeed, you have to place one stone on top of another, then start over, and then start over again. It is under these conditions that Burkina Faso is proud today to have increased the percentage of children in school from 10 percent to nearly 22 percent, thanks to the numerous schools and classrooms we have built with our own hands, right here and now. We have been able to build many dams, many small water dams that, although they're not the size of those great works that are spoken of so widely in the world, have their merits, and inspire

---

1. A reference in Greek mythology to someone who was condemned for eternity to roll a huge boulder up a hill, only to have it roll down again right before it reached the top. The term has come to symbolize fruitless labor.

us, legitimately I believe, with pride.

It is again with the courage of our hands and the faith of our hearts that we have built a primary health care station in every village of Burkina Faso. It is with determination that we have vaccinated millions and millions of children of this country and neighboring countries. The list would be long but, alas, it would not be enough to represent one step, even one step of our vast and ambitious program. In other words, the road is a long one, a very long one.

Mr. François Mitterrand:

We hope you will be able to get to know these realities by coming to Burkina Faso. That is what we hope you will be able to take back to France and elsewhere. In the turmoil of struggle, in the cacophony of aggression, it is useful for accurate, sound, and relevant accounts to tell things the way they are. And by choosing you as interpreter and spokesperson, we also want to emphasize the constant battles that have characterized your political career and your life itself. We are familiar with these battles and they also inspire us, those of us from Burkina Faso.

You like to speak, sometimes stubbornly in certain recalcitrant milieus, of the rights of the peoples of the world. You like to speak of the debt in a clear manner that we have appreciated. You also like to speak of cooperation, and of the Third World. That's good. When we learned that Mr. François Mitterrand was going to set foot on the soil of Burkina Faso, we told ourselves that even though reasoning together might preclude oratorical eloquence, nevertheless the noble sense of combat—I'm speaking here of oratorical duels—would succeed in drawing us closer, because we so appreciate those whose discourse avoids wheeling and dealing, tricks and deceit.

In the French region of Berry, I believe, your name,

Mitterrand, means "mid-sized field"—or perhaps "grain measurer." In any case, a man of common sense. Common sense that is close to the men who are tied to the land, the land that never tells lies. Whether it is grain or whether it is a field, we think that the constant factor is that you yourself remain tied to the land. That is why, when speaking of the rights of the peoples of the world—a subject that is dear to you—we say that we have listened to you and have appreciated the calls you have issued, and which you have repeated since May 1981.

Each day we also follow and assess what is actually done. Along with the other peoples of the world, France is committed to the struggle for peace, and that is why, as we meet today, it is worth recalling that others, elsewhere, know nothing of this peace—and for how much longer?

First, there are the Palestinians. The Palestinians, men and women who roam from place to place, the wandering people of Zionism. These men and these women who are forced to seek refuge, these men and these women for whom the nights are a succession of nightmares, and the days an avalanche of mortar shells.

Peace—that also means Nicaragua. You yourself, in one of your speeches, spoke forcefully of the support you extended to Nicaragua against the mining of its harbor and against all the actions that are conducted from the outside against the Nicaraguans. You yourself, in your numerous discussions with Commander Ortega, have shown compassion for this people, which has not ceased to suffer and which has not ceased being subjected to the actions of barbarians who come from not very far away—because they are Nicaraguans—but who are strongly supported by others.

Peace also means Iran and Iraq. Complex, fratricidal, incomprehensible fighting, where one no longer knows who is in which camp, so entangled is the situation. But where one may simply observe that these arms, the cocking of which means death, also sing a sad song for the women, the children, and the elderly. Those arms are furnished every day by those who feed on the blood of others, by those who cheer when the sword kills and the fire blazes.[2]

Peace in the world also means that tormented region of southern Africa—as if through some sort of spell incompatible factors had been concentrated there in confusion and in battles that become larger and more numerous by the day. Not long ago we were filled with dismay by the death of Samora Machel. At the same time we saw a message there, a sign—the necessity of fighting against a barbaric, evil, and backward order, of fighting against an order that civilized peoples—and we count France among such peoples—have the duty to combat every inch of the way, be it by economic sanctions, be it by political and diplomatic measures, or be it also by direct and open armed combat against racism and apartheid in South Africa.

It is in this context, Mr. François Mitterrand, that we did not understand how bandits like Jonas Savimbi and killers like Pieter Botha, have been allowed to travel up and down France, which is so beautiful and so clean. They have stained it with their blood-covered hands and feet. All those who have made it possible for them to carry out these actions will bear full responsibility here and everywhere, today and forever.

We know that this question has been amply discussed and we are familiar with the positions of the various parties. But our sadness is simply immense. Those men have no right to speak of compatriots who have died for peace because they do not know what peace is. Those who have

---

2. France was one of the main suppliers of arms to Iraq during Baghdad's war against Iran.

died for peace are resting in peace and together, every day, we see to it that their memory is kept alive thanks to what each of us tries to do to further the same ends.

Peace in the world also means the Saharawi Arab Democratic Republic where—and this we don't understand—a people, the Saharawi people, still has not been able, still has not found out how to achieve self-determination because strongly backed and supported opposition forces intervene and get in their way.[3]

Peace in this region also means Libya which was bombed, with houses destroyed, but above all, a pointless slaughter that did not even allow its authors to succeed, to get their way, while it deprived the people of their closest relatives of their friends, and of their achievements.[4]

Peace also means Chad. Chad, where constructions and destructions succeed one another. Chad, where military operations and expeditions also succeed one another. Chad will therefore never find peace, happiness, and development as long as Chadians have not had the opportunity to choose a road and a path of national construction for themselves.[5]

For all these stormy areas, and I believe, Mr. President, for many others, your efforts can only be of considerable aid due to the importance of your country, and also due

---

3. In 1986 the government of France politically and militarily supported the occupation of Western Sahara by Morocco.

4. On April 15, 1986, the U.S. Air Force bombed Libya, killing over 100. While formally condemning the bombing, French officials stated they favored instead "a more ambitious and hard-hitting action against Libya," designed to "actually bring down the Qaddafi government."

5. After having militarily intervened there several times, the French government based a permanent military contingent of 1,200 soldiers in Chad in February 1986.

to the direct or indirect involvement of your country in those areas. I would like to assure you that, for our part, in Burkina Faso, we are fully ready to lend a hand, to give our assistance to whomever requests it, as long as the fight to be waged is a fight that reminds us of the France of 1789. It is for this reason that I would like to say to you that Burkina Faso is prepared to sign a defense agreement with France to allow all these arms you possess to come and be stationed here, in order to continue on to Pretoria, where peace calls us.

Mr. President:

I would like to continue to address the man. You speak much and often of the debt, of the development of our countries, and of the difficulties we encounter during international forums, such as the meeting of the "Big Powers" in Tokyo.[6] You are said to have defended our cause there and we are grateful for that. We request that you continue doing so, because today we are victims of the errors, of the thoughtlessness of others.

We are supposed to pay twice for actions to which we never committed ourselves. We were not at all responsible for these loans, these debts of yesterday. They were recommended to us and granted to us under conditions we no longer know. Except that today we must suffer over and over again. But we believe these questions will never be resolved through incantations, moans, pleas, and speeches.

To the contrary, such detours risk the grave consequence of lulling to sleep the conscience of the peoples of the world, who must struggle to free themselves from

6. A reference to the meeting of the heads of state of the Group of Seven, or G7 (Canada, France, Italy, Japan, United Kingdom, United States, and West Germany) in May 1986 in Tokyo.

this domination, from these forms of domination. You yourself have written somewhere in the many pages you have given French literature that all prisoners aspire to be free, that only combat can make one free.

Together, let us organize and bar the way to exploitation. Together, let us organize—you from over there and us from here—against these temples of money. No altar, no belief, no holy book, neither the Koran nor the Bible nor the others, have ever been able to reconcile rich and poor, exploiter and exploited. And if Jesus himself had to take the whip to chase them from his temple, it is indeed because that is the only language they hear.

Mr. President:

On the subject of the cooperation between France and the Third World, but mainly between France and Burkina Faso, I would like to say that we welcome with open arms all those who, as they travel through here, are willing to come contribute with us to the success of this vast construction project that is Burkina Faso.

In that sense, France will always be welcome in our home. It will always be welcome in ways that we like to think of as more flexible and that will draw French and Burkinabè closer together. We are not asking for aid that would drive Burkinabè and French apart. That would be historically self-defeating. We are not asking, as has been done previously, that the French authorities cozy up to the Burkinabè and African authorities, only to have French public opinion a few years later, through its press, widely condemn what was called "aid," but what was only an ordeal and torture for the people.

Some time ago a certain idea was born in France, called "Cartierism." Unfortunately, "Cartierism" was also able to emerge because of the inability of Africans, who were unable to take advantage of the cooperation between France and the African countries.[7]

This is just to say that both sides are to blame. In our "Song of Victory," our national anthem, we call those who bear full responsibility here in Africa local lackeys. Because, subject to a master, and without understanding their actions, they executed orders here that went against their people.

Mr. President:

You have written somewhere that currently the amount of French aid is declining and, unfortunately, you add, the amount of aid evolves according to France's political ambitions and, worst of all—sorry, you said and emphasized, what is worse—it's the capitalists who profit from this. Well, we believe that is also right. You wrote it, I believe, in that book *Ma part de vérité* [My share of truth]. This small share of the truth is a truth. It is indeed the capitalists who profit from this, and we are ready to fight together against them.

Mr. President:

We are eager to hear from you, to hear you tell what you have gotten out of these few hours spent in Burkina Faso, to also hear you tell us what this tour that finishes here in Burkina Faso means. In six days you have traveled throughout a good part of Africa. On the seventh day you will rest.

We want to spare a thought for all those in France who do honest work to draw distant peoples—such as the peoples of Africa, such as the people of Burkina Faso—together with the French people, who are courageous and of great merit. We want to think of, we want to address our thoughts to all those over there who are cut to the quick every day, whose souls are wounded, because somewhere a

---

7. See glossary, Cartierism.

Black or a foreigner in France was the victim of a barbaric act taken without any consideration for his human dignity.

We know that in France, many French suffer when they see that. You yourself have clearly said what you thought of certain recent decisions, such as the deportations of our Malian brothers.[8] We are hurt that they were deported and we are grateful that you did not give your backing to such decisions, to such actions reminiscent of days gone by.

As for the immigrants in France, although they are there for their happiness—like any man seeking sunnier horizons and greener pastures—they are also helping and building France for the French. A France, which has, as always, welcomed freedom fighters from all countries on its soil.

Here in Burkina Faso, French people are struggling seriously at the side of Burkinabè, often in nongovernmental organizations. Although, it must be said, not all these nongovernmental organizations represent respectable institutions in our view—some of them are purely and simply reprehensible liars—there are some that have great merit. And those make it possible for us to get to know France better, to get to know the French better. We are also thinking of those people. We are thinking, too, of all those who believe in joint action for a better world.

Every year, in a ritual manner and with the precision of a metronome, you go to Solutré.[9] You go there regularly, and watching these repetitive actions teaches us that it is

---

8. A month earlier, on October 18, 101 immigrant workers from Mali had been deported by French authorities.

9. Every year on the same day, Mitterrand climbed the Solutré Rock in Burgundy to commemorate his participation in the resistance against the occupation of France by Nazi Germany during the Second World War. He joined the French Resistance in November 1943, while he was an administrator in the French fascist Vichy regime.

necessary to use "the great wind of effort, the shelter of friendship, and the unity of minds." That, too, you wrote. I am borrowing it from you. We hope that you will take back with you to France this feeling of friendship, and that your stopover in Ouagadougou will have been in the shelter of friendship.

That is why I would like to request, Mr. President, Madame, and gentlemen, that you raise your glasses to drink to the friendship between the people of France and the people of Burkina Faso. Let us drink to friendship and to unity in struggle against those who, here, in France, and elsewhere, exploit us and oppress us. For the triumph of just causes, for the triumph of greater liberty, for the triumph of greater happiness.

Homeland or death, we will win!

Thank you.

The revolution cannot triumph without the emancipation of women

On International Women's Day
March 8, 1987

This speech was given in Ouagadougou on International Women's Day to a meeting of several thousand women from across the country. The text, including subtitles, is taken from a pamphlet published in 1987 by the National General Secretariat of the Committees for the Defense of the Revolution.

It is not an everyday occurrence for a man to speak to so many women at once. Nor does it happen every day that a man suggests to so many women new battles to be joined. A man experiences his first bashfulness the minute he becomes conscious he is looking at a woman. So, sisters, you will understand that despite the joy and the pleasure it gives me to be speaking to you, I still remain a man who sees in every one of you a mother, a sister, or a wife.

I hope, too, that our sisters here from Kadiogo province who don't understand French—the foreign language in which I will be giving my speech—will be patient with us, as they always have been. After all, it is they who, like

Speaking on International Women's Day, Ouagadougou, March 8, 1987.

our mothers, accepted the task of carrying us for nine months without complaint. [*Sankara then explains in the Mooré language that these women would receive a translation.*]

Comrades, the night of August 4 gave birth to an achievement that was most beneficial for the Burkinabè people. It gave our people a name and our country new horizons. Imbued with the invigorating sap of freedom, the men of Burkina, the humiliated and outlawed of yesterday, received the stamp of what is most precious in the world: honor and dignity. From this moment on, happiness became accessible. Every day we advance toward it, heady with the first fruits of our struggles, themselves proof of the great strides we have already taken. But this selfish happiness is an illusion. There is something crucial missing: women. They have been excluded from this joyful procession.

Though our men have already reached the edges of this great garden that is the revolution, our women are still confined to a depersonalizing darkness. Among themselves, in voices loud or soft, they talk of the experiences that have enveloped Burkina—experiences that are, for them, for the moment, merely a rumble in the distance. The revolution's promises are already a reality for men. But for women, they are still merely a rumor. And yet the authenticity and the future of our revolution depend on women.

These are vital and essential questions, because nothing whole, nothing definitive or lasting can be accomplished in our country as long as a crucial part of ourselves is kept in this condition of subjugation—a condition imposed over the course of centuries by various systems of exploitation.

Starting now, the men and women of Burkina Faso should profoundly change their image of themselves. For they are part of a society that is not only establishing new social relations but is also provoking a cultural transformation, upsetting the relations of authority between men and women and forcing both to rethink the nature of each.

This task is formidable but necessary. It will determine our ability to bring our revolution to its full stature, unleash its full potential, and show its true meaning for the direct, natural, and necessary relations between men and women, the most natural of all relations between one human being and another. This will show to what extent the natural behavior of man has become human and to what extent he has realized his human nature.

This human being, this vast and complex combination of pain and joy; solitary and forsaken, yet creator of all humanity; suffering, frustrated, and humiliated, and yet endless source of happiness for each one of us; this source of affection beyond compare, inspiring the most unexpected courage; this being called weak, but possessing untold ability to inspire us to take the road of honor; this being of flesh and blood and of spiritual conviction—this being, women, is you! You are our source of comfort and life companions, our comrades in struggle who, because of this fact, should by rights assert yourselves as equal partners in the joyful victory feasts of the revolution.

It is in this light that all of us, men and women, must define and assert the role and place of women in society. Therefore, we must restore to man his true image by making the reign of freedom prevail over differentiations imposed by nature and by eliminating all systems of hypocrisy that reinforce the shameless exploitation of women.

In other words, posing the question of women in Burkinabè society today means posing the abolition of the system of slavery to which they have been subjected for millennia. The first step is to try to understand how this system functions, to grasp its real nature in all its subtlety, in order then to work out a line of action that can lead to women's total emancipation.

In other words, in order to win this battle common to men and women, we must be familiar with all aspects of the woman question on a world as well as a national scale. We must understand how the struggle of Burkinabè women today is part of the worldwide struggle of all women and, beyond that, part of the struggle for the full rehabilitation of our continent. The condition of women is therefore at the heart of the question of humanity itself, here, there, and everywhere. The question is thus universal in character.

The class struggle and the worldwide status of women

We undoubtedly owe a debt to dialectical materialism for having shed the greatest light on the problem of the conditions women face, allowing us to understand the exploitation of women as part of a general system of exploitation. Dialectical materialism defines human society not as a natural, unchanging fact, but as the exact opposite.

Humankind does not submit passively to the power of nature. It takes control over this power. This process is not an internal or subjective one. It takes place objectively in practice, once women cease to be viewed as mere sexual beings, once we look beyond their biological functions and become conscious of their weight as an active social force. What's more, woman's consciousness of herself is not only a product of her sexuality. It reflects her position as determined by the economic structure of society, which in turn expresses the level reached by humankind in technological development and the relations between classes.

The importance of dialectical materialism lies in going beyond the inherent limits of biology, rejecting simplistic theories about our being slaves to the nature of our species, and, instead, placing facts in their social and economic context.

From the beginning of human history, man's mastering of nature has never been accomplished with his bare hands alone. The hand with the opposable thumb is extended by the tool, which increases the hand's power. It was thus not physical attributes alone—musculature or the capacity to give birth, for example—that determined the unequal status of men and women. Nor was it technological progress as such that institutionalized this inequality. In certain cases, in certain parts of the globe, women were able to eliminate the physical difference that separated them from men.

It was the transition from one form of society to another that served to institutionalize women's inequality. This inequality was produced by our own minds and intelligence in order to develop a concrete form of domination and exploitation. The social functions and roles to which women have been relegated ever since are a living reflection of this fact. Today, her childbearing functions and the social obligation to conform to models of elegance determined by men prevent any woman who might want to from developing a so-called male musculature.

For millennia, from the Paleolithic to the Bronze Age, relations between the sexes were, in the opinion of the most skilled paleontologists, positive and complementary in character. So it was for eight millennia. Relations were based on collaboration and interaction, in contrast to the patriarchy, where women's exclusion is a generalized characteristic of the modern historical era.

Frederick Engels not only traced the evolution of technology but also of the historic enslavement of women, which was born with the arrival of private property, owing to the transition from one mode of production to another, and from one form of social organization to another.

With the intensive labor required to clear the forests, cultivate the fields, and put natural resources to best use, a division of labor developed. Selfishness, laziness, looking for the easy way out—in short, taking the most with the least effort—emerged from the depths of the human spirit and became elevated into principles.

The protective tenderness of women toward the family and the clan became a trap that delivered her up to domination by the male. Innocence and generosity fell victim to deceit and base motives. Love was made a mockery. Dignity was tarnished. All genuine feelings were transformed into objects of barter. From this moment on, women's hospitality and desire to share succumbed to the trickery of the deceitful.

Though conscious of this deceit, which imposed on them an unequal share of the burdens, women followed men in order to care for and raise all that they loved. For their part, men exploited women's great self-sacrifice to the hilt. Later, this seed of criminal exploitation established terrible social imperatives, going far beyond the conscious concessions made by women, who had been historically betrayed.

Humankind first knew slavery with the advent of private property. Man, master of his slaves and of the land, also became the owner of the woman. This was the great historic defeat of the female sex. It came about with the upheaval in the division of labor, a result of new modes of production and a revolution in the means of production.

In this way, paternal right replaced maternal right. Property was now handed down from father to son, rather than as before from the woman to her clan. The patriarchal family made its appearance, founded on the sole and personal property of the father, who had become head of the family. Within this family the woman was oppressed. Reigning supreme, the man satisfied his sexual whims by mating with his slaves or concubines. Women became his booty, his conquest in trade. He profited from their labor power and took his fill from the myriad of pleasures they afforded him.

For their part, as soon as the masters gave them the chance, women took revenge in infidelity. Thus adultery became the natural counterpart to marriage. It was the woman's only form of defense against the domestic slavery to which she was subjected. Her social oppression was a direct reflection of her economic oppression.

Given this cycle of violence, inequality can be done away with only by establishing a new society, where men and women enjoy equal rights, resulting from an upheaval in the means of production as well as in all social relations. That is, women's lot will improve only with the elimination of the system that exploits them.

In fact, throughout the ages and wherever the patriarchy triumphed, there has been a close parallel between class exploitation and women's oppression. Of course, there were brighter periods where women, priestesses or female warriors, broke out of their oppressive chains. But the essential features of her subjugation survived and were consolidated, both in everyday activity and in intellectual and moral repression. Her status overturned by private property, banished from her very self, relegated to the role of child raiser and servant, written out of history by philosophy (Aristotle, Pythagoras, and others) and the most entrenched religions, stripped of all worth by mythology, woman shared the lot of a slave, who in slave society was nothing more than a beast of burden with a human face.

So it is not surprising that in its ascending phase the capitalist system, for which human beings are just so many numbers, should be the economic system that has exploited women the most cynically and with the most sophistication. So, we are told, manufacturers in those days employed only women on their mechanized looms. They gave preference to women who were married and, among them, to those with a family at home to support. These women paid greater attention to their work than single women and were more docile. They had no choice but to work to the point of exhaustion to earn the barest subsistence for their families.

In this way the woman's particular attributes are used against her, and all the most moral and delicate qualities of her nature become the means by which she is enslaved. Her tenderness, her love for her family, the meticulous care she brings to her work—all this is used against her, as she guards against any flaws she may have.

Thus, throughout the ages and throughout different types of society, women suffered a sorry fate, in a continually reinforced position of inferiority to men. Though the inequality was expressed in many and varied ways, it continued to exist nevertheless.

In slave society, the male slave was looked upon as an animal, a means of production of goods and services. The woman, whatever her social rank, was crushed within her own class and outside of that class. This was the case even for women who belonged to the exploiting classes. In feudal society, women were kept in a state of absolute dependence on men, justified by their supposed physical and psychological weakness. Often seen as a defiled object and a primary agent of indiscretion, women, with a few rare exceptions, were kept out of places of worship. In capitalist society, the woman, already morally and socially persecuted, is also subjugated economically. Kept by the man if she does not work, she remains under a man's domination even when she works herself to death. We will never be able to paint an adequate picture of the misery women suffer, nor show too strongly that women share the misery of proletarians as a whole.

The specific character of women's oppression

Woman's fate is bound up with that of the exploited male. This interdependence arises from the exploitation that both men and women suffer, exploitation that binds them together historically. This should not, however, make us lose sight of the specific reality of women's situation. The conditions of their lives are determined by more than economic factors, and they show that women are victims of a specific oppression. The specific character of this oppression cannot be explained away by equating different situations through superficial and childish simplifications.

It is true that both the woman and the male worker are condemned to silence by their exploitation. But under the current system, the worker's wife is also condemned to silence by her worker-husband. In other words, in addition to the class exploitation common to both of them, women must confront a particular set of relations that exist between them and men, relations of conflict and violence that use physical differences as their pretext.

It's clear that the difference between the sexes is a feature of human society. It's also clear that this difference determines the particular relations that prevent us from viewing women, even in the framework of economic production, as simply female workers. Privileged relations, perilous relations—the net result is that women's reality constitutes an ongoing problem.

The male uses the complex nature of these relations as an excuse to sow confusion among women. He takes advantage of all the shrewdness that class exploitation has to offer in order to maintain his domination over women. This is the same method used elsewhere by men to rule over other men. They succeeded in imposing the idea that certain men, by virtue of their family origin and birth, or by divine right, were superior to others. This was the basis for the feudal system. Other men have managed to enslave whole peoples in this way. They used their origins, or arguments based on their skin color, as a supposedly scientific justification to rule over those who were unfortunate enough to have skin of a different color. That's colonial rule. That's apartheid.

We must pay close attention to the situation of women because it pushes the best of them to talk of a war of the sexes, when what we really have is a war of social groups and of classes that should simply be waged together, with men and women complementing each other. We have to say frankly that it's the attitude of men that makes such confusion possible. That in turn paves the way for the bold assertions made by feminism, some of which have not been without value in the fight that men and women are waging against oppression. This fight is one we can and will win—if we understand that we need one another and are complementary, and finally, if we understand that we are condemned to being complementary.

For the time being, we have no choice but to recognize that male behavior—made up of vanity, irresponsibility, arrogance, and violence of all kinds toward women—can in no way result in coordinated action against women's oppression. What can be said of these attitudes, which can sink to the level of stupidity, and which in reality are nothing but a safety valve for oppressed males, who, through brutalizing their wives, hope to regain some of the human dignity denied them by the system of exploitation. This male stupidity is called sexism or machismo.

It includes moral and intellectual impoverishment of all types, even (acknowledged or not) physical powerlessness, which often compels politically conscious women to consider it their duty to fight on two fronts.

To fight and win, women must identify with the oppressed layers and classes of society—workers, peasants, and others. The man, however, no matter how oppressed he is, has another human being to oppress: his wife. Saying this means, without any doubt, asserting a terrible fact. When we talk about the disgusting system of apartheid, for example, our thoughts and emotions turn to the exploited and oppressed Blacks. But we forget, unfortunately, the Black woman who has to endure her husband—this man who, armed with his passbook, allows himself all kinds of reprehensible escapades before returning home to the woman who, suffering and destitute, has waited for him with dignity. We should keep in mind, too, the white woman of South Africa. Aristocratic, no doubt materially satisfied, she is, unfortunately, a tool for the pleasure of the lecherous white man. The only thing these men can do to forget their crimes against Blacks is to get wildly and perversely drunk from bestial sexual behavior.

Moreover, there is no lack of examples of men, even though progressive, who live cheerfully in adultery, yet would be ready to murder their wives on the merest suspicion of infidelity. Many men in Burkina seek so-called consolation in the arms of prostitutes and mistresses of all kinds. This is not to mention the irresponsible husbands whose wages serve only to keep mistresses and make the bars richer.

And what can be said of those little men, also progressive, who get together and talk lewdly about the women they have taken advantage of. They believe that in this way they'll be able to measure up to other men and even humiliate some of them, by seducing married women. In reality, such men are pitiful and insignificant. They would not even enter our discussion if it were not for the fact that their criminal behavior undermines the morale and virtue of many women of great merit, who would have been highly useful to our revolution.

And then there are those more-or-less revolutionary militants—much less revolutionary than more—who do not accept their wives being politically active; or who allow them to be active by day, and by day only; or who beat their wives because they've gone out to a meeting or demonstration in the evening. Oh, these suspicious, jealous men! What narrow-mindedness! And what a limited, partial commitment! For is it only at night that a disappointed and determined woman can cheat on her husband? And what kind of political commitment is it that expects political activity to cease at nightfall, to resume only at daybreak?

And finally, what should we make of remarks about women made by all kinds of militants, the one more revolutionary than the next. Remarks such as "women are despicably materialist," "profiteers," "actors," "liars," "gossips," "schemers," "jealous," and so on? Maybe this is all true of women. But surely it is equally true of men.

Could our society be any less perverse than this when it systematically places burdens on women, keeps them away from anything that is supposed to be serious and of consequence, and excludes them from anything other than the most petty and minor activities?

When you are condemned, as women are, to wait for your master of a husband in order to feed him and receive his permission to speak and to live, what else do you have to keep you occupied and to give you at least the illusion of being useful or important other than meaningful glances, gossip, small-talk, quarrels, furtive and envious glances, followed by malicious comments on the desire of others to be stylish and on their private lives? The same attitudes are found among men placed in the same situation.

Another thing we say about women is that, unfortunately, they are forgetful. We even call them birdbrains. But we must never forget that a woman's life is taken up, even tormented, by a fickle spouse, an unfaithful and irresponsible husband, and by her children and their problems. Worn out by taking care of the entire family, how could she not have haggard eyes that reflect distraction and absentmindedness. For her, forgetting becomes an antidote to pain, a relief from the harshness of her existence, a vital part of self-preservation.

But there are forgetful men, too—a lot of them. Some because of drink or drugs, others through indulging in various kinds of perversity while racing through life. However, no one ever says these men are forgetful. What vanity! What banality! Banalities men revel in and that demonstrate the weaknesses of the masculine world. Because in a society of exploitation the masculine world needs women prostitutes. The women who are defiled and, after being used, are sacrificed on the altar of prosperity of a system built on lies and plunder—they are merely scapegoats.

Prostitution is nothing but the microcosm of a society where exploitation is a general rule. It is a symbol of the contempt men have for women. And yet this woman is none other than the painful figure of the mother, sister, or wife of other men, thus of every one of us. In the final analysis, prostitution reflects the unconscious contempt we have for ourselves. There can be prostitutes only as long as there are "prostituters" and pimps.

Who goes to see prostitutes?

First, there are the husbands who commit their wives

to chastity while they relieve their depravity and debauchery upon the prostitute. This allows them to treat their wives with seeming respect, while they reveal their true nature at the bosom of the lady of so-called pleasure. So on the moral plane prostitution becomes the counterpart to marriage. Tradition, customs, religion, and moral doctrines alike seem to have no difficulty adapting themselves to it. This is what our church fathers mean when they explain that "sewers are needed to assure the cleanliness of the palace."

Then there are the unrepentant and intemperate pleasure seekers who are afraid to take on the responsibility of a home with its ups and downs, and who flee from the moral and material responsibility of fatherhood. So they exploit a discreetly located brothel as a treasure trove of liaisons without consequences.

There is also the group of men who, publicly at least and in "proper" company, subject women to vicious public attack. Either because of some disappointment that they did not have the strength of character to surmount, thus losing confidence in all women, who then became "tools of the devil." Or else out of hypocrisy, proclaiming their contempt for the female sex too often and categorically, a contempt they strive to assume in the eyes of society, from which they force admiration on false pretenses. All these men end up night after night in brothels until, occasionally, their hypocrisy is discovered.

Then there is the weakness of the man who is looking for a polyandrous arrangement. Far be it from us to make a value judgment on polyandry, which was the dominant form of relations between men and women in certain societies. What we are denouncing here are the flocks of idle, money-grubbing gigolos lavishly kept by rich ladies.

Within this same system, prostitution can, economically

speaking, include both the prostitute and the "materialist-minded" married woman. The only difference between the woman who sells her body through prostitution and she who sells herself in marriage is the price and duration of the contract.

So, by tolerating the existence of prostitution, we lower all our women to the same level, whether prostitute or wife. The only difference between the two is that the legal wife, though still oppressed, at least has the benefit of the stamp of respectability that marriage confers. As for the prostitute, all that remains for her is the exchange value of her body, a value that fluctuates according to what's in the male chauvinist's wallet.

Isn't she just an object, taking on more or less value according to the degree to which her charms fade? Isn't she governed by the law of supply and demand? Prostitution is a concentrated, tragic, and painful summary of female slavery in all its forms.

We should therefore see in every prostitute an accusing finger pointing at society as a whole. Every pimp, every partner in prostitution, turns the knife in this festering and gaping wound that disfigures the world of man and leads to his ruin. By fighting prostitution, by holding out a helping hand to the prostitute, we are saving our mothers, our sisters, and our wives from this social leprosy. We are saving ourselves. We are saving the world.

Women's reality in Burkina Faso

While society sees the birth of a boy as a "gift from God," the birth of a girl is greeted as an act of fate, or at best, a gift that can be used to produce food and perpetuate the human race.

The little male will be taught how to want and get, to speak up and be served, to desire and take, to decide things on his own. The future woman, however, is dealt blow after blow by a society that unanimously, as one man—and "as one man" is the appropriate term—drums into her head norms that lead nowhere. A psychological straitjacket called virtue produces a spirit of personal alienation within her. Concern with being protected is nurtured in the child's mind, inclining her to seek the supervision of a protector or negotiations for a marriage. What a monstrous mental fraud!

And so this child knows no childhood. From the age of three, she must meet the requirements of her role in life: *to serve and be useful.* While her brother of four or five or six will play till he drops from exhaustion or boredom, she, with little ceremony, will enter the process of production. She already has a trade: assistant housewife. It is of course an unpaid position, for isn't it generally said that a housewife "does nothing"? Don't we write "housewife" on the identity cards of women who have no income, meaning they have no job? That they are "not working"? With the help of tradition and obligatory submissiveness, our sisters grow up more and more dependent, more and more dominated, more and more exploited, and with less and less leisure or free time.

While the young man's road includes opportunities to blossom and take charge of his life, at every new stage of the young girl's life the social straitjacket is pulled tighter around her. She will pay a heavy price for having been born female. And she will pay it throughout her whole life, until the weight of her toil and the effects—physical and mental—of her selflessness lead her to the day of eternal rest. She is an instrument of production at the side of her mother, who, from that moment on, is already more a boss than a mother. She will never sit idle, nor be left alone to her games and toys like her brother.

Whichever direction we turn—from the central plateau in the northeast, dominated by societies where power is highly centralized; to the west, where the powers of the village communities are decentralized; or to the southwest, the land of the so-called segmental communities—traditional social organization has at least one point in common: the subordination of women. In our 8,000 villages, on our 600,000 plots of land, and in our million-plus households, on the question of women we can see identical or similar approaches. From one end of the country to the other, social cohesion as defined by men requires the submission of women and the subordination of the young.

Our society—still too primitively agrarian, patriarchal, and polygamous—turns the woman into an object of exploitation for her labor power and of consumption for her biological reproductive capacity.

How does the woman manage to live out this peculiar dual identity, which makes her the vital link that keeps the whole family together, the link whose presence and attention guarantees the family's fundamental unity, while at the same time guaranteeing she will be marginalized and ignored? The woman leads a twofold existence indeed, the depth of her social ostracism being equaled only by her stoic endurance. To live in harmony with the society of man, to conform with men's demands, she resigns herself to a self-effacement that is demeaning, she sacrifices herself.

Woman—source of life, yet object. Mother, yet servile domestic. Nurturer, yet trophy. Exploited in the fields and at home, yet playing the role of a faceless, voiceless extra. The pivot, the link, yet in chains. Female shadow of the male shadow.

The woman is the pillar of family well-being, the midwife, washerwoman, cleaner, cook, errand-runner, matron, farmer, healer, gardener, grinder, saleswoman, worker. She is labor power working with obsolete tools, putting in hundreds of thousands of hours for an appalling level of production.

Our sisters, fighting as they are on the four fronts of our war against disease, hunger, poverty, and degeneracy, feel the pressure of changes over which they have no control. For every single one of the 800,000 males who emigrate, a woman takes on an additional load. The two million Burkinabè men who live outside the country thus exacerbate the imbalance in the sex ratio that puts women today at 51.7 percent of the total population, or 52.1 percent of the resident population that is potentially part of the workforce.[1]

Too busy to give the necessary attention to her children, too exhausted to think of herself, the woman continues to slave away—wheel of fortune, wheel of friction, drive wheel, spare wheel, ferris wheel. Broken on the wheel and bullied, women, our sisters and wives, pay for having created life. Socially relegated to third place, after the man and the child, they pay for sustaining life. Here, too, a Third World is arbitrarily held back to be dominated, to be exploited.

Subjugated, the woman goes from a protective guardian who exploits her to one who dominates her and exploits her even more. She is first to work and last to rest. She is first to go for water and wood, first at the fire, yet last to quench her thirst. She may eat only if there is food left and only after the man. She is the keystone of the family, carrying both family and society on her shoulders, in

---

1. Some 800,000 inhabitants of Upper Volta were estimated to be working in neighboring countries in the mid-1970s, with a total of two million living abroad. The majority were men.

her hands, and in her belly. In return, she is paid with oppressive, pro-birth ideology, food taboos and restrictions, overwork, malnutrition, dangerous pregnancies, depersonalization, and innumerable other evils that make maternal deaths one of the most intolerable, unspeakable, and shameful defects of our society.

Given this foundation of alienation, the intrusion of predators from afar encourages the isolation of women, making their condition even more precarious. The euphoria of independence left women behind in a bed of dashed hopes. Forced into segregated discussions, absent from decisions, vulnerable (and thus the primary victim), they remained at the mercy of family and society. Capital and bureaucracy have banded together to keep women subjugated. Imperialism has done the rest.

Only half as likely as men to attend school, women are 99 percent illiterate, have little training in trades, are discriminated against in employment, are confined to the worst jobs, and are the first to be harassed and fired. Yet burdened as they are by a hundred traditions and a thousand excuses, women have continued to rise to meet challenge after challenge. They have had to keep going, whatever the cost, for the sake of their children, their family, and for society in general. Through a thousand nights without a dawn.

Capitalism needed cotton, shea nuts, and sesame for its industries. And it was women, it was our mothers, who in addition to all the tasks they were already carrying out, found themselves responsible for harvesting these products too. In the towns, where civilization is supposedly a liberating force for women, they found themselves decorating bourgeois living rooms, selling their bodies to survive, or serving as commercial bait in advertising.

Women from the petty bourgeoisie in the towns no

doubt live better on a material level than women in the countryside. But are they really freer, more liberated, more respected, or entrusted with more responsibility? We must do more than ask questions in this regard. We must provide a way forward.

Many problems still persist, whether they concern jobs, access to education, women's status in legal codes, or even just at the level of everyday life: the Burkinabè woman still remains the one who comes after the man, rather than alongside him.

The different neocolonial governments that were in power in Burkina never went beyond a bourgeois approach to women's emancipation, one that offers only an illusion of freedom and dignity. A few petty-bourgeois women from the towns were concerned with the latest fashion in feminist politics—rather, primitive feminism—which demanded the right of the woman to be masculine. Thus the creation of the Ministry of Women's Position in Society, headed by a woman, was touted as a victory.

But was women's position in society understood? Was it understood that the position of women in society means the condition of 52 percent of the Burkinabè population? Was it understood that this condition was the product of social, political, and economic structures, and of prevailing backward conceptions? And that the transformation of this position therefore could not be accomplished by a single ministry, even one led by a woman?

This was so true that Burkinabè women could plainly see after several years of this ministry's existence that their condition had in no way changed. And it could not be otherwise, given that the approach to the question of women's liberation that led to the creation of this token ministry refused to recognize, show, and take into account the real causes of women's subjugation and exploitation.

So we should not be surprised that, despite the existence of this ministry, prostitution grew, women's access to education and jobs did not improve, their civil and political rights continued to be ignored, and the general conditions of their lives in town and country alike improved not one iota.

Female trinket, token female politician in the government, female temptress used to influence elections, female robot in the kitchen, female frustrated by the submission and restrictions imposed on her despite her open mind—wherever the female finds herself in the spectrum of pain, whether urban or the rural, she continues to suffer.

But one single night placed women at the heart of the family's resurgence and at the center of national solidarity. The dawn that followed the night of August 4, 1983, brought liberty with it, calling all of us to march together side by side in equality, as a single people joined by solidarity in common goals. The August revolution found the Burkinabè woman in her state of subjugation, exploited by a neocolonial society deeply imbued with the ideology of backward social forces. The revolution owed it to itself to break with the reactionary policies on women's emancipation that had been advocated and followed up to then, by clearly defining new, just, and revolutionary policies.

Our revolution and the emancipation of women

On October 2, 1983, in the Political Orientation Speech, the National Council of the Revolution clearly laid out the main axis of the fight for women's liberation. It made a commitment to work to mobilize, organize, and unify all the active forces of the nation, particularly women.

The Political Orientation Speech had this to say specifically in regard to women: "They will be involved in all the battles we will have to wage against the various shackles of neocolonial society in order to build a new society. They will be involved—at all levels in conceiving projects, making decisions, and implementing them—in organizing the life of the nation as a whole. The final goal of this great undertaking is to build a free and prosperous society in which women will be equal to men in all spheres."

There can be no clearer way to conceive of and explain the question of women and the liberation struggle ahead of us. "The genuine emancipation of women is one that entrusts responsibilities to women, that involves them in productive activity and in the different fights the people face. The genuine emancipation of women is one that compels men to give their respect and consideration."

What is clearly indicated here, comrade militants, is that the struggle to liberate women is above all your struggle to deepen our democratic and popular revolution, a revolution that grants you from now on the right to speak and act in building a society of justice and equality, in which men and women have the same rights and responsibilities. The democratic and popular revolution has created the conditions for such a fight. It now falls to you to act with the greatest sense of responsibility in breaking through all the chains and shackles that enslave women in backward societies like ours and to assume your share of the responsibilities in the political fight to build a new society at the service of Africa and at the service of all humanity.

In the very first hours of the democratic and popular revolution we said, "Emancipation, like freedom, is not granted, it is conquered. It is for women themselves to put forward their demands and mobilize to win them." In this way, our revolution has not only laid out the goal to be attained in the struggle for women's liberation but has also indicated the road to follow and the methods to use, as well as the main protagonists of this battle.

We have now been working together, men and women, for four years in order to achieve success and come closer to our final goal. We should be conscious of the battles that have been waged, the successes that have been achieved, the setbacks that have been suffered, and the difficulties that have been encountered. This will aid us in further preparing and leading future struggles.

What work has the democratic and popular revolution accomplished with respect to women's emancipation? What are the strong points, the weak points?

One of the main gains of our revolution in the struggle for women's emancipation has been, without doubt, the establishment of the Women's Union of Burkina [UFB]. The creation of this organization constitutes a major gain because it has given the women of our country a framework and sound tools for waging a successful fight. The creation of the UFB represents a big victory because it makes possible mobilizing all women militants around well-defined and just goals in the fight for liberation, under the leadership of the National Council of the Revolution.

The UFB is the organization of militant and serious women who are determined to work for change, to fight to win, to fall down repeatedly, but to get back on their feet each time and go forward without retreating. This is the new consciousness that has taken root among the women of Burkina, and we should all be proud of it. Comrade militants, the Women's Union of Burkina is your combat organization. It's up to you to sharpen it further so its blade will cut more deeply, bringing you more and more victories.

The different initiatives for women's emancipation that the government has been able to take over a little more than three years are certainly insufficient. But they have made it possible to take some steps, to the point where our country can today present itself as being in the vanguard of the battle to liberate women. Our women participate more and more in decision making and in the real exercise of popular power. The women of Burkina are present everywhere the country is being built. They are part of the projects—the Sourou [valley irrigation project], reforestation, the vaccination brigades, the "clean town" operations, the Battle for the Railroad, and so on.

Little by little the women of Burkina have stood up and asserted themselves, demolishing in the process all the male-chauvinist, backward conceptions of men. And this will go on until women are present in Burkina's entire social and professional fabric. For three and a half years our revolution has worked continually to eliminate all practices that demean women, such as prostitution and related problems, like vagrancy and female juvenile delinquency, forced marriages, female circumcision, and the particularly difficult living conditions women face.

By working to solve the water problem everywhere, by helping to install mills in the villages, popularizing the improved cookstoves, creating popular day-care centers, carrying out regular vaccinations, and encouraging a healthy, abundant, and varied diet, the revolution has no doubt greatly contributed to improving the quality of life of the Burkinabè woman. Women, in turn, should commit themselves to greater involvement in putting into practice the slogans of the fight against imperialism. They should be firm in producing and consuming Burkinabè goods by always asserting their role as major economic players— both as producers and consumers of locally made goods.

Though the August revolution has undoubtedly done much for the emancipation of women, this is still far from adequate. Much remains for us to do. To better appreciate what remains to be done, we must be more aware of the difficulties still to be overcome. There are many obstacles and difficulties. At the top of the list are the problems of illiteracy and low political consciousness—both of which are intensified by the inordinate influence that reactionary forces exert in backward societies like ours. We must work with perseverance to overcome these two main obstacles. Because as long as women don't have a clear appreciation of the just nature of the political battle to be fought and don't see clearly how to take it forward, we can easily stop making headway and eventually slip backward.

This is why the Women's Union of Burkina should fully live up to its role. The women of the UFB should strive to overcome their own weaknesses and break with the kind of practices and behavior traditionally thought of as female—behavior we unfortunately often still see today in the things many women say and the way they act. I'm talking here about all those petty meannesses like jealousy, exhibitionism, unremitting empty, negative, and unprincipled criticism, mutual defamation, supersensitive subjectivity, rivalries, and so on. Revolutionary women should reject such behavior, which is particularly pronounced among petty-bourgeois women. It's liable to jeopardize any collective effort, while the fight for women's liberation is precisely one that requires an organized effort, and therefore help from all women.

Together we must collectively take care that women retain access to work. It is work that emancipates and liberates women by assuring them economic independence and a greater social role, as well as a more complete and accurate understanding of the world.

Our view of women's economic capacities has nothing in common with the crude greed and crass materialism that turns some women into market speculators or walking safes. These are women who lose all dignity, all self-control, and all principles as soon as they hear the clinking of jewelry or the crinkling of bank notes. Some of them unfortunately push men deep into debt, even to embezzlement and corruption. These women are like a dangerous mud, slimy and foul, that stifles the revolutionary fervor of their husbands or companions who are militants. There have been sad cases where revolutionary flames have burned out, and where the husband's commitment to the cause of the people has been abandoned for the sake of a selfish, cantankerous, jealous, and envious woman.

Education and economic emancipation, if not well understood and channeled in a constructive direction, can be a source of misfortune for the woman and thus for society as a whole. The educated and economically independent woman is sought after as lover and wife in good times and abandoned as soon as bad times arrive. Society passes a merciless judgment on them. An educated woman "has trouble finding a husband," it is said. A wealthy woman is suspect. They are all condemned to remaining single— which in itself would not be a problem if it didn't express a general ostracism on the part of all of society directed against people, innocent victims, who don't understand their "crime" or their "flaw," frustrated because every day douses their emotions, which turn into sour tempers and hypochondria. For many women great knowledge has been the cause of heartbreak, and great fortune has spawned many a misfortune.

The solution to this apparent paradox lies in the ability of these unfortunate rich and educated women to place their great knowledge and wealth at the service of the people. By doing this, they will be all the more appreciated and admired by the many people to whom they will have brought a little happiness. How could they possibly feel alone in these conditions? How could they not know emotional fulfillment when they have taken their love of and for themselves, and turned it into love of and for others?

Our women should not retreat in face of the many-sided struggles that lead a woman to take charge of herself fully and proudly, so as to discover the happiness of being herself, not the domesticated female of the male. Today, many of our women still seek the protective cover of a man as the safest way out from the oppression of "What will people say?" They marry without love or joy, just to serve some crude, dreary male who is far removed from real life and the struggles of the people. Quite often, women will arrogantly demand their independence while asking at the same time for protection, or even worse, to be put under the colonial protectorate of a male. They do not believe they can live otherwise.

No! We must say again to our sisters that marriage, if it brings society nothing positive and does not bring them happiness, is not indispensable and should even be avoided. To the contrary, let's show them our many examples of bold, fearless pioneers, single women with or without children, who are radiant and blossoming, overflowing with richness and availability for others—even envied by unhappily married women, because of the warmth they generate and the happiness they draw from their freedom, dignity, and willingness to help others.

Women have shown sufficient proof of their ability to take care of the family and raise children—in short, to be responsible members of society—without the oppressive tutelage of a man. Our society is surely sufficiently advanced to put an end to this banishment of the single woman. As revolutionaries, we should see to it that marriage is a choice that adds something positive, and not some kind of lottery where we know what the ticket costs us, but have no idea what we'll end up winning. Human feelings are too noble to be subjected to such games.

Another problem doubtlessly lies in the feudal, reactionary, and passive attitude of many men who by their behavior continue to hold things back. They have no intention of jeopardizing the total control they have over women, either at home or in society in general. In the battle to build a new society, which is a revolutionary battle, the conduct of these men places them on the side of reaction and counterrevolution. For the revolution cannot triumph without the genuine emancipation of women.

So, comrade militants, we must be highly conscious of all these difficulties in order to better face the battles to come. Women, like men, have qualities and weaknesses—which undoubtedly proves they are equal to men. Placing the emphasis deliberately on women's qualities in no way means we have an idealistic vision of them. We simply aim to single out the qualities and capacities that men and society have always hidden in order to justify their exploitation and subjugation of women.

How should we organize ourselves to accelerate the march forward to emancipation?

Though our resources are ridiculously small, our goals are ambitious. The will to go forward and our firm conviction are not sufficient to make our wager succeed. We must marshal our forces—all our forces—organize them, and channel them toward winning our struggle.

Emancipation has been a topic of discussion in our country for more than two decades now. There has been much emotion. Today, we should approach the question in its overall context. We should avoid shirking responsibilities, which has led to a failure to bring all forces into the struggle and to making this pivotal question of women's emancipation into a marginal one. We must also avoïd rushing ahead, leaving far behind those, especially the women, who should be on the front lines.

On the governmental level, guided by the directives of the National Council of the Revolution, a coherent plan of action to benefit women will be implemented. All ministerial departments will be involved, and each will be assigned short- and medium-term responsibilities. Far from being a list of pious wishes and other expressions of pity, this plan of action should be a guide to stepping up revolutionary action. It's in the heat of struggle that important and decisive victories are won.

This plan of action should be conceived by us and for us. Our wide-ranging, democratic discussions should produce bold resolutions that make clear our confidence in women. What do men and women want for women? This is what we will include in our plan of action. This plan, by involving all the ministerial departments, will be a sharp break from the approach of relegating the question of women's equality to the side, relieving of responsibility officials who, through their daily activity, should have and could have made a significant contribution to solving this problem.

This new many-sided approach to the question of women flows directly from our scientific analysis of its origins, its causes, and the importance it has within the framework of our plans for a new society rid of all forms of exploitation and oppression. We are not pleading for anyone to condescendingly do women a favor. We are demanding, in the name of the revolution—whose purpose is to give, not to take—that justice be done to women.

From now on, the activity of every ministry and the administrative committee of each ministry, in addition to the usual overall assessment we make, will be judged according to its success in implementing this plan. For this purpose, our statistical analyses will necessarily include action taken of direct benefit or concern to women. The question of women's equality must be in the minds of all decision-makers, at all times, and in all the different phases of conceiving and executing plans for development. Conceiving a development project without the participation of women is like using only four fingers when you have ten. It's an invitation to failure.

In the ministries responsible for education, we should take special care to assure that women's access to education is a reality, for this reality constitutes a qualitative step toward emancipation. It is an obvious fact that wherever women have had access to education, their march to equality has been accelerated. Emerging from the darkness of ignorance allows women to take up and use the tools of knowledge in order to place themselves at the disposal of society. All ridiculous and backward concepts that hold that only education for males is important and profitable, and that educating women is an extravagance, must disappear in Burkina Faso.

Parents should accord the same attention to the progress of their daughters at school as they do to their sons, their pride and joy. Girls have proven they are the equals of boys at school, if not simply better. But above all they have the right to education in order to learn and know— to be free. In future literacy campaigns, the rate of participation by women must be raised to correspond with their numerical weight in the population. It would be too great an injustice to maintain such an important part of the population—half of it—in ignorance.

In the ministries responsible for labor and justice, texts should constantly be adapted to the transformation our society has been going through since August 4, 1983, so that equality between men and women is a tangible reality. The new labor code, now being drawn up and debated, should express how profoundly our people aspire to social justice. It should mark an important stage in the work of destroying the neocolonial state apparatus—a class apparatus fashioned and shaped by reactionary regimes to perpetuate the system that oppressed the popular masses, especially women.

How can we continue to accept that a woman doing the same job as a man should earn less? Can we accept the *levirate*[2] and dowries, which reduce our sisters and mothers to common commodities to be bartered for? There are so many things that medieval laws continue to impose on our people, on women. It is only just that, finally, justice be done.

In the ministries in charge of culture and family affairs, particular emphasis will be put on developing a new mentality in social relations, in close collaboration with the Women's Union of Burkina. Mothers and wives in the revolution have specific and important contributions to make in the framework of the revolutionary transformations being carried out. Children's education, efficient management of the family budget, family planning, the forging of a family spirit, patriotism—these are all important attributes that should effectively contribute to the birth of revolutionary moral values and an anti-imperialist lifestyle, preludes to a new society.

In the home, women should take particular care to participate in improving the quality of life. As Burkinabè, living well means eating well and dressing well by using Burkinabè products. It means keeping up a clean and

---

2. The levirate is a marriage in which the widow weds a brother of the deceased, with varying degrees of compulsion.

pleasant living environment, because the living environment has a big impact on relations within the family.
Living in squalor produces squalid relations. Look at the
pigs if you don't believe me.

The transformation of mentalities would be incomplete
if the new woman has to live with the old kind of man.
Where is men's real superiority complex more pernicious,
yet at the same time more decisive, than in the home—
where the mother, a guilty accomplice, teaches her off-
spring sexist, unequal rules? Women perpetuate sexual
complexes right from the beginning of a child's education and the formation of its character.

Moreover, what use would our efforts be to draw someone into political activity during the day if this novice
were to find himself with a reactionary and demobiliz-
ing woman at night!

And what about the all-consuming and mind-deadening
housework that tends to turn you into a robot and to
leave no time or energy to think! This is why resolute action must be undertaken aimed at men and at setting up
a large-scale network of social facilities such as nurseries,
day-care centers, and cafeterias. This would allow women
to more easily take part in revolutionary debate and action. Each child, whether rejected as the mother's failure
or doted on as the father's pride, should be of concern to
society as a whole, everyone the object of society's attention and affection. Men and women will, from now on,
share all the tasks in the home.

The plan of action in favor of women should be a revolutionary tool for the general mobilization of all the political and administrative structures in the effort to liberate women. I repeat, comrade militants: before it can
correspond to the real needs of women, this plan must
be subjected to a democratic discussion at every level of

the UFB's structures.

The UFB is a revolutionary organization. As such, it is a school for popular democracy, governed by the organizational principles of criticism and self-criticism and democratic centralism. It intends to differentiate itself from those organizations where mystification has won out over concrete goals. But such a differentiation can be effective and permanent only if the comrades of the UFB carry out a resolute struggle against the weaknesses that unfortunately still persist in some female milieus. Because we are not talking at all here about bringing women together for the sake of appearances or for any other electoralist, demagogic, or otherwise reprehensible ulterior motive.

We are talking about bringing together women fighters to win victories. We are talking about fighting in an organized way and on the basis of a series of activities decided democratically within their committees, taking fully into account each revolutionary structure's own organizational autonomy. Every UFB official must have fully absorbed her role in her structure in order to be effective in action. This requires that the Women's Union of Burkina carry out vast campaigns of political and ideological education of its officials, so as to strengthen the UFB structures on all levels.

Comrade militants of the UFB, your union—our union—should participate fully in the class struggle on the side of the popular masses. Those millions whose consciousness was dormant and who have now been awakened by the coming of the revolution represent a formidable force. On August 4, 1983, we Burkinabè made a decision to rely on our own resources, which means in large part on the resources that you women represent. To be useful, your energies have to be focused on the struggle to eliminate every breed of exploiter and imperialism's economic domination. As a structure for mobilization, the UFB will have to forge a highly developed political awareness among its militants, so they can make a completely revolutionary commitment as they carry out the different actions initiated by the government to improve the position of women.

Comrades of the UFB, only the revolutionary transformation of our society can create conditions favorable for your liberation. You are dominated both by imperialism and by men. In every male sleeps the soul of a feudal lord, a male chauvinist, which must be destroyed. This is why you must eagerly embrace the most advanced revolutionary slogans to make your liberation real and to advance toward it more rapidly. This is why the National Council of the Revolution notes with joy how intensely you are participating in the big national development projects and encourages you to give ever greater support to the August revolution, which is above all yours.

By participating massively in these projects you are showing yourselves to be all the more worthy, given that in its division of labor, society has always sought to relegate you to the least important tasks. Your apparent physical weakness is nothing more than the result of norms of appearance and fashion that society has imposed on you because you are women.

As we go forward, our society should break from all those feudal conceptions that lead to ostracizing the unmarried woman, without realizing that this is merely another form of appropriation, which decrees each woman to be the property of a man. This is why young mothers are looked down upon as if they were the only ones responsible for their situation, whereas there is always a guilty man involved. This is how childless women are oppressed due to antiquated beliefs, when there is a scientific explanation for their infertility, which science can overcome.

In addition, society has imposed on women norms of beauty that violate the integrity of their bodies, such as female circumcision, scarring, the filing of teeth, and the piercing of lips and noses. Practicing these norms of beauty is of dubious value. In the case of female circumcision, it can even endanger a woman's ability to have children and her love life. Other types of bodily mutilation, though less dangerous, such as the piercing of ears and tattoos, are no less an expression of women's conditioning, imposed by society if a woman wants to find a husband. Comrade militants, you look after yourselves in order to win a husband. You pierce your ears and do violence to your body in order to be acceptable to men. You hurt yourselves so that men can hurt you even more!

Women, my comrades-in-arms, it's you to whom I am speaking.

You, who lead miserable lives in town and village alike.

You, in the countryside, who sag under the weight of the various burdens of dreadful exploitation that is "justified" and "explained."

You, in the towns, who are supposedly happy, yet deep down are miserable day in and day out, laden down with tasks. Because as soon as you rise from bed, you turn round in front of your wardrobe like a spinning top, wondering what to wear. Not so as to be dressed and to protect yourself from the elements, but to please men. Because every day you are supposed to—compelled to—please men.

You, who, when it is time to rest, have the sad look of one who has no right to rest.

You, who are compelled to ration yourself, to exercise self-restraint, to diet to maintain a figure men will desire.

You, who at night, before going to bed, cover yourselves with makeup, with those many products you detest so much—we know you do—but whose purpose is to hide an indiscreet wrinkle, an unfortunate sign of age always considered to have come too soon, age that has started to show, or a premature plumpness. There you are—made to go through a two-hour ritual every night to preserve your best attributes, only to be ill-rewarded by an inattentive husband. And to start all over again at the break of dawn.

Comrade militants, yesterday in speeches given by the Directorate for Mobilization and Organization of Women, and in accordance with the general statutes of the CDRs, the National Secretariat of the CDRs succeeded in setting up committees, subcommittees, and sections of the UFB. The Political Commission, which is in charge of organization and planning, will be responsible for completing your organizational pyramid by setting up a national executive committee of the UFB.

We have no need of a feminized apparatus to bureaucratically manage women's lives or to issue sporadic statements about women's lives by smooth-talking functionaries. What we need are women who will fight because they know that without a fight the old order will not be destroyed and no new order will be built. We are not looking to organize what exists but to definitively destroy and replace it.

The National Executive Committee of the UFB should be made up of convinced and determined cadres who will always be available, so great is the task to be undertaken. And the struggle begins at home. These militants should be conscious that in the eyes of the masses they represent the image of the emancipated, revolutionary woman and should conduct themselves accordingly.

Comrade militants, women and men: experience shows us more and more that in changing the classical order of things, only the organized people are capable of wielding power democratically. The basic principles of this change—justice and equality—allow women to show that societies are wrong not to have confidence in them on the political as well as the economic level. Women, wielding the power they have seized as part of the people, are in a position to redeem all women condemned by history. Our revolution has begun to profoundly and qualitatively change our society. This change must necessarily take into account the aspirations of Burkinabè women.

Comrades, the future demands that women be liberated, and the future, everywhere, brings revolutions. If we lose the fight to liberate women we will have lost all right to hope for a positive and superior transformation of our society. Our revolution will then no longer have any meaning. It is to wage this noble struggle that all of us, men and women, are summoned.

Let our women move up to the front line! Our final victory depends fundamentally on their capacities, their wisdom in struggle, their determination to win. Let each woman be able to get a man to reach the height of his possibilities. And to do that, let each woman draw from her immense well of affection and love, let her find the strength and the know-how to encourage us when we are advancing and to replenish our energy when we show signs of weakening. Let each woman advise a man, let each woman be a mother to each man! It is you who brought us into the world, who educated and made men of us.

Let each woman—you who have guided us to where we are today—continue to play the role of mother and guide. Let women remember what they are capable of. Let each woman remember she is the center of the earth. Let each woman remember she lives in the world and for the world. Let each woman remember that the first to cry for a man is a woman. It is said, and you will remember this comrades, that at the moment of death each man calls out the name of a woman—his mother, his sister, or his companion—with his last breath.

Women need men to win. And men need women's victories to win. At the side of every man, comrades, there is always a woman. The woman's hand that cradled the man's child will cradle the entire world. Our mothers have given us life. Our wives give birth to our children, feed them at their breasts, raise them, and make them into responsible beings. Women assure the continuity of our people. Women assure the destiny of humanity. Women assure that our work will go forward. Women thus assure the pride of every man.

Mothers, sisters, companions:

There can be no proud man without a woman at his side. Every proud man, every strong man, draws his energy from a woman. The endless source of virility is femininity. The endless source, the key to victories always lies in the hands of a woman. It is at the side of a woman, sister, or companion that each one of us finds a burst of honor and dignity.

It is always at the side of a woman that each of us returns to find consolation and the courage and inspiration to dare to go back to battle, to receive the advice that will temper our recklessness or some presumptuous irresponsibility. It is always at the side of a woman that we become men again, and every man is a child for every woman.

He who does not love women, who does not respect women, who does not honor women, despised his own mother. Thus, he who despises women despises and destroys the very place from which he has come. That is, having come from the generous womb of a woman, he kills himself because he believes he has no right to exist. Comrades, woe to he who despises women! The same to all men, here and elsewhere, to all men of any social condition, whatever hut they may come from, who despise women, who do not know and forget what women are: "You have struck a rock. You have dislodged a boulder. You will be crushed."[3]

Comrades, no revolution—starting with our own—will triumph as long as women are not free. Our struggle, our revolution will be incomplete as long as we understand liberation to mean essentially that of men. After the liberation of the proletariat, there remains the liberation of women.

Comrades, every woman is the mother of a man. I would not presume, as a man and as a son, to give advice to a woman or to indicate which road she should take. This would be like giving advice to one's own mother. But we know, too, that out of indulgence and affection, a mother listens to her son, despite his whims, his dreams, and his vanity. And this is what consoles me and makes it possible for me to address you here. This is why, comrades, we need you in order to achieve the genuine liberation of us all. I know you will always find the strength and the time to help us save our society.

Comrades, there is no true social revolution without the liberation of women. May my eyes never see and my feet never take me to a society where half the people are held in silence. I hear the roar of women's silence. I sense the rumble of their storm and feel the fury of their revolt. I await and hope for the fertile eruption of the revolution through which they will transmit the strength and the

---

3. Words taken from a song made famous in South Africa on August 9, 1956, when twenty thousand women, led by the African National Congress, protested the apartheid regime's notorious pass laws, which forced Blacks to carry special identification with them at all times. August 9 is celebrated today as South African Women's Day.

rigorous justice issued from their oppressed wombs.

Comrades, forward to conquer the future.

The future is revolutionary.

The future belongs to those who struggle.

Homeland or death, we will win!

A united front against the debt

At Organization of African Unity conference,
Addis Ababa
July 29, 1987

This speech was given in Addis Ababa, Ethiopia, at the twenty-fifth conference of member states of the Organization of African Unity (OAU). Kenneth Kaunda, president of Zambia, chaired the session. The text of Sankara's address was published in Paris in February 1989 in the magazine *Coumbite.*

Mr. President;
Heads of delegations:

I would like at this moment for us to take up the other question that plagues us, the question of the debt, the question of Africa's economic situation. As much as peace, resolving this is an important condition for our survival. That is why I thought I should impose a few additional minutes on you, so we could take this up.

Burkina Faso would like to begin by expressing its fear. The fear that as successive OAU gatherings take place, they're all the same, but there is less and less financial participation in what we do.

Mr. President:

How many heads of state are present here, after being duly invited to come discuss Africa, in Africa?[1]

Mr. President:

How many heads of state are ready to dash off to Paris, London, or Washington when called to meetings there, but are unable to attend a meeting here in Addis Ababa, in Africa? This is very important. [*Applause*] I know some have valid reasons for not attending. That's why I would like to propose, Mr. President, that we establish a scale of sanctions for the heads of state who fail to respond to an invitation to attend. Let's make it so that with a certain number of points for good behavior, those who come regularly—like us for example [*Laughter*]—can get backing for some of their projects. For example, the proposals we submit to the African Development Bank would be affected by a coefficient of Africanness. [*Applause*] The least African would be penalized. If we did that, everyone would come to the meetings.

I would like to tell you, Mr. President, that the question of the debt is a question we cannot lose sight of. You yourself know something of this in your own country, where you have had to make courageous decisions, even risky ones—steps that seem completely out of keeping with your age and white hair. [*Laughter*] His Excellency President Habib Bourguiba, who didn't come but sent us an important message, gave Africa another example when he, too, had to make courageous decisions in Tunisia for economic, social, and political reasons.[2]

---

1. Only 16 heads of state, out of the 50 members of the OAU at the time, were in attendance at the meeting.

2. In Zambia in 1986, the government of Kenneth Kaunda abolished food subsidies in an attempt to meet demands of the International

But Mr. President, are we going to continue to allow heads of state to seek individual solutions to the problem of the debt, at the risk of creating, in their own countries, social conflicts that could endanger their stability and even the building of African unity? The examples I have cited—there are many more—indicate it would be well worth it for OAU summits to give a reassuring reply to each of us on the question of the debt.

We believe analysis of the debt should begin with its roots. The roots of the debt go back to the beginning of colonialism. Those who lent us the money were those who colonized us. They were the same people who ran our states and our economies. It was the colonizers who put Africa into debt to the financiers—their brothers and cousins. This debt has nothing to do with us. That's why we cannot pay it.

The debt is another form of neocolonialism, one in which the colonialists have transformed themselves into technical assistants. Actually, it would be more accurate to say technical assassins. They're the ones who advised us on sources of financing, on underwriters of loans. As if there were men whose loans are enough to create development in other people's countries. These underwriters were recommended to us, suggested to us. They gave us enticing financial documents and presentations. We took on loans of fifty years, sixty years, and even longer. That is, we were led to commit our peoples for fifty years and more.

The debt in its present form is a cleverly organized

Monetary Fund. A popular rebellion followed, which was put down brutally by the Zambian police. On May 1, 1987, the government suspended the measures.

In Tunisia in January 1984, after several days of protests throughout the country, the government of Bourguiba canceled a doubling of the price of bread and grain it had announced a month earlier.

reconquest of Africa under which our growth and development are regulated by stages and norms totally alien to us. It is a reconquest that turns each of us into a financial slave—or just plain slave—of those who had the opportunity, the craftiness, the deceitfulness to invest funds in our countries that we are obliged to repay. Some tell us to pay the debt. This is not a moral question. Paying or not paying is not a question of so-called honor at all.

Mr. President:

We listened to and applauded the prime minister of Norway when she spoke right here. She said, and she's a European, that the debt as a whole cannot be repaid. I just want to develop her remarks further by saying that none of the debt can be repaid. The debt cannot be repaid, first of all, because, if we don't pay, the lenders won't die. Of that you can be sure. On the other hand, if we do pay, we are the ones who will die. Of that you can be equally sure. Those who led us into debt were gambling, as if they were in a casino. As long as they were winning, there was no problem. Now that they're losing their bets, they demand repayment. There is talk of a crisis. No, Mr. President. They gambled. They lost. Those are the rules of the game. Life goes on. [*Applause*]

We cannot repay the debt because we have nothing to pay it with. We cannot repay the debt because it's not our responsibility. We cannot repay the debt because, on the contrary, the others owe us something that the greatest riches can never repay—a debt of blood. It is our blood that was shed.

People talk of the Marshall Plan, which rebuilt the economy of Europe.[3] But they don't mention the African

---

3. Launched by Washington in April 1948 as an early move in the emerging Cold War, the Marshall Plan financed reconstruction and

Plan, which enabled Europe to face Hitler's hordes at a time when their economies were under siege, their stability threatened. Who saved Europe? It was Africa. There is very little talk about that. There is so little talk that we can't become accomplices ourselves of this ungrateful silence. If others can't sing our praise, we have the duty, at the very least, to point out that our fathers were courageous and that our veteran fighters saved Europe and ultimately allowed the world to rid itself of Nazism.

The debt is also the product of confrontations. When people talk to us today about economic crisis, they forget to mention that the crisis didn't appear overnight. It has been with us for a long time, and it will deepen more and more as the popular masses become increasingly aware of their rights in face of the exploiters.

There is a crisis today because the masses refuse to allow wealth to be concentrated in the hands of a few individuals. There is a crisis because a few individuals hold colossal sums of money in foreign banks—enough to develop Africa. There is a crisis because in face of these individual fortunes, whose owners we can name, the popular masses refuse to live in ghettos and slums. There is a crisis because people everywhere refuse to stay in Soweto when Johannesburg is directly opposite them. That is, there is struggle, and the deepening of this struggle leads to worries among the holders of financial power.

They ask us today to collaborate in the search for stability. Stability to the benefit of the holders of financial power. Stability to the detriment of the popular masses. No, we can't be accomplices in this. No, we can't go along with those who suck the blood of our peoples and who

---

rearmament of capitalist Europe, much of which was destroyed during the Second World War.

live off the sweat of our peoples. We can't go along with their murderous ventures.

Mr. President:

We hear talk of clubs—the Club of Rome, the Club of Paris, the Club of Everywhere. We hear talk of the Group of Five, of Seven, of the Group of Ten, perhaps the Group of One Hundred. Who knows what else? It's normal that we too have our own club, our own group. Starting today, let's make Addis Ababa a similar seat, the center from which will come a breath of fresh air, the Club of Addis Ababa. We have the duty to create the united front of Addis Ababa against the debt. This is the only way we can say today that, by refusing to pay, we're not setting out on a course of war but, on the contrary, a fraternal course of explaining the facts as they are.

What's more, the popular masses of Europe are not opposed to the popular masses of Africa. Those who want to exploit Africa are the same ones as those who exploit Europe. We have a common enemy. Our Club of Addis Ababa must tell both sides that the debt cannot be paid. When we say the debt cannot be paid we are in no way against morality, dignity, or respect for one's word. It's our view that we don't have the same morals as the other side. The rich and the poor don't share the same morals. The Bible and the Koran can't serve in the same way those who exploit the people and those who are exploited. There will have to be two editions of the Bible and two editions of the Koran. [*Applause*]

We can't accept their morals. We can't accept their talking to us about dignity. We can't accept their talking to us about the merits of those who pay and about a loss of confidence in those who don't pay. On the contrary, we must explain that it's normal these days to favor the view that the richest people are the biggest thieves. A poor man who steals commits no more than larceny, a petty crime, just to survive, out of necessity. The rich are the ones who rob the tax revenue and customs duties. They are the ones who exploit the people.

Mr. President:

My proposal does not aim simply to provoke or to create a spectacle. I am trying to say what each of us thinks and hopes for. Who here doesn't want to see the debt written off, pure and simple? Anyone who doesn't want that can leave, take his plane, and go directly to the World Bank to pay it off. [*Applause*] I hope you don't take the proposal from Burkina Faso as something coming from immature youth, who have no experience. I also hope you don't think only revolutionaries speak in this manner. I hope you acknowledge that it's simply a matter of objectivity and of duty.

I can give you examples of both revolutionaries and nonrevolutionaries, of both young and old, who have called for not paying the debt. I could mention Fidel Castro, for example. He has said not to pay. He's not my age, even if he is a revolutionary. François Mitterrand has also said the African countries cannot pay, the poor countries cannot pay. I could cite the madam prime minister of Norway. I don't know her age, and I would hesitate to ask. [*Laughter and applause*] I could also cite President Félix Houphouët-Boigny. He isn't my age. But he has officially and publicly declared that, at least as far as his country is concerned, the debt cannot be paid. Now, the Ivory Coast is counted as one of the wealthier countries in Africa, at least in French-speaking Africa. That's why, moreover, it's no surprise that it no longer pays its dues here. [*Applause*]

Mr. President:

This is not a provocation. I hope you can very wisely offer us solutions. I hope our conference sees the necessity of stating clearly that we cannot pay the debt. Not in a warmongering or warlike spirit. This is to avoid our going off to be killed one at a time. If Burkina Faso alone were to refuse to pay the debt, I wouldn't be at the next conference. On the other hand, with the support of all, which I greatly need [*Applause*], with the support of all, we can avoid paying. And if we can avoid paying, we can devote our meager resources to our development.

I would like to close by saying that when we tell countries we're not going to pay the debt, we can assure them that what is saved won't be spent on prestige projects. We don't want any more of those. What is saved will be used for development. In particular we will avoid going into debt to buy arms. Because an African country that buys arms can only be doing so to use them against an African country. What African country here can arm itself to defend against the nuclear bomb? No country is capable of that, from the best armed to the least armed. Every time an African country buys a weapon, it's for use against another African country. It's not for use against a European country. It's not for use against an Asian country. So in preparing the resolution on the debt we must also find a solution to the question of armaments.

I am a soldier, and I carry a gun. But Mr. President, I wish we would disarm. Because I carry the only weapon I own. Others have camouflaged the weapons they own. [*Laughter and applause*] So dear brothers, with everyone's support we can make peace at home.

We can also use Africa's immense latent resources to develop the continent, because our soil and subsoil are rich. We have the means to do that and we have an immense market, a vast market from north to south, east to west. We have sufficient intellectual capacities to create technology and science, or at least to adopt it wherever we find it.

Mr. President:

Let's assemble this united front of Addis Ababa against the debt. Let's organize so that beginning in Addis Ababa we make the decision to limit the arms race between weak and poor countries. The clubs and swords we buy are of no use. Let's make sure that the African market is a market for Africans. Let's produce in Africa, transform in Africa, consume in Africa. Produce what we need and consume what we produce, in place of importing it.

Burkina Faso has come to show you the cotton produced in Burkina Faso, woven in Burkina Faso, sewn in Burkina Faso to clothe the Burkinabè. My delegation and I were clothed by our weavers, our peasants. Not a single thread comes from Europe or America. [*Applause*] I'm not here to put on a fashion show; I simply want to say that we should undertake to live as Africans. It is the only way to live free and to live in dignity.

Thank you, Mr. President.

Homeland or death, we will win!

[*Ovation*]

We can count on Cuba

Interview with Radio Havana
August 1987

Radio Havana correspondent Claude Hackin conducted this interview in Ouagadougou. It appeared in the August 4, 1987, issue of *Granma*, the daily newspaper of the Communist Party of Cuba.

RADIO HAVANA: Comrade Thomas Sankara, you have met with President Fidel Castro several times. Would you please tell us about your first meeting with him, which took place in New Delhi in March 1983 at the Seventh Summit Conference of Nonaligned Countries—before you became leader of the revolution in Burkina Faso.

THOMAS SANKARA: For me this was and remains a memorable meeting. As I recall, he was very much in demand. There were a great number of people around him, and I thought it would be impossible to talk with him since he didn't know me. I did, however, get the chance to meet with Fidel.

In this first conversation, I realized Fidel has great

human feeling, keen intuition, and that he understood the importance of our struggle and the problems of my country. I remember all this as though it were yesterday. And I've happily reminded him of it each time I've seen him since then. We're great friends, thanks to the revolution that guides both Burkina Faso and Cuba.

RADIO HAVANA: After August 4, 1983, new relations opened up between Cuba and Burkina Faso. How do you view the development of these collaborative ties?

SANKARA: Cooperation between Cuba and Burkina Faso has reached a very high level. We attach great importance to this because it puts us in contact with a sister revolution. We like feeling at ease with each other. Nobody likes to feel alone. Knowing we can count on Cuba is an important source of strength for us.

A variety of economic cooperation programs have been established in sectors like sugarcane production, a Cuban specialization, and ceramics. In addition, Cuban specialists have done studies in areas like rail transport, for the construction of railroad ties, and the production of prefabricated units for housing construction. Then there's the social sector: health and education. Many Cubans here are involved in training technical cadres. And we also have many students in Cuba. Cuba is very close to us today.

RADIO HAVANA: Do you believe it's necessary to build a vanguard party in Burkina Faso?

SANKARA: We have to build a vanguard party. We have to create a structure based on organization, because our achievements will remain fragile if we have nothing to defend them with, nothing to educate the masses with so as to score new victories.

We do not see the formation of a party as a distant or impossible thing. We're quite close to this objective. But there are still a whole number of small-group conceptions, and in this regard, we'll have to wage a serious drive for agreement, regroupment, and unity.

The nature of the party, how it's conceived, and how it's built will certainly not be the same as it would have been had we built a party before coming to power. We'll have to take a lot of precautions in order to avoid falling into leftist opportunism. We can't let the masses down. We have to be very careful, selective, and demanding.

RADIO HAVANA: In various speeches you've referred to the class struggle in your country. What are the elements of this struggle today?

SANKARA: In our country the question of the class struggle is posed differently from the way it's posed in Europe. We have a working class that's numerically weak and insufficiently organized. And we have no strong national bourgeoisie either that could have given rise to an antagonistic working class. So what we have to focus on is the very essence of the class struggle: in Burkina Faso it's expressed in the struggle against imperialism, which relies on its internal allies.

RADIO HAVANA: What are these social groups that are opposing the revolution?

SANKARA: They are the feudal-type forces that cannot applaud when faced with the disappearance of their privileges. We also have a bureaucratic bourgeoisie, which is still here, hiding. It has experience in administrative work in the state apparatus. You'll find it in various places in state administration, and it never ceases to harass us and create difficulties for us, with imperialism's backing. In addition, there are the big landowners, who are not very numerous, and some sectors of the religious hierarchy, who more or less openly oppose the revolution.

RADIO HAVANA: What is democracy, in your opinion?

SANKARA: Democracy is the people, with all their strength

and potential. Ballot boxes and an electoral apparatus in and of themselves don't signify the existence of democracy. Those who organize elections every so often, and are concerned about the people only when an election is coming up, don't have a genuinely democratic system. But wherever people can say what they think every day, that's where there's genuine democracy—because you have to earn the people's trust every day. Democracy can't be conceived of without total power resting in the hands of the people—economic, military, political, social, and cultural power.

RADIO HAVANA: How did you come to Marxism?

SANKARA: It was very simple—through discussion, through friendship with a few men. It was also a result of my social experience. I listened to these men discuss and propose solutions to society's problems clearly and logically. Gradually, thanks to reading, but above all thanks to discussions with Marxists on the reality of our country, I came to Marxism.

RADIO HAVANA: There's a street in Ouagadougou named after Ernesto Che Guevara. What does this eminent Latin American patriot mean to you?

SANKARA: This man, who gave himself entirely to the revolution, with his eternal youth, is an example. For me the most important victory is the one conquered deep inside yourself. I admire Che Guevara for having done this in an exemplary way.

RADIO HAVANA: In the context of Africa, what does Patrice Lumumba mean to you?

SANKARA: Patrice Lumumba is a symbol. When I see African reactionaries who were contemporaries of this hero and who were unable to evolve even a little upon contact with him, I see them as wretched, despicable people who stood before a work of art and did not even manage to appreciate it.

Lumumba was in a very unfavorable situation. He grew up under conditions in which Africans had practically no rights whatsoever. Largely self-educated, Patrice Lumumba was one of the few who learned more or less how to read and managed to become conscious of the situation of his people and of Africa.

When you read the last letter Lumumba wrote to his wife, you ask yourself: How could this man have come to an understanding of so many truths other than by experiencing them inwardly and wholeheartedly?

It makes me extremely sad to see how some people use his image and name. There should be a court to judge those who dare use the name of Patrice Lumumba to serve the base, vile causes they promote.

RADIO HAVANA: Comrade President, if you could step back four years, would you do the same thing, follow the same road?

SANKARA: I'd take a different road in order to do much more than I've accomplished, because in my opinion what's been done is not enough. A lot of mistakes have held up the process, when progress could have been greater and more rapid. So if we had everything to do all over again with the experience we have today, we'd fix a lot of things. But we would never abandon the revolution. We would make it deeper, stronger, and more beautiful.

Our revolution needs a people who are convinced, not conquered

On fourth anniversary of revolution
August 4, 1987

The following was given on the fourth anniversary of the revolution in Bobo-Dioulasso, the capital of Houet province.

In this speech and in the next one in this collection, given October 2, Sankara refers to the growing differences over the course of the revolution between himself and the majority of members of the National Council of the Revolution (CNR), as well as of the political organizations participating in it. These included the Union of Burkinabè Communists, the Union of Communist Struggle, and the Burkinabè Communist Group, all of whose origins were Maoist. Most members of the CNR and the leaders of these political groups supported the October 15 coup led by Blaise Compaoré in which Sankara was assassinated.

Among the disagreements dividing the CNR were Sankara's proposal, made later in this speech, for "a pause in the pursuit of a certain number of projects . . . in order to devote our energies to the tasks of political and ideological organization"; the proposal Sankara would make to the CNR on August 21 to consider rehiring teachers and government employees who had been dismissed "for their acts and words against the revolution"; and Sankara's determination to create a united revolutionary organization that reached more deeply into the popular masses and would group together all those actively involved "in economic, social, health, and cultural battles," a topic he would come back to in his October 2 speech.

The speech was published in the August 21, 1987, edition of *Carrefour africain.*

Honorable guests from the Soviet Union, Togo, Benin, Niger, Ivory Coast, Guinea-Bissau, Cape Verde, Angola, Ethiopia, the Saharawi Arab Democratic Republic, Libya, Algeria, Iran, Cuba, France, Italy;

Dear friends of Burkina Faso who have come from Senegal, Belgium, and Spain;

Comrade militants of the democratic and popular revolution:

Today, August 4, 1987, we are celebrating the fourth anniversary of our revolution, the August revolution, the democratic and popular revolution. We let our hearts guide the way to this gathering of joy and jubilation. Our hearts led us to Bobo-Dioulasso, this historic and exuberant town whose name is inextricably linked to the Africa of anticolonial struggle, the Africa of unity, the Africa of federations, in short, the Africa of invigorating pan-Africanism.[1]

Thank you all for coming. Thanks to all those who have become Burkinabè for the day and those who are Burkinabè forever. Thanks to all those who could not make the trip to Bobo-Dioulasso, but who are certainly with us in spirit—with us humbly and unobtrusively by choice or by necessity, but with solemnity and dignity.

---

1. Bobo-Dioulasso had been a center of anticolonial resistance and then the struggle for independence, going back to the end of the nineteenth century.

Thanks also to all those who were unable to celebrate with us today, due to illness and other hardships, and who stoically cherish the hope of better days. Thank you to those who are no longer with us, but who were able to savor the delights of our victories. In memory of all the militants who left us prematurely, let us observe a minute of silence.

Thank you.

Comrades, the fourth anniversary of our revolution takes place under the banner of our dynamic peasantry. The peasantry—the community of those who solve the concrete question of food concretely every day for everyone.

Yes, it is this peasantry, emerging from the shadows of the Middle Ages and backwardness, that, under the most precarious conditions, beats the odds every year one way or another. This peasantry, our peasantry, makes up the largest part of our population. It is the part that has been subjected to—and continues to be subjected to—the most intense exploitation at the hands of the remnants of feudal-type forces and of imperialism. It is this part that has suffered the most from the ills we inherited from colonial society: illiteracy, obscurantism, pauperization, cruelty in many forms, endemic diseases, and famine.

So it comes as no surprise that our peasantry today is a force that wants change, revolutionary change, because only the revolution, by overturning the old order, can satisfy the peasantry's legitimate aspirations. In order to respond to this legitimate desire and mobilize all available energies, the democratic and popular revolution has transformed the peasantry into an organized political force by creating the National Union of Peasants of Burkina.[2]

The axis of this political force must be to strengthen

---

2. The National Union of Peasants of Burkina was created in April 1987.

the revolutionary process by forging a conscious commitment to the revolution on the part of every poor peasant. In the course of the past year many fine initiatives have been taken toward accomplishing this task—a very important and complex one. We'll need to come back to it at another time during Year Five of the revolution in order to define it more fully and in greater depth.

The celebration of Year Four, with its focus on the peasantry, should mark the birth of a new kind of peasant in harmony with the new society that is being built. We are not celebrating the backward peasant, who is resigned to his fate, naive, a slave to obscurantism, and ferociously conservative. We are celebrating the birth of the new peasant, serious and aware of his responsibilities, a man who turns to the future by arming himself with new technologies. Moreover, the increasingly widespread application of the slogan "Produce and consume Burkinabè" is already helping to create this new image of the peasant, a major player in and beneficiary of the policy of building an independent national economy, as laid out by the Second National Conference of the Committees for the Defense of the Revolution.[3]

The implementation of the first five-year popular development plan that's part of this new economic policy, should therefore provide us all with an occasion for learning how to produce what we need for ourselves—and to constantly improve the quality of our work. So the five-year plan should not be implemented with the sole concern of making it possible to compile statistics someday.

Thanks to this all-embracing transformation and its consequences, the term *peasant* should cease to be the

---

3. The Second National Conference of the CDRs was held March 30–April 3, 1987.

derogatory term we know today and should become a synonym for respect—the respect owed a proud and worthy combatant who defends just causes and who successfully meets the targets for his part in social production as a member of the great body that is the people.

The peasantry should not be left to fight this battle alone. The working class and the revolutionary, intellectual petty bourgeoisie should assume their historic responsibility, and work to reduce the gap between town and country through selflessness and sacrifice. The working class and the revolutionary, intellectual petty bourgeoisie should consider this celebration an important milestone in the process of strengthening their strategic alliance with the peasantry. Today is the festival of the peasantry and therefore of its allies, too—symbolized by our emblem, the emblem of the democratic and popular revolution.[4]

Comrades, today we should take a look at four years of revolution, not so much to mechanically praise our victories—though justifiable pride pushes us to do so—but to draw the lessons in order to shed more light on our road to progress.

We have initiated and achieved many concrete transformations to the benefit of the masses. We do not owe these results to more plentiful or exceptional equipment. We owe them to the actions of men. Yesterday these men were resigned, silent, fatalistic, and passive. Today they're standing tall, involved in concrete revolutionary struggle on different projects. The victories we've registered are the fruit of their labor, the projection in real life of their creative genius and their revolutionary enthusiasm.

These results are proof that our revolution is a people's revolution, because it draws its richness, strength, and

---

4. See note on page 157.

invincibility from the masses. This is why we should salute all the courage and selflessness, all the sacrifices and the devotion of the militants of the democratic and popular revolution.

We're not saluting them just to be nice. The results we have achieved can be explained scientifically. Power, whether it comes from muscles or is produced by machines, can be measured and compared and is therefore substitutable. Others before us have demonstrated this, and we had only to apply it to our concrete reality. Doing so has required that the mentality of the Burkinabè cease being a reproduction of the culturally alienated and politically servile individual created to perpetuate imperialist domination in the newly independent countries.

This transformation of our mentality is far from complete. There are still many among us who make foreign norms their touchstone when judging the quality of their social, economic, and cultural lives. They're in Burkina Faso yet refuse to live within the concrete reality of our country. To achieve the new society, we need a new people, a people who have their own identity, a people who know what they want, who know how to assert themselves, and who know what is needed to reach the goals they've set for themselves.

After four years of revolution, our people have begun to forge themselves as this new people. The unprecedented decline of passive resignation registered among our people is a tangible sign of this. The Burkinabè people as a whole believe that a better future is possible. On this point, we've even managed to convince reactionaries of yesterday—people who today, drawn into the workings of history's march forward, join us in looking to the future with optimism, forgetting that only yesterday they were preaching submission to imperialism and perpetual begging as a means to develop the country. The construction of our homeland has strengthened our collective consciousness of the need to depend on our own resources and to emphatically reject resorting to blind and servile mimicry, or to humiliating and degenerate groveling.

Comrade militants, the political year drawing to a close on this fourth anniversary, has certainly been stormy. Without going back over the details of conflicts that arose, or over the quality of the solutions found to resolve them, we must assimilate the main lesson of this experience.

The democratic and popular revolution needs a convinced people, not a conquered people—a convinced people, not a submissive people passively enduring their fate.

Since August 4, 1983, revolutionary Burkina Faso has emerged on the African and international scene, especially and above all thanks to its intellectual genius, and to the moral and human virtues of its leaders and organized masses. We've overcome adversities and triumphed over base and determined opponents who were armed to the teeth. We've succeeded in being firm in defending our principles without ever giving in to anger. We've defended ourselves without hatred and with respect for the dignity of others, because dignity is sacred in Burkina.

The main thing we need to do now is to remember the diverse forms hostile forces can take, and to learn from that to fortify ourselves, since tomorrow's battles will undoubtedly be harder and more complex.

During the past four years of revolution, we have constantly had to confront reaction and imperialism. They have hatched the most vile plots aimed at hindering our work—or worse, at overthrowing our revolution. Imperialism and reaction are, and will remain, fiercely opposed to the transformations taking place every day in our country, threatening their interests.

Yet for the past four years our people have constantly proven that with the revolution, it's possible to end exploitation, do away with misery, and create happiness for all through the power of our hands and hearts. Those living in luxury based on the exploitation of others have opposed our struggle and will do so even more tomorrow.

What have they not done, what are they not doing even today, to stop our forward march? The economic sabotage, the smear campaigns, the corruption, the provocations of all sorts, the blackmail, and the threats are among the many enemy maneuvers we've encountered and confronted during these four years of revolutionary struggle.

We have also known adversity within our beloved Burkina Faso, within our own ranks, in the camp of the revolution. Erroneous ideas and practices have indeed developed among the masses and among revolutionaries, and have caused the revolution harm. We have had to combat these problems despite the relative fragility of our own ranks. We have seen some appalling about-faces. Confrontations have followed provocations. There have even been rifts, though nothing is ever permanent.

We have come up against opportunism and watched it operate. It works in various ways to get us to desert the revolutionary struggle and abandon an intransigent defense of the people's interests in favor of a frenetic search for selfish personal gain. The systematic defense of our revolutionary orientation demands that we combat any idea or any behavior that runs counter to the deepening of the revolution.

As a result of having chosen to follow this path rather than the easier road of demagogy, we've been subjected to ever more slanderous attacks from both our traditional enemies and from elements springing from the ranks of the revolution itself; from impatient people infected with the dubious zeal of the novice, when it's not from a frenzy of schemers with undisguised personal ambitions.[5]

Opportunism, like the counterrevolution, is a thornbush habitually found in the path of the revolution. And until the revolution reaches its final goal, the creation of a new society where there is no exploitation of man by man, opportunism will continue to show itself at different moments, under different circumstances, and in extremely varied forms, all the way from its most right-wing expressions to its most ultraleft and radical.

The difficulties of the struggle, the demands of political activity, the harshness of the class struggle—all these factors have led some comrades to desert our ranks pure and simple, to take premature initiatives, or even to go after the wrong target pure and simple.

Others dream of throwing in the towel but have qualms about how they should do it. They also try to theorize in advance about their desertion of the revolutionary struggle. This is why so many theories and ideas, all thoroughly imbued with opportunism, have been, and still are, circulating.

All of this has given rise to the obstacles we've had to combat in order to go forward. Yet we continue to think and believe that it's only other revolutions that have suffered and are suffering setbacks, defeats, cooptation by the bourgeoisie, fatal deadlocks, and betrayals.

Our revolution, just like others, is constantly threatened

---

5. Beginning in June 1987, anonymous flyers increasingly began to circulate in the country. Often of a scurrilous nature, these unsigned flyers consisted of personal and political attacks against Sankara and other leaders of the revolution. Several well-documented accounts published after the downfall of the revolution state that some of these leaflets were issued by organizations within the National Council of the Revolution.

by all kinds of counterrevolutionary dangers. We must be conscious of this, highly conscious, and firmly commit ourselves to the permanent defense of the correct perspective that will guide us to the ultimate goal. Above all, we must be aware that these problems are created dialectically by the sharpening class struggle, and that, on the contrary, if there were no such problems, it would actually signify the underhanded suppression of the revolutionary struggle in favor of class collaboration.

Comrades, we must take time today to draw the lessons and learn from our past activity in order to enrich our revolutionary theory and practice, and deepen our commitment to the struggle in an organized, more scientific, and more resolute manner.

Many tasks—and complex ones—lie ahead of us. The enemies of our people and revolution have redoubled their energies and ingenious efforts to bar our road forward. And we'll need more courage, more conviction, and more determination to keep marching forward. This determination and conviction will come, in part, from the lessons we're able to draw from four years of struggle. This is why we need to make our revolution's Year Five a year of assessment, a year of scientifically organized ideological and political work. Yes, we need such an assessment.

In four years of revolution we've carried out many important revolutionary transformations. We've laid the basis for solving numerous problems facing our people. We've been very active throughout different sectors of our society. We've given the impression that we want to change everything, and do it immediately. We've been criticized sometimes, and we understand that very well. Furthermore, we ourselves have noticed that other important tasks have been neglected or downplayed. We must devote Year Five specifically to carrying out tasks of a political, ideological, and organizational character.

The deepening of our revolution and the future success of our political activity will depend on how well we solve these issues of organization and ideological orientation in our country. The revolution cannot go forward and achieve its goals without a vanguard organization able to guide the people in all its battles and on all fronts. Forging such an organization will require a big commitment on our part from now on.

Based on the work we've already undertaken to find solutions to the organizational question, revolutionaries in our country must join forces in order to overcome the defects and inadequacies we all share. Unity among revolutionaries is undoubtedly a stage we'll have to go through in order to advance further toward organizing the vanguard. I'm delighted to note that the basis has been laid for building real unity on this fourth anniversary of our revolution, a militant unity of all the revolutionary forces in our country.

We should, however, guard against making unity into a dry, paralyzing, sterilizing, monochromatic thing. On the contrary, we would rather see a manifold, varied, and enriching expression of many different ideas and diverse activities, ideas and activities that are rich with a thousand nuances, all submitted courageously and sincerely, accepting differences, respecting criticism and self-criticism—all directed toward the same radiant goal, which can be none other than the happiness of our people.

Comrades, the ideological, political, and organizational tasks we must accomplish are of great importance for strengthening our revolution and for sustaining our people's overwhelming conscious support for the revolutionary policies we will continue to put into practice. It will take persistent, rigorous political and ideological work to convince the masses and tear them away from all kinds of medieval conceptions that hamper their full commitment to the building of a new society. While the revolution means repression of the exploiters, of our enemies, it must mean only persuasion for the masses—persuasion to take on a conscious and determined commitment.

Our revolution's ideological and political tasks are the duty of all revolutionaries, above all of the political leadership. The political leadership of our revolution must strengthen itself and become more efficient and rigorous in accomplishing its mission. Year Five calls on us to throw all our energies into the organizational fight, into political and ideological consolidation, into the overriding importance of political leadership.

In terms of structured political organization, however, what we are saying here means that we cannot plunge headlong into theoretical schemas and intellectually seductive configurations of no interest to the daily lives of the masses. Let's take advantage of the experience of other revolutions that popular history gives us to learn from. In particular, let's take into account the experience of those like us—and there are many—who have had to equip themselves either with a variety of organizations each united, or with one united organization full of variety. All the while organizing and defending the state power conquered with dignity through fierce struggle. So let's avoid ethereal ramblings that give rise to useless theoretical flow charts devoid of interest to the masses, simply destined for contemplation by a few dreamers and self-gratifying fanatics.

On the contrary, our revolution is first and foremost a qualitative revolution, a qualitative transformation of minds that translates into the practical building of a new Burkinabè society. It's the quality of life that's changing in Burkina, and that's the result of a qualitative evolution of minds.

The myth of getting rich through a dog-eat-dog struggle, based on what happened in the capitalist jungle of the postwar years, has disappeared forever from Burkina. Our homeland has become one vast construction site where the criteria of morality, concern for social justice, and respect for everyone's fundamental right to live and to enjoy a better and better existence are not just empty words, but find material expression in the social activity of each of us.

What gives our revolution its specific character, what makes it an example and accounts for its spreading influence are the cardinal values we've succeeded in fiercely defending up to now. We must continue being revolutionaries, that is, continue being above all men of flesh and blood, men of feelings and of pure emotions.

It's true, in the recent past we sometimes made errors. This should never happen again on the sacred soil of Faso. All of us must have room in our hearts for those who are not yet in perfect agreement with the Political Orientation Speech and the goals of our five-year plan. It's up to us to go to them and win them to the revolutionary cause of the people.

The revolution does not look for short cuts. It requires that we all march together, united in thought and in deed. This is why the revolutionary must be a perpetual teacher, and a perpetual question mark. If the masses do not yet understand, it's our fault. We must take the time to explain, and take the time to convince the masses so that we can act with them and in their interests.

If the masses have trouble understanding, it's still our fault. We have to correct errors, be more precise, adapt ourselves to the masses, and not try to adapt the masses to our own desires and our own dreams. Revolutionaries are not afraid of their mistakes. They have the political courage to admit them publicly, because doing so means a commitment to correcting them and to doing better. We should prefer one step forward together with the people to ten steps forward without the people.

We still have a lot of political work to do to further broaden out the ranks of militants, male and female. There are still thousands of comrades to mobilize, to reorganize, and politicize for revolutionary action. This action will represent a further consolidation and deepening of the indisputable gains of our revolution.

After four years, we must increase tenfold our efforts to think critically about what has been accomplished. We should reject all triumphal and superficial balance sheets, which are so dangerous over time. Perseverance, tolerance, criticism of others, self-criticism—this is the difficult fight to wage, the revolutionary fight.

As revolutionaries we have chosen the difficult road, which means we must surpass ourselves, we must surpass ourselves individually and collectively. There are easier and quicker roads, but they only create illusions and bitter tomorrows. We will succeed thanks to our revolutionary structures in the workplaces, in the towns and villages, thanks to our Committees for the Defense of the Revolution, thanks to the National Movement of Pioneers, thanks to the National Union of Elders of Burkina, and thanks to the National Union of Peasants of Burkina. These structures need to be perfected and completed. Those whose construction needs more effort, those who are most in need of our daily efforts, will get our attention throughout Year Five of our revolution.

Comrades, dear friends from countries in Africa, Europe, America, and Asia:

In the name of our people and the National Council

of the Revolution, I would like to reiterate all our thanks for the support you bring to this struggle, and to repeat our sincere desire and our wish to maintain the friendliest of relations with the peoples of your respective countries. Burkina Faso, land of peace and dignity, will always be present where fraternity and militant, active solidarity are being defended.

Comrade militants from Houet province, through your enthusiastic work and your mobilization you have made this fourth anniversary of our revolution an important milestone on the long road of our people's struggle for a radiant future. I congratulate you and encourage you to redouble your vigilance and fighting spirit so that you may register ever more spectacular successes.

Comrade militants of the democratic and popular revolution:

The revolution is neither sadness nor bitterness. On the contrary, it is the embodiment of the enthusiasm and pride of an entire people taking responsibility for itself, and thereby discovering its own dignity. This is why I invite you to the festival, a festival that is the logical conclusion of work done well and that marks the beginning of new and demanding battles full of promise.

Comrades, I invite you to commit yourselves to the work of Year Five. I invite you to stand firm together in order to pursue the march we have begun at an even more accelerated pace, but which at the same time is experiencing a pause—a pause in the pursuit of a certain number of projects, a pause we need in order to devote our energies to the tasks of political and ideological organization.

I invite you to step forward. To step into the new year that is beginning, a year that will be one of struggles, a year in which we'll anchor our revolution more firmly and put ourselves at the disposal of all the peoples of the world as a contribution to humanity's quest for the happiness denied them by the enemies of the people, and that we, the peoples, have a duty to build here today, now, and for everyone.

For unity with Ghana! [*Shouts of "Forward!"*]

For a conscious, organized, and mobilized peasantry! [*Shouts of "Forward!"*]

For strengthening the National Union of Peasants of Burkina! [*Shouts of "Forward!"*]

For reducing the gap between town and country! [*Shouts of "Forward!"*]

Let us produce! [*Shouts of "Burkinabè!"*]

Let us consume! [*Shouts of "Burkinabè!"*]

Live with the masses!

Triumph with the masses!

Homeland or death, we will win!

Thank you.

Eight million Burkinabè,
eight million revolutionaries

On fourth anniversary
of Political Orientation Speech
October 2, 1987

The following speech was given on the fourth anniversary of the Political Orientation Speech (DOP) in Tenkodogo, capital of Boulgou province. The text was published in the October 8, 1987, issue of *Sidwaya*.

Comrade militants, women and men, of the democratic and popular revolution;
Dear friends of Burkina Faso:

Today we celebrate the fourth anniversary of our guide, our guide to revolutionary action, our ideological guide— the Political Orientation Speech.

Tenkodogo was chosen to host these events, to serve as a focus for the thoughts of the Burkinabè, to receive the greetings and best wishes of our friends. Tenkodogo was selected in order to bring to life all the thinking that has gone into four years of revolutionary initiative, four years of struggle. I would like to congratulate the militants of Boulgou province who mobilized together night and day

Just before
speaking in
Tenkodogo,
October 2, 1987.

so the DOP's fourth anniversary could be celebrated with all the magnificence its importance demands. Their work also ensured that the anniversary celebrations would illustrate the glorious march of our people toward happiness.

The militants of Boulgou province deserve our praise in more than one regard. This is especially true when we take into account all the plots that were made to bar the road to their initiatives, to block their efforts, to discourage their sacrifices, to make a failure of this impressive event that marks the fourth anniversary of the Political Orientation Speech.

Our comrades in Boulgou province, and the revolutionary structures they have created, give us reason to hope, to believe, to have confidence in the future, to have confidence in our masses, wherever they are to be found, geographically speaking. Boulgou province also allows us to believe in miraculous transformations, in leaps forward with the people, always with the people, without surging ahead prematurely. Boulgou province welcomes us under conditions that make it an exemplary province in more than one regard, a deserving province in more than one regard: not only because of its social and economic achievements, but above all because it has mobilized in a political and consistent, confident and determined manner.

If there was a setback in Tenkodogo, if there was a setback in Boulgou province, it was a setback for those—of both the right and the left—who tried in one way or another to disrupt the course of the revolution, believing they could mislead the popular masses, deceive the militants, and use the confusion they themselves artificially created to control them.

The revolution is invincible. It will conquer in both town and country. It will conquer in Burkina Faso because in Boulgou it has already won.

Comrades:

In speaking to the popular masses of Boulgou province, I simply say thank you. Thank you for your enthusiastic welcome, thank you for having begun the celebration under this life-giving rain. An elder reminded me just a moment ago that the first anniversary of the DOP was celebrated in the rain. Today as well we celebrate the fourth anniversary in the rain. It's a welcome element of the celebration. Our peasant masses on whom we rely, our peasant masses who see rain as a fundamental material element of our agricultural system, will certainly not contest us on this point.

Those who twist and turn revolutionary phrases will, unfortunately, see the rain as a symbol of the ceremony's disruption, of the bamboula's[1] disruption. For the peasant, rain means joy, rain means hope, rain means victory and happiness. We are with our people, we fight alongside our people, distancing ourselves from all erroneous ideas. That's why we're happy in Tenkodogo, in the rain, on the fourth anniversary of the DOP.

Comrades:

The Political Orientation Speech, our guide to revolutionary action, is at the disposal of the Burkinabè. It's at the disposal of all revolutionaries. Our guide joins humanity's effort to attain great happiness, to fight the forces of domination, to fight the forces of oppression. That's why our outlook is international. That's why we see the DOP as a link to, an affirmation of the fact that we belong to the collective struggle of all humanity, the humanity of the popular masses, the humanity of peoples in struggle.

That's why we salute the qualitative support, the fraternal and friendly support of our neighboring peoples.

---

1 A word from the Bantu language group meaning "popular festival."

Peoples who, in one way or another, joined with us, crossing the artificial boundaries that separate us in order to extend a hand to that concrete reality—the courage of the Burkinabè. Togolese, friends of Burkina, have come from Togo. We thank them. Ghanaians, fighting alongside us for the African revolution, have come from Ghana. Brothers in combat, in victories, they have also willingly shared our setbacks, which are no more than indications to all of us of the need to continually move forward. We extend greetings to these friends. We extend greetings to all our other friends, so many in number that there's no way to mention them by name.

The Political Orientation Speech serves as our guide. It's the collective achievement of the Burkinabè. It's the collective thinking of all who are a conscious part of making the democratic and popular revolution. That's why the Political Orientation Speech must be our point of reference, our North Star, guiding us and pointing the road forward; the star that keeps us from losing our way. The Political Orientation Speech teaches us that we have to go beyond mere rebellion, that we have to chart a scientific course, a rigorous, methodical course in order to accurately say where we have come from and where we are going. If we don't, our revolution will be no more than a subjective outburst, an outburst by rebels that will have been little more than a brush fire, in other words, it will die a slow death, unable to breathe, unable to catch the breath that enables a revolution to continue going forward, to light the way, and rekindle itself.

The revolutionary guide to action unites us, educates us, and calls on us to act in a disciplined way within the ranks of the revolution. By drawing on the Political Orientation Speech we can help those who have slipped, those who have lost their way, to return to the straight and narrow path.

The Political Orientation Speech rekindles us, brings us warmth—warmth that enables the fearful to regain their footing in struggle and have confidence in the revolution. That's why we must continually go back to the Political Orientation Speech. We not only have to constantly open its pages, read them, and understand them. Above all, we must apply them to the concrete realities around us—realities that evolve, change, become transformed—because we are material beings. Reality is not an idea floating in the air, an idea we can interpret according to our dreams or visions.

The Political Orientation Speech has a past. It's already four years old. That's a lot for a country like ours. But if it has a past, the Political Orientation Speech also has a present—its task today of uniting all revolutionaries. Above all it has a future. What is the future of the Political Orientation Speech?

The future of the Political Orientation Speech depends on the efforts of revolutionaries—efforts to deepen it; continual efforts to make ourselves equal to the battles we face; efforts to bring it to the forefront of today's battles, giving revolutionaries answers to the theoretical and practical questions posed by the many problems besieging us. The aim of the Political Orientation Speech is also to unite, to bring revolutionaries together. It's around the Political Orientation Speech—by consistently refining it, by deepening it in a responsible way—that revolutionaries can transform the reality of Burkina Faso for the Burkinabè people.

Our revolution is not a public-speaking tournament. Our revolution is not a battle of fine phrases. Our revolution is not simply for spouting slogans that are no more than signals used by manipulators trying to use them as catchwords, as codewords, as a foil for their own display. Our revolution is, and should continue to be, the collective effort of revolutionaries to transform reality, to improve the concrete situation of the masses of our country. Our revolution will be worthwhile only if, in looking back, in looking around, in looking ahead, we can say that the Burkinabè are, thanks to the revolution, a little happier. Happier because they have clean water to drink, because they have abundant, sufficient food, because they're in excellent health, because they have education, because they have decent housing, because they are better dressed, because they have the right to leisure, because they have enjoyed more freedom, more democracy, more dignity. Our revolution will have a reason to exist only if it can respond concretely to these questions.

As long as the revolution cannot bring material and moral happiness to our people, it will be no more than the activity of a bunch of people—a collection of people of some merit or other—but really just a bunch of mummies who represent nothing but a lifeless collection of decaying values, incapable of moving and driving forward, incapable of transforming the reality we confront. The revolution is happiness. Without happiness, you cannot talk about success. Our revolution has to answer these questions concretely.

That's why it's so important to make the Political Orientation Speech known to everyone, so it can play its role of rousing and rallying our forces. Of course we run into difficulties all along, as we take action. We have already experienced difficulties in and outside our ranks. These difficulties should not stop us. These difficulties should not discourage us. These difficulties should not become a brake, an insurmountable obstacle for us. On the contrary, they simply teach us that we are indeed involved in revolutionary struggle. That is, they teach us to confront each day the same obstacles that prevented others from reaching the happiness they had promised, because they stuck to words and did not engage in action with and for the people.

We will unite around the Political Orientation Speech. We use it to strengthen the bonds between us. And we use it as the starting point for explaining, for discussing our disagreements, our differences, our points of view, because we share a single goal and it remains the same. Today in Burkina Faso any disagreement that can't be worked out in the framework of the Political Orientation Speech is a disagreement about goals that are different, pure and simple. If the goals are the same, the Political Orientation Speech will provide a way for our methods of action to converge.

Our unity will be forged for the benefit of our people. Our unity won't be like a soccer match played by teams that may be brilliant, certainly outstanding, but that offer only a ninety-minute show, with possible overtime, and may even conclude with a penalty kick. No, our unity will be forged through struggle together with the people, and under their scrutiny. That is to say, we unite as revolutionaries, and only revolutionaries will respond to this unity.

Who then will be a revolutionary? Revolutionaries will be those who in action, in practice, but also in their consciousness, succeed in taking effective, indisputable, unquestionable positions in the course of our struggle, which is a concrete one. It is the struggle, for example, to build dams and reservoirs by the hundreds and thousands. It is the struggle to lay tracks with our own hands to win the Battle for the Railroad, to make it a success. It is the struggle to open up roads, to build health clinics, to pass on some of what we've learned to our brothers, our comrades who haven't had the opportunity to get access to education.

That's where we'll find revolutionaries. We'll find them

in battles on the economic, social, sanitation, and cultural fronts. Opening struggles elsewhere would not be useful. We must see the difference between struggles that are useful to us, and other struggles. The struggles we are interested in are those that make us happier each day, that make our people independent as they struggle fiercely against imperialism.

We will find revolutionaries among those who say no to the products that imperialism dumps on our people so as to continue capitalism's domination over us. Those who accept the rigorous demands of the transformations we're undergoing, those who choose as their duty to give up the habits of a consumer lifestyle in order to live alongside the masses—those will be the revolutionaries. Not everyone is capable of living up to our slogan "Consume Burkinabè." There are many who pay only lip service to "Consume Burkinabè," saving their tongues and mouths for the true delights of imperialist consumption. They are not revolutionaries. They are the ones we're going to unmask. They are the ones who must be pushed aside.

Our peasants in Burkina Faso will never win the battle to free themselves until we, the urban consumers, are ready, for example, to drink beverages produced from their harvests. Why do people want to make us consume products from far away?

This is very serious, unacceptable. It's even more criminal when it is comrades, revolutionaries, who are the transmission belts of this pressure, the transmission belts of this domination. It means these comrades have not grasped the depth and meaning of their own high-quality, high-level speeches. It means we need debate. Let's go back to the Political Orientation Speech. Let's look at the Political Orientation Speech again. It will show us the way. It's unique, and leads us to a single goal—the happiness of our people.

Our unity will be forged in combat, in struggle, with scrupulous respect for our organizational statutes and methods of work. We must be firmly organized around our organizational statutes. Clear statutes will spotlight plots and intrigues, which consistent revolutionaries will fight with legitimate anger. Our unity will be forged around the program of Burkina Faso revolutionaries by applying revolutionary ethics, by applying revolutionary moral values.

Revolutionary moral values will tell us our rights, but more importantly, our duties. Revolutionary moral values will tell us how we must conduct ourselves in society for the masses to evaluate us, positively or negatively; for the masses to continue to come to us not because we've conquered them but because we've convinced them by our example. The Political Orientation Speech should be used to open this door. That door is already there in each line, in each page of our DOP. Let's make the best use of it we can.

Our revolution is a revolution that cannot declare itself exempt from preexisting scientific laws that govern all revolutions. In fact, it's when we fail to apply these scientific laws that we go astray. Without revolutionary theory there can be no revolution. However far it may advance, one day our revolution will certainly meet up with other revolutions through the application of revolutionary theory, through the deepening of our Political Orientation Speech.

We've experienced difficulties—there's no need to hide them—difficulties that have led to confrontations here and there, confrontations among individuals who are good, valuable, and committed to the revolutionary process. These are people we must have confidence in. Whenever we let ourselves fall prey to the idea that only a certain nucleus, only a certain group, is worth anything and that all the others are just complainers and failures, we isolate ourselves. That is, we jeopardize the revolution.

The goal of the revolution is not to scatter revolutionaries. The goal of the revolution is to consolidate our ranks. We are eight million Burkinabè; our goal is create eight million revolutionaries. And no revolutionary has the right to sleep until the last reactionary in Burkina Faso can capably explain the Political Orientation Speech. It's not reactionaries who have to make the effort to understand the speech. It's revolutionaries who have to make the effort to get them to understand. The reactionary has chosen his reactionary position. The revolutionary has chosen his revolutionary position, that is, of going to others to win them over. If he can't win reactionaries to the revolution, the forces of reaction will grow through the world.

Therefore, the duty of every revolutionary is to prevent the revolution from turning in on itself, to prevent the revolution from ossifying, to prevent the revolution from shriveling up like a dried fig. Otherwise a thousand of us would become five hundred, and five hundred no more than two. Our democratic and popular revolution sets itself apart from all sects and sectarian groupings. Each and every day, from the Pioneer movement to the UNAB, we should be able to say we have more and more militants.

Of course, not everyone will be on the same level. It would be utopian, we would be dreaming, to think that everyone could be on the same level of commitment and understanding. It's up to revolutionaries, every day, to never become discouraged, to never become weary, and to make the physical, moral, and intellectual effort to reach out to others. This will frequently require that we be hard on ourselves: explain and explain again. Lenin said something we often forget, "At the root of any revolution you will find pedagogy." Let's never forget that. The art of teaching is repetition. We have to repeat and repeat again.

The Political Orientation Speech also clearly explains the need for us to be resolute in living up to our responsibilities in the class struggle facing us. In Bobo-Dioulasso on August 4, 1987, I invited you to strengthen the revolutionary struggle, in order to win more revolutionaries to our revolution. I invited you to understand that we need a convinced people, not a conquered people. A conquered people means an endless series of prisons; that is, we'd need to find an endless supply of jailers. If we put four million Burkinabè in prison, we'd need twice that many jailers to guard the prisons.

This does not mean we shouldn't know how to deal ruthlessly with those who believe the revolution is synonymous with weakness, those who confuse democratic discussion—which we need—with condescension and sentimentality. Those people will reap what they sow. If they have to be punished, they will be punished, inside or outside Burkina. We know at times we won't be understood. But we also know that sanctions can be educational. We should take action against those who are wrong, who stand in the way of the revolution in order to disrupt it.

We'll come back to them when time permits. What's more, and we've proven this, we've never declared a single person to be a definitive enemy. We've always tried to win back those we could win back. And we'll continue to do so whenever conditions permit. Don't ask us to run and scratch an itch at the same time. Don't ask us to focus on those who are already way ahead, and, at the same time, stop to pay attention to those who are pulling backward, those recalcitrants who are digging in their heels.

We must have the courage to look all this calmly in the face. That's why every militant should understand that every Burkinabè should have a thorough political education. Political education means first of all that all those who favored punishment—without trying to win people over—should systematically rethink their approach. We should try to convince the person who has been punished, to say something about the way they act, their shortcomings, and give them advice that can help them redeem themselves.

Let's educate our people. Let's educate, through democratic discussion, those we're punishing. Once we've been through that process, as revolutionaries, we'll find out if the person punished has made honorable amends and can be redeemed. The best redemption is a process you undertake yourself, not something that comes from others. It means recognizing your errors and solemnly pledging never to repeat them. It also means every day living the life of a revolutionary who has recognized his errors. Under these conditions revolutionaries will value, and make decisions favorable to, those who have been punished.

But first of all, wherever we have attained a certain degree of organization, we should begin using these structures to ask questions about all revolutionaries. Beginning today, October 2, 1987, we invite the people of Burkina, the militants of Burkina, to organize themselves, because the National Council of the Revolution is going to ask them to review the work of every revolutionary. It will be the responsibility of the CDRs to report on the social and revolutionary conduct of individual militants at their workplaces or in their geographic sectors.

Comrades:

The revolution cannot confer state power, it cannot confer power of any kind, it cannot confer even the possibility of taking action except to those who are willing to do so in the interests of our people. We cannot give any responsibility whatsoever, at any level, to those who are working against our people. From now on, no one can be given responsibility at any level without the CDRs or our other organizations having first given their evaluation of the comrade in question.

From time to time we will go back to the ranks to see if such-and-such comrade is a good militant. What do you think of this comrade? Is he a good militant? Does he take part in your evening discussions?[2] Does he play a concrete role in your conferences? Does he take part in your community projects? Does he help resolve problems in his area of work or sector? Does he set a good example? Is he on time? Does he respect the guidelines set by the National Council of the Revolution? That is, does he fight imperialism consistently? From now on, that will be determined through the eyes and ears—the infallible senses—of our people.

The evaluations will be democratic and popular. Then we can say to each person—whether a director, head of a workplace, or an official—"Comrade, over the course of the year your conduct has been in keeping with the Political Orientation Speech, with the organizational statutes, with the program, with revolutionary ethics." Or we can say, "Comrade, we regret to tell you that you have been acting out of step with, in contradiction to, your revolutionary commitments." And we'll take the necessary measures.

This means that from now on all those who have been punished—dismissed, released from responsibility, suspended—must be called before the CDR to see what has become of them, what they are doing for the revolution. Those who are doing nothing are actually doing something against the revolution. For the revolution, each one

---

2. These were events organized by the Committees for the Defense of the Revolution, usually in the form of a presentation on a specific theme followed by a question-and-discussion period.

must answer to the popular organizations. Because there are some who believe, erroneously, that once a sanction had been taken against them, they had become enemies of the revolution and had to act as enemies of the revolution. Yes, a sanction was imposed, but the revolution still needs them. Because the supreme sanction is to do away with your enemy completely. But the revolution offers people who have been sanctioned the advantage of remaining with us to see, to hear, and to understand, in order to redeem themselves. So they really must be followed up on, not to make life difficult for them, but so we know exactly what they're doing for the revolution.[3]

The Political Orientation Speech is there for all of us. No one can live off the backs of our people and claim it was because he was pushed to the sidelines. Those who have sought out the sidelines will be found by the people. The people have been given the mission to act, to seek out, and to educate all those who have tried to bury themselves in some hole or other. That's how we can be sure we've really tried to educate, because some people who were punished say they were simply pushed to the sidelines. Well, how many of them are willing to take part in community projects? How many are willing to make their contribution to moving the revolution forward?

Comrades:

The revolution is constantly victorious. Having established its control over the situation, the revolution can allow some people to redeem themselves. That's why, on

---

3. On August 21, 1987, Sankara asked government ministers to review requests for reinstating teachers and civil servants who had been fired for their opposition to the revolution. Sankara's proposal met strong opposition within the National Council of the Revolution and most of the political organizations within it.

this fourth anniversary of the Political Orientation Speech, I would like to announce two measures.

The first is the freeing of detainees whose social behavior harmed our people, that is, detainees who had committed actions, crimes, and violations of common law against men, women, and goods belonging to our people. We're going to set them free because we've watched them during the process of social reintegration. This reintegration is happening everywhere and must be continued. For revolutionaries, victory lies in the disappearance of prisons.

For reactionaries, victory lies in the construction of a maximum number of prisons. That's the difference between them and us. We will free eighty-eight people. The minister of justice will publish the names of these eighty-eight who conducted themselves well at work on the construction sites. Each day they appreciated more the mistake they had made, and understood that work makes us free. Of course, there are always individuals who will not know how to take advantage of the revolution's clemency. And, of course, they'll be put back where they came from. But I'm sure the majority, perhaps all, will take advantage of this act of clemency, so we can free others as well.

The second measure concerns the stockbreeders. For a long time we've had a tax that weighed heavily on stockbreeders. The National Council of the Revolution has decided to just abolish this tax. We're abolishing it not because the state's coffers are full. We're abolishing this tax because it hurts us and causes our people unnecessary suffering. It demobilizes the section of the peasantry that breeds livestock. It hurts our economy by disrupting the raising of livestock. So we're abolishing it.

We invite the organizations concerned—the Ministry of Agriculture and Stockbreeding, the Secretariat of State for Stockbreeding, the Ministry of the Peasant Question, and all the other organizations—to help us draw maximum benefit from abolishing the tax, as opposed to simply accepting that administration and funding have become more difficult. I invite employees of the tax office, for example, to use their imagination to come up with other ways of mobilizing our resources so we can do an even better job of building our Faso.

Joy for some should not mean sadness for others. Every one of us—those directly engaged in stock raising, those who live off or draw profit from it, whether upstream or downstream, whether behind, in front of, or under the cattle benefit from the measure. And I thank you, comrades, for the support you have given this measure.

Comrades, at last the Political Orientation Speech has been made available in translation in the national languages of Fulfulde, Diula, and Mooré. That's a way to reach more people, more Burkinabè. I would like to thank all who helped in this work. To adapt and translate concepts that were often new in our milieu, to render them equally accessible, without pedantry, this was an intellectual task that surely required great effort, a lot of work, and a lot of thought. I congratulate those involved because they have created something useful. I also congratulate those who took the initiative in the project of translating the DOP.

I congratulate, in advance, those who work every day to help our people become more literate—the ministries of National Education, of Higher Education and Scientific Research, and of the Peasant Question. That's their direct contribution to enriching the DOP. If the peasants don't know how to read the speech—because they've never learned how to read—there would be little interest in the fact the DOP has been translated into the national languages. They would remain blind. To offer someone who cannot read an untranslated copy of the DOP would be like insulting a blind man by offering him a flashlight. First, the blind man needs to be able to see, then he needs the flashlight to see better. First, let's help all who are illiterate learn how to read. Then we'll give them sound material to read, useful material, like the DOP translated into the national languages.

Comrades of Boulgou:

I extend my congratulations again to the high commissioner and to the provincial PRP.[4] I extend my congratulations again to the provincial Committees in Defense of the Revolution. I extend my congratulations again to the provincial section of the National Union of Elders of Burkina. I extend my congratulations again to the provincial section of the Women's Union of Burkina. I extend my congratulations again to the National Union of Peasants of Boulgou. And I won't forget the Pioneers, who brought us so much pleasure in this celebration and show us that the future is full of hope.

I won't forget the workers, particularly the engineer who was seriously injured in the course of building the October 2 monument in Tenkodogo. Despite his injury he returned to the job immediately after receiving a bit of medical care, to make sure the finishing touches on the monument were done right. The miracle happened. The monument was erected in a matter of days. And the forked tongues of our enemies were cut to pieces. From now on, we'll congratulate those who have excelled at their work more often by awarding medals, as we've just done.

---

4. The Provincial Revolutionary Government (PRP) was the governing body of revolutionary power in every province. Each was presided over by a high commissioner appointed by the National Revolutionary Council. The PRP was composed of all those in charge of government services in the province.

Comrades, this morning at the unveiling of the October 2 monument the comrade minister of state[5] spoke of the meaning of this symbol. I'm certain he planted a little seed of feeling in each of you that will encourage you to advance even further. And that's why it's natural, easy, and a pleasure for me to say to you today:

Comrades, forward to a thousand anniversaries of the DOP!

Forward to a DOP that's even deeper, even more capable of uniting us despite all that may be done to divide us!

Forward to a DOP that will be the material basis for the moral and material happiness of our people!

Forward to a DOP that will be the beacon guiding us and other peoples to the happiness in which we all have such faith!

Homeland or death, we will win!

Thank you.

5. Blaise Compaoré.

You cannot kill ideas

A tribute to Che Guevara
October 8, 1987

A week before the overthrow of the revolutionary government and Sankara's assassination, he gave this speech in
Ouagadougou at the inauguration of an exhibition honoring
the life of Cuban revolutionary leader Ernesto Che Guevara, who
had been killed exactly twenty years earlier. A Cuban delegation that included Guevara's son, Camilo Guevara March, was
in attendance. Inaudible passages in the tape-recording of the
speech are indicated by ellipses.

We've come this morning, in a modest way, to open this
exhibition that seeks to trace the life and work of Che. At
the same time, we want to tell the whole world today that
for us Che Guevara is not dead. Because throughout the
world there are centers of struggle where people strive for
more freedom, more dignity, more justice, and more happiness. Throughout the world, people are fighting against
oppression and domination; against colonialism, neocolonialism, and imperialism; and against class exploitation.

Dear friends, we join our voices with everyone in the world who remembers that one day a man called Che Guevara . . . his heart filled with faith, took up the struggle alongside other men and, in so doing, succeeded in creating a spark that powerfully disturbed the forces of occupation in the world.

We simply want to say that a new era in Burkina Faso has come, a new reality is on the march in our country. That's how Che Guevara's call to action must be understood—Che, who wanted to light fires of struggle throughout the world.

Che Guevara was cut down by bullets, imperialist bullets, under Bolivian skies. And we say that for us, Che Guevara is not dead.

One of the beautiful phrases often recalled by revolutionaries, by the great Cuban revolutionaries, is the one that Che's friend, his companion in struggle, his comrade, his brother, Fidel Castro himself repeated. He heard it from the mouth of a man of the people one day during the struggle—one of Batista's officers who, despite being part of that reactionary, repressive army, managed to connect with the forces fighting for the well-being of the Cuban people. Right after the assault on the Moncada garrison had failed, when those who had attempted it were about to be put to death by the guns of Batista's army— they were going to be shot—the officer said simply, "Don't shoot, you cannot kill ideas."[1]

---

1. On July 26, 1953, some 160 combatants led by Fidel Castro attacked the Moncada garrison in Santiago de Cuba, and the garrison in the nearby town of Bayamo, with the goal of initiating a popular uprising against the U.S.-backed dictatorship of Fulgencio Batista. After the attack, Batista's forces massacred more than fifty of the captured revolutionaries. Despite its failure, the Moncada attack marked the opening volley of the revolutionary struggle that culminated less than six years later in the overthrow of the dictatorship in January 1959.

It's true, you cannot kill ideas. Ideas do not die. That's why Che Guevara, an embodiment of revolutionary ideas and self-sacrifice, is not dead. You have come here today [from Cuba], and we draw inspiration from you.

Che Guevara, an Argentine according to his passport, became an adopted Cuban through the blood and sweat he shed for the Cuban people. He became, above all, a citizen of the free world—the free world that we're building together. That's why we say that Che Guevara is also African and Burkinabè.

Che Guevara called his beret *la boina*. He made that beret and its star known almost everywhere in Africa. From the north to the south, Africa remembers Che Guevara.

Bold young people—young people thirsting for dignity, thirsting for courage, thirsting also for ideas and for the vitality he symbolized in Africa—sought out Che Guevara in order to drink from the source, the invigorating source represented in the world by this revolutionary captain. Some of the few who had the opportunity and honor of being in Che's presence, and who are still alive, are here among us today.

Che is Burkinabè. He is Burkinabè because he participates in our struggle. He is Burkinabè because his ideas inspire us and are inscribed in our Political Orientation Speech. He is Burkinabè because his star is stamped on our banner. He is Burkinabè because some of his ideas live in each of us in the daily struggle we wage.

Che is a man, but a man who knew how to show us and teach us that we can dare to have confidence in ourselves and our abilities. Che is among us.

What is Che, I'd like to ask? Che, to us, is above all conviction, revolutionary conviction, revolutionary faith in what you're doing, the conviction that victory belongs to us, and that struggle is our only recourse.

Che is also a sense of humanity. Humanity—this expression of generosity and self-sacrifice that made Che not only an Argentine, Cuban, and internationalist combatant, but also a man, with all the warmth of a man.

Che is also, and above all, demanding. The demanding character of one who had the good fortune to be born into a well-to-do family . . . Yet he was able to say no to those temptations, to turn his back on the easy road in order, on the contrary, to assert himself as a man of the people, a man who makes common cause with the people, a man who makes common cause with the suffering of others. Che's demanding character is what should inspire us the most.

Conviction, humanity, a demanding character—all this makes him Che. Those who are capable of mustering these virtues within themselves, those who are capable of mustering these qualities within themselves—this conviction, this humanity, and this demanding character—they can say that they are like Che—men among men, but, above all, revolutionaries among revolutionaries.

We have just looked at these pictures that trace part of Che's life as best they can. Despite their forceful expression, these images remain silent on the most crucial part of the man, the very part against which imperialism took aim. The bullets were aimed much more at Che's spirit than at his image. His picture is found the world over. His photo is in everyone's mind, and his silhouette is one of the best known. So let's see to it that we're able to get to know Che better.

Let's draw closer to Che. Let's draw closer to him, not as we would a god, not as we would an idea—an image placed above men—but rather with the feeling that we're moving toward a brother who speaks to us and to whom we can also speak. We must see to it that revolutionaries draw inspiration from Che's spirit, that they too become internationalists, that they too, together with other men, learn how to build faith—faith in the struggle for change, in the struggle against imperialism and against capitalism.

As to you, Comrade Camilo Guevara, we certainly cannot speak of you as an orphaned son. Che belongs to all of us. He belongs to us as a heritage belonging to all revolutionaries. So you cannot feel alone and abandoned, finding as you do in each of us—we hope—brothers, sisters, friends, and comrades. Together with us today you are a citizen of Burkina, because you have followed resolutely in Che's footsteps—the Che who belongs to all of us, a father to us all.

Finally, let us remember Che simply as an embodiment of eternal romanticism, of fresh and invigorating youth, and at the same time of the clear-sightedness, wisdom, and devotion that only profound men, men with heart, can possess. Che was the seventeen-year-old youth. But Che was also the wisdom of a man of seventy-seven. This judicious combination is something we should achieve all the time. Che was both the heart that spoke, and the bold and vigorous hand that took action.

Comrades, I would like to thank our Cuban friends for the efforts they made to be with us. I would like to thank all those who traveled thousands of kilometers and crossed oceans to come here to Burkina Faso to remember Che.

I would also like to thank everyone whose personal contributions will ensure that this day will not be a mere date on the calendar, but will, above all, become days, many days in the year, many days over the years and centuries, making Che's spirit live eternally.

Comrades, I would finally like to express my joy that we have been able to immortalize Che's ideas here in Ouagadougou by naming this street after Che Guevara.

Every time we think of Che, let's try to be like him, and make this man, the combatant, live again. And especially, every time we think of acting in his spirit of self-sacrifice, by rejecting material goods that seek to alienate us, by refusing to take the easy road, by turning instead to education and the rigorous discipline of revolutionary morality—every time we try to act in this way, we will better serve Che's ideas, we will spread them more effectively.

Homeland or death, we will win!

Glossary

African Development Bank – Created 1964 by newly independent African governments with stated aim of providing loans and assistance for social and economic projects in Africa. Headquarters in Abidjan, Côte d'Ivoire.

African Independence Party/Patriotic Development League (PAI/Lipad) – Political organization looking to ex–Soviet Union. Led a number of unions prior to revolution. Part of National Council of the Revolution 1983–84. Rallied to Blaise Compaoré regime after October 1987 coup.

African National Congress (ANC) – Formed 1912, led South African antiapartheid struggle. Legalized 1990 after 30-year ban. Became governing party in 1994, after first elections not limited to whites.

Allende, Salvador (1908–1973) – Leader of Socialist Party of Chile. Elected president of Chile September 1970. Killed during military coup September 1973.

Apartheid – Social and political system in South Africa based on racial separation, institutionalized after 1948, with aim of maintaining domination by white minority. Overthrown after decades of struggle, registered by first nonracial elections in 1994 that brought African National Congress to power with Nelson Mandela as president.

Batista, Fulgencio (1901–1973) – Military strongman in Cuba 1934–44. Led coup on March 10, 1952, establishing military-police tyranny. Fled Cuba January 1, 1959, in face of advancing Rebel Army and popular insurrection.

Bishop, Maurice (1944–1983) – Central leader of New Jewel Movement of Grenada. Prime minister of popular revolutionary government brought to power after March

1979 overthrow of U.S.-backed dictatorship. Headed workers and farmers government until October 1983, when coup led by Bernard Coard overthrew it and murdered Bishop, opening door to U.S. invasion of island days later.

Botha, Pieter (1916–2006) – Prime minister (1978–84) then president (1984–89) of apartheid regime in South Africa.

Bourguiba, Habib (1903–2000) – Prime minister of Tunisia 1956; president 1957–87.

Cabral, Amilcar (1924–1973) – Founder in 1956 of African Party for Independence of Guinea-Bissau and Cape Verde (PAIGC), which took up arms against Portuguese rule in 1963. Assassinated January 13, 1973, in Conakry by agents of Portuguese imperialism.

Carrefour africain – French-language periodical published in Ouagadougou from 1960 until early 2000s.

Cartierism – Named after journalist Raymond Cartier (1904–1975), who waged a campaign in 1950s and '60s against all aid by French government to its former African colonies, under pretext that doing so only heightened corruption in the newly independent regimes.

Castro, Fidel (1926–2016) – Led revolutionary war in Cuba against U.S.-backed Batista dictatorship. Prime minister from 1959 to 1976, since then president of Council of State and Council of Ministers, 1976–2008, Commander in chief of Revolutionary Armed Forces, 1959–2008, and first secretary of Communist Party of Cuba, 1965–2011.

Castro, Raúl (1931–) – A central leader of Cuba's revolutionary war. Minister of the Revolutionary Armed Forces since 1959. Vice premier 1959–76, then vice president of Council of State and Council of Ministers. Second secretary of Communist Party of Cuba since 1965.

Committees for the Defense of the Revolution (CDRs) – Mass organizations developed after revolutionary victory, based in neighborhoods, villages, workplaces, schools, and army units throughout country, and among Burkinabè abroad. Mobilized participation in social programs of revolutionary government; drew population into political activity. Organized militia out of their ranks. Dissolved by Compaoré regime March 1988.

Compaoré, Blaise (1951–) – Burkina Faso's head of state since 1987 coup that overthrew revolutionary government, in which Sankara was assassinated. As commander of National Commando Training Center at Pô military base, led August 4, 1983, march on Ouagadougou that opened way to victory of revolution. Became member of National Council of Revolution and minister of justice.

Contadora Group – Established 1983 by Mexico, Venezuela, Colombia, and Panama. Sought to organize negotiations between conflicting forces in contra war in Nicaragua and civil war in El Salvador. Sandinista-led government's defeat of contras led to signing of accord in August 1987 by Costa Rica, El Salvador, Guatemala, Honduras, and Nicaragua.

Contadora Support Group – Formed 1985 by governments of Argentina, Brazil, Peru, and Uruguay to support Contadora Group.

Contras – Counterrevolutionary army fighting Sandinista-led government in Nicaragua in 1980s. Financed, organized, trained, and armed by Washington and its client regimes in region. Militarily defeated by early 1987.

Council of Popular Salvation (CSP) – Government established after coup by Gabriel Somé Yoryan, November 7, 1982. Jean-Baptiste Ouédraogo became president, Jean-Baptiste Lingani, general secretary. Sankara was named prime minister, January 10, 1983. Dissolved after May 17, 1983, coup, when Sankara and Lingani were arrested.

Diakité, Moussa – From Mali, director of West African Economic Community's Solidarity, Development and Compensation Fund. Tried and convicted by People's Revolutionary Courts in 1986 for embezzlement of

6 billion CFA francs, sentenced to 15 years in prison.

Diallo, Hama Arba (1939–2014) – Leader of Patriotic Development League (Lipad), an organization that supported new government in August 1983. Minister of foreign affairs from August 1983 until dissolution of first cabinet of National Council of the Revolution in August 1984. Arrested at end of 1984, freed in early 1985. Rallied to support of new regime after October 1987 counterrevolution.

Diawara, Mohamed – Businessman, former minister of economic planning in Côte d'Ivoire. Put on trial by People's Revolutionary Court for defrauding West African Economic Community of 6 billion CFA francs. Sentenced to 15 years in prison in 1986.

Engels, Frederick (1820–1895) – Lifelong collaborator of Karl Marx and cofounder with him of modern communist workers movement.

Entente Council – Founded in 1959 under domination of Paris. Includes Benin, Burkina Faso, Côte d'Ivoire, Niger, and Togo. Primarily takes up technical and economic questions.

Eyadéma, Gnassingbe (1935–2005) – President of Togo 1967–2005.

Five-year plan – Launched 1986 to improve peasants' living conditions and develop agricultural production. Replaced Popular Development Program.

Foccart, Jacques (1913–1997) – In charge of African and Malagasy affairs for French presidents Charles de Gaulle and Georges Pompidou 1958–74. Built political, military, and financial networks in Africa that enabled Paris to create, topple, and control governments in former French colonies.

Fonseca, Carlos (1936–1976) – Founded Sandinista National Liberation Front (FSLN) of Nicaragua in 1961. Was its central leader until his death in combat against U.S.-backed Somoza dictatorship.

Frontline States – Grouping of African countries in geographic proximity to South African apartheid state: Angola, Botswana, Mozambique, Tanzania, Zambia, and Zimbabwe. Were targets of repeated military attacks and economic pressure by apartheid regime.

Gandhi, Indira (1917–1984) – Prime minister of India 1966–77, and from 1980 until her assassination.

Group of 77 – Committee formed 1964 by 77 semicolonial UN-member countries, with goal of presenting common front at UN conferences on economic development. In 2007 the Group had more than 130 members.

Guevara, Ernesto Che (1928–1967) – Argentine-born leader of Cuban Revolution. Promoted to rank of commander in revolutionary war 1956–58. After 1959 was head of National Bank and then minister of industry. Beginning in April 1965 led Cuban internationalist volunteers in Congo, then Bolivia. Wounded and captured by Bolivian army October 8, 1967. Murdered next day on Washington's orders.

Hart, Armando (1930–2017) – Founding member of July 26 Movement in Cuba and a leader of clandestine urban struggle during revolutionary war. Minister of culture 1976–97; Communist Party of Cuba Central Committee member, 1965 until his death. Political Bureau member, 1965-91

Houphouët-Boigny, Félix (1905–1993) – Côte d'Ivoire (Ivory Coast) president from independence in 1960 until his death. Faithful ally of French imperialism.

International Monetary Fund (IMF) – Imperialist financial organization founded 1945. Through loans and "structural adjustment policies," has saddled semicolonial countries with debt and interest payments, while pressing cuts in social expenditures and sale of state-owned enterprises to private capitalists.

Kaunda, Kenneth (1924–) – First president of independent Zambia 1964–91.

Kérékou, Mathieu (1933–2015) – President of Benin 1972–91, 1996–2006.

Ki-Zerbo, Joseph (1922–2006) – Burkinabè historian. Founder of National Liberation Movement in 1958, then of Voltaic Progressive Front in 1980. Supported November 25, 1980, coup. Opposed National Council of the Revolution after August 1983. Chose to live in exile during revolution.

Kountché, Seyni (1931–1987) – President of Niger 1974–87.

Lamizana, Aboubakar Sangoulé (1916–2005) – Military officer, took power in 1966 coup after overthrow of Maurice Yaméogo government. Elected president in 1978, overthrown by November 1980 coup led by Sayé Zerbo. Acquitted of fraud charges by Popular Revolutionary Courts in 1984. Leader of Union of Burkinabè Elders in 1986.

League for Patriotic Development (Lipad). *See* African Independence Party/Patriotic Development League

Lenin, V.I. (1870–1924) – Founder of Bolshevik Party. Central leader of 1917 October Revolution in Russia. Chair of Council of People's Commissars (Soviet government) 1917–24; member of Executive Committee of Communist International 1919–24.

Lingani, Jean-Baptiste Boukary (d. 1989) – Military commander, became general secretary of Popular Council of Salvation after November 7, 1982, coup. Arrrested at same time as Sankara during May 1983 coup. Became CNR member and army chief of staff after August 4 revolution. Member of Blaise Compaoré government after Sankara's assassination. Executed without trial September 1989.

Lumumba, Patrice (1925–1961) – Leader of Congo's fight for independence from Belgian rule. Became first Congolese prime minister June 1960. Overthrown in September in coup led by Joseph Mobutu and murdered in January 1961 with support and aid of U.S. and other imperialist governments and with complicity of UN troops.

Machel, Samora (1933–1986) – Commander of armed forces of Frelimo liberation movement in Mozambique 1966–75. Became Frelimo president 1970. President of country from independence in 1975 until his death in October 1986 in plane crash over South African territory that many African and antiapartheid leaders considered a political assassination.

Mandela, Nelson (1918–2013) – Leader of antiapartheid struggle and African National Congress in South Africa. Arrested 1962 and imprisoned until 1990, freed under impact of growing international campaign and rising revolutionary struggle. Elected president of South Africa 1994 in first nonracial elections, serving until 1999.

Martí, José (1853–1895) – Cuba's national hero. Revolutionary, poet, writer, speaker, journalist, and combatant. Founded Cuban Revolutionary Party in 1892 to fight Spanish colonial rule and oppose U.S. designs on Cuba. Organized and planned independence war in 1895 and died in combat.

Marx, Karl (1818–1883) – Founder with Frederick Engels of modern communist workers movement and architect of its programmatic foundations.

Military Committee for Redressment and National Progress (CMRPN) – Highest government body under Upper Volta regime of Col. Saye Zerbo, November 25, 1980, to November 7, 1982, following coup against President Sangoulé Lamizana.

Mitterrand, François (1916–1996) – Post–World War II leader of Socialist Party in France. As interior minister organized repression at start of Algerian independence fight 1954 and opposed independence for Vietnam and other French colonies. Became first secretary of Socialist Party 1971; president of France 1981–95.

Mobutu Sese Seko (1930–1997) – Army colonel, organized September 1960 coup against Patrice Lumumba in Congo. Directly involved in Lumumba's 1961 murder in collaboration with Belgian and U.S. imperialism. President of Congo, which he renamed Zaïre, 1965–97. Overthrown 1997, died in exile.

Mondlane, Eduardo (1920–1969) – Founder and first president of Frelimo liberation movement, waging independence struggle in Mozambique against Portuguese colonial rule. Assassinated in Dar es Salaam by agents of Portuguese imperialism, February 1969.

Mozambique Liberation Front (Frelimo) – Founded 1962, launched armed struggle against Portuguese colonial rule in 1964. Became governing party in 1975 when Mozambique gained independence.

Mugabe, Robert (1924–2019) – A leader of struggle against white minority regime in Rhodesia since early 1960s. Prime minister 1980–87; president 1987–2017.

Namibia – Southern African state, won independence in 1990 after decades-long struggle waged by SWAPO against colonial domination by South Africa.

Nasser, Gamal Abdel (1918–1970) – Egyptian army officer who led overthrow of monarchy in 1952. Prime minister 1954–56; president 1956–70. In 1956 nationalized British- and French-owned Suez Canal. A founder of Nonaligned Movement.

National Council of the Revolution (CNR) – Highest body of government, established by Thomas Sankara and his collaborators on taking power August 4, 1983. Dissolved during October 15, 1987, coup.

National Movement of Pioneers (MNP) – Mass movement created May 1985 for children between 6 and 12.

National Union of African Teachers of Upper Volta (SNEAHV) – Union of elementary school teachers. Its leadership was strongly influenced by Voltaic Progressive Front.

National Union of Peasants of Burkina (UNPB) – Created April 1987 to involve peasants in revolution, especially in land reform.

Nehru, Jawaharlal (1889–1964) – Prime minister of India, from independence in 1947 until his death. A founder of Nonaligned Movement.

Ngom, Moussa – Senegalese politician, secretary general of West African Economic Community beginning in 1976. Tried for fraud in Burkina Faso by Popular Revolutionary Courts in April 1986. Sentenced to 15 years in prison.

Nkrumah, Kwame (1909–1972) – Led Ghana to independence from United Kingdom in 1957; president until overthrown in U.S.-backed military coup February 1966. Proponent of Pan-Africanism. A founder of Nonaligned Movement. Died in exile.

Nonaligned Countries, Movement of – Founded 1961 by representatives of 25 governments and national liberation movements in colonies and semicolonies, at initiative of governments of Egypt, Ghana, India and Yugoslavia. More than 100 member governments and national liberation movements took part in its eighth conference, held 1986 in Harare, Zimbabwe.

Organization of African Unity (OAU) – Founded in Addis Ababa, Ethiopia, in 1963. In 1983 included all independent states and African liberation movements except for South Africa. Became African Union in 2002.

Ortega, Daniel (1945–) – Leader of Sandinista National Liberation Front and of workers and peasants government established in 1979. President of Nicaragua 1984–90. Almost two decades after demise of revolutionary government, elected president in 2006.

Ouédraogo, Jean-Baptiste (1942–) – Military commander. President of Upper Volta after November 1982 coup, and creation of Council of Popular Salvation. Participated in May 1983 coup. Overthrown by August 4, 1983, revolution.

Palestine Liberation Organization (PLO) – Founded in 1964 as umbrella organization of groups fighting for Palestinian national rights against colonial-settler state of Israel.

Patriotic Development League. *See* African Independence Party/ Patriotic Development League

Penne, Guy (1925–2010) – Adviser to French president Mitterrand on African affairs 1981–86. Present in Ouagadougou during proimperialist May 1983 coup.

People's Revolutionary Courts (TPRs) – Established October 1983 by National Council of the Revolution. Convened by government order, each court was composed of seven members named by Council of Ministers: a judge, a soldier or police officer, and five CDR members. Dealt mainly with counterrevolutionary activities and serious cases of corruption.

Pinochet, Augusto (1915–2006) – Chilean general; led bloody U.S.-backed coup in 1973; dictator of Chile until 1990.

Polisario Front. *See* Saharawi Arab Democratic Republic

Popular Courts of Conciliation (TPC) – Neighborhood courts dealing with domestic or community conflicts. Its members were elected by popular assemblies.

Popular Development Program (PPD) – Launched in October 1984 by National Council of the Revolution, lasted 15 months, and mobilized population through Committees for the Defense of the Revolution to carry out small-scale projects in road building and construction of water reservoirs, sports facilities, and rural health clinics.

Popular Investment Effort (EPI) – Deductions from pay of workers and government employees to fund development programs.

Qaddafi, Muammar al- (1942–2011) – Libyan army officer who led military coup that overthrew monarchy in 1969; nationalized country's oil in 1973; Libya's head of state 1969 until his death.

Rawlings, Jerry (1947–2020) – Flight lieutenant in Ghanaian armed forces. In 1981 became president of National Provisional Defense Council of Ghana, set up by junior army officers and civilians. President of Ghana 1993–2001.

Revolutionary Solidarity Fund (CSR) – Created November 1983 to aid rural populations threatened by drought and famine. Financed by voluntary contributions; had collected nearly 500 million CFA francs by mid-1985.

Saharawi Arab Democratic Republic (SADR) – Established by Polisario Front 1976 in former Spanish colony of Western Sahara to counter invasions by Morocco and Mauritania; the latter withdrew in 1979. Became a full member of Organization of African Unity in 1984. Continues to fight U.S.- and French-backed occupation by Morocco.

Sahel – Semiarid region of Africa along southern edge of Sahara Desert. Covers parts of Burkina Faso, Chad, Ethiopia, Mali, Mauritania, Niger, Nigeria, Senegal, and Sudan. Has suffered increasing desertification since end of 1960s and recurring major droughts.

Sandinista National Liberation Front (FSLN) – Founded in 1961 by Carlos Fonseca to organize struggle against U.S.-backed Somoza dictatorship. Led workers and peasants government following 1979 revolutionary victory. By late 1980s the revolutionary course FSLN had initially followed had been reversed, leading to downfall of workers and peasants government and subsequent FSLN defeat in 1990 elections.

Sandino, Augusto César (1895–1934) – Led six-year guerrilla struggle in Nicaragua against U.S. Marines and proimperialist forces 1927–33. Murdered on orders of U.S.-backed dictator Anastasio Somoza.

Sassou Nguesso, Denis (1943–) – Army colonel; president of Congo Brazzaville 1979–92 and from 1997.

Savimbi, Jonas (1934–2002) – Founded National Union for the Total Independence of Angola (UNITA) in 1966 to fight Portuguese rule of Angola. Once independence was won in 1975, became ally of South African apartheid regime and U.S. imperialism against the new government. Killed in ambush by Angolan armed forces.

Sidwaya – French-language daily published in Ouagadougou since 1984.

Somé Yoryan, Gabriel (d. 1983) – Army colonel, initiated November 1982 coup that put Council of Popular Salvation in power. Organized May 1983 coup against then–prime minister Thomas Sankara. Arrested after August 4, 1983, revolution. Shot August 9.

Somoza Debayle, Anastasio (1925–1980) – Last of family of dictators ruling Nicaragua since 1936. President from 1967 to 1979, overthrown by Sandinista revolution.

SWAPO (South West African People's Organisation) – National liberation movement formed 1960 to fight for Namibia's independence from South African colonial rule. Fought alongside Cuban-Angolan forces in southern Angola. Governing party in Namibia since independence in 1990.

Tito, Josip Broz (1892–1980) – Led Partisan struggle against Nazi occupation of Yugoslavia during World War II. Prime minister of Yugoslavia 1945–53, president from 1953 until his death. A founder of Nonaligned Movement.

Touré, Soumane (1948–) – Leader of Patriotic Development League (Lipad); secretary general of Confederation of Voltaic Unions (became Confederation of Burkinabè Unions in 1985) 1976–84. Following series of clashes with government, was imprisoned without charges or trial January 1985–October 1986.

Traoré, Moussa (1936–) – Installed as president of Mali in 1968 coup, overthrown by coup in 1991.

UNAB (National Union of Elders of Burkina) – Created November 1986 to involve the elderly in the revolution.

UNITA (National Union for the Total Independence of Angola) – Founded 1966 to fight Portuguese colonial rule. When independence was won in 1975, allied itself with the South African apartheid regime and U.S. imperialism against new government. Over next 25 years waged a terrorist war, killing hundreds of thousands.

Voltaic Progressive Front (FPV) – Procapitalist, proimperialist organization led by Joseph Ki-Zerbo. Founded 1958 as National Liberation Movement, became FPV in 1980. Banned by National Council of the Revolution in 1983.

West African Economic Community (CEAO) – Replaced West African Customs and Economic Union in January 1974. Members are Côte d'Ivoire, Mali, Mauritania, Niger, Senegal, and Upper Volta.

Women's Union of Burkina (UFB) – Mass organization created 1986.

Zerbo, Saye (1932–2013) – Army colonel, overthrew Sangoulé Lamizana regime in 1980 and was himself overthrown in November 1982 by Somé Yoryan. Sentenced to 15 years imprisonment for corruption in May 1984 by People's Revolutionary Courts.

Zongo, Henri (d. 1989) – Army captain, organized resistance in Ouagadougou after proimperialist coup in May 1983. Became minister of economic development in National Council of the Revolution after August 4, 1983. Participated in regime created by October 1987 counterrevolution. Executed without trial September 1989.

Index

RELATED READING

We Are Heirs of the World's Revolutions

Speeches from the
Burkina Faso Revolution, 1983–87

THOMAS SANKARA

How peasants and workers in this West African country established a popular revolutionary government and began to fight hunger, illiteracy, and economic backwardness imposed by imperialist domination. They set an example not only for workers and small farmers in Africa, but their class brothers and sisters the world over. $10. Also in Spanish, French, and Farsi.

Maurice Bishop Speaks

The Grenada Revolution and Its Overthrow, 1979–83

The triumph of the 1979 revolution in the Caribbean island of Grenada under the leadership of Maurice Bishop gave hope to millions throughout the Americas. Invaluable lessons from the workers and farmers government destroyed by a Stalinist-led counterrevolution in 1983. $20

Capitalism and the Transformation of Africa

Reports from Equatorial Guinea

MARY-ALICE WATERS, MARTÍN KOPPEL

Describes how, as Equatorial Guinea is pulled into the world market, both a capitalist class and a working class are being born. Also documents the work of volunteer Cuban health-care workers there—an expression of the living example of Cuba's socialist revolution. $10. Also in Spanish and Farsi.

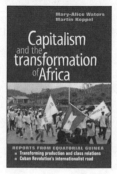

THE WORKING CLASS
AND FIGHTING JEW-HATRED

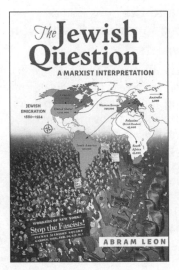

The Jewish Question
A Marxist Interpretation

ABRAM LEON

Why is Jew-hatred still raising its ugly head? What are its class roots—from antiquity through feudalism, to capitalism's rise and current crises? Why is there no solution under capitalism? The author, Abram Leon, was killed in the Nazi gas chambers. Revised translation, new introduction, and 40 pages of illustrations and maps. $17. Also in Spanish and French.

The Low Point of Labor Resistance Is Behind Us
The Socialist Workers Party Looks Forward

JACK BARNES, MARY-ALICE WATERS
STEVE CLARK

The global order imposed by Washington in the aftermath of its victory in World War II is shattering. A long retreat by the working class and unions has come to an end. More and more workers of all ages, skin colors, and both sexes are saying, "Enough is enough!" This book highlights opportunities ahead for building a mass proletarian party able to lead the struggle to end capitalist rule, opening a future for humanity. $10. Also in Spanish and French.

On the Jewish Question

LEON TROTSKY

"Now more than ever, the fate of the Jewish people is indissolubly linked with the emancipation struggle of the international proletariat," wrote Leon Trotsky. A selection of the exiled Bolshevik leader's writings from the 1930s. $5

CUBA'S SOCIALIST REVOLUTION

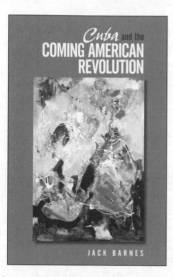

Cuba and the Coming American Revolution

JACK BARNES

This is a book about the struggles of working people in the imperialist heartland, the youth attracted to them, and the example set by the Cuban people that revolution is not only necessary—it can be made. It is about the class struggle in the US, where the revolutionary capacities of workers and farmers are today as utterly discounted by the ruling powers as were those of the Cuban toilers. And just as wrongly. $10. Also in Spanish, French, and Farsi.

From the Escambray to the Congo
In the Whirlwind of the Cuban Revolution

VÍCTOR DREKE

Dreke was second in command of the internationalist column in the Congo led in 1965 by Che Guevara. He recounts the creative joy with which working people have defended their revolutionary course—from Cuba's Escambray mountains to Africa and beyond. $15. Also in Spanish.

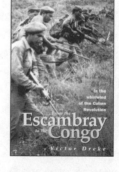

Cuba and Angola
Fighting for Africa's Freedom and Our Own

FIDEL CASTRO, RAÚL CASTRO
NELSON MANDELA

In March 1988, the army of South Africa's apartheid regime was dealt a crushing defeat by Cuban, Angolan, and Namibian combatants in Angola. Here leaders and participants tell the story of the 16-year-long internationalist mission that strengthened the Cuban Revolution as well. $12. Also in Spanish.

LABOR'S TRANSFORMATION OF NATURE

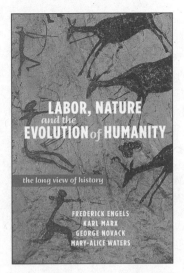

Labor, Nature, and the Evolution of Humanity

The Long View of History

FREDERICK ENGELS, KARL MARX
GEORGE NOVACK
MARY-ALICE WATERS

Without understanding that social labor, transforming nature, has driven humanity's evolution for millions of years, working people are unable to see beyond the capitalist epoch of class exploitation that warps all human relations, ideas, and values. Only the revolutionary conquest of state power by the working class can open the door to a world free of capitalist exploitation, degradation of nature, subjugation of women, racism, and war. A world built on human solidarity. A socialist world. $12. Also in Spanish and French.

The Communist Manifesto

KARL MARX AND FREDERICK ENGELS

Communism, say the founding leaders of the revolutionary workers movement, is not a set of ideas or preconceived "principles" but workers' line of march to power, springing from a "movement going on under our very eyes." $5. Also in Spanish, French, Farsi, and Arabic.

Our Politics Start with the World

JACK BARNES

The huge economic and cultural inequalities between imperialist and semicolonial countries, and among classes within them, are accentuated by the workings of capitalism. To build parties able to lead a successful revolutionary struggle for power in our own countries, vanguard workers must be guided by a strategy to close this gap. In *New International* no. 13. $14. Also in Spanish, French, Farsi, and Greek.

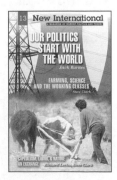

CAPITALIST CRISIS AND THE FIGHT FOR WORKERS POWER

Are They Rich Because They're Smart?
Class, Privilege, and Learning under Capitalism

JACK BARNES

In battles forced on us by the capitalists, workers will begin to transform our attitudes toward life, work, and each other. We'll discover our worth, denied by the rulers and upper middle classes who insist they're rich because they're smart. We'll learn in struggle what we're capable of becoming. $10. Also in Spanish, French, Farsi, and Arabic.

The Clintons' Anti-Working-Class Record
Why Washington Fears Working People

JACK BARNES

What working people need to know about the profit-driven course of Democrats and Republicans alike over the last three decades. And the political awakening of workers seeking to understand and resist the capitalist rulers' assaults. $10. Also in Spanish, French, Farsi, and Greek.

Malcolm X, Black Liberation, and the Road to Workers Power

JACK BARNES

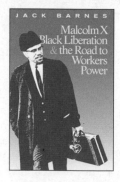

Drawing lessons from a century and a half of struggle, this book helps us understand why it is the revolutionary conquest of power by the working class that will make possible the final battle against class exploitation and racist oppression and open the way to a world based on human solidarity. A socialist world. $20. Also in Spanish, French, Farsi, Arabic, and Greek.

toshak – A narrow mattress used in Afghan homes as a chair or bed.

tuberculosis – A contagious bacterial infection that usually attacks the lungs.

UN – The United Nations, an international organization that promotes peace, security and economic development.

UNHCR – The United Nations High Commission on Refugees.

UNICEF – The United Nations International Children's Emergency Fund, an agency that helps governments (especially in developing countries) improve the health and education of children and mothers.

visa – A document that allows a person to enter another country.

warlord – A military commander who acts in his own interests rather than in the interests of the national government.

About the Author

Deborah Ellis is the author of more than two dozen books, including *The Breadwinner*, which has been published in twenty-five languages and was adapted into a feature-length animated film and a graphic novel. She has won the Governor General's Award, the Middle East Book Award, the Peter Pan Prize, the Jane Addams Children's Book Award and the Vicky Metcalf Award for a Body of Work. She has received the Ontario Library Association's President's Award for Exceptional Achievement, and she has been named to the Order of Canada. She has donated more than $2 million in royalties to organizations such as Women for Women in Afghanistan, UNICEF and Street Kids International.

Deborah lives in Simcoe, Ontario.